GUINNESS WORLD RECORDS 2021

Fastest electric ice-cream van
On 17 Mar 2020, inventor Edd China (UK) reached a peak speed of 118.964 km/h (73.921 mph) in *Edd's Electric Ices*, as confirmed by the UK Timing Association at Elvington airfield in North Yorkshire, UK. The vehicle began life as a diesel-engined Mercedes-Benz Sprinter van built by Whitby Morrison (UK) before Edd converted it to electric drive. A separate battery pack powers the soft-ice-cream machine.

Destinations

All aboard the 2021 edition of the world's **best-selling annual book**, fully updated for a new decade with thousands of the latest records! Across 12 superlative-packed chapters, you'll discover the world's most astonishing, surprising and inspiring achievements... and also get the chance to take on some record attempts of your own.

Our Animals chapter (pp.48–67) brings you fascinating facts about the world's fauna. This year, we're focusing on how animals' outer layers work. From fur and spines to skin and scales, we've got it covered!

GWR Hall of Fame
This year, we've inducted 12 more high-profile record-breakers into the GWR Hall of Fame. Among those honoured are explorer Victor Vescovo, conservationist Jane Goodall and activist Greta Thunberg, plus the world's most dysfunctional family (see p.210).

The book is crammed with jaw-dropping photography of the most remarkable record-breakers. Also, look out for some never-before-seen images shot by our global team of photographers.

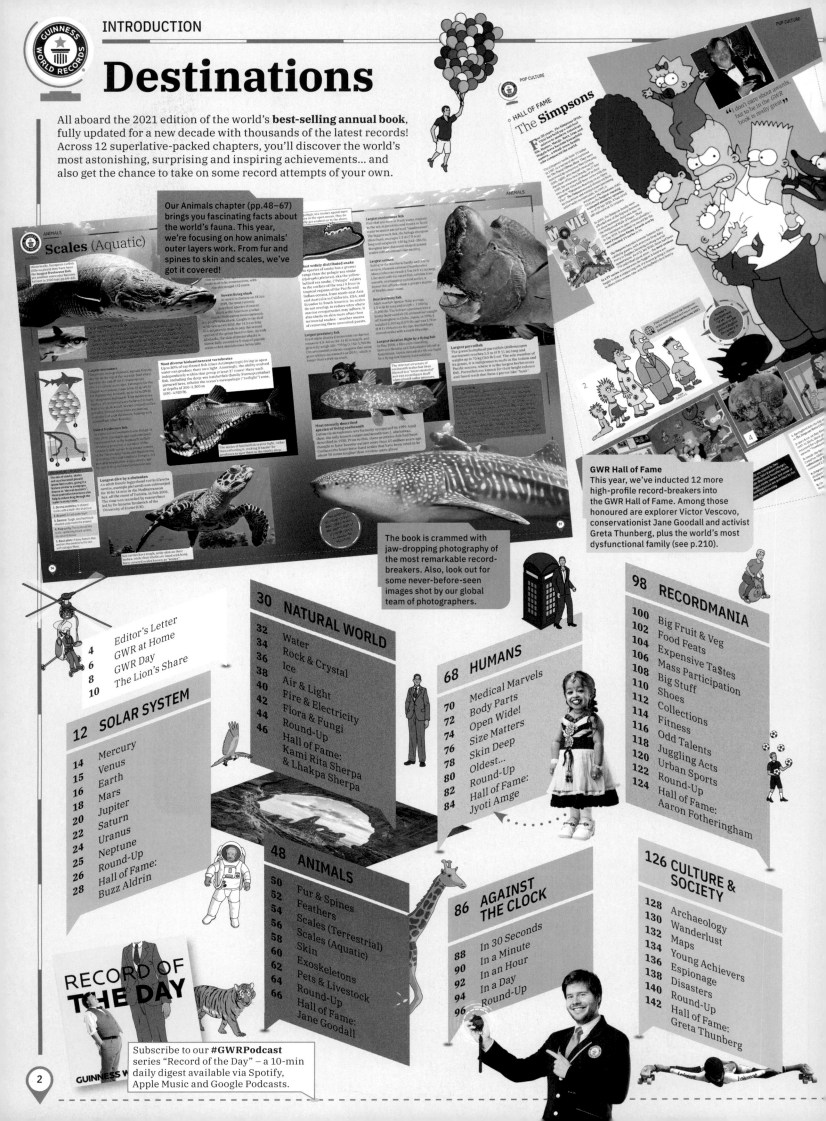

RECORD OF THE DAY

Subscribe to our **#GWRPodcast** series "Record of the Day" – a 10-min daily digest available via Spotify, Apple Music and Google Podcasts.

Travel light years without even leaving your chair! GWR brings you the very latest scientific discoveries about our neighbours in the Solar System.

Jupiter

Augmented-reality planets!
We've partnered with augmented-reality (AR) experts Peapodicity to bring our superlative Solar System (pp.12–27) to life with a free app. Just follow these simple steps:
• Download *AugmentifyIt®* for free from the App Store (iOS), Google Play (Android) or Amazon Appstore.
• Open the app on your device, then use the camera to scan an AR card like this one (right); it will be marked with the blue "scan" icon (above left).
• After a few seconds, the celestial body will pop up on screen, where it can be enjoyed in all its 3D glory.
• Want more? Check out peapodicity.com.

You'll find plenty of extra bite-size facts, figures and statistics scattered throughout the book.

Against the Clock
This special chapter is jam-packed with records achieved in a set time frame, along with tips and official GWR guidelines. Married martial artists Chris and Lisa Pitman (above) have each set the ▶ **most pine boards broken in a minute with one hand**, but don't worry, we don't expect you to go to these lengths! Instead, we offer up a series of records that you can take on at home. The timer starts on p.86…

Continue the story online…
Whenever you see this symbol, visit **guinnessworldrecords.com/2021** for bonus video content. Our digital team has curated a selection of clips from the world's most awe-inspiring record holders, so don't miss the chance to see these records in action.

How big? Discover the true scale of some of our biggest and smallest record holders wherever you see the 100% icon.

100%

Editor's Letter

Welcome to *Guinness World Records 2021* – a fully updated compendium of the world's most extraordinary achievements... compiled in the most extraordinary of circumstances.

As we go to press with the 67th edition of the **biggest-selling annual book**, the world has been turned upside down by COVID-19. With lockdowns firmly in place, we've had to rethink how to keep the cogs turning across every aspect of what we do at GWR. Luckily, the editors and designers have been able to work from their homes – I'm writing this at my kitchen table – and we've all had to very quickly adapt to the "new normal".

In terms of the Records Management Team it's business as usual, at least in one sense: records still need to be researched and ratified. In the past year, we've had to process 32,986 applications from across the globe – perhaps two- or three-thousand fewer than the same time last year. But that's still around 90 records per day. We may all be in lockdown, but the appetite for record-breaking continues to keep our adjudicators and researchers busy. On pp.6–7, you'll see how GWR has kept record-breaking alive during these challenging times.

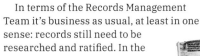

Call the Midwife
GWR played a starring role in the *Call the Midwife* 2019 Christmas special. When Reggie Jackson (played by Daniel Laurie, above second from right) receives a copy of the 1964 edition of the book (inset), he is inspired to attempt the world record for the **longest paper chain** and succeeds in bringing the whole community together.

Blue Peter
On 5 Sep 2019, the **longest-running children's magazine TV programme** (which celebrated its 61st birthday in Oct 2019) helped launch *GWR 2020*. Adjudicator Alan Pixsley oversaw presenter Richie Driss (far right) as he set the **fastest time to dress as a goalkeeper**, in 40.16 sec, while magician Martin Rees pulled off the **most cards identified in one minute (trick)** – 18.

Inspiring the selection of chapters and features in *GWR 2021* is the theme of "Discover Your World", which kicks off before you even open the book. For this year's cover, we wanted to shake things up so we asked the award-winning illustrator Rod Hunt to visualize what he thought of Guinness World Records in his own inimitable style. Find out more on p.256.

Inside, you'll find 12 chapters, each curated with the idea of "discovery" in mind. We begin with 17 pages dedicated to the Solar System (pp.12–29), which is enhanced with a free augmented-reality (AR) app for your smartphone or tablet. We've partnered with the boffins at Peapodicity to send you on a virtual journey of discovery through the Solar System without leaving your home. Find out how to access the *AugmentifyIt®* app on p.3.

Britain's Got Talent
The 13th series of ITV's talent show was won by Colin Thackery, whose performance of songs such as "We'll Meet Again" won the nation's hearts. On 20 Sep 2019, Thackery (b. 9 Mar 1930) became the **oldest person to release a debut album**, aged 89 years 195 days old, with *Love Changes Everything*.

Strictly: It Takes Two
On 18 Oct 2019, a troupe of 14 professional dancers from BBC's *Strictly Come Dancing* vied to pull off the **most Botafogo dance steps in 30 seconds**. It was Graziano Di Prima (ITA) who prevailed, with 90. Di Prima is pictured below, with GWR's Mark McKinley and hosts Zoe Ball and Rylan Clark-Neal.

The Gadget Show
To celebrate its 400th episode, on 12 Nov 2019 Channel 5's technology show staged the **longest ramp jump by a remote-controlled model car** – clearing a distance of 40.21 m (131 ft 11 in). The car was built by Team Associated RC8 T3.1e and controlled by Jon Howells. Host Ortis Deley (inset) was on hand to present the GWR certificate.

At the end of each chapter, you'll meet the latest additions to the GWR Hall of Fame, including pioneers such as Moon-walker Buzz Aldrin (pp.28–29), Everest climbers Kami Rita Sherpa and Lhakpa Sherpa (pp.46–47), and deep-sea explorer Victor Vescovo (pp.160–61). Among the other inductees are activist Greta Thunberg (pp.142–43), the **shortest woman**, Jyoti Amge (pp.84–85), and gymnastics sensation Simone Biles (pp.242–43).

If you're a gamer, head over to our expanded section dedicated to videogaming, starting on p.178. Seven key genres – plus a feature curated by our partners at Speedrun.com – should keep you occupied if you're stuck at home. And if the grown-ups complain about the amount of time you're spending on your console, just show them the teenager who made over $1 million playing *Fortnite* (pp.190–91)!

While many parts of this year's book have relied upon the proactive record-breaking

Scrambled!
The CITV Saturday morning show loves a record-breaking challenge, and on 4 Mar 2020 presenters Robyn Richford and Kerry Boyne teamed up to achieve the **most badges pinned on to a person in one minute** – 25. Newcomer host Robyn affixed the badges on to Kerry. For a one-minute challenge *you* can try at home, turn to p.91.

efforts of the public, the majority of the records have been curated by our vast network of consultants. New additions to this year's panel include Stuart Ackland, Curator of Maps at the Bodleian Library (see pp.132–33), Dr Christopher Moran, Reader in US National Security at the University of Warwick, who helped with the top-secret Espionage feature (pp.136–37), and Dr Alexandra Jones of Archaeology in the Community (pp.128–29), who you might recognize from TV show *Time Team America*. You'll find more consultants and contributors who've helped with this year's book on pp.250–51. Thank you all.

Indeed, thank you to *everyone* who's helped with this year's book. But a special thanks to all of our record-breakers, who, despite the upheavals and lockdowns, have continued to be Officially Amazing!

Craig Glenday
Craig Glenday
Editor-in-Chief

Capital FM
On 25 Oct 2019, breakfast-show host Sonny Jay achieved the **most Justin Bieber songs identified from their lyrics in one minute** – 22. He had finally made it into the "GWR club", joining his Capital FM co-hosts Roman Kemp and Vick Hope, who have both set their own records.

Twinkl
On 7 Nov 2019, the educational publisher Twinkl did their bit for BBC Children in Need by organizing the **most people in a singing relay (multiple songs)** – 384 – in Sheffield, South Yorkshire. The choir, drawn from local schools and businesses, sang four numbers, with each person contributing a single word of the lyrics in turn.

WELSH WONDERS

In 2020, GWR teamed up with Welsh-language broadcaster S4C to celebrate St David's Day on 1 Mar in superlative style. A total of seven world records were broken across Wales. At the National Waterfront Museum in Swansea, clog dancer Tudur Phillips broke his own record for the **most candles extinguished by heel-click jump in one minute** with 55 (**1**). Strongwoman Nicky Walters set the **fastest 50 m pulling a narrowboat (female)** in 1 min 35.53 sec (**2**) on the Pontcysyllte Aqueduct in Llangollen – which, standing 38.4 m (126 ft) off the ground, is the **tallest navigable canal aqueduct**. The **longest human archway relay** was created on Aberystwyth Promenade, consisting of 164 pairs (**3**), including S4C's Rhianna Loren and Alun Williams (above). In Portmeirion, freestyle footballer Ash Randall set two records: the **most knee catches in 30 seconds** – 23 – and the **most "hotstepper" ball-control tricks in one minute** – 56 (**4**).

Fun Kids Radio
On 8 Aug 2019, four **one-minute** world records were broken by presenters at Fun Kids Radio. From left to right: the **most Taylor Swift songs identified from their lyrics** – 27, by Dan Simpson; the **most football teams identified by team badge** – 28, by Conor Knight; the **tallest staircase built in *Minecraft* (console)** – 28 blocks, by Sean Thorne; and the **most young-adult authors identified by book title** – 32, by Bex Lindsay.

GWR at Home

The year 2020 saw everyone's lives affected by the coronavirus outbreak, restricting us to our homes as never before. But people just *won't* stop breaking records. And as long as they are, GWR will find ways of adjudicating them...

In truth, even when not faced with a global pandemic, we're always evolving inventive and innovative ways to help people become record-breakers. A recent project that started off as a way to create records for kids only – by using online tools and video submissions – suddenly found a much wider use with the onset of the COVID-19 outbreak. The result is the "GWR at Home" project and the online #GWRchallenge records, which are seeing new categories being adjudicated via video every week.

We've also adapted to the lockdown by carrying out virtual certificate presentations to the likes of fitness guru Joe Wicks, inspirational people's hero

Captain Tom Moore, and the newly proclaimed **oldest man**, Robert Weighton.

As you'll see opposite, with the world gradually adapting to staying indoors for long periods at a time, we've taken to TikTok. And we've enjoyed record-breaking concerts by famous names to celebrate the health workers at the front line in the fight against the virus.

From its inception in 1955, GWR has continually adapted to mirror the real world, and we're doing what we can to keep record-breaking alive, even in a worldwide crisis. To find out more, or to get inspiration, visit **guinnessworldrecords.com/records/ GWR-at-home**.

#GWRchallenge
Whatever the circumstances, spending hours indoors provides a golden opportunity for record-breaking. We've encouraged our online audience to put any spare time to good use in our weekly record challenge (**guinnessworldrecords.com/ records/GWR-at-home**). Among those who became GWR online title holders are:
1. Vikas Saini (IND): **fastest time to put on 10 socks** – 9.23 sec.
2. Jed Hockin (AUS): **most football (soccer) touches in 30 seconds with a toilet roll** – 84.
3. Jesse Horn (USA): **fastest time to make a 10-can pyramid** – 3.09 sec.

GWR Kids
We've come up with an exciting new plan to create record titles specifically aimed at younger people, so that they won't have to compete unfairly alongside adults. This project has been launched with 20 different titles, to challenge kids across a range of activities. They also coincide with a revamp of our kids website, and readers can go there for more information – check out **kids.guinnessworldrecords. com**. Pictured here are two categories with young people in mind: **fastest time to stack 20 LEGO® bricks in a right-angle tower** and **most soft toys caught blindfolded**. Why not start your GWR adventure with one of these?

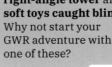

Most live streams of a fitness workout on YouTube

To stay fit while quarantined indoors, many people looked online for help and inspiration. Exercise guru Joe "The Body Coach" Wicks (UK) became an internet sensation after he began streaming a daily fitness class from home, racking up nearly 1 million viewers for the 24 Mar 2020 session. Below, GWR Editor-in-Chief Craig Glenday (virtually) hands over Joe's certificate. Find out more on p.114.

Most musical acts to perform at a remote music festival

Website and app Global Citizen offers a way of bringing people together to help those locked into poverty. On 18 Apr 2020, in conjunction with the World Health Organization, it hosted the all-star online concert *One World: Together at Home*. Curated by Lady Gaga (below), a record 72 acts including The Rolling Stones, Elton John, Taylor Swift and Coldplay's Chris Martin (below right) took part in an 8-hr show that raised $127.9 m (£102.4 m) for coronavirus relief efforts.

Oldest man

Another recipient of a virtual GWR certificate was Robert Weighton (UK, b. 29 Mar 1908), who was 112 years 1 day old on 30 Mar 2020, as verified in Alton, Hampshire, UK. Sadly, we weren't able to present it to Robert in person, but we wished him many happy returns of the day via video, and he replied with a recorded message of his own, thanking us for the certificate.

Editor-in-Chief takes to TikTok

GWR has 8 million followers on TikTok, so on 1 Apr 2020, Craig Glenday took the opportunity to go live to a virtual classroom. As part of EduTok – TikTok's educational offering – Craig lectured on GWR's history, suggested some ideas for home-based record attempts, and fielded questions from attendees.

Most money raised by a charity walk (individual)

One of the most inspirational and heart-warming responses to the COVID-19 crisis came from a 99-year-old veteran in the UK. As of 30 Apr 2020, Captain Tom Moore had raised more than £32.79 m ($40.82 m) in donations for the UK's NHS by walking lengths of his 25-m (82-ft) garden in Marston Moretaine, Bedfordshire, UK. Find out about another of his records on p.80.

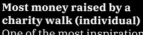

Captain Tom was made an honorary colonel on 30 Apr, his 100th birthday, in recognition of his achievement.

GWR DAY

Each year, thousands of people around the world attempt a mind-boggling variety of challenges as part of Guinness World Records Day. And for the first time in 2019, we introduced a theme: "Spirit of Adventure".

Our annual day of record-breaking was inaugurated in 2005 to mark the anniversary of *Guinness World Records* becoming the **best-selling annual book**. It was created to give you the chance to have a go at an official GWR title while highlighting a good cause, raising money for charity, bringing together friends or colleagues, or just for fun. For GWR Day 2019, we also took the opportunity to present certificates to those record-breakers we felt truly embodied the "Spirit of Adventure" theme throughout the year...

▶ **Fastest circumnavigation by tandem bicycle (male)**
Lloyd Edward Collier and Louis Paul Snellgrove (both UK) went around the world on a two-man bike in 281 days 22 hr 20 min. They started and ended in Adelaide, Australia, from 7 Aug 2018 to 16 May 2019. Turn to pp.154–55 for more.

▶ **Fastest 400 m on roller skates blindfolded (female)**
Ojal Sunil Nalavadi (IND) completed a 400-m (1,312-ft) course on roller skates while blindfolded in 51.25 sec in Hubballi, Karnataka, India, on 14 Nov 2019.

▶ **Longest journey on an electric scooter**
Over the course of 64 days, Song Jian (CHN) travelled from the east to the west of China on his electric scooter, covering a total distance of 10,087.2 km (6,267 mi). He started out in Fuyuan, Heilongjiang, and arrived in Kashgar, Xinjiang Autonomous Region, on 7 Sep 2019. Song almost doubled his own previous record, set in 2018.

Oldest person to climb Mount Kilimanjaro
On GWR Day, we first published the story of Anne Lorimor (USA, b. 11 Jun 1930), who had summitted Africa's highest mountain on 18 Jul 2019 aged 89 years 37 days. Anne set out on 12 Jul and scaled Kilimanjaro (5,895 m; 19,340 ft) in a round trip from base to summit and back in nine days.

The Harlem Globetrotters
They may be synonymous with the USA, but the exhibition basketball team have certainly lived up to their name. Since 1926, the Globetrotters have chalked up the **most sovereign countries played in by a basketball team** – 101. For GWR Day 2019, Rochell "Wham" Middleton (USA, below left) completed the ▶ **most bounced basketball figure eight moves blindfolded in one minute** – 63 – in Prescott Valley, Arizona, USA. Teammate Chris "Handles" Franklin (USA, below right) sank the ▶ **farthest kneeling basketball shot made backwards** – 19.39 m (63 ft 7 in).

▶ **Longest open-ocean journey by jet ski (unsupported)**
Between 18 Sep and 2 Oct 2019, Lucas Del Paso Cánovas (ESP) rode his Yamaha VX Deluxe jet ski a distance of 3,602 km (2,238 mi) from Sagres in Portugal to Sapri in Italy. Lucas's epic journey was part of a project called Blue4green, which involved him picking up all the waste he spotted in the sea as he went. Money was also donated for planting trees, as a way of offsetting the jet ski's carbon footprint.

▶ **Fastest time to swim 5 km pulling a canoe**
Ex-Royal Marine Nick Watson (UK) celebrated his 50th birthday in style – swimming 5 km while towing his son Rio in a canoe in 2 hr 42 min 48 sec in Dubai, UAE. Nick is part of Team Angel Wolf, which promotes inclusion of people with disabilities. He went on to set the **10 km** record in 6 hr 6 min 52 sec.

The team may be Globetrotters but they originated in Chicago, Illinois, rather than Harlem, New York City!

Most people sport stacking (multiple venues)

Each year, the World Sport Stacking Association (USA) hosts its "STACK UP!" event on GWR Day. In 2019, sport stackers in 20 countries joined in the fun, with a total number of 638,503 participants – almost 15,000 more than in 2018.

▶ Farthest distance cycling with one leg in one hour

Mark Newman (UK) cycled 20.345 km (12.64 mi) in 60 min at Preston Park Velodrome in Brighton, East Sussex, UK, on 14 Nov 2019. His other foot did not touch the pedal at any time.

Mark's record was one of four attempted at Preston Park velodrome on GWR Day. Others included the **farthest distance on a penny farthing bicycle in one hour (no hands)** – 26 km (16.15 mi), by Neil Laughton (UK). Both Neil and Mark have played penny farthing bicycle polo for England. Turn to pp.92–93 for more.

Most people doing double under-rope skips in a relay

Professional rope skipper Hijiki Ikuyama and Tsukishima Daini Elementary School (both JPN) teamed up to perform 188 double under-rope skips in a relay in Tokyo, Japan. Tsukishima Daini Elementary School used GWR Day to encourage rope skipping as part of an educational programme, while Hijiki wanted to show students that teamwork is the best way to overcome challenges.

Oldest person to swim the Oceans Seven

The Oceans Seven is a set of marathon open-water channel swims located around the world. Elizabeth Fry (USA, b. 28 Oct 1958) completed the challenge aged 60 years 301 days on 25 Aug 2019 by swimming the 35-km (21.7-mi) North Channel between Northern Ireland and Scotland, UK, in 11 hr 13 min 11 sec. On GWR Day, we presented Elizabeth with her two titles: **oldest female** and **overall**.

Fastest journey by helicopter through 48 contiguous US states

Yosuke Chatmaleerat (THA) piloted his helicopter across the territory of the 48 adjoining US states (i.e., excluding Hawaii and Alaska) in 12 days 14 hr 59 min between 25 Sep and 7 Oct 2019. Yosuke had to navigate thunderstorms, haze and extreme headwinds – and all in his first three days!

Most one-arm push-ups in three minutes (male)

Powerlifting teacher Sverre Diesen (NOR) completed 126 one-arm push-ups in 180 sec on 14 Nov 2019 in Larvik, Norway. He beat the previous best by 19.

Sverre is the holder of several GWR titles, including the **most one-arm push-ups carrying an 80-lb pack in one minute** – 26 – which he set on 10 Dec 2018.

▶ Fastest speed in a body-controlled jet-engine-powered suit

On 14 Nov 2019, real-life Iron Man Richard Browning (UK) took to the skies above Brighton Beach in East Sussex, UK, piloting his flying suit to a speed of 136.89 km/h (85.06 mph). Browning smashed his own record of 51.53 km/h (32.02 mph), set two years earlier on GWR Day 2017. Improvements in the technology and stabilizing fins on his legs enabled Browning to reach much higher speeds than before.

The sparks coming from the suit are decorative. Richard built a pyrotechnic device into his shoe.

Browning named his suit *Daedalus* after the Greek mythological character who learned to fly using wings made from string, wax and feathers.

The Lion's Share

The Lion's Share · UNDP · GUINNESS WORLD RECORDS

Launched in Jun 2018, The Lion's Share is a UN-backed project to encourage the advertising and media industries to give something back to nature. Guinness World Records is delighted to count itself among many global brands to have heeded the call and pledged to support this worthy cause.

"T is for tiger"... It's one of many such expressions we learn at school or when reading with our families. But what if we lived in a world where animal icons – in our books, TV shows and advertising campaigns – no longer existed? That was the wake-up call for Australian film-makers Christopher Nelius and Rob Galluzzo, who decided it was high time that advertisers were given a chance to assure the future of their wild stars.

The principle behind the initiative is simple: any company that uses an animal in its advertising or branding donates 0.5% of a campaign's media budget to the fund. It may sound very little, but a staggering 20% of adverts feature an animal, so the scope is huge.

All the donations are administered by the UN Development Programme, which calls on its network of NGOs, government contacts and grass-roots partners to action real change in the field (see right).

The Lion's Share has lofty ambitions, not least to "create a world where nature flourishes". Among its more specific aims are to help abandoned pets, secure 1 million ha (2.4 million acres) of wilderness and safeguard the remaining 4,000 or so wild tigers.

With more than 25 partners already on board, there's renewed hope that we will be able to enjoy all the animals from A to Z – record holders or not – for many generations to come.

1955

2021

GWR's debt to animals

The *Guinness World Records* book has changed a lot since the first volume (inset top) launched 65 years ago. But one thing hasn't changed: our annuals would be all the poorer without record-breaking animals inside. In the panel below, we highlight just a few superlative species that are currently under threat, according to the International Union for Conservation of Nature (IUCN) Red List. You can read more about The Lion's Share and GWR's collaboration at **www.guinnessworldrecords.com/2021**.

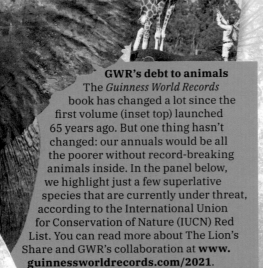

The Lion's Share has a long-term plan to help the most threatened animals and habitats, but certain record-breaking species are already reaping the rewards.

1. Rangers at Mozambique's Niassa Reserve have received new digital communications equipment to help them in their fight against poaching. Although primarily introduced to help protect the reserve's elephants, all wildlife there stands to gain. This includes endangered painted dogs (*Lycaon pictus*), which are the **most successful predators**.

2. Coral reefs are among the most biodiverse ecosystems on Earth. The Lion's Share is actively researching marine areas that it can support, including the sealife-rich "Coral Triangle" located in south-east Asia.

WILD RECORD-BREAKERS IN PERIL

Largest land animal
African bush elephant (*Loxodonta africana*)
Status: Vulnerable

Oldest land animal
Jonathan: Seychelles giant tortoise (*Aldabrachelys gigantea hololissa*)
Status: Vulnerable

Most primitive bear
Giant panda (*Ailuropoda melanoleuca*)
Status: Vulnerable

Smallest natural range for a vertebrate
Devils Hole pupfish (*Cyprinodon diabolis*)
Status: Critically Endangered

Fastest land mammal (short distance)
Cheetah (*Acinonyx jubatus*)
Status: Vulnerable

Rarest parrot
Spix's macaw
(*Cyanopsitta spixii*)
Status: Extinct in
the Wild

SIR DAVID ATTENBOROUGH: WHY SHARING IS CARING

Naturalist and environmental campaigner Sir David Attenborough (UK) needs no introduction. He has guided us around the world's natural wonders for more than six decades, giving him the **longest career as a TV presenter**. His debut was on *Animal Disguises* (BBC, UK) in 1953 and he is still active more than 66 years later, most recently in the BBC series *Seven Worlds, One Planet* in 2019.

"Retirement" is clearly not a word in 94-year-old Sir David's vocabulary. In 2020, he narrated *Wild Karnataka*, a film focusing on iconic Indian fauna, as well as starring in the feature-length documentary *A Life on Our Planet*, produced with the WWF. Although its planned premiere had to be postponed owing to lockdown measures during the COVID-19 pandemic, it is slated to be released at cinemas and on Netflix later in the year.

Sir David has also placed his wholehearted support behind The Lion's Share, serving as its first Special Ambassador. This was his rallying cry: "In 2015, the world adopted a new global development agenda with an ambitious set of 17 sustainable development goals. Now, through The Lion's Share, advertisers have a real opportunity to act and deliver on these sustainable development goals by making a small change in the way they recognize animals in their advertisements. I urge you – every brand and every CEO out there – to join us and sign up to this profoundly game-changing initiative, so that we might help protect Earth's habitats, animals and wildlife as we head into this new century."

▶ **Tallest animal**
Giraffe (*Giraffa camelopardalis*)
Status: Vulnerable

> " I urge... every brand and every CEO out there to... sign up to this profoundly game-changing initiative "

3. A tract of rainforest has been purchased in the Leuser Ecosystem of Sumatra in Indonesia to provide some sanctuary for threatened species, such as Sumatran rhinos (the **smallest rhinoceros species**; see p.59) and orangutans (see p.50), the **largest arboreal mammals**.

4. Working with the Jaguar Corridor Legacy Partnership, The Lion's Share is seeking to limit habitat fragmentation in South America's Pantanal – the planet's **largest swamp**. Jaguars (*Panthera onca*) are the third-biggest wild cats after tigers (see below) and lions, and those found in the Pantanal are the **largest jaguar subspecies**.

▶ **Largest genome**
Axolotl (*Ambystoma mexicanum*)
Status: Critically Endangered

▶ **Largest wild cat**
Tiger (*Panthera tigris*)
Status: Endangered

Most northerly penguin
Galápagos penguin
(*Spheniscus mendiculus*)
Status: Endangered

Largest primate
Eastern lowland gorilla
(*Gorilla beringei graueri*)
Status: Critically
Endangered

Solar System

The Sun

At the heart of our Solar System is a G-type main-sequence star (or "yellow dwarf") which we call the Sun. Although fairly unremarkable as stars go (the **largest star**, UY Scuti, is at least 1,500 times larger), the Sun is nonetheless the **largest object in the Solar System**, with a mass more than 1,000 times greater than the planet Jupiter (see pp.20–21), which is the next-largest object. As the centre point around which all the planets rotate, the Sun (also called "Sol") is the obvious starting point for our record-breaking tour of the Solar System.

Sun ("Sol")

The star at the centre of our Solar System is a ball of hot plasma around 330,000 times heavier than Earth. Its mass accounts for *c.* 99.86% of the total mass of the Solar System.

Distance from galactic core
2.46×10^{17} km (25,766 light years)

Equatorial diameter
1,391,016 km

Mass
1.98×10^{30} kg

Surface gravity
274.0 m/s^2

Rotation period (day)
609 hr 7 min (25.3 Earth days; varies with latitude)

Orbital period (year)
230 million Earth years (relative to galactic core)

SUN

See the planets in 3D

For each of the planets in the Solar System, our partners at Peapodicity have an animated model that can be viewed in augmented reality using a phone or tablet. Just use the free *AugmentifyIt®* app (details on p.3) to scan each of these picture cards and the planet (or star in this case) will transform from 2D to 3D.

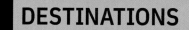

DESTINATIONS

Mercury

Smallest planet in the Solar System
With a diameter of just 4,879 km (3,031 mi) – about as wide as the Atlantic Ocean – Mercury is not only smaller than all the other planets, it is not even as big as the two largest planetary moons (Ganymede and Titan). Though small, Mercury has a lot of mass and is the second-densest body in the Solar System after Earth.

Shortest year
Mercury is both the **closest planet to the Sun,** orbiting at an average distance of 57.9 million km (35.9 million mi), and the **fastest planet**, with an orbital velocity of 170,496 km/h (105,941 mph). This means that it completes a full orbit around the Sun every 87 days 21 hr.

Largest planetary core
Research published in *Geophysical Research Letters* on 15 Mar 2019 revealed that Mercury's core makes up 85% of the planet's total volume, and has a diameter of around 4,000 km (2,480 mi).

Most eccentric planet
Mercury has an orbital eccentricity of 0.205, on a scale where 0 is a perfect circle and 1 is a parabola (Earth's eccentricity is 0.01). Its orbit brings it to within 46 million km (28.58 million mi) of the Sun at its closest point (perihelion) and out as far as 69.81 million km (43.37 million mi) from the Sun at its most distant (aphelion).

First Mercury orbiter
On 18 Mar 2011, NASA's *Messenger* probe became the first spacecraft to be placed in orbit around Mercury. Reaching the planet was an impressive feat of mission design: it launched in 2004 but had to make six gravity-assist manoeuvres over seven years to get into position. It remained active for more than four years.

Greatest temperature range
Surface temperatures on Mercury range from 427°C (800.6°F) in the daytime to -173°C (-279.4°F) during the Mercurian night.

First meteorite from Mercury
Discovered in Morocco in 2012, NWA 7325 is the first meteorite thought to have originated from the planet Mercury. Chemical studies of the space rock show its composition is consistent with the geology of Mercury. The meteorite is estimated to be around 4.56 billion years old.

First topographic map of Mercury
On 6 May 2016, NASA's Planetary Data System published a 3D map of Mercury's surface. It was created by analysing the shadows and topographic details in more than 100,000 images taken between 2011 and 2015 by NASA's *Messenger* orbiter (see above right). The map is shown above, with high altitudes in yellow.

Largest impact basin on Mercury
The Caloris basin was formed 3.8–3.9 billion years ago when an object at least 100 km (62 mi) wide struck the planet. It was first spotted in pictures taken by *Mariner 10* (which made the **first fly-by of Mercury** in 1974) and mapped in detail by *Messenger*, which determined that it measured 1,550 km (963 mi) across. It is surrounded by 2,000-m-tall (6,561-ft) mountains.

Mercury	
Scorched by its proximity to the Sun, Mercury is a cratered rocky world, about the same size as our Moon, where heat and solar radiation have burned away any chance of life.	
Average distance from the Sun	0.38 au (57.9 million km)
Equatorial diameter	4,879.4 km
Mass	3.301 x 10²³ kg
Surface gravity	3.7 m/s²
Rotation period (day)	58 Earth days 15 hr (see below)
Orbital period (year)	87 Earth days 21 hr
Number of moons	0

MERCURY

Mercury's rotation and its day/night cycle don't line up. It rotates every 58 Earth days, but a day/night cycle takes 176 Earth days.

Venus

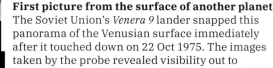

Hottest planet in the Solar System
On the surface of Venus, the average temperature is a furnace-like 473°C (884°F) – hot enough to melt lead and make timber spontaneously ignite. The planet's thick, carbon-dioxide-rich atmosphere creates a powerful greenhouse effect, preventing heat from being lost from the night side of the planet.

First picture from the surface of another planet
The Soviet Union's *Venera 9* lander snapped this panorama of the Venusian surface immediately after it touched down on 22 Oct 1975. The images taken by the probe revealed visibility out to around 100 m (328 ft) and light levels comparable to a heavily overcast day on Earth, which surprised many scientists.

Brightest planet from Earth
Venus is one of the brightest objects in the night sky, outshone only by the Moon. It stands out particularly clearly just before sunrise, earning it the traditional name "morning star". In astronomical terms, it has an apparent magnitude of -4.14, making it more than three times brighter than Jupiter.

First detection of lightning on Venus
On 26 Oct 1975, four days after it released its lander, the Soviet Union's *Venera 9* spacecraft detected a series of bright lightning flashes from the night side of Venus.

More than three years later, another Soviet mission heard the **first extraterrestrial thunder**. *Venera 11*'s lander recorded two 82-dB thunderclaps on 25 Dec 1978.

Most acidic rain
The clouds that swirl through the Venusian atmosphere are made of concentrated sulphuric acid (H_2SO_4). The rain from these clouds may have a pH as low as -1.2. This precipitation boils away in the searing lower atmosphere before it ever reaches the surface.

Most cloud cover for a terrestrial planet
The surface of Venus is perpetually hidden by a layer of cloud that covers 100% of the planet. Earth's cloud cover, by contrast, covers around 67% of the planet's surface (...though it feels like more than that in London).

Longest rotation period
Venus takes 243 Earth days to spin just once on its axis. It rotates in the opposite direction to its orbit, however, meaning that the planet's solar day (a single day/night cycle) is shorter at 116 Earth days.

Tallest mountain on Venus
Skadi Mons is an 11,520-m (37,795-ft) peak located in the Maxwell Montes, a mountain massif on Venus's Ishtar Terra. Heights of features on Venus are measured relative to the planet's average radius.

Longest time survived on Venus by a spacecraft
Given the brutally harsh atmosphere of the planet, the *Venera 13* lander was only expected to survive for about 30 min. It managed to keep transmitting data for 127 min after it landed on 1 Mar 1982, thanks to its rugged design, which was more like a deep-sea submarine than a satellite.

Venus	
Despite having been visited by 26 successful robotic missions, our closest planetary neighbour still holds many secrets beneath its smotheringly thick atmosphere.	
Average distance from the Sun	0.72 au (108.2 million km)
Equatorial diameter	12,103 km
Mass	4.86 x 10^{24} kg
Surface gravity	8.87 m/s²
Rotation period (day)	243 Earth days
Orbital period (year)	224 Earth days 13 hr
Number of moons	0

VENUS

Largest impact crater on Venus
Mead is a shallow multi-ringed impact crater in Venus's northern hemisphere. It measures roughly 280 km (174 mi) in diameter. There are many craters on the surface of Venus, but none are smaller than 2 km (1.2 mi). This is because small meteors burn up in the planet's thick atmosphere.

Earth

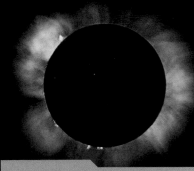

Most solar eclipses viewed from within the Moon's umbral shadow

Glenn Schneider and John Beattie (both USA) have each witnessed 35 solar eclipses from within the darkest part of the shadow created by the Moon as it passes in front of the Sun. Their latest trip into the "path of totality" (the track of the Moon's shadow across Earth's surface) took place on 2 Jul 2019 on board a special flight to Easter Island.

Largest crater in the Solar System

The South Pole-Aitken basin is a gigantic impact scar located in the lower southern hemisphere of the Moon's far side. The basin measures some 2,500 km (1,553 mi) in diameter and, with a depth of up to 13 km (8 mi), it is also the **deepest impact crater**. Despite having existed for around 3.9 billion years, this major feature of our planetary companion was totally unknown to science until 1959, when the Soviet Union's *Luna 3* spacecraft took the **first pictures of the far side of the Moon**.

Longest day on Earth

The tidal bulges in Earth's oceans, caused by the gravitational effect of the Moon, are gradually transferring momentum from Earth's rotation to the Moon's orbit. As a result, Earth's rotation is slowing by around 0.0018 sec per century and each day is a tiny bit longer than the one before. Therefore, the longest day on Earth is always today.

Largest moon compared to its planet

At 3,474 km (2,158 mi) across, the Moon's diameter is 27% of that of Earth. Around 4.51 billion years old, it is the largest of the three moons in the inner Solar System and the only other world that humans have visited. Just 12 men have walked on its surface – the **last man on the Moon**, Gene Cernan (USA), commander of the Apollo 17 mission, left on 14 Dec 1972.

First supercontinent

Over geological time, as the continents drift they occasionally connect together. The first time such a supercontinent formed was around 3.1 billion years ago; geologists refer to it as Vaalbara.

The **most recent supercontinent**, Pangea, formed around 300 million years ago, in the Late Permian period. The continental crust gathered in the southern hemisphere to create Pangea, which began to break apart some 175 million years ago.

Longest ice age

Between 2.29 and 2.25 billion years ago, Earth endured its most severe ice age, known as the Huronian Glaciation. During this period, much of the planet was probably covered in ice, possibly 1 km (0.6 mi) deep.

Largest rocky planet

Earth has a diameter of 12,742 km (7,917.5 mi) and a mass of around 5.972×10^{21} tonnes (6.5832×10^{21} US tons). It is also the **most geologically active inner planet**, with 1,500 potentially active volcanoes. It orbits the Sun at an average distance of around 150 million km (93.2 million mi). As a result, it takes sunlight approximately eight minutes to reach us.

Longest-lasting space station

The first habitable configuration of the *International Space Station* (*ISS*) was completed on 19 Oct 2000. It was still operational as of 12 Dec 2019, 19 years 54 days later. The ongoing development of the *ISS*, and the operations required to keep it crewed and supplied, means that as of the same date it had been 19 years 42 days since every human being was on Earth at the same time – the **longest uninterrupted human presence in space**.

The name "Earth" is *c.* 1,000 years old and has its roots in Old English and Proto-Germanic nouns. All other planets in the Solar System bear Greek or Roman titles.

First sculpture on the Moon

Fallen Astronaut is an 8.5-cm-long (3.3-in) aluminium figurine of an astronaut made by Belgian artist Paul Van Hoeydonck. It was left on the Moon by David Scott and James Irwin of Apollo 15 at 12:18 a.m. GMT on 2 Aug 1971 and lies at the Hadley-Apennine landing site. Nearby is a small plaque in memory of 14 US and Soviet astronauts who had died in service.

100%

Most liquid water in the Solar System

There is an estimated 1,361,620,510 km³ (326,670,132 cu mi) of liquid water lying on or inside Earth, or within its surrounding atmosphere. Around 99.2% of this is salt water in the planet's oceans, seas, saline lakes and aquifers.

Liquid fresh water accounts for only 0.8% of Earth's liquid water because most of it remains frozen in the form of permafrost, glaciers and ice caps. The **largest body of fresh water** is the Antarctic Ice Sheet, which contains around 24 million km³ (5.7 million cu mi), or roughly 68% of the world's total.

Densest planet

Earth has an average density of 5,513 kg/m³ (344 lb/cu ft), or more than five times that of water. For the **least dense planet**, see p.22.

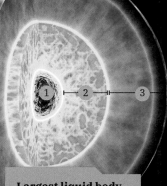

Largest liquid body on Earth

Our planet's solid inner core **(1)** is enclosed by a fluid outer core **(2)** 2,259 km (1,403 mi) thick, with a volume of 1.719×10^{11} km³ (4.12×10^{10} cu mi). Mostly iron and nickel, it represents around 29.3% of Earth's mass and 16% of its volume.

The **largest region of Earth's interior** is the mantle **(3)**, making up 84% of our planet's volume. It is 2,900 km (1,800 mi) deep, from just below the crust **(4)** down to the outer core.

Largest impact crater on Earth

Of around 200 impact craters identified so far on Earth, the largest is the Vredefort Crater (above left), near Johannesburg in South Africa. Its estimated diameter of 250–300 km (155–186 mi) is equal to the distance from London to Manchester, or New York to Baltimore. This huge, eroded structure was formed around 2 billion years ago, when an asteroid or comet collided with Earth.

Earth

Our planet is the fifth-largest world in the Solar System and the third from the Sun. It's also the only celestial body known to have liquid water – which covers 70% of its surface – and life.

Average distance from the Sun
1 au (1.49×10^8 km)

Equatorial diameter
12,742 km

Mass
5.972×10^{24} kg

Surface gravity
9.80665 m/s²

Rotation period (day)
24 hr

Orbital period (year)
365.25 days

Number of moons
1

EARTH

Earth's oceans hold 97% of all the water on the planet. They are around 4 km (2.5 mi) deep on average.

First full-disc image of Earth (taken by humans)

NASA's Apollo 17 mission was the last flight to the Moon by humans. The geometry of the Solar System during the flight was such that, with the Sun behind them, the full Earth was visible for the first time to people beyond our planet's orbit. En route to the Moon, the crew captured an iconic image of Earth, known as the "Blue Marble". It was taken on 7 Dec 1972 from a distance of around 45,000 km (27,960 mi).

Mars

Closest moon to a planet
Phobos orbits just 5,981 km (3,716 mi) above the Martian surface. This small, irregularly shaped world is dark and covered with dusty craters. Believed to be an asteroid captured by Mars's gravity, Phobos is on a collision course with the planet, nearing it at a rate of 1.8 m (6 ft) every 100 years.

First spacecraft to orbit another planet
On 14 Nov 1971, *Mariner 9* was placed into Mars orbit by a 15-min orbital-insertion burn initiated at 00:17:39 UTC. Both NASA and the Soviet Union had sent probes to other planets before (the first being the Soviet probe *Venera 3*), but *Mariner 9* was the first mission to carry out the complex manoeuvres required to enter a stable orbit.

The **longest-functioning Mars orbiter** is NASA's *Mars Odyssey*, which entered orbit on 24 Oct 2001 – a total of 18 years 74 days ago, as of 6 Jan 2020. One of its functions is to serve as the primary communications relay for landers on the Martian surface, such as the *Curiosity* rover.

First spacecraft to land on Mars
On 2 Dec 1971, the Soviet *Mars 3* lander touched down on the Red Planet. It deployed successfully, but suddenly stopped transmitting data after just 20 seconds.

The **first successful Mars lander** is *Viking 1*, which reached the surface on 20 Jul 1976. A stationary lander fitted with cameras and scientific instruments, *Viking 1* completed its planned objectives and remained active on Mars for 7 years 85 days.

Highest clouds in the Solar System
In Aug 2006, European scientists reported faint clouds 90–100 km (55–62 mi) above the surface of Mars. Detected by the ESA's *Mars Express* orbiter, the clouds are composed of carbon-dioxide ice crystals.

Most probed planet
As of 6 Jan 2020, a total of 25 successful or partially successful robotic exploration missions had been launched to Mars. These missions have placed 14 orbiters around the Red Planet and nine at least partially successful landers on the surface. Several other space missions have made it as far as Mars's gravitational sphere of influence, but failed before they could transmit back any data.

Largest impact basin on Mars
Located in the southern hemisphere of the planet, the Hellas Basin (aka the Hellas Planitia) has a diameter of 2,299 km (1,428 mi) and is 7.15 km (4.44 mi) deep, as measured from Martian zero elevation. The red circle on the inset map shows how large this asteroid impact scar would be relative to North America.

Mars
The fourth planet from the Sun is a cold and dusty world with a thin atmosphere. Known as the Red Planet, it owes its distinct colouration to the oxidized (rusty) iron minerals in the Martian soil.

Average distance from the Sun	1.52 au (228 million km)
Equatorial diameter	6,779 km
Mass	6.4171×10^{23} kg
Surface gravity	3.71 m/s^2
Rotation period (day)	24 hr 37 min 22 sec
Orbital period (year)	1.88 Earth years
Number of moons	2

MARS

Perseverance
With a launch window of 17 Jul–5 Aug 2020, NASA's latest mission to Mars is scheduled to land in the Red Planet's Jezero Crater on 18 Feb 2021. The new Mars rover, called *Perseverance* (a name suggested by Virginia middle-schooler Alexander Mather), should surpass the 900-kg (1,984-lb) and 3-m-long (9-ft 10-in) *Curiosity* as the **largest planetary rover**.

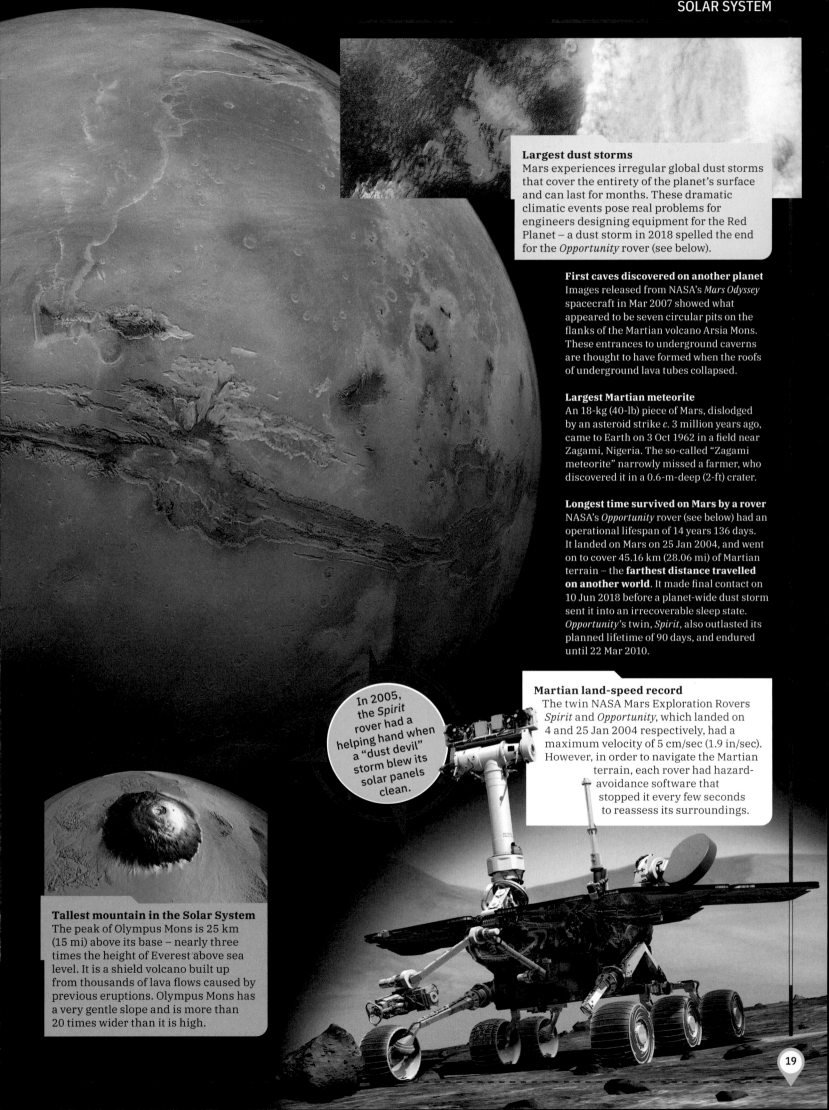

Largest dust storms

Mars experiences irregular global dust storms that cover the entirety of the planet's surface and can last for months. These dramatic climatic events pose real problems for engineers designing equipment for the Red Planet – a dust storm in 2018 spelled the end for the *Opportunity* rover (see below).

First caves discovered on another planet

Images released from NASA's *Mars Odyssey* spacecraft in Mar 2007 showed what appeared to be seven circular pits on the flanks of the Martian volcano Arsia Mons. These entrances to underground caverns are thought to have formed when the roofs of underground lava tubes collapsed.

Largest Martian meteorite

An 18-kg (40-lb) piece of Mars, dislodged by an asteroid strike *c.* 3 million years ago, came to Earth on 3 Oct 1962 in a field near Zagami, Nigeria. The so-called "Zagami meteorite" narrowly missed a farmer, who discovered it in a 0.6-m-deep (2-ft) crater.

Longest time survived on Mars by a rover

NASA's *Opportunity* rover (see below) had an operational lifespan of 14 years 136 days. It landed on Mars on 25 Jan 2004, and went on to cover 45.16 km (28.06 mi) of Martian terrain – the **farthest distance travelled on another world**. It made final contact on 10 Jun 2018 before a planet-wide dust storm sent it into an irrecoverable sleep state. *Opportunity*'s twin, *Spirit*, also outlasted its planned lifetime of 90 days, and endured until 22 Mar 2010.

In 2005, the *Spirit* rover had a helping hand when a "dust devil" storm blew its solar panels clean.

Martian land-speed record

The twin NASA Mars Exploration Rovers *Spirit* and *Opportunity*, which landed on 4 and 25 Jan 2004 respectively, had a maximum velocity of 5 cm/sec (1.9 in/sec). However, in order to navigate the Martian terrain, each rover had hazard-avoidance software that stopped it every few seconds to reassess its surroundings.

Tallest mountain in the Solar System

The peak of Olympus Mons is 25 km (15 mi) above its base – nearly three times the height of Everest above sea level. It is a shield volcano built up from thousands of lava flows caused by previous eruptions. Olympus Mons has a very gentle slope and is more than 20 times wider than it is high.

Jupiter

Largest planet in the Solar System
Jupiter has an equatorial diameter of 139,822 km (86,881 mi), making it 11 times wider than Earth. It has more than twice the mass of all the other Solar System planets combined. Spacecraft from Earth harness Jupiter's intense gravity to slingshot themselves farther into space.

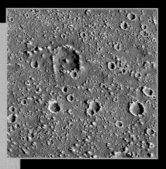

Most craters on any moon
The icy surface of Callisto is 100% covered with impact craters. No evidence of any other geological processes have been discovered, meaning that this moon's pock-marked landscape is likely the oldest surface in the Solar System. Callisto is the outermost of Jupiter's four Galilean moons, and was discovered – along with Io, Ganymede and Europa – by Galileo Galilei in 1610.

Planet with the shortest day
Jupiter spins around on its axis once every 9 hr 55 min 29.69 sec, making a Jovian day less than half the length of one on Earth.

Strongest magnetic field
Jupiter's magnetic field is a little less than 3,000 times stronger than Earth's, and extends several million kilometres into space from the planet's cloud tops. The field is generated by the **largest metallic hydrogen ocean**, which resides within Jupiter's interior and has a depth of up to 55,000 km (34,175 mi). At pressures

exceeding around 4 million bar (400,000,000 kilopascal) – 3,600 times the pressure at the **deepest point in Earth's oceans**, the Challenger Deep – hydrogen atoms become ionized, giving the liquid hydrogen metallic properties and making it an electrical conductor.

Largest moon in the Solar System
Ganymede has a mean diameter of 5,262.4 km (3,269.9 mi). Larger than the planet Mercury (see p.14), it is the ninth-largest object in the Solar System. It is also the only moon with its own magnetic field.

Jupiter

The fifth planet from the Sun, Jupiter is a gas giant composed primarily of hydrogen and helium. Its extreme environment is unable to support human life, but its moons may be another story...

Average distance from the Sun	5.2 au (778 million km)
Equatorial diameter	139,822 km
Mass	1.8982×10^{27} kg
Surface gravity	27.79 m/s²
Rotation period (day)	9 hr 55 min 29.69 sec
Orbital period (year)	11 Earth years 314 days
Number of moons	79

JUPITER

Most powerful auroras in the Solar System
The Jovian auroras are driven by electric potentials of up to 400 kiloelectronvolts, some 10 to 30 times stronger than those measured on Earth. The auroras form when energized particles are accelerated into Jupiter's atmosphere by its powerful magnetic field. These particles collide with atoms near the poles, creating flashes of light.

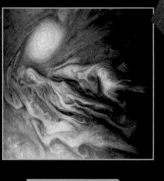

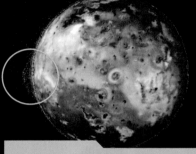

Most distant solar-powered spacecraft

As it orbits Jupiter, NASA's *Juno* space probe is carried as far as 816.62 million km (507.42 million mi) from the Sun. Pictures of Jupiter from the JunoCam imager have been colour-enhanced by citizen scientists Gerald Eichstädt and Seán Doran to highlight the swirling clouds and storms rippling above the planet's surface (inset).

Densest moon in the Solar System

Io has an average density of 3,530 kg/m³ (220 lb/cu ft). Earth's own Moon is the second densest, at 3,346 kg/m³ (208 lb/cu ft).

Planet with the most Trojan asteroids

Trojan asteroids are clusters of small bodies that circle the Sun in the same orbit as a planet. They sit in areas of stability called the L_4 and L_5 Lagrange points, where the gravitational forces of Jupiter and the Sun are balanced. As of 10 Dec 2019, some 7,284 Trojan asteroids had been discovered sharing Jupiter's orbit. Neptune had 23, Mars nine, while Earth and Uranus had one each.

Most spacecraft to visit an outer planet

Jupiter has been visited by nine unmanned spacecraft. *Pioneer 10* performed the **first Jupiter fly-by** on 3 Dec 1973, followed by *Pioneer 11* in 1974 and *Voyagers 1* and *2* in 1979. *Ulysses* achieved two long-distance fly-bys in 1992 and 2004 and the *Galileo* spacecraft orbited the gas giant from 1995 to 2003. *Cassini-Huygens* and *New Horizons* used Jupiter as a slingshot during fly-bys in 2000 and 2007, on their way to Saturn and Pluto respectively. The most recent craft to visit is *Juno*, which entered Jupiter's orbit on 4 Jul 2016 (see above).

Most volcanically active body in the Solar System

Photographs of Jupiter's moon Io taken by NASA's *Voyager 1* probe in 1979 revealed volcanic eruption plumes reaching several hundred kilometres into space (circled above). Io's activity is driven by gravitational interactions between Jupiter, Io and its close neighbour Europa.

Io is home to the **most powerful volcano in the Solar System**, Loki Patera, which emits more heat than all of Earth's active volcanoes put together. It has an enormous caldera (volcanic crater) which measures more than 10,000 km² (4,000 sq mi) and is regularly flooded with lava.

On 6 Aug 2001, while performing a close fly-by of Io, NASA's *Galileo* spacecraft passed through the top of a 500-km-high (310-mi) volcanic plume – the **highest measured volcanic eruption**.

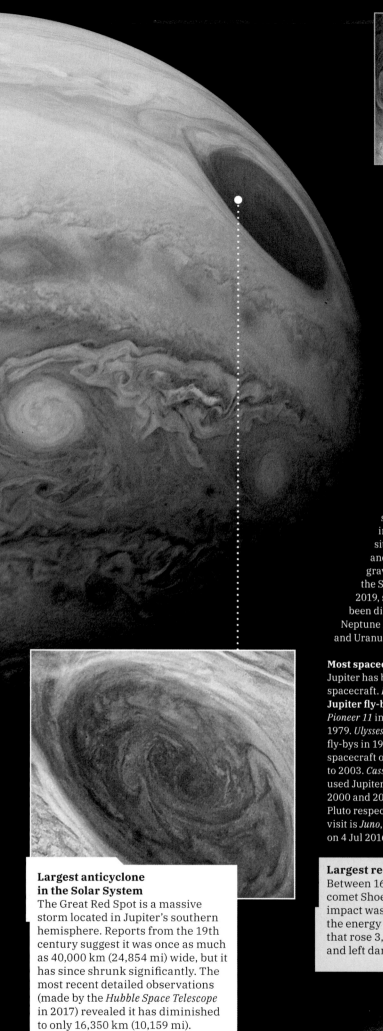

Largest anticyclone in the Solar System

The Great Red Spot is a massive storm located in Jupiter's southern hemisphere. Reports from the 19th century suggest it was once as much as 40,000 km (24,854 mi) wide, but it has since shrunk significantly. The most recent detailed observations (made by the *Hubble Space Telescope* in 2017) revealed it has diminished to only 16,350 km (10,159 mi).

Largest recorded impact in the Solar System

Between 16 and 22 Jul 1994, more than 20 fragments of comet Shoemaker-Levy 9 collided with Jupiter. The greatest impact was made by the "G" fragment, which exploded with the energy of *c.* 6 million megatons of TNT. It caused a fireball that rose 3,000 km (1,864 mi) above the Jovian cloud tops and left dark impact scars in the atmosphere (see below).

Saturn

Least dense planet

Saturn is composed mostly of hydrogen and helium, the lightest elements in the universe. As a result, it has an average density of only 687 kg/m³ (42.8 lb/cu ft) – water has a typical density of 997 kg/m³ (62.2 lb/cu ft). Saturn's low density, combined with its very fast rotation, has made it the **least round planet**, with a polar diameter that is only 90% of its equatorial diameter.

The dark gap in the ring system is called the Cassini Division, after astronomer Giovanni Cassini.

Saturn

This gloriously ringed gas giant is the second-largest planet in the Solar System. It is surrounded by a record-setting number of moons, including some that may be capable of supporting life.

Average distance from the Sun
9.53 au (1,426 million km)

Equatorial diameter
116,464 km

Mass
5.68319 x 10²⁶ kg

Surface gravity
10.44 m/s²

Rotation period (day)
10 hr 40 min

Orbital period (year)
29.44 Earth years

Number of moons
82 (see right)

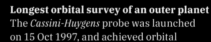

SATURN

♄

Longest orbital survey of an outer planet

The *Cassini-Huygens* probe was launched on 15 Oct 1997, and achieved orbital insertion around Saturn on 1 Jul 2004. It was finally deorbited on 15 Sep 2017, after 13 years 76 days studying the gas giant and its moons.

Cassini sent more than 635 gigabytes of data back to Earth over the years, resulting in 3,948 scientific papers and many new discoveries. It also carried the *Huygens* lander, which made its descent on to Titan on 14 Jan 2005, setting the record for **most distant soft landing** in the process.

Tallest eye-wall clouds

Over the exact location of Saturn's south pole, there is a massive hurricane-like vortex of clouds. It was first observed by the *Cassini* spacecraft on 11 Oct 2006, which measured eye-wall clouds with a vertical extent of between 35 and 70 km (18–46 mi). Although large storms are known to exist on other planets, none exhibits the largely cloud-free eye of a terrestrial storm. Follow-up observations revealed that this storm is the **warmest spot on Saturn** (see opposite), though the reason for this is still unknown.

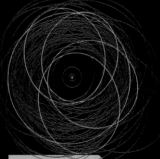

Most moons

On 7 Oct 2019, the International Astronomical Union's Minor Planet Center acknowledged 20 new satellites orbiting Saturn, bringing the planet's total number of moons to 82 (Jupiter only has 79 known moons). The image above – created by the Carnegie Institution for Science team that discovered the new satellites – shows the orbital tracks of all 82 moons.

Largest ring system in the Solar System

The extensive system of rings around Saturn have a combined mass of around 15.4 quintillion kg (16 quadrillion US tons). While this is more than can be found in the rings of any other planet, these discs of ice and debris only account for a tiny fraction of the mass orbiting Saturn. The moon Titan (see right) by itself is around 8,700 times more massive than the ring system.

Largest moon of Saturn

With a diameter of 5,149 km (3,199 mi), Titan is the largest of Saturn's satellites. Its dense atmosphere (see opposite) hides an active world with a hydrologic cycle similar to that of Earth. The difference is that because Titan is so cold (-176°C; -284°F), the working fluid in this cycle is methane rather than water. This means that Titan has methane clouds whose rain feeds methane rivers, lakes and seas. The **longest known extraterrestrial river** is Titan's Vid Flumina, which flows for 412 km (265 mi) through deep canyons to a methane sea called the Ligeia Mare.

Longest-lasting lightning storm

The *Cassini* probe observed many large lightning storms on Saturn, the longest of which raged from mid-Jan to Sep 2009 – more than eight months of almost constant lightning strikes.

Most distant planetary ring

The Phoebe Ring is a nearly imperceptible ring of dust located around 12.95 million km (8.05 million mi) above Saturn's surface. The ring, formed by impacts on the outer moon Phoebe, was discovered in 2009.

Closest moon to Saturn

The moonlet S2009/S1 orbits Saturn around 56,700 km (35,230 mi) above its cloud-tops. It orbits within the B ring. With a diameter of just 300 m (984 ft), S2009/S1 is also the **smallest moon of Saturn** whose existence had been confirmed as of Dec 2019.

Satellite with the thickest atmosphere

Titan, the **largest moon of Saturn** (see above right), has a surface atmospheric pressure of 144 kiloPascals (1.42 atm) – that's more

Largest hexagon in the Solar System

Saturn's north pole is capped by a 29,000-km-wide (18,000-mi) hexagonal cloud system. It is not known how this feature formed, and further studies have only added to the mystery. In 2005, researchers reported the **highest temperatures recorded on Saturn**, -122°C (-188°F), over the southern pole, as well as a similar heat spike over the north, where temperatures would be expected to be at their lowest (infra-red image, above right).

than 40% greater than Earth's. The moon's combination of a dense atmosphere and weak gravity means that very little energy would be required to fly on Titan. In 2019, NASA announced it will be sending a 450-kg (900-lb) multi-rotor drone called *Dragonfly* to explore the moon's surface in the 2020s.

Smallest rounded world

Mimas, the 20th-largest moon in the Solar System, is just 396.6 km (246.4 mi) across. Despite its diminutive size, it has just enough mass for the force of its own gravity to have pulled it into a more or less spherical shape. Less dense or smaller objects remain in irregular shapes.

Tallest ridge in the Solar System

On 31 Dec 2004, observations of Saturn's moon Iapetus by *Cassini* revealed a huge ridge approximately 20 km (12 mi) tall. It is at least 1,300 km (800 mi) long; Iapetus itself is only 1,400 km (890 mi) across.

Most geysers on a moon

At the south pole of Enceladus there is a series of cracks (see inset, right) that cut deep into the moon's icy crust. These fissures are punctuated by geysers, which vent water from the moon's subsurface ocean into space. *Cassini* made 23 passes by Enceladus, including flights through the plumes (below). From the data gathered on these passes, researchers have identified 101 distinct geysers, and there may be more.

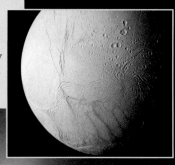

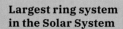

The ice crystals from Enceladus' plumes have spread out to form a faint ring around Saturn called the E ring.

Uranus

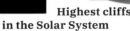

Longest period of daylight and darkness on any planet in the Solar System

Owing to Uranus's pronounced axial tilt (see below), its polar regions take turns to point almost directly at the Sun. Over the course of the planet's 84-year-long orbit of the Sun, this means each pole receives 42 years of non-stop sunlight, followed by 42 years of non-stop darkness.

First fly-by of Uranus

On 24 Jan 1986, NASA's *Voyager 2* spacecraft made its closest approach to Uranus. The probe came within 81,500 km (50,640 mi) of the cloud tops of the planet. To date, *Voyager 2* remains the only robotic probe to reach Uranus.

Voyager 2 was launched on 20 Aug 1977, and was joined by its twin *Voyager 1* just over two weeks later on 5 Sep. Their long-duration mission was to perform fly-bys of the giant outer planets Jupiter, Saturn, Uranus and Neptune. On 25 Aug 2012, *Voyager 1* became the **first probe to leave the Solar System**, and remains the **most distant artificial object**. It is 22.1 billion km (13.7 billion mi) from the Sun as of 13 Dec 2019.

Largest tilt of any planet

Uranus spins on an axis that is slanted 97.77° relative to its orbital plane; by way of comparison, Earth's axial tilt is 23.5° at present. Astronomers have speculated that Uranus's extreme tilt is the consequence of a collision with an Earth-sized planet, likely during the early formation of the Solar System, which knocked Uranus on its side.

Highest cliffs in the Solar System

Uranus's moon Miranda has a surface comprising of a jumble of bizarre geological features. One of the most prominent is an enormous cliff with a vertical relief of about 20 km (12 mi). Named Verona Rupes, it is more than 10 times higher than the walls of the Grand Canyon in Arizona, USA.

Coldest atmospheric temperature on a planet

In Jan 1986, *Voyager 2* recorded a temperature of -224°C (-371°F) on Uranus. Despite being 1.62 billion km (1 billion mi) closer to the Sun than Neptune, Uranus has a cooler core, meaning that the average temperature on the two planets is more or less the same. Uranus may have lost a significant amount of heat and energy in the hypothetical collision event mentioned above.

Uranus	
Uranus is the first of the Solar System's two "ice giants" – cold and distant worlds that formed from heavier elements than their inner neighbours Jupiter and Saturn.	
Average distance from the Sun	19.8 au (2.87 x 10⁹ km)
Equatorial diameter	50,724 km
Mass	8.68103 x 10²⁵ kg
Surface gravity	8.87 m/s²
Rotation period (day)	17 hr 14 min
Orbital period (year)	84 Earth years 6 days
Number of moons	27

URANUS

First planet discovered by telescope

On 13 Mar 1781, British astronomer William Herschel observed a "star" from his garden in Bath, Somerset, UK. He originally reported it as a newly discovered comet, although it was later recognized as a new planet and named Uranus. It is possible to see Uranus with the naked eye, and countless people would have observed it before Herschel.

Largest moon of Uranus

Titania, the largest of Uranus's 27 moons, has a diameter of 1,578 km (980 mi) and orbits the planet at a mean distance of 435,000 km (270,300 mi). It was discovered in 1787 by William Herschel. Images returned by *Voyager 2* revealed a surface of impact craters and tectonic features, including the trench-like Messina Chasmata, some 1,490 km (925 mi) long.

William Herschel's sister Caroline, who assisted him, was the first woman to be awarded the Royal Astronomical Society's gold medal.

Neptune

Farthest planet in the Solar System
Since the demotion of Pluto as a planet in 2006, Neptune is now the farthest major planet from the Sun. At 4.498 billion km (2.8 billion mi) from the heart of our Solar System, it circles the Sun at 19,566 km/h (12,158 mph), taking 164 years 288 days to complete one orbit. Although first seen in 1846, Neptune's existence had been mathematically predicted beforehand.

First fly-by of Neptune
On 25 Aug 1989, *Voyager 2* made its closest approach to Neptune following a three-and-a-half-year cruise from Uranus. The probe came within 4,800 km (2,980 mi) of the cloud tops above the planet's north pole, the closest *Voyager 2* had been to any planet since it left Earth in 1977.

Most distant moon from a planet
Neso, the 13th moon of Neptune, was first observed on 14 Aug 2002 and officially recognized in 2003. It circles Neptune at an average distance of 48,370,000 km (30,055,724 mi), taking 9,374 days (25 years 240 days) to make one orbit. Neso is around 60 km (37 mi) in diameter.

Tallest nitrogen geysers
When *Voyager 2* encountered Neptune's large moon Triton in 1989, the probe's cameras discovered active cryovolcanism in the form of geysers of nitrogen gas and snow. Reaching heights of up to 8 km (5 mi) into Triton's thin atmosphere, these eruptions

Fastest winds in the Solar System
Measured by NASA's *Voyager 2* probe in 1989, the winds circulating around Neptune blow at around 2,400 km/h (1,500 mph), propelling frozen methane clouds across the surface. That's around five times faster than the **fastest estimated wind speed on Earth** – a gust of *c.* 486 km/h (302 mph) measured in a tornado in Oklahoma, USA, in 1999 (see p.39).

Largest retrograde satellite
When a moon orbits in the opposite direction to its planet's rotation, its orbit is described as "retrograde". Triton, the largest of Neptune's satellites, measures 2,706 km (1,681 mi) across. Triton's unusual retrograde orbit implies that it was once a Kuiper Belt object that was "captured" by Neptune's gravity.

are believed to be caused by weak sunlight heating nitrogen ice lying just below the moon's surface.

These ejections of frigid nitrogen gas also represent the **coldest observed geological activity**. With a surface temperature of only -235°C (-391°F), Triton is so cold that lakes of water are frozen as hard as steel, and retain impact craters that are millions of years old.

Closest moons to each other
The nearest approach between two satellites occurs roughly every five days between Naiad and Thalassa, two small moons of Neptune. Naiad, the innermost of the two, orbits Neptune at a slightly faster rate than Thalassa. Each time it overtakes Thalassa, they pass within 3,540 km (2,200 mi) of each other.

Most eccentric satellite
In this context, "eccentric" describes the degree to which a body's orbit deviates from a perfect circle. Nereid, the third-largest moon of Neptune, has a mean eccentricity of 0.7507. Its highly elliptic orbit brings it to within 1,372,000 km (852,500 mi) of Neptune before swinging out to a distance of 9,655,000 km (6,000,000 mi). Nereid was discovered on 1 May 1949 by Dutch-American astronomer Gerard Kuiper.

Most planets visited by one spacecraft
NASA's *Voyager 2* spacecraft, which was launched in 1977, visited all four of the outer gas giants (Jupiter, Saturn, Uranus and Neptune) between 1979 and 1989. In Nov 2018, it left the Solar System and entered interstellar space – a region beyond the Sun's influence – as its fellow probe *Voyager 1* had in Aug 2012.

Neptune
The most distant known planet, Neptune is an ice giant some 30 times farther from the Sun than Earth. Its atmosphere is a mix of methane (which creates its blue hue), hydrogen and helium.

Average distance from the Sun	30 au (4.498 x 10⁹ km)
Equatorial diameter	49,244 km
Mass	1.0241 x 10²⁶ kg
Surface gravity	11.15 m/s²
Rotation period (day)	16 hr
Orbital period (year)	164 Earth years 288 days
Number of moons	14

NEPTUNE

Round-Up

First pictures taken on the surface of an asteroid
At 02:44 UTC on 22 Sep 2018, Japan's *HIBOU* rover began taking images from asteroid 162173 Ryugu, having been launched from the Japanese Space Agency's *Hayabusa2* probe the previous day. The main photograph above shows a close-up of Ryugu's rocky surface; the white patches in the inset picture are sunlight.

revealed that 243 Ida, which is 59.8 km (37.1 mi) along its longest axis, has its own natural satellite. Since named Dactyl, it has an average diameter of just 1.6 km (0.9 mi).

Largest source of comets
Beyond Neptune's orbit lies the Oort Cloud, an icy, spherical shell composed of thousands of billions of cometary nuclei. It begins more than 300 billion km (185 billion mi) from the Sun and extends far into

Largest crater on Pluto
Highlighted above, Sputnik Planum in Pluto's northern hemisphere measures *c.* 1,050 x 800 km (650 x 495 mi). It was formed by an impact with a body 10 km (6.2 mi) across, about 90 times longer than an American football field. The bright surface is dominated by nitrogen ice, while its smoothness suggests that it is under 10 million years old.

First asteroid landing
The *NEAR-Shoemaker* spacecraft touched down on asteroid 433 Eros on 12 Feb 2001, shortly before the end of its mission. The spacecraft took pictures during its descent, but as *NEAR*'s only camera faced towards Eros (i.e., straight down), it returned no images from the surface.

Eros was the **first near-Earth asteroid discovered**. Astronomers Carl Gustav Witt (DEU) and Auguste Charlois (FRA)

independently detected its presence in 1898. The curious orbit of 433 Eros brings it within the orbit of Mars and closer to Earth than any other planet or asteroid. It was named after the Greek god of love.

First asteroid found to have a moon
While en route to Jupiter, NASA's *Galileo* spacecraft performed a flyby of the asteroid Ida in 1993. On 17 Feb 1994, examination of the images from the flyby

interstellar space. The Oort Cloud is believed to be the source of most of the comets that visit the inner Solar System. NASA's *Voyager 1* probe, which is currently travelling at 62,140 km/h (38,612 mph), will take about 300 years to reach the inner edge of the Oort Cloud.

Smallest quasi-satellite of Earth
Quasi-satellites orbit the Sun on a path that never takes them too far from a particular planet, but never near enough for them to become locked into orbit around it. On 27 Apr 2016, the *Pan-STARRS 1* survey telescope on Haleakala in Hawaii, USA, discovered a small asteroid estimated to measure *c.* 40–100 m (130–320 ft) across. Named 469219 Kamo`oalewa, it is the fifth quasi-satellite of Earth discovered to date. It orbits the Sun in exactly one year, during which time it loops around Earth, trailing the planet for half of its orbit and leading it for the other half. It has been estimated that during this "orbital dance" with Earth, the asteroid never approaches closer than 14.5 million km (9 million mi) and never recedes to farther than about 38.6 million km (23.9 million mi).

First image from the surface of a comet
On 12 Nov 2014, the *Philae* lander alighted on comet 67P/Churyumov-Gerasimenko. Unfortunately, *Philae*'s touchdown left it in shadow and tilted, making it impossible for its cameras to take a 360° panorama of the landing site. The first image released, on 13 Nov 2014, was a mosaic from two of *Philae*'s cameras, showing the cliff face it had landed next to, as well as part of the lander itself.

First all-female spacewalk
On 18 Oct 2019, NASA astronauts Jessica Meir (left) and Christina Koch (both USA) performed a spacewalk to replace a malfunctioning battery-charge unit on the exterior of the *International Space Station* (*ISS*). They began their extra-vehicular activity at 11:32 UTC, and returned to the airlock with the faulty component 7 hr 23 min later.

The **first woman to perform a spacewalk** was Soviet cosmonaut Svetlana Savitskaya, outside the *Salyut 7* space station on 25 Jul 1984.

While outside the *ISS*, Meir and Koch paid tribute to Alexei Leonov (RUS), who carried out the **first spacewalk** on 18 Mar 1965. He had died a week earlier.

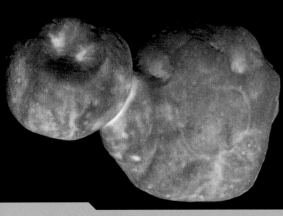

Most distant Solar System object to be explored

On 1 Jan 2019 at 05:33 UTC, the space probe *New Horizons* visited an asteroid in the Kuiper Belt that was initially nicknamed "Ultima Thule" but later given the name "Arrokoth", after a Native American word for "sky". The probe collected around 50 Gbit of data about the asteroid. An initial batch of downlinked images have revealed it to be a "contact binary" consisting of two connected spheres *c.* 31 km (19 mi) long.

Smallest astronomical object with rings

The remote asteroid 10199 Chariklo has a diameter of 248 km (154 mi). Two distinct rings orbiting it were spotted by the European Southern Observatory (ESO), who published their findings in *Nature* on 26 Mar 2014. The ESO trained their telescopes on the star UCAC4 248–108672 on 3 Jun 2013, as it was predicted that an astronomical object would pass in front of the star. Astronomers at seven different locations

saw the light from the star blocked by the object, but also detected two very short dips in its apparent brightness. These were later identified as rings orbiting Chariklo.

Smallest object orbited by a spacecraft

At 19:44 UTC on 31 Dec 2018, the NASA spacecraft *OSIRIS-REx* executed an 8-sec thruster firing that inserted the vessel into orbit around an asteroid known as 101955 Bennu. The latter has a mass of 73.2 million tonnes (80.7 million US tons) and a diameter of 510 m (1,673 ft) measured from pole to pole.

ARROKOTH

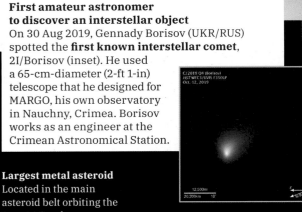

First amateur astronomer to discover an interstellar object

On 30 Aug 2019, Gennady Borisov (UKR/RUS) spotted the **first known interstellar comet**, 2I/Borisov (inset). He used a 65-cm-diameter (2-ft 1-in) telescope that he designed for MARGO, his own observatory in Nauchny, Crimea. Borisov works as an engineer at the Crimean Astronomical Station.

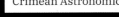

Largest metal asteroid

Located in the main asteroid belt orbiting the Sun, 16 Psyche measures some 279 x 232 x 189 km (173 x 144 x 117 mi). Radar observations indicate that it is probably 90% iron. In Jan 2017, NASA approved a mission to this body, which may be a suitable candidate for future asteroid mining.

Nearest extrasolar planet

On 24 Aug 2016, astronomers announced their discovery of a planet orbiting Proxima Centauri, outside our Solar System. Around 4.224 light years

(39.9 trillion km; 24.8 trillion mi) away, Proxima Centauri b is similar in size to Earth. Its presence was confirmed using a number of facilities, including the European Southern Observatory's 3.6-m-diameter (11-ft 9-in) telescope at La Silla in Chile.

Excluding the Sun, Proxima Centauri is the **nearest star**, but it would still take a craft going as fast as *Voyager 1* about 73,000 years to get there.

Dwarf planets

There are five of these astronomical bodies in the Solar System. Pluto **(1)** is the **largest dwarf planet** with an average diameter of *c.* 2,376 km (1,476 mi). It also has the **most moons for a dwarf planet**: five. They are Charon, Hydra, Kerberos, Nix and Styx. While it has a smaller diameter than Pluto, Eris **(2)** is the **most massive dwarf planet** at 1.66×10^{22} kg (1.82×10^{19} US tons). Haumea **(3)**, which spins so fast it has been distorted into an oval, is the **first dwarf planet with a ring** – of icy particles. All three, like Makemake **(4)**, are located in the Kuiper Belt, a region beyond Neptune that is home to thousands of frozen cosmic bodies dating from the early Solar System. Finally, with an average diameter of 941 km (584.7 mi), Ceres **(5)** is the **smallest dwarf planet** but also the **largest body in the main asteroid belt** between Mars and Jupiter.

A dwarf planet is a body large enough to have been rounded by its own gravity, but not large enough to have cleared its orbit of debris.

HALL OF FAME

Buzz Aldrin

In the history of human exploration, few have pushed the limits of discovery further than the Moon. In 1969, two US astronauts became the first crewed mission to land on another world: Commander Neil Armstrong, and lunar module pilot ⊙ Dr Buzz Aldrin.

I n the history of human exploration, few have pushed the limits of discovery further than the Moon. In 1969, two US astronauts became the first humans to step foot on another world ⊙ Dr Buzz Aldrin.

Before joining NASA, Buzz had flown fighter planes for the US Air Force in the Korean War. In 1966, he flew into space for the first time, on the Gemini 12 mission. Three years later, he joined Neil Armstrong and Michael Collins as they blasted off for the Moon.

Before joining NASA, Buzz earned a doctorate in orbital dynamics. Buzz and Armstrong and Michael Collins (Coordinated Universal Time), Buzz and for the first time, and Michael Collins as they blasted off for the Moon.

On 20 Jul 1969, at 20:18 UTC (Coordinated Universal Time), Buzz and Armstrong landed Apollo's lunar module, the *Eagle*, on the surface at the Moon's Sea of Tranquility. Following two astronauts spent more than two hours 02:56 UTC on 21 Jul, Buzz recalled. "Very clear. No collecting samples...terrain," Buzz recalled. "Very clear. No black sky, the sunlit terrain."

On 20 Jul 1969, at 20:18 UTC (Coordinated Universal Time), Buzz and Armstrong landed Apollo's lunar module, the *Eagle*, on the surface at the Moon's Sea of Tranquility. Following two astronauts spent more desolate: the 02:56 UTC on 21 Jul, "Nothing," Buzz recalled. "Very clear. No collecting samples...terrain," black sky. No life.

The astronauts returned safely to Earth on 24 Jul, whereupon they received a hero's welcome. Yet atmosphere.

The astronauts returned safely to Earth on 24 Jul, whereupon they received the world – and the Buzz's drive to discover remained undimmed.

Buzz's drive to discover the world undimmed. He dived to both the wreck of the *Titanic* and South Poles. universe – around him advocate for the North and travelled to both the North advocate for the He also became a passionate about Mars. As Buzz puts it: the explore, or we expire. "We explore, or we expire."

He also became a passionate about Mars. He explore, or we expire. "We explore, or we expire."

The first crewed mission to land on the Moon was Apollo 11, which touched down on 20 July 1969 (EDT). On board the Eagle Lunar Module were Neil Armstrong and Buzz Aldrin, who subsequently became the first humans to walk on the Moon, while Michael Collins remained in orbit in the Command Module.

OFFICIALLY AMAZING

Buzz was given his nickname by his sister, who mispronounced "brother" as "buzzer".

On behalf of the next generation of space pioneers, Buzz has spent years devising a transportation system between Earth and Mars. He believes the best system employs a fleet of spacecraft "cycling" between Earth and Mars, with the gravity of the two planets. This would involve using the gravity of Mars and Earth to loop between the two planets, virtually no fuel consumption.

In 1998, Buzz joined the crew of a Russian ice breaker to visit the North Pole. He ate a meal on the ice and even joined in with an impromptu softball game. Two years earlier, Buzz had dived 3,810 m (12,500 ft) in a French minisubmarine, the *Nautile*, to explore the wreck of the *Titanic* in the North Atlantic Ocean.

1: Buzz on the Moon's surface, as photographed by Neil Armstrong.

2: A hologram Buzz acts as a guide through his virtual-reality vision for a human settlement on Mars.

3: On 13 Nov 1966, during a tethered Gemini 12 mission, Buzz takes the **first selfie in open space.**

4: The three-man crew of Apollo 11: left to right, Neil Armstrong, Michael Collins and Buzz Aldrin.

5: In 2016, at the age of 86, Buzz becomes the **oldest person to visit both poles.** the **oldest person to visit the South Pole** and the **oldest person to visit both poles.**

Find out more about Buzz in the Hall of Fame section at **www.guinnessworldrecords.com/2021**

Apollo 11's Michael Collins (centre) piloted the Command Module Columbia and did not set foot on the Moon.

Natural World

Largest concentration of sandstone pillars
Situated in north-west Hunan, China, Zhangjiajie Sandstone Peak Forest Geopark contains more than 3,100 natural quartz sandstone pillars and columns – with an average density of 37.5 peaks per square km (97.1 peaks per square mi). More than 1,000 of these reach at least 120 m (393 ft) in height, and 45 soar to 300 m (984 ft). The topography is thought to have formed predominantly through physical erosion caused by expanding ice in winter and plant growth in spring.

As well as its breathtaking natural wonders, the park is home to the Zhangjiajie Grand Canyon Glass Footbridge – the **highest footbridge**, at 260 m (853 ft) – and the Bailong Elevator (right), which at 326 m (1,070 ft) is the ◗ **tallest outdoor elevator**, standing higher than London's Shard.

Zhangjiajie is one of 147 UNESCO Global Geoparks. It was recognized in 2004.

DESTINATIONS

Zhangjiajie's landscape was the inspiration for Pandora's Hallelujah Mountains in the sci-fi blockbuster *Avatar* (USA, 2009).

Water

Saltiest lake

Located in the Danakil Depression in the Afar Region of Ethiopia, the Gaet'ale Pond has 43.3% salt by weight. This is nearly twice the salinity of the Dead Sea.

The Danakil Depression is one of the hottest and driest places in the world. It is also the centre of the **newest-forming ocean**. Following the opening of a 56-km (35-mi) rift in 2005, tectonic shifts beneath the surface indicate that the region will one day be flooded with water.

Deepest river

The Congo River spans 10 countries in Africa and has a maximum depth of at least 220 m (721 ft) based on measurements taken in Jul 2008.

Africa is also home to the **longest river**. The Nile snakes northwards 6,695 km (4,160 mi) from Burundi to the Mediterranean Sea on Egypt's coast.

Most alkaline lakes

The Rift Valley of Kenya and Tanzania contains saline bodies of water that reach 50°C (122°F) and pH levels of 10 to 12 – strong enough to burn skin. The corrosiveness is caused by high concentrations of sodium carbonate (soda), chlorine and phosphorus produced by local volcanoes. The deep red colour of Lake Natron (below) is the result of pigments produced by algae that thrive in the hypersaline environment.

Largest hyperacid lake

Found on the Indonesian island of Java, the crater lake in the Kawah Ijen volcano has an area of 0.6 km² (0.2 sq mi), a maximum depth of 200 m (660 ft) and a volume of 27.5 million m³ (971 million cu ft). Its waters have a pH of less than 0, corrosive enough to eat through metal. Upon exposure to oxygen-rich air, the sulphuric gases burn with an electric blue flame, with some of the gas condensing into molten sulphur (see inset).

Lowest river

The mouth of the Jordan River lies *c.* 430 m (1,410 ft) below sea level. It is the only major water source that flows into the Dead Sea, the **lowest exposed body of water**. The hot climate evaporates the water flowing in from the Jordan before the lake can overflow. For the **highest river**, see right.

Largest concentration of geysers

Yellowstone National Park, which lies mostly in Wyoming, USA, contains more than 10,000 thermal features including 500 geysers – two-thirds of the planet's total.

One of the most notable is Steamboat Geyser, whose jets can reach in excess of 91.4 m (300 ft) – making it the **tallest active geyser**. Steamboat erupted 48 times in 2019, breaking its record for a calendar year.

Largest hot spring (surface area)

Frying Pan Lake (aka Waimangu Cauldron) is a natural hot spring covering *c.* 38,000 m² (409,000 sq ft) with an average water temperature of 50–60°C (122–140°F). It is found in the Echo Crater of the Waimangu Volcanic Rift Valley in New Zealand.

Highest river

Known as the "Everest of Rivers", the Yarlung Zangbo has a source lying some 6,020 m (19,750 ft) above sea level, at the foot of the Angsi Glacier in Tibet Autonomous Region, China. It flows east across the Tibetan Plateau and through the **deepest canyon** (see p.35) before crossing into India, where it is known as the Brahmaputra River.

Widest waterfall

The Khône Falls on the Mekong River in Laos have a total width of 10.78 km (6.7 mi). This is almost the same distance as the depth of the Challenger Deep, the **deepest point in the sea** (see pp.160–61). The falls comprise a series of rapids and waterfalls – the tallest of which is about 21 m (69 ft) high – that weave between numerous small islands and rocky outcrops.

LONGEST UNDERWATER CAVE SYSTEM EXPLORED

In 2019, naturalist Steve Backshall led an elite team of divers through the flooded caves of Sistema Sac Actun in Mexico's Yucatán Peninsula for the BBC show *Undiscovered Worlds*. The system had 371.95 km (231.1 mi) of recorded tunnels as of Jul 2019. He talked to GWR about his experience.

How did these caves compare to those you've explored previously?
I'd done a lot of training and cave dives in the past, but actually exploring new systems is a notch up.

Describe the conditions.
There's no light. The water temperature is pretty constant, and comfortable unless you end up on a long dive, or stop moving. Then it starts to feel super cold!

What was running through your mind when you temporarily got stuck in a narrow passage?
Don't panic! I just had to keep focusing on my gauges and move slowly backwards and forwards until the cave let me go!

What wildlife did you see?
Way more than I expected: crocodiles, turtles, tarpon, shrimp and isopods in the darkness. We didn't find any new species, but in one cave we found so many thousands of blind cave fish that my expert buddy could not believe his eyes!

How did the Mexican underwater caves rate compared to your other "undiscovered worlds"?
We were only a stone's throw from hundreds of tourists on the beach and yet we were in places no human has ever been. That's quite something.

First proven "rogue wave"
Long deemed a maritime myth, rogue, or freak, waves are unpredictable and far bigger than the ones that precede and follow them. On 1 Jan 1995, the first confirmed measurement of this rare phenomenon occurred when a 25.6-m-tall (84-ft) wave struck the Draupner oil rig in the North Sea.

Tallest multi-tiered waterfall
Located in South Africa's Drakensberg ("Dragon's Mountains"), Tugela Falls is Earth's second-tallest waterfall. It descends 948 m (3,110 ft) over a series of five drops.
    The **tallest waterfall** is Venezuela's Kerepakupai Merú – aka Angel Falls. Its full drop has been measured at 979 m (3,212 ft).

Warmest ocean
The Indian Ocean has a minimum surface temperature of around 22°C (72°F) and can reach as high as 28°C (82°F) towards the east. At 73,556,000 km² (28,400,000 sq mi), it covers approximately 20% of Earth's surface but has no contact with the icy Arctic Ocean, which helps to maintain its warm temperatures throughout the year.

Largest underwater waterfall (by volume)
The 3.5-km-high (2.17-mi) Denmark Strait Cataract carries around 5 million m³ (176.5 million cu ft) of water every second. The submarine waterfall occurs where the icy Greenland Sea meets the warmer Irminger Sea. The colder water molecules, being less active and more dense, slide under the warmer molecules and over a great drop in the ocean floor.

Deepest blue hole
Blue holes are circular marine caverns or sinkholes notable for their dark blue waters. Dragon Hole, situated off the Paracel Islands in the South China Sea, reaches a depth of 301 m (987 ft) – the same height as the Eiffel Tower.

1960 **2011**

Greatest shrinkage of a lake
Located on the border between Uzbekistan and Kazakhstan, the Aral Sea was once the fourth-largest freshwater lake on Earth. But when Soviet authorities diverted away feeder rivers for land irrigation, it caused an 85% decrease in the Aral Sea's surface area between 1960 and 2011 – from 67,499 to 10,317 km² (26,061 to 3,983 sq mi). The lake bed is now largely desert, though World Bank aid has enabled Kazakhstan to build the Kok-Aral Dam, boosting water levels in the sea's northern section.

During monsoon season, the Khône Falls disappear completely beneath the swollen river.

GREATEST RAINFALL IN...*

96 hr
4,936 mm
*24–27 Feb 2007
Réunion Island, Indian Ocean*

72 hr
3,930 mm
*24–26 Feb 2007
Réunion Island, Indian Ocean*

48 hr
2,493 mm
*15–16 Jun 1995
Cherrapunji (aka Sohra), India*

24 hr
1,825 mm
*7–8 Jan 1966
Réunion Island, Indian Ocean*

1 min
31.2 mm
*4 Jul 1956
Unionville, Maryland, USA*

Record rainfalls are scrutinized to ensure that the rain-gauge instrumentation and timings are correct. Three of the records above were set on the Indian Ocean island of Réunion, whose steep mountains and valleys give rise to high precipitation levels and torrential rainstorms known as *avalasses*.

* Source: all rainfall records verified by the World Meteorological Organization

Rock & Crystal

Highest mountain tabletop
Straddling the borders of Venezuela, Guyana and Brazil, the sandstone plateau of Monte Roraima soars 2,810 m (9,219 ft) above sea level. It is the loftiest example of a *tepui*, a form of flat-top mountain, or mesa, unique to northern South America. According to the local indigenous Pemón tradition, *tepuis* are the abodes of the gods.

The cloud-piercing Monte Roraima is believed to have been the inspiration for the setting of Arthur Conan Doyle's 1912 novel *The Lost World*.

Largest amethyst geode
Weighing some 13 tonnes (28,660 lb) – about the same as two American school buses – and measuring longer than a three-seater sofa, this enormous amethyst-lined rock was found in Uruguay. It is now displayed at the Shandong Tianyu Museum of Natural History in Shandong, China. The institution is also home to the **largest turquoise**, a 225-kg (496-lb) stone that is 1.03 m (3 ft 5 in) long.

Oldest rock
Dating minerals is fraught with difficulty. There is no universally accepted technique for doing so, and it's hard to know whether you're ageing the rock or the material that it formed from (i.e., the "precursor").

Pieces of zircon from the Jack Hills region of Western Australia have been estimated at 4.3–4.4 billion years old. At only about the width of a human hair across, though, these crystals are not considered "rocks", but rather chips off older blocks, making them the **oldest fragments of Earth**. Although their precise age is debated, a 2014 paper that used atom-probe tomography to try to settle the argument determined them to be 4.374 billion years old (give or take 6 million years); this would make them only 160 million years younger than Earth itself.

When it comes to the **oldest rock**, one contender is bedrock taken from the Nuvvuagittuq Greenstone Belt on the shore

of Hudson Bay in Quebec, Canada, dated at 4.28 billion years old using isotopic techniques. Another is gneiss from an island in the Acasta River in Canada's Northwest Territories, with an upper age limit of 4.03 billion years calculated with radiometric dating.

The **oldest Earth rock on the Moon** came to light in Mar 2019. The study, published in *Earth and Planetary Science Letters*, focuses on a 4.011-billion-year-old chunk of felsite that was collected on the Apollo 14 mission in 1971. Its composition of quartz, zircon and feldspar (all of which are rare lunar minerals) and high oxygen content indicate it most likely formed on Earth. It is believed that the rock was blasted up to our planet's satellite after a powerful impact event.

Largest glacial erratic boulder
Glacial erratics are rocks that have been relocated by the movement of glaciers. The Okotoks Erratic, which now sits in the prairieland of Alberta, Canada, measures

Most natural arches in one region
Inaugurated in 1971, Arches National Park in Utah, USA, was so-named for the 2,000-plus sandstone arches with a span of at least 0.9 m (3 ft) within its borders. Its longest specimen – and the largest of its kind in North America – is the 88.3-m (290-ft) Landscape Arch. That puts it in fifth place globally, behind four longer arches in China.

around 41 m long, 18 m wide and some 9 m high (135 x 59 x 30 ft). It's been estimated to weigh 16,500 tonnes (18,200 US tons) – the same as 29 fully loaded Airbus A380s.

Largest single cave chamber (surface area)
Malaysia's Sarawak Chamber has an estimated surface area of 154,530 m² (1.66 million sq ft), which is around twice the size of the floor area of Buckingham Palace in London, UK. The Sarawak cave comes in second place in terms of volume (see opposite).

Largest cannonball concretions
Spherical masses of rock, known as cannonball concretions, formed millions of years ago after loose sediment became cemented together by a mineral such as calcite leaching from buried fossils or shells. As softer rock like sandstone erodes over time, the more robust boulders within are left exposed. The biggest examples, spanning up to 6 m (19 ft 8 in), can be seen in Rock City Park (above) in Minneapolis, Kansas, USA.

Tallest volcanic columns
Devils Tower (aka Bear Lodge) in Wyoming, USA, stands 264.2 m (867 ft) above its surrounding plains. The monolith's life began as a subterranean eruption of magma that then solidified. Over 50 million years, erosion wore away the softer sedimentary rock around it, leaving the tougher igneous rock behind, looming almost three times the height of the Statue of Liberty.

Apollo 17, the **longest crewed Moon mission**, carried back 110.4 kg (243 lb) of lunar material – the **most Moon rock returned** in one go.

In Oct 2019, reports emerged from Russia of an unprecedented gem: the **first diamond inside a diamond**. Read more on p.45.

Hardest mineral
According to the Mohs "scratch" hardness test, no mineral is harder than diamond, a form of carbon, with a rating of 10. Because the Mohs scale is not absolute, diamond is actually about *700 times* harder than the **softest mineral**, talc, with its score of 1. Diamonds formed more than 1 billion years ago in Earth's mantle under immense heat and pressure, before volcanic upheaval pushed them to the surface.

Deepest canyon
Situated at the eastern end of the Himalayas, the Yarlung Tsangpo Gorge in Tibet Autonomous Region, China, plunges to 5,382 m (17,657 ft) at its most extreme point. That's more than three times the deepest parts of the Grand Canyon in the USA. The Yarlung Tsangpo River, the world's **highest river** known as the "Everest of Rivers" (see p.32), flows through the valley base.

Largest uncut...
• **Piece of jade**: A single lens of nephrite jade weighing 577 tonnes (636 US tons) was found in Canada's Yukon Territory in Jul 1992. It is owned by Yukon Jade (CAN).
• **Ruby**: A corundum owned by Rajiv Golcha (IND) weighed 21.95 kg (48 lb 6 oz) and measured 31 x 16.5 x 14 cm (12.2 x 6.5 x 5.5 in), as confirmed on 3 Jun 2009.
• **Piece of amber**: Owned by Joseph Fam (SGP), it weighed 50.4 kg (111 lb 1 oz) when assessed by members of the International Amber Association on 26 Feb 2017.
• **Goshenite**: A beryl owned by Wing Kiat Cheong (SGP) tipped the scales at 1.3 kg (2 lb 13 oz) on 13 Mar 2018.

If Nanga Parbat and Everest continue to grow at their current rates, the former will surpass the latter in *c.* 200,000 years to become the **highest mountain**.

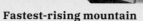

Fastest-rising mountain
Located in Pakistan and marking the westernmost point of the Himalayan range, the 8,126-m (26,660-ft) Nanga Parbat ("Naked Mountain") is growing by about 7 mm (0.27 in) per annum. That is because the collision between the Eurasian and Indian continental plates that created the Himalayas some 50 million years ago is ongoing. The **highest mountain**, Everest (see pp.46–47) – some 1,450 km (900 mi) east – is also still rising, but only by about 4 mm (0.1 in) per year.

Largest single cave chamber (volume)
The Miao Room – part of the Gebihe cave system in Ziyun Getu He National Park in Guizhou, China – has a volume of 10.78 million m³ (380.7 million cu ft), or around 10 times the capacity of the UK's Wembley Stadium. The chamber was mapped with 3D laser scanners by a British-led geology team in 2013. The Miao Room also features some of the world's tallest stalagmites, up to 45 m (148 ft) high.

Tallest granite monolith
El Capitan in Yosemite National Park, California, USA, towers 1,095 m (3,593 ft) – twice the height of Toronto's CN Tower – above the valley floor. Its summit stands 2,307 m (7,569 ft) above sea level. A magnet for extreme climbers, the natural feature is estimated to be around 100 million years old.

Ice

The previous record holder was drilled at Dome C in Antarctica and announced in 2004. Dating back 740,000 years, it remains the **oldest continuous ice core**.

Largest tropical glacier
In 2017, the Coropuna Ice Cap had a surface area of 44 km² (16.9 sq mi) – large enough to fit Vatican City inside it 100 times over. Coropuna is located in the Peruvian Andes, together with the previous record holder, Quelccaya Ice Cap. Both glaciers are shrinking, but Coropuna's rate of ice melt is slower.

Largest documented iceberg ever
On 12 Nov 1956, crew on the USS *Glacier* sighted a tabular iceberg estimated to be more than 31,000 km² (12,000 sq mi) – which would have made it larger than Belgium. The iceberg was 335 km (208 mi) long and 97 km (60 mi) wide. It was seen west of Scott Island in the Southern Ocean.

Fastest-moving glacier
The Jakobshavn Isbræ glacier ("Sermeq Kujalleq" in Greenlandic) reached a reported speed of 45 m (148 ft) per day in Aug 2004. This rapid flow has been attributed to an influx of warm ocean water into Disko Bay, on Greenland's western coast. The glacier has since slowed dramatically, especially in the aftermath of an extreme cold spell in 2013. It is possible that the RMS *Titanic* was sunk by an iceberg that had calved from Jakobshavn Isbræ.

Thickest ice
The Antarctic Ice Sheet has been measured at a thickness of 4,897 m (16,066 ft) over a region known as the Astrolabe Subglacial Basin, to the south of the Adélie Coast. This is thicker than Mount Vinson – the **highest Antarctic mountain** – stands tall (4,892 m; 16,050 ft). The basin takes its name after *Astrolabe*, the flagship of the French Antarctic Expedition (1837–40).

Largest glacial meltwater flood
Between late Sep and mid-Oct 1996, the Grímsvötn volcano erupted under the Vatnajökull glacier, the largest ice cap in Iceland. As a result, meltwater was discharged at a peak rate of some 45,000 m³ (1.58 million cu ft) – or about 18 Olympic-sized swimming pools – per second. An eruption in 1918 beneath the much smaller Mýrdalsjökull ice cap in Iceland may have generated as much as 400,000 m³ (14.12 million cu ft) per second.

1. A68A iceberg
2. Weddell Sea
3. Sea ice
4. Antarctic Peninsula

Oldest glacier ice
Ice cores are tubes of ice drilled out of glaciers that can reveal a lot about Earth's changing climate. On 15 Aug 2017, scientists announced they had uncovered "blue ice" fragments in Antarctica containing gas bubbles dated at 2.7 million years old. This beat the previous record by some 1.7 million years. Blue ice forms from snow that settles on a glacier and becomes compressed, resulting in a blueish tint to our eyes. Such ice is typically found at shallow depths, just below the snowy surface.

Largest supraglacial lake
A lake forms every year on top of the Amery Ice Shelf in eastern Antarctica during the summer months, when the surface snow and ice melts and water collects in a large trough. The largest extent of this lake was 71.5 km² (27.6 sq mi), recorded in Jan 2017 during the height of the Antarctic summer.

The **largest subglacial lake** lies more than 3.7 km (2 mi) beneath the East Antarctic Ice Sheet. The Vostok Subglacial Lake covers an area of some 14,000 km² (5,405 sq mi) and has a depth of at least 100 m (330 ft).

Highest glacier
The head of the Khumbu Glacier in north-east Nepal reaches an altitude of around 8,000 m (26,247 ft) above sea level. The 17-km-long (10.5-mi) glacier is fed by ice and snowfall from the Western Cwm valley, which lies between Mount Everest and the Lhotse-Nuptse Ridge.

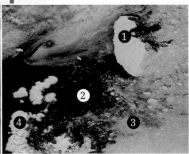

Largest satellite-measured iceberg
In Jul 2017, a chunk of ice spanning seven times the size of New York City calved from the Larsen C Ice Shelf on the Antarctic Peninsula. Soon afterwards, the A68 iceberg split into two major pieces: A68A and A68B. As of 7 Feb 2020, A68A (the larger of the two) measured 82 km (50.9 mi) long and 26 km (16.1 mi) wide, according to NOAA's National Ice Center. It is now heading north, towards the South Atlantic's "Iceberg Alley".

When A68 first detached from the Larsen C Ice Shelf in 2017, it was estimated to weigh about 1 trillion tonnes (1.1 trillion US tons).

FIRST ICE CLIMB OF NIAGARA FALLS

On 27 Jan 2015, extreme adventurer Will Gadd (CAN) climbed Niagara Falls' semi-frozen Horseshoe Falls on the US/Canadian border. He was followed up shortly after by his partner Sarah Hueniken (CAN), who achieved the female record.

What drew you to ice climbing?
I grew up climbing in the Rockies [in North America] with my dad, and started ice climbing when I was 16. I loved the way it made ice – something that's normally dangerous and difficult to even walk on – so much fun!

What were the greatest challenges of scaling Niagara Falls?
It took two years of work to organize all the permits, safety planning and logistics. Then the climbing was unknown – how the water would fluctuate, ice quality. It was a huge leap for us and took a lot of thought and careful planning to execute safely and well. The ice was really fragile, as it forms mostly from spray from the running water, so we had to be extra careful.

How did it feel to make history with your partner, Sarah?
Great! To share a huge dream with your partner is a special thing.

What is the most difficult ice climb that you've done beyond Niagara?
Probably Helmcken Falls [in British Columbia, Canada], which also forms as spray ice. That was where we learned how to climb [this type of ice] safely.

Can anyone learn to be an ice climber?
If you can walk up and down a couple of flights of stairs, you can climb ice. What I do is on the edge of the sport, but at a basic level it's not *that* hard – and it's pretty cool!

What's the next challenge?
I'm going back to Africa in a couple of months to climb the last ice on top of Mount Kilimanjaro. There are always new projects and places to explore, and I'm really, really excited to do more of it.

Heaviest hailstones
On 14 Apr 1986, the Gopalganj area of Bangladesh was hit by hailstones weighing up to 1.02 kg (2 lb 3 oz), according to the World Meteorological Organization. A reported 92 people were killed.

Pictured above to scale is the heaviest hailstone to have been recorded in the Western Hemisphere. It fell on 23 Jul 2010 in Vivian, South Dakota, USA, and weighed 0.88 kg (1 lb 15 oz).

Deepest permafrost
Permafrost, or permanently frozen ground, accounts for around 15% of Earth's land surface. The most extensive permafrost is found in Siberian Russia, where the ground is constantly frozen to a depth of around 1 km (0.6 mi).

This frozen ground serves as an effective "deep freeze" for ancient organisms. In Jun 2018, the **oldest liquid blood** was extracted from a young male Lenskaya horse unearthed from the permafrost of the Batagai depression in Sakha Republic, Russia. The animal has been dated to between 41,000 and 42,000 years old.

From the same region, and dated to the same age, were two species of nematode (roundworm) – *Panagrolaimus aff. detritophagus* and *Plectus aff. parvus*, found in 2015. Incredibly, the nematodes were brought back to life (reanimated) – the **longest animal cryobiosis** – as reported in *Doklady Biological Sciences* in May 2018.

100%

First formation of a brinicle filmed
In 2011, the BBC's *Frozen Planet* team recorded a "brinicle" growing under Antarctic sea ice in McMurdo Sound. Brinicles are pipes of ice that form when super-cold, super-saline water sinks and freezes. If a brinicle reaches the ocean floor in shallow conditions, super-cold water can spread across the seabed, killing any lifeforms in its path.

Most southerly exposed active volcano
Antarctica's second-tallest volcano, the 3,794-m (12,447-ft) Mount Erebus, is located on Ross Island at a latitude of 77.5°S. The stratovolcano's 500-m-wide (1,640-ft) main crater is also home to the **most southerly lava lake**, a molten pool (sometimes referred to as Ray Lake) with an estimated surface extent diameter of 40 m (131 ft).

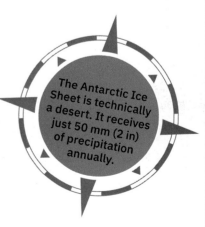

The Antarctic Ice Sheet is technically a desert. It receives just 50 mm (2 in) of precipitation annually.

Air & Light

Highest atmospheric phenomenon

Aurorae – also known as the northern and southern lights – occur some 400 km (250 mi) above Earth's surface. These dazzling light shows, most prevalent towards the poles, are created when solar winds carrying charged particles from the Sun collide with Earth's upper atmosphere.

Largest steam rings

Mount Etna in Sicily, Italy, can emit vapour rings with a diameter of around 200 m (650 ft). The rings can last for around 10 minutes, drifting to a height of 1,000 m (3,280 ft) above the volcanic vent. The precise reason for this unusual phenomenon remains unknown.

Longest single clouds

"Morning Glory" are backward-rolling cloud formations best known from the Gulf of Carpentaria in Australia, which can reach 1,000 km (620 mi) in length – the distance between London, UK, and Monaco.

The **tallest clouds** are cumulonimbus clouds. In the tropics, they have been observed to reach a height of nearly 20,000 m (65,600 ft). This is more than twice the height of Mount Everest.

Noctilucent clouds are the **highest clouds**, forming at altitudes of *c.* 80 km (50 mi) above 99.9% of Earth's atmosphere.

City with the highest $PM_{2.5}$ air pollution

Kanpur in India had an average $PM_{2.5}$ level of 173 micrograms per m^3 in 2016, according to a 2018 World Health Organization (WHO) report. This is more than 17 times higher than the WHO's advised maximum. Industrial burning and vehicle emissions contribute to Kanpur's polluted air.

Coldest cloud tops

At 04:21 UTC (Coordinated Universal Time) on 30 Nov 2019, the Visible Infrared Imaging Radiometer Suite on board the polar-orbiting *NOAA-20* satellite recorded an infrared temperature of -109.35°C (-164.83°F) in a Category 1 storm system in the west Pacific Ocean. The high-altitude cloud was associated with Typhoon Kammuri. Scientists estimated that the cloud tops were around 19,500 m (64,000 ft) above Earth's surface at their coldest point.

Smallest hole in the ozone layer

On 8 Sep 2019, NOAA and NASA scientists reported that the hole in the ozone layer above Antarctica had reached a peak size of 16.4 million km^2 (6.3 million sq mi), the smallest observed since 1982. Over the next two months, it shrank further still to less than 10 million km^2 (3.9 million sq mi).

The **largest hole in the ozone layer** measured 29.9 million km^2 (11.54 million sq mi) – about three times the area of the USA – as verified on 9 Sep 2000.

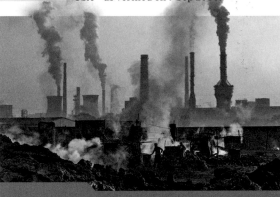

Highest annual atmospheric CO_2 concentration

Average levels of carbon dioxide (CO_2) in the atmosphere reached 407.8 ppm (parts per million) in 2018, according to the World Meteorological Organization's *Greenhouse Gas Bulletin*. This was a rise of 0.57% from the previous highest level, recorded in 2017, and is up 147% since pre-industrial levels in 1750. Preliminary reports indicate that levels were 409.5 ppm in 2019.

Fastest jet stream on Earth

A jet stream is a narrow channel of very fast-moving air, normally found at high elevations in the atmosphere, caused largely by heat differential between the equator and the poles. Based on data collected by the Integrated Global Radiosonde Archive since 1905, the fastest jet stream recorded by a weather balloon is 115.7 m/s (416.5 km/h; 258.8 mph). The reading was taken at a pressure of 250 millibars, which corresponds to an altitude of around 10,400 m (34,120 ft), near Yonago in Tottori, Japan, from where it launched on 5 Feb 2004. Climate change may be strengthening the intensity of jet streams – something that pilots are able to take advantage of to expedite long-haul flights (see p.169).

The term $PM_{2.5}$ describes particulate matter with a diameter of less than 2.5 micrometres (µm; 1 millionth of a metre), such as fine soot. PM_{10}, meanwhile, refers to larger pollutants up to 10 µm in diameter, such as dust or pollen.

LONGEST CAREER AS A HURRICANE HUNTER

Eighty-six-year-old meteorologist Dr James McFadden (USA) had worked at the National Oceanic and Atmospheric Administration as a "hurricane hunter" for 52 years 352 days, as of his flight into Tropical Storm Jerry on 22 Sep 2019.

Tell us about your flight into Hurricane Dorian in 2019.
Dorian was the most savage hurricane of the season, causing massive destruction to the islands just east of the Florida coast. My last flight into it was very rough, with wind speeds between 130 and 156 mph [209–251 km/h]. One could only imagine what the folks on the ground were going through.

What's the strongest hurricane you've ever flown into?
The most terrifying was Hurricane Hugo in 1989. It was a Category 5 storm – the strongest on the Saffir-Simpson scale. We entered the eyewall at 1,500 ft [457 m] and encountered winds in excess of 200 mph [321 km/h], along with severe turbulence. We suffered an engine failure at a critical time and there were a few anxious moments before the pilots regained control.

Has anything ever gone majorly wrong during one of your flights?
Three engines failed within four minutes during a night flight over the Atlantic in February 2007, but the flight crew was able to restart all three and get us back to base.

Are hurricanes getting more severe? Is this a knock-on effect of climate change?
It's complicated and I think one has to be careful to blame climate change for all of it – but as global temperatures rise, I believe that the catalyst is there for stronger storms.

What does it take to be a hurricane hunter?
Being smart and being safe. They go hand in hand, and without them you can get into a world of hurt.

Do you foresee yourself still flying on missions for years to come?
In 2022, we'll be introducing a new high-altitude jet, a Gulfstream 550, into the hurricane programme. That may be worth waiting around to see.

Greatest display of solar haloes

On 11 Jan 1999, at least 24 types of solar halo were witnessed at the Geographic South Pole. Solar haloes are formed by the reflection and refraction of sunlight by ice crystals in the atmosphere, causing rings around the Sun and brightly coloured patches in the sky. The rings tend to be positioned 22° from the Sun, so scientists call them "22° haloes".

Fastest recorded wind speed

On 10 Apr 1996, a weather station on Barrow Island off Western Australia logged a 408-km/h (253-mph) gust during Tropical Cyclone Olivia. This is the strongest surface wind measurement taken by an anemometer *not* associated with a hurricane.

Scientists from the University of Oklahoma recorded the **fastest estimated wind speed** on 3 May 1999. A tornado that struck near Bridge Creek in Oklahoma, USA, peaked at 486 km/h (301 mph) – give or take 32 km/h (20 mph) – according to a "Doppler on Wheels" mobile weather observatory.

Most tornadoes in 24 hours

During a four-day "super outbreak" of storms over southern USA, the WMO logged 207 distinct twisters over a 24-hr period on 27–28 Apr 2011. More than 300 people were killed and the total cost of the damage was $11 bn (£6.6 bn).

The **most tornadoes spawned by a hurricane** is 119, by Hurricane Ivan on 15–17 Sep 2004 in the Caribbean Sea.

The **largest tornado** had a diameter of 4.18 km (2.59 mi), as measured on 31 May 2013 using Doppler radar by the US National Weather Service in El Reno, Oklahoma, USA.

Deadliest dust devil

Dust devils are short-lived whirlwinds with a primarily upward motion that tend to form over hot, dry surfaces. There are only two recorded incidents of fatalities caused by dust devils – both in the USA: on 19 May 2003, a house fell in and killed a man in Lebanon, Maine; and on 18 Jun 2008, a woman died in a collapsed shed in Casper, Wyoming.

Longest "cloud street"

A series of swirling cloud eddies over the Norwegian island of Jan Mayen extended for *c.* 300 km (186 mi) in Jun 2001. Such vortices are a feature of "cloud streets", parallel rows of marine stratocumulus that can form when air currents encounter isolated islands or mountains.

Longest-lasting rainbow

On 30 Nov 2017, a rainbow over Yangmingshan in Chinese Taipei was continuously observed for 8 hr 58 min by members of the Atmospheric Sciences department of Chinese Culture University (TPE). It was believed to have been caused by a seasonal monsoon wind carrying water vapour from the sea.

Largest source of dust storms

The Bodélé Depression is a former lake bed on the southern edge of the Sahara Desert, located between two mountainous regions. Winds funnelling through this area disturb the surface sediments, whipping up around 100 dust storms each year and injecting some 700,000 tonnes (771,600 US tons) of dust into the atmosphere every day. Pictured is a dust storm rolling across Erg Chebbi in Saharan Morocco.

Longest-lasting non-tropical thunderstorms

Supercells are powerful thunderstorms that form around deep, rotating updrafts known as mesocyclones. They can measure kilometres across and last for several hours, producing torrential rainfall, hail and high winds. Around 30% of supercells spawn tornadoes. They often occur on the Great Plains of the USA, in the area known informally as "Tornado Alley".

An average-sized cumulonimbus cloud weighs around the same as an Airbus A380 passenger airliner!

Fire & Electricity

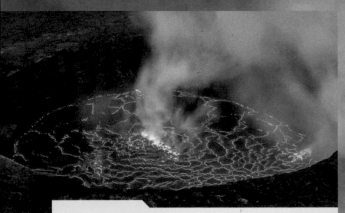

Largest lava lake
The shield volcano Mount Nyiragongo in the Democratic Republic of the Congo houses an active lava lake in its crater approximately 250 m (820 ft) wide. The volcano has erupted at least 34 times since 1882. When it did so on 10 Jan 1977, the lava – which is very fluid, owing to low silica content – raced down the mountain's flank at speeds of 60–100 km/h (37–62 mph): the **fastest lava flow**.

Largest active volcano
Mauna Loa in Hawaii, USA, is a broad, gentle dome 120 km (75 mi) long and 50 km (31 mi) wide, with hardened lava flows that occupy more than 5,125 km² (1,980 sq mi) – bigger than metropolitan Los Angeles. Its volume is 42,500 km³ (10,200 cu mi), of which 84.2% is below sea level. It last erupted in 1984.

Greatest heat output for a volcano
On 28 Jan 2015, *Geophysical Research Letters* published a paper by US and UK geologists in which they analysed 95 of Earth's most active volcanoes. Their data came from readings of thermal flux taken by the spectroradiometers on NASA's *Terra* and *Aqua* Earth-monitoring satellites between 2000 and 2014. In that period, Hawaii's Kīlauea volcano emitted 9.8 x 10¹⁶ joules of thermal energy, which is enough to power New York City for about six months.

Hottest place on Earth
For a fraction of a second, the air around a lightning strike is heated to approximately 30,000°C (54,000°F) – roughly five times hotter than the visible surface of the Sun or the temperature of Earth's inner core.

Farthest lightning flash
The longest confirmed distance spanned by a single lightning bolt is 321 km (199.5 mi). The flash spread horizontally east to west over central Oklahoma, USA, on 20 Jun 2007 at 06:07:22 UTC. A committee convened by the UN's World Meteorological Organization (WMO) ruled that the discharge, detected with VHF radio receivers, lasted for 5.7 sec.

In Sep 2016, the WMO announced a new record for the **longest-lasting lightning flash**. On 30 Aug 2012, over south-east France, a cloud-to-cloud bolt travelled horizontally for 200 km (124 mi) and lasted 7.74 sec; an average flash lasts 0.2 sec.

In Aug 2019, reports emerged of two lightning flashes that could almost double both the distance and duration records, but these are yet to be ratified by the WMO.

Most common type of lightning
Intra-cloud lightning, otherwise known as sheet lightning, occurs within a cloud and does not reach the ground. It accounts for as much as 90% of all lightning flashes.

Longest-burning methane crater
The Darvaza Crater, which has been ablaze since 1971, is located within a natural gas field in Turkmenistan's Karakum Desert. It is thought to have formed after the ground collapsed when drilling equipment breached an underground void. To prevent a large leak of methane gas, geologists set the crater on fire, believing that it would soon run out of fuel, but it has remained alight. Some 69 m (226 ft) across and 30 m (98 ft) deep, the fiery pit has been dubbed "The Door to Hell" – and one person has dared to venture inside (see opposite).

Longest-burning fires
Ignited coal seams smoulder underground at very slow burn rates. One example, located underneath Mount Wingen (aka "Burning Mountain", above) in New South Wales, Australia, is believed to have started *c.* 6,000 years ago. It is thought to have been ignited by lightning striking an exposed coal seam.

Most northerly lightning
On 9–13 Aug 2019, a series of thunderstorms were recorded by the US National Weather Service unusually high within the Arctic Circle. The most extreme lightning flash occurred at a latitude of 89.53°N – a mere 52 km (32 mi) from the Geographic North Pole – at 09:26 UTC on 13 Aug. The discharges were picked up by the GLD360 lightning detection network, created and managed by the Finnish environmental monitoring company Vaisala.

First confirmed fire tornado
Wildfires can generate pyrocumulonimbus clouds (see opposite), from which fiery rotating plumes known as "firenadoes" can emerge. They are far more powerful than fire whirls (aka "fire devils") – short-lived whirlwinds that do not extend from the ground to the cloud base like a true tornado.

In early 2003, a bushfire outbreak struck near Australia's capital, Canberra. Radar data and footage confirmed that a fire tornado arose near McIntyres Hut in Brindabella National Park on 18 Jan 2003. It moved at around 30 km/h (18.6 mph) and, at its peak, was *c.* 0.5 km (0.3 mi) wide at the base. The tornado was powerful enough to move cars and tear the roofs off houses.

Largest grassland wildfire (mega-complex)
Beginning in mid-2019, unprecedentedly high temperatures and a prolonged drought led to devastating bushfires in south-eastern Australia, which set state and national records. It's likely, however, that history's greatest mega-complex grassland fire (i.e., an outbreak of wildfires that occurs concurrently in a single region) took place in the summer season of 1974–75 (left). It burned a swathe of approximately 117 million ha (289.1 million acres) across central Australia. The area of bush burned represented around 15% of the entire island continent – almost equivalent to the size of the UK, France and Italy combined.

Instruments on the *International Space Station* detected that smoke reached an altitude of 23,000 m (75,460 ft) two months after the PNE – unprecedented for a wildfire.

Earliest known wildfire

The oldest confirmed wildfire smouldered *c.* 419 million years ago, during the Silurian period, when oxygen levels may have been higher than today. A team of scientists from Cardiff University's School of Earth and Ocean Sciences (UK) found ancient charcoal from a low-intensity burn, probably started by a lightning strike, while studying three-dimensional charred fossils of small plants found in rocks near Ludlow in Shropshire, UK, in Apr 2004.

Largest forest wildfire (single fire)

Wildfires can be measured in various ways and historically are notoriously difficult to compare, but two contenders stand out for the title of largest forest fire. The Chinchaga Fire began on 1 Jun 1950 in wood debris in British Columbia, Canada, but soon escalated. It spread to Alberta, where rain and cooler weather extinguished it on 31 Oct. By then, *c.* 1.2 million ha (3 million acres) of forest had been lost.

The 1987 Daxing'anling Wildfire (aka the Great Black Dragon Fire) burned a similar-sized area of pine forest. It raged through the Greater Khingan mountain range of north-east China and across the border into the Siberian region of the USSR (now Russia) between 6 May and 2 Jun 1987. In excess of 200 people were reportedly killed, with more than 250 injured and tens of thousands displaced.

Tallest volcanic fire fountain

A fire fountain is a violent, geyser-like outburst of incandescent lava, different from an ash column. In Nov 1986, as Japan's Izu-Ōshima volcano erupted, the lava reached up to 1.6 km (1 mi) above the caldera. That's about twice as high as the **tallest building**, the Burj Khalifa in the UAE (see pp.170–71).

Largest stratospheric smoke injection by a wildfire

On 12 Aug 2017, forest fires burned over swathes of British Columbia in Canada and Washington State, USA. Dubbed the Pacific Northwest Event (PNE), it injected approximately 100,000–300,000 tonnes (110,000–330,000 US tons) of smoke aerosol particles into the lower stratosphere. The conflagration induced five concurrent pyrocumulonimbus clouds in the sky above the blazes, soaring up to 12,000 m (39,370 ft) high.

Highest clouds formed by wildfires

The intense heat from wildfires can make their own weather. The powerful updrafts of air can carry water vapour and ash high into the atmosphere, creating a type of cumulus cloud known as pyrocumulus. These clouds can reach the lower stratosphere at around 10,000 m (32,800 ft) above the ground. Still more powerful are pyrocumulonimbus clouds (pictured above), which can attain altitudes in excess of 16,000 m (52,500 ft).

Most powerful lightning

Less than 5% of all lightning strikes are "positive", where protons from the top of a storm cloud are transferred to the ground. Such strikes can be 10 times more powerful than the far more common "negative" flashes. Positive lightning can produce an electrical current of 300,000 amps and strikes registering up to 1 billion volts.

First person to explore the bottom of the Darvaza Crater

On 6 Oct 2013, Canadian adventurer George Kourounis touched base at the burning Darvaza Crater (see opposite). Using an insulated aluminium suit and a Kevlar climbing harness, Kourounis descended into the gas crater to collect rock samples. Later lab tests revealed that bacteria lived on the rocks there, proving that life can survive in extreme temperatures reaching in excess of 1,000°C (1,830°F).

The expression "bolt from the blue" is most associated with positive lightning, which can strike many miles away from its original cloud, even from clear skies.

The background image on these pages was taken as fires ravaged Australia in 2019–20.

As of Jan 2020, at least 10.3 million ha (25.5 million acres) – an area the size of South Korea – had been devastated by the fires in Australia.

Flora & Fungi

100%

Oregon, USA, covers 965 ha (2,385 acres) – equivalent to around 1,350 soccer fields. Scientists believe that this fungus is between 2,400 and 8,650 years old. Interestingly, this species is one of only around 80 fungi with the ability to produce its own light (i.e., bioluminescence), though the ethereal green glow it emits is usually too weak for the human eye to detect.

Smallest seed
Epiphytic orchids – non-parasitic plants that grow on others – produce seeds that are the size of a speck of dust, with some 992 million of them per gram (28,129 million per ounce). As they contain no nutritional tissue, the seeds need to lodge in a certain type of fungus in order to flourish. This may require a journey of hundreds of miles, but their light weight makes them ideal for wind dispersal.

Smallest flowering plant
A watermeal (genus *Wolffia*) is less than 1 mm long and 0.3 mm wide. Related to duckweed (genus *Lemna*), these rootless aquatic plants form a mat on ponds and calm streams.

Watermeals produce a tiny flower that develops into the **smallest fruit**, which takes up much of its parent plant's body. The fruit of *W. angusta* is only 0.25 mm long and weighs about 70 micrograms, only a fraction more than a grain of sand.

Largest living organism (by area)
A specimen of honey fungus (*Armillaria ostoyae*) growing in the Malheur National Forest in the Blue Mountains of eastern

Largest water lily
Native to shallow freshwater lakes and bayous in the Amazon basin, the giant water lily (*Victoria amazonica*) has floating leaves that measure up to 3 m (10 ft) across, and are held in place upon an underwater stalk 7–8 m (23–26 ft) long. The undersurface of its pads are supported by rib-like ridges.

100%

Smallest water lily
Nymphaea thermarum (the thermal lily) has pads a mere 10–20 mm (0.3–0.7 in) across. It is now believed to be extinct in the wild. Horticulturist Carlos Magdalena was able to save this aquatic plant from total extinction by germinating stored seeds at Kew Gardens in London, UK, in Nov 2009.

Fastest-growing plant
Some of the 1,400 or so grass species in the bamboo subfamily (Bambusoideae) grow at a rate of 91 cm (2 ft 11 in), or 0.00003 km/h (0.00002 mph), per day. That's more than 1,800 times quicker than human hair grows.

Greatest tree girth
The trunk of El Árbol del Tule in Oaxaca, Mexico, had a circumference of *c.* 36.2 m (118 ft) when measured by arborist Robert Van Pelt in 2005. As of the same date, this 2,000-year-old Montezuma cypress (*Taxodium mucronatum*) stood 35.4 m (116 ft) tall. The tree has become a local landmark in the town of Santa María del Tule.

Fastest-growing marine plant
The giant kelp (*Macrocystis pyrifera*) has a peak growth rate of 50 cm (1 ft 7.6 in) per day as the fronds approach the surface of the sea where there is more sunlight. It is also the **longest seaweed**, with one specimen measured at 60 m (197 ft). The superlative seaweed is found near rocky shores in the Pacific Ocean.

Also called "string kelp", this algae has no roots. Instead, it absorbs nutrients from the surrounding water and anchors itself to rocks with root-like growths known as haptera.

WAY TO GROW!

▼ Largest single flower
In Jan 2020, a specimen of *Rafflesia arnoldii* with a 111-cm (3-ft 7-in) flower was discovered in a rainforest in West Sumatra, Indonesia. The species has no leaves, stem or roots, but grows parasitically inside jungle vines. Its foul aroma has led it to being dubbed the "corpse flower", an epithet that it shares with another superlative plant (see bottom).

▶ Largest seed
The seeds of the rare coco-de-mer palm (*Lodoicea maldivica*) may reach 50 cm (1 ft 7 in) in length and weigh 25 kg (55 lb) – about the same weight as 16 coconuts. The palm is very slow-growing and the fruits can take up to six years to develop.

▲ Largest puffball
Native to temperate areas worldwide, the giant puffball (*Calvatia gigantea*) fungus has a spheroid fruiting body that may attain a diameter of 1.5 m (4 ft 11 in) and weigh 20 kg (44 lb). Its spores develop inside this receptacle, which grows during late summer and autumn, and occurs in meadows and deciduous forests.

▶ ◐ Tallest bloom
Louis Ricciardiello (USA) grew a titan arum (*Amorphophallus titanum*) measuring 3.1 m (10 ft 2 in) tall, as confirmed on 18 Jun 2010. It was measured when on display at Winnipesaukee Orchids in Gilford, New Hampshire, USA.

A. titanum is also regarded as the ◐ **smelliest plant** – hence its nickname, "corpse flower". When in bloom, it releases a pungent odour, comparable to rotten flesh, that can be smelled around 0.8 km (0.5 mi) away.

Most poisonous fungus

Found globally, the death cap (*Amanita phalloides*) accounts for 90% of fatal poisonings caused by fungi. Its total dry-weight toxin content is 7–9 mg (0.1–0.13 grains), whereas the estimated amount of amatoxins (a set of related poisons) considered lethal for humans is just 5–7 mg (0.07–0.1 grains). Cooking does not neutralize its poison. If eaten, it can cause liver and kidney failure.

Tallest tree

A coast redwood (*Sequoia sempervirens*) named "Hyperion" measured 115.85 m (380 ft 1 in) as of 2017. This arboreal behemoth was discovered on 25 Aug 2006 by Chris Atkins and Michael Taylor (both USA) in Redwood National Park, California, USA. They measured its height at 115.24 m (378 ft), although a subsequent reading in 2017 resulted in a revised figure of 115.85 m (380 ft 1 in) – twice the height of Italy's Leaning Tower of Pisa. Later measurements confirm that the vertiginous redwood is active and still growing.

After a five-year genetic study, in Apr 2019 it was announced that the coast redwood has the **largest plant genome** (a species' total genetic material). The species boasts 26.5 gigabases, or 26.5 billion base pairs – the basic building blocks of DNA. This is around nine times the size of the human genome.

The world's **tallest tropical tree** was also verified in Apr 2019. A yellow meranti (*Shorea faguetiana*) in Sabah, Malaysia, was confirmed to stand 100.8 m (330 ft) – twice the height of Nelson's Column in London, UK. As much as 95% of this tree's mass is estimated to lie in its trunk.

Thickest tree bark

With age, the bark of the giant sequoia (*Sequoiadendron giganteum*) can vary between 25 cm and 121 cm (10 in–4 ft). These lofty trees grow in the Sierra Nevada mountains of California, USA.

Largest fern fronds

Australian giant ferns (*Angiopteris evecta*) can grow to 3 m (10 ft) tall, while their huge fronds reach in excess of 8 m (26 ft) – about the length of a school bus. Although found in south-east Asia, the biggest specimens are reported to grow in Queensland, Australia.

Largest prey of carnivorous plants

Nepenthes rajah and *N. rafflesiana* pitcher plants have been known to trap and digest large frogs, birds and even rats. They are commonly found in the rainforests of Asia, notably Borneo, Indonesia and Malaysia.

Fastest predatory plant

Aquatic bladderworts (genus *Utricularia*) use suction-based traps to capture insects, small crustaceans and even young tadpoles. One species (*U. australis*, aka the southern bladderwort) has been recorded ensnaring victims in just 5.2 milliseconds (ms), though 9 ms is more typical. In comparison, the clamshell-like leaves of the Venus flytrap (*Dionaea muscipula*) shut in 100 ms from the moment they are stimulated.

The **fastest terrestrial predatory plant** is the pimpernel sundew (*Drosera glanduligera*, inset) of southern Australia. Its "snap tentacles" enable it to capture small insects, such as flies and ants, within 75 ms. The fast-moving appendages catapult bugs on to shorter tentacles covered in a glue-like substance where they meet a sticky end, carried towards the centre of the sundew to be digested.

As the name suggests, an undivided leaf is one whole blade, whereas a divided leaf comprises multiple leaflets.

Largest undivided leaf

A specimen of *Alocasia macrorrhiza* (example pictured) found in 1966 had a 3.02-m-long (9-ft 11-in) leaf with a surface area of 3.17 m² (34 sq ft) – around the same as a king-size bed. It grew in Sabah, Malaysia.

The **largest leaves** overall are those of the raffia palm (*Raphia farinifera*) of the Mascarene Islands in the Indian Ocean, and the Amazonian bamboo palm (*R. taedigera*) of South America and Africa. Their compound foliage can reach 20 m (65 ft) long in total, with 4-m (13-ft) petioles – the stalks by which palm fronds affix to the trunk.

Round-Up

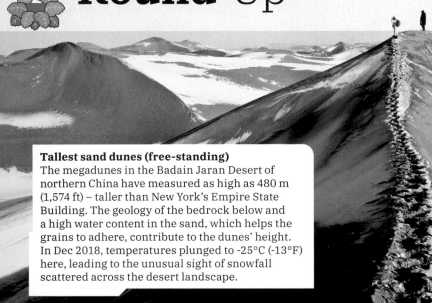

THE RISE AND RISE OF GLOBAL WARMING

Average worldwide temperatures have increased consistently over the past decade, with 2019 seeing the **warmest month** in history (see below). In that year, the six countries shown here experienced their hottest days on record. Even Earth's coldest locations are feeling the heat. Preliminary data from a research base in northern Antarctica suggests that it registered 18.3°C (64.9°F) on 6 Feb 2020 – although this is still pending ratification. The previous Antarctic high, set in Mar 2015, was 17.5°C (63.5°F).

India
51.0°C (123.8°F) in Phalodi, Rajasthan, on 30 May

France
46.0°C (114.8°F) in Vérargues, Hérault, on 28 Jun

Germany
42.6°C (108.7°F) in Lingen, Lower Saxony, on 25 Jul

Belgium
41.8°C (107.2°F) in Begijnendijk, Flemish Brabant, on 25 Jul

Netherlands
40.7°C (105.3°F) in Gilze en Rijen, North Brabant, on 25 Jul

UK
38.7°C (101.7°F) in Cambridge, Cambridgeshire, on 25 Jul

Tallest sand dunes (free-standing)
The megadunes in the Badain Jaran Desert of northern China have measured as high as 480 m (1,574 ft) – taller than New York's Empire State Building. The geology of the bedrock below and a high water content in the sand, which helps the grains to adhere, contribute to the dunes' height. In Dec 2018, temperatures plunged to -25°C (-13°F) here, leading to the unusual sight of snowfall scattered across the desert landscape.

Oldest stardust
In Jan 2020, a report revealed that scientists had found microscopic grains (or stardust) 7 billion years old, pre-dating the birth of our Solar System. Researchers analysed rare, so-called "pre-solar" grains in the Murchison meteorite, which struck Australia in 1969, to calculate how long they had been exposed to high-energy cosmic rays in space. When some of these rays encounter matter, they create new elements; the longer the exposure, the more elements are made. By examining how many new elements were present, scientists were able to ascertain the stardust's age.

Oldest fossilized forest
Petrified tree roots found in 2009 at a quarry near Cairo in New York, USA, have been dated to *c.* 386 million years old, placing them in the mid-Devonian era. The period represents a transition phase in Earth's history when forests rapidly spread across the planet, some 150 million years before dinosaurs emerged. The findings were published in *Current Biology* on 19 Dec 2019.

Most thermogenic plants
Thermogenesis is an organism's ability to produce heat, and is quite rare in flora. Among plants, heat output can be measured in various ways:
• In terms of the maximum rate of heat production across the entire flower, titan arums (*Amorphophallus titanum*) can generate 34.53 W of energy; see more on this behemoth bloom on p.42.
• The male florets of *Arum concinnatum* output up to 0.43 W/g at night, which is the highest rate of heat production relative to mass.
• Based on the difference between a flower and ambient temperature, the eastern skunk cabbage (*Symplocarpus foetidus*, below) has been measured in the wild at 25.6°C (78.1°F) warmer than the air surrounding it – enough to melt overlying snow.

Largest non-nacreous pearl
Nacre (aka mother-of-pearl) is a substance secreted by certain molluscs that lends "true pearls" their iridescence. Some pearls, however, are non-nacreous, formed instead of the less-lustrous calcium carbonate, though these gems are still highly prized. The weightiest example is the 27.65-kg (60-lb 15-oz) "Giga Pearl". It belongs to Abraham Reyes (CAN), who also commissioned the gold octopus that now serves as its setting. The pearl's weight was ratified on 20 Aug 2019.

Oldest fungi
Samples of microfossil fungi in dolomite shale from the Democratic Republic of the Congo were aged at *c.* 715–810 million years old. They consist of narrow carbonaceous filaments less than 5 micrometres wide. The discovery was announced in Feb 2020.

Warmest average global ocean temperature
In 2019, the heat content for the upper 2,000 m (6,560 ft) of Earth's oceans

Warmest month
Temperature analysis by the National Oceanic and Atmospheric Administration (NOAA) has concluded that Jul 2019 was the hottest month in history, as reported by its National Centers for Environmental Information on 15 Aug 2019. The average global temperature in Jul 2019 was 0.95°C (1.71°F) above the 20th-century average of 15.7°C (60.3°F), making it the hottest July in the 140 years since meteorological records began in 1880.
The **warmest decade** on record is 2010–19, which had a temperature anomaly of 0.80°C (1.44°F) above the 20th-century average.

"Barnum" (see right) is part of the **largest collection of coprolites**. As of the last official count in 2015, this stood at 1,277 prehistoric poos, but now numbers in the region of 7,000!

The Malham Cave was formed some 7,000 years ago when rain seeped from the surface via cracks and then hollowed out channels in the rock salt, which lead down to the Dead Sea.

For such a gem to form, its crystallization must have been interrupted. Perhaps the smaller stone was surrounded by a weaker mineral that later disintegrated, but only after the larger diamond had developed around it.

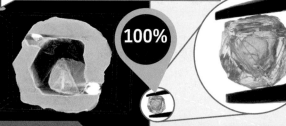

100%

First diamond inside a diamond
In Oct 2019, reports emerged of a unique double diamond mined in eastern Russia. The larger gem weighs 0.62 carats and is 4.9 mm (0.19 in) across – as wide as a rice grain. Its 0.02-carat companion is just 2.1 mm (0.08 in). The find was dubbed the "Matryoshka diamond" after Russian nesting dolls.

Longest salt cave
Located beneath Mount Sodom in Israel, the *c.* 10-km-long (6.2-mi) Malham Cave was recognized as the world's longest salt cave on 28 Mar 2019. The announcement was made by the Hebrew University of Jerusalem (ISR), following a two-year survey. The largest single chamber within the cave measures 5.6 km (3.5 mi) long.

was 0.075°C (0.135°F) warmer than the 1981–2010 average, according to NOAA. Such a rise is the result of absorbing 228 zettajoules (228 billion trillion joules) of energy owing to global warming; for context, annual worldwide human energy usage is about 0.5 zettajoules.

Ocean warming is the chief cause of coral bleaching, in which reefs' colour-producing algae loses its pigment or is expelled. In 2019, marine biologists reported that not even the **most southerly coral reef** has escaped this fate. The reef is located at 31.53°S, off Australia's Lord Howe Island in the Tasman Sea, where cooler waters would normally protect it. But, near the shore, up to 90% of the coral had been affected.

Lowest point on land
NASA's project "BedMachine Antarctica" is creating high-precision maps of the bedrock under the Antarctic Ice Sheet. As reported in Dec 2019, it has revealed an ice-filled trench beneath the Denman Glacier in East Antarctica extending more than 3,500 m (11,480 ft) below sea level, which is 2,000 m (6,560 ft) farther than thought. That equates to more than eight times the depth of the **lowest exposed land** – the shoreline of the Dead Sea (see right).

But you'd have to go a *lot* lower to reach the **deepest point in the sea**: the Challenger Deep at the bottom of the Pacific Ocean. US explorer Victor Vescovo dived into it in 2019 – read the full story on pp.160–61.

Deepest hypersaline lake
The Dead Sea on the Israel-Jordan border reaches depths of 306 m (1,003 ft). It is also the **lowest exposed body of water**, around 430 m (1,410 ft) below sea level. Salinity here averages almost 10 times greater than that of typical sea water.

▶ Largest coprolite from a carnivore
Based on its dimensions, the largest coprolite (fossilized poo) from a carnivorous animal measures 67.5 cm (2 ft 2.5 in) along the central curve and up to 15.7 cm (6.2 in) wide, as confirmed on 2 Mar 2020. The enormous excretion was discovered on a private ranch near the town of Buffalo in South Dakota, USA, in the summer of 2019. Now known as "Barnum" – after palaeontologist Barnum Brown, who unearthed the first *Tyrannosaurus rex* remains in 1902 – its proud owner is coprolite collector George Frandsen (USA, right). The petrified droppings of prehistoric creatures offer us insights into the range and habitat of long-extinct animals. Traces of undigested food, known as "inclusions", also provide invaluable information about ancient diets.

Its size, the site of its discovery and its high bone content all suggest that "Barnum" came from a *T. rex*.

100%

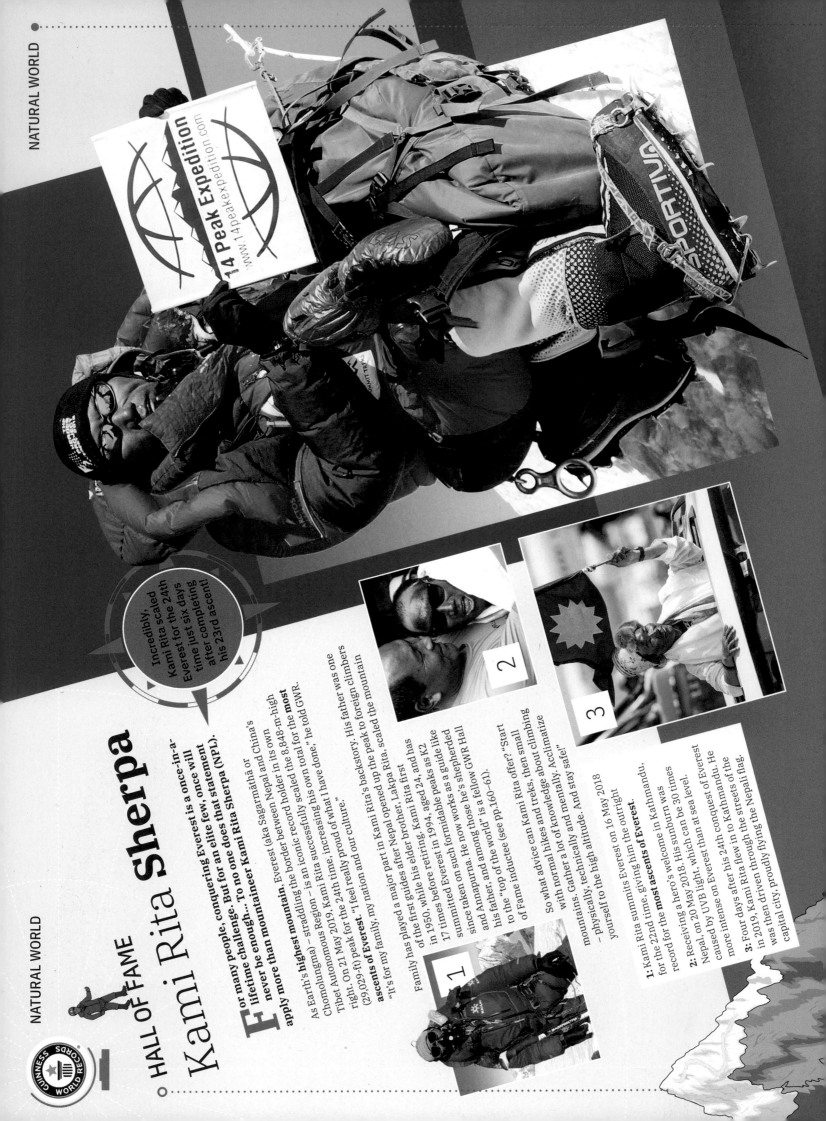

HALL OF FAME

Kami Rita Sherpa

For many people, conquering Everest is a once-in-a-lifetime challenge. But for an elite few, once will never be enough… To no one does Kami Rita Sherpa (NPL) apply more than mountaineer.

F

As Earth's **highest mountain**, Everest (aka Sagarmāthā or Chomolungma) – straddling the border between Nepal and China's own Tibet Autonomous Region – is an iconic record holder in its own right. On 21 May 2019, Kami Rita successfully scaled the 8,848-m-high peak for the 24th time, increasing his own total for the **most ascents of Everest**. "I feel really proud of what I have done," he told GWR.

"It's for my family, my nation and our culture." His father was one of the first climbers.

Family has played a major part in Kami Rita's backstory. His father was one of the first guides after Nepal opened up the peak to foreign climbers in 1950, while his elder brother, Lakpa Rita, scaled the mountain 17 times before retiring. Kami Rita first summitted Everest in 1994, aged 24, and has since taken on such formidable peaks as K2 and Annapurna. He now works as a guide like his father, and among those he's shepherded to the "top of the world" is a fellow GWR Hall of Fame inductee (see pp.160–61).

So what advice can Kami Rita offer? "Start small with normal hikes and treks, then climbing mountains. Gather a lot of knowledge. Acclimatize yourself to the high altitude. And stay safe!" – physically, technically and mentally.

1: Kami Rita summits Everest on 16 May 2018 for the 22nd time, giving him the outright record for the **most ascents of Everest**.

2: Kami Rita flew in to Kathmandu. Receiving a hero's welcome in Kathmandu. His sunburn was caused by UVB light, which can be 30 times more intense on Everest than at sea level. Four days after his 24th conquest of Everest on 20 May 2018.

3: Kami Rita flew through the streets of the capital city, proudly flying the Nepali flag. in 2019, driven flying the Nepali flag. was then driven through the streets of the capital city.

Incredibly, Kami Rita scaled the 24th Everest for the 24th Everest just six days time just completing after completing his 23rd ascent! his 23rd ascent!

Lhakpa Sherpa

Find out more about Kami Rita and Lhakpa in the Hall of Fame section at **www.guinnessworldrecords.com/2021**

This inspiring Nepali mountaineer first topped Everest in 2000. "It was a long-time dream," she enthuses, telling me all my life that it wasn't possible."

"I felt like a champion when I reached the summit," she tells GWR. "And I was able to do it despite people made her the most ascents of Everest (female), completing her ninth climb on 16 May 2018. Lhakpa is currently planning a 10th ascent and – having founded her own guide company in 2019 – Cloudscape Climbing along with her. may take clients along with her.

"That Everest (Pasang first woman from Nepal to return alive in 1993). She's now Lhamu Sherpa died during her descent in 1993). She's now
"like I was born from Nepal to
"I was born to a champion when I reached the mountains."

Lhakpa was born in 1973, two years before Junko Tabei (JPN) became the **first woman to ascend Everest**. Although she's determined to tackle the **highest mountain** again, she admits, "It's a little harder each time, I think due to my age." But Lhakpa's made one ascent while of strong stuff: she made the birth of just eight months after and another second! her first daughter, and her second with two months pregnant to show that her first daughter, and and she's determined to show that And she's determined to compete with female mountaineers: "I want to break their male counterparts and challenge realistic more records and challenge it's a game."
men's records. I feel like it's a game."

"My friends and family are supportive. They also worry, but they know that they can't keep me from climbing."

When not with her 'head in the clouds', US-based Lhakpa takes whatever odd jobs she can to help finance future expeditions. In her downtime, her hobbies include hiking, cooking and singing, including washing dishes and working at a local grocery store. In and she has just recently learned to swim.

1: Lhakpa conquers Everest for the seventh time on 20 May 2016. She'd actually retired, after mountaineering 10 years earlier, but the lure of Everest proved too powerful.

2: On 29 May 2018, Lhakpa and Kami Rita Sherpa meet up for a rally on International Everest (Sagarmāthā) Day. The event marks her sixth ascent from mountaineering, but the lure of Everest the anniversary of the **first ascent of Everest**, by Edmund Hillary (NZ) and Tenzing Norgay (IND/Tibet) in 1953.

3: Lhakpa with her daughters Shiny (left) and Sunny (centre) at an awards ceremony in Connecticut, USA, in Apr 2019. She also has a son called Nima.

CERTIFICATE

GUINNESS WORLD RECORDS

The most ascents of Everest by a woman was achieved by Lakpa Sherpa (Nepal), who successfully climbed the 8,848-m-high (29,029-ft) summit of Everest on for the sixth time on 11 May 2006

OFFICIALLY AMAZING

Animals

DESTINATIONS

Tallest giraffe

A 12-year-old giraffe (*Giraffa camelopardalis*) named Forest measures 5.7 m (18 ft 8 in) to the top of his ossicones – the bony protuberances on his head – as verified at Australia Zoo in Queensland on 4 Dec 2019. Native to the dry savannah of sub-Saharan Africa, giraffes are the world's **tallest animals.** Adult males, or "bulls", typically reach between 4.6 and 5.5 m (15–18 ft); even newborns stand a lofty 1.8 m (6 ft) – the same as an adult man.

Here, for context, Forest is pictured with fellow giraffe Kebibi and the park's Senior Africa Section Keeper, Kat Hansen. Australia Zoo is owned by the Irwin family. The late Steve Irwin was the star of TV's *Crocodile Hunter* and his family continues his passion for wildlife. His daughter, Bindi, is the **most followed TV naturalist on Instagram,** with 3,334,904 followers as of 4 Mar 2020.

Despite their stature, giraffes only have seven vertebrae in their necks – just like humans!

Fur & Spines

Longest hair
There are several contenders for the longest hair in the animal kingdom, including the tails of domestic horses, the overcoats of muskoxen (*Ovibos moschatus*) – see opposite – and the tail tuft of giraffes (*Giraffa*), which are used as a defence against bugs. However, the animals with the greatest hair length on record are, in fact, humans (*Homo sapiens*). When measured on 8 May 2004, the hair on the head of Xie Qiuping (CHN) had grown to 5.627 m (18 ft 5.5 in) – the same height as a whole giraffe! An Indian monk named Swami Pandarasannadhi may have had even longer locks, reported to be 7.9 m (26 ft) in 1949. Evidence suggests that he had a condition known as plica caudiformis, where the hair matts together to form a single mass.

Oldest bat
A Brandt's bat (*Myotis brandtii*) found in a cave in Russian Siberia in 2005 was aged at least 41 years old, having been banded in 1964. This bat's small size – only weighing 5–7 g (0.1–0.2 oz) – and long lifespan defy convention among mammals; more diminutive species tend to die young. Based on its "longevity quotient", it lived almost 10 times longer than expected!

Largest porcupine
North African crested porcupines (*Hystrix cristata*) measure around 90 cm (3 ft) long, minus the tail. The black-and-white striped quills are modified hairs with a hard outer layer of keratin and pointed tips; the longest of these measure more than this opened book. Under threat, the porcupine raises its spines into a defensive crest.

Finest animal hair
Endemic to the Tibetan Plateau, the chiru (*Pantholops hodgsonii*) boasts the finest natural fibre, with soft undercoat hairs 7–10 micrometres in diameter; that's about 10 times thinner than the average human hair. The trade in this mountain-dwelling antelope's wool – known as *shahtoosh* – has led to a dramatic decline in its numbers.

Longest whiskers
Pinnipeds (i.e., seals, sea lions and walruses) have the largest whiskers, or vibrissae, of all mammals. None exceeds those of the Antarctic fur seal (*Arctocephalus gazella*). Typical length for males is 35 cm (13.7 in), though in females that decreases to 13–22 cm (5.1–8.6 in). One exceptional bull from South Georgia, described in *British Antarctic Survey Scientific Reports* in 1968, had one 48-cm (1-ft 7-in) whisker. The full span of his titanic 'tache was 106.5 cm (3 ft 6 in).

Rarest great ape
Only formally recognized as a new species in 2017, the Tapanuli orangutan (*Pongo tapanuliensis*) is listed as Critically Endangered. Its single population in north-west Sumatra, Indonesia, comprises fewer than 800 individuals. As well as DNA tests, its frizzier coat and more prominent moustache helped to distinguish this species from the Sumatran orangutan (*P. abelii*).

Most whiskers on a pinniped
Whiskers are special hairs that have evolved to act as sensory organs. They are found to some extent on all mammals (bar monotremes and humans). The walrus (*Odobenus rosmarus*) has 400–700 quill-like whiskers on its face, taking the form of a bushy moustache. Each averages only 8 cm (3 in) long but is 3 mm (0.11 in) thick – 30 times the diameter of a human hair.

Anatomy of... fur
Along with mammary glands, fur (or hair) is a defining feature of most mammals. Although predominantly made of the protein keratin (as are feathers and horns), hair comes in many forms, including spines.

1. **Follicle:** The living portion of hair from which the shaft grows

2. **Hair shaft:** Comprises three layers: a medulla, cortex and the external cuticle

3. **Sebaceous gland:** Produces oily sebum to keep the skin moist

4. **Sweat gland:** Helps to regulate body temperature in some mammals; others pant, roll in mud or radiate heat from their bodies

5. **Arrector pili:** Muscles that cause hair to stand on end when cold (i.e., goosebumps) or on edge

6. **Blood vessels**

7. **Nerves**

8. **Subcutaneous fat**

A walrus uses its whiskers to detect bivalves such as clams on the murky sea floor. They are sensitive enough to differentiate shells that are millimetres apart in size.

Smallest primate

Discovered in the deciduous forests of western Madagascar in 1992, the Madame Berthe's mouse lemur (*Microcebus berthae*) is the smallest primate. It has a total length of around 21 cm (8.3 in), more than 50% of which is tail. At 30.6 g (1.1 oz), adults weigh about half the size of a plum.

FAUX FUR

▶ "Furriest" crustacean
The yeti lobster (*Kiwa hirsuta*) lives on hydrothermal vents in the South Pacific Ocean. Its long claws and shorter thoracic limbs are covered in blond bristles called setae. The strands harbour a colony of bacteria that the crustacean may farm as a food source.

◀ "Furriest" frog
What appears to be hair on the hind legs and midriff of male hairy frogs (*Trichobatrachus robustus*) is actually a mass of tiny skin filaments, supplied with blood. Scientists believe that the frogs use these as supplementary respiratory aids, like gills.

▶ "Furriest" fish
Fish too can occasionally have a shaggy appearance, though none seen to date has actual hair. One contender for the "furriest" title is the striated frogfish (*Antennarius striatus*), whose dermal spinules help it to blend in among coral and seaweed.

MOST NORTHERLY...

Ungulate

In colder climes experienced at more extreme latitudes, fur is essential for survival. Among hoofed animals, none ventures farther north than the muskox (*Ovibos moschatus*), found at 83°N in Arctic Canada and Greenland. Muskoxen have a double-layered coat to keep -40°C (-40°F) temperatures at bay. The annually shed woolly underlayer, known as *qiviut*, is said to be eight times warmer than sheep's wool, while the outer guard hairs are among the longest in the animal kingdom; around the skirt, they can reach some 60 cm (2 ft).

Bear

Polar bears (*Ursus maritimus*) live on ever-shrinking Arctic sea-ice at 65–85°N, though on 5 Aug 2001, an adult was spotted swimming at 89.775°N. Approximately 24 km (14.9 mi) from the North Pole, this is the northernmost sighting ever recorded for any bear.

These large carnivores are well equipped to cope with subzero conditions, boasting the **most efficient insulation** among their kind. As well as a 10-cm (4-in) layer of blubber beneath the skin – fed by their **most fatty diet** of seals – their two-layered pelage plays a pivotal role in keeping them warm.

Despite appearances, their fur is *not* white as you may assume but mainly transparent. It only appears white because when sunlight hits their coat, some photons get trapped in the hair follicles and causes them to luminesce. The naturally off-white colour of keratin in the hair also contributes to polar bears' perceived colouration.

Most northerly lagomorph

Of the 90 or so species of rabbit, hare and pika (order Lagomorpha), the Arctic hare (*Lepus arcticus*) is found the farthest north. Its boreal range extends to 89°N, at the very northern tip of Greenland. For year-round camouflage on the tundra, it has a white coat in winter and grey-brown fur in summer (inset).

Densest fur

To withstand the frigid waters of the northern Pacific, the sea otter (*Enhydra lutris*) has up to 160,000 hairs per cm² (>1 million per sq in), though thickness varies across its body. Compare that with about 18,500 per cm² (60,000 per sq in) on a domestic cat's belly. The fur traps a layer of insulative air close to their bodies; this stands in for blubber, which sea otters lack.

On top of their thick coats, sea otters have to eat up to 25% of their body weight per day to keep warm!

Feathers

100%

Longest beak relative to overall body length

Found in the Andes from Venezuela to Bolivia, the sword-billed hummingbird (*Ensifera ensifera*) has a 10.2-cm (4-in) beak – longer than its body, if the tail is excluded.

At more than 25 cm (9.8 in) from the end of its tail to the tip of its prodigious bill, it is also the **longest hummingbird**.

First feathered animal

In Jun 2000, scientists announced their discovery of "proto-feathers" on a 220-million-year-old fossilized animal. Named *Longisquama insignis*, it had appendages on its back that were hollow, along with other characteristics consistent with the plumage of modern birds. This creature probably used its feathers to glide between trees 75 million years before the first birds evolved.

The **largest feathered animal ever** was the dinosaur *Yutyrannus huali*. This ancestor of *Tyrannosaurus rex* was covered in filamentous, downy feathers, measured 9.1 m (29 ft 10 in) long and weighed some 1,400 kg (3,100 lb). It was officially described in Apr 2012, having been discovered in north-eastern China's Yixian Formation fossil deposit, which dates from *c.* 125 million years ago.

First dinosaur tail found in amber

On 8 Dec 2016, a team of scientists led by the China University of Geosciences published their analysis of a sample of amber containing preserved feathers unearthed in 2015. Dating back 99 million years to the mid-Cretaceous era, it held part of a tail covered in small chestnut-brown feathers, with a whitish underside, that probably belonged to a juvenile coelurosaur.

A new contender for the title of **oldest feathers in amber** came to light in a paper published in *Nature Communications* on 10 Dec 2019. Two pieces of Myanmar amber that were aged *c.* 100 million years old contained not just dinosaur feathers but also previously unknown lice-like bugs, named *Mesophthirus engeli*. Strong, chewing mouthparts, along with signs of damage to the feathers, indicate that these parasites are the **oldest feather-feeding insects**.

Greatest recovery by a bird species

By 1980, the Chatham Island robin (*Petroica traversi*), endemic to the South Pacific, had a population of just five birds. As of Nov 2015, the number of adults had risen to 289. The bird's startling comeback was aided by an innovative technique of "cross-fostering": eggs and hatchlings were given to similar species to brood and raise.

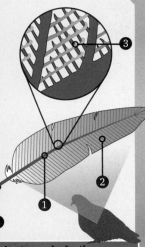

Greatest wingspan for an owl

Large adult female Eurasian eagle owls (*Bubo bubo*, pictured) and Blakiston's eagle owls (*B. blakistoni*) can attain a total wingspan of up to 2 m (6 ft 6 in).

The Eurasian eagle owl is also the world's **largest owl**, with an average length of 66–71 cm (2 ft 2 in–2 ft 4 in) and weighing up to 4 kg (8 lb 13 oz) – 40 times heavier than a blackbird (*Turdus merula*). It has been known to abduct small pet cats.

Anatomy of... feathers

Like their beaks and talons, birds' feathers are composed of keratin, which is both light and durable. Soft, downy plumage provides birds with warmth; tougher, longer feathers are used in flight.

1. Rachis: Central shaft from which paired branches shoot off

2. Barbs: Small, parallel branches that project from the rachis that together form a feather's "vane"

3. Barbules: Extensions from each barb. Some of these have hooklets, which help to connect adjoining barbules

4. Calamus: A hollow stalk, also known as the quill, connecting the feather to the bird's body

Largest puffin super-colony

There are some 830,000 breeding pairs of Atlantic puffins (*Fratercula arctica*) in Vestmannaeyjar (aka the Westman Islands), off south-west Iceland, during the April–August nesting season. This figure represents approximately 20% of the species' global population and is based on "apparently occupied burrows", or AOBs – the standard measurement unit for assessing puffin populations.

As it preens itself, a puffin coats its feathers with oil secreted by a gland near its tail, to keep them waterproofed.

Heaviest parrot

The kākāpo (*Strigops habroptila*), aka the owl parrot, is now only found in the wild on three tiny islets off New Zealand. Males are larger than females, weighing up to 4 kg (8 lb 13 oz) at maturity.

Identified from two fossilized leg bones unearthed on New Zealand's South Island in 2008, the **heaviest parrot ever** was *Heracles inexpectatus*. It weighed an estimated 6.96 kg (15 lb 5.5 oz) – around twice as much as the kākāpo – and stood *c.* 1 m (3 ft 3 in) tall, as described in the journal *Biology Letters* in Aug 2019. The silhouettes above show both birds in comparison to an adult man.

Longest feathers on a bird

In 1972, the tail covert of a phoenix fowl, aka Yokohama chicken – a domestic strain of red jungle fowl (*Gallus gallus*) – was measured at 10.6 m (34 ft 9.3 in). It was owned by Masasha Kubota (JPN).

The central tail feathers of Reeves's pheasant (*Syrmaticus reevesii*) may exceed 2.4 m (8 ft), the **longest feathers on a wild bird**. If thrown up in flight, they act as a brake, allowing it to rapidly alter trajectory.

A tail feather from this bird would be 30 times longer than the **smallest parrot** stands tall. Adult buff-faced pygmy parrots (*Micropsitta pusio*) can be as short as 8 cm (3.1 in) and weigh half that of an AA battery!

Highest density of feathers

This record has long been attributed to the emperor penguin (*Aptenodytes forsteri*), with 11–12 feathers per cm² (70–77 per sq in). On land, the feathers stay erect to trap air to insulate the birds – vital in their native Antarctica, where temperatures can plummet below -40°C (-40°F). In the water, which may be as cold as -1.8°C (28.7°F), the feathers flatten to form a watertight barrier. Some scientists now believe that this density has been overestimated, however. Other contenders for the title include the white-throated dipper (*Cinclus cinclus*). Research is ongoing as we go to press.

Largest peafowl species

The green peafowl (*Pavo muticus*) is native to south-east Asia. The male, or peacock, can grow to 3 m (9 ft 10 in) long, including its spectacular train or tail covert, which alone may reach 1.6 m (5 ft 3 in). The biggest male specimens are one of the largest flying birds alive today.

Strongest bird of prey

Female harpy eagles (*Harpia harpyja*) are capable of hunting animals of equal or superior size – up to 9 kg (20 lb). Quarry includes sloths and howler monkeys, which are among the **largest eagle prey**. The female's lower legs may be as large in diameter as a child's wrist, while individual talons can be as long as 12.5 cm (5 in). Female harpy eagles are much larger than males.

Tallest flying bird

Cranes belong to the family Gruidae. The largest specimens, such as sarus cranes (*Antigone antigone*, pictured), stand up to 1.8 m (5 ft 10 in) – as tall as the average adult man. They are native to the Indian subcontinent, northern Australia and south-east Asia.

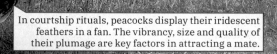

In courtship rituals, peacocks display their iridescent feathers in a fan. The vibrancy, size and quality of their plumage are key factors in attracting a mate.

Scales (Terrestrial)

As well as serving as dermal armour, crocodilians' osteoderms also help them to regulate body temperature.

Largest claws on a living animal
The anterior talons on the third digit of the giant armadillo (*Priodontes maximus*) can grow 20.3 cm (8 in) long. Native to South America, it uses its talons to dig and rip apart termite mounds. Its tough carapace is composed of bony scales called osteoderms (or "scutes").

Earliest land-walking fish
There's a good reason that scales are a defining feature of early reptiles and all their descendants today: tetrapods (four-limbed animals) evolved from bony fish that transitioned from an aquatic to a terrestrial environment.

The first fish with the capability to traverse land was *Tiktaalik roseae*, a species of sarcopterygian that lived *c.* 375 million years ago, in what is now the Canadian Arctic. Its pectoral fins possessed primitive wristbones not seen in true fishes but present in tetrapods; the fins themselves were notably muscular, with highly developed shoulder bones, and also exhibited functional elbows. All of this would have enabled it to support itself in shallow water, and perhaps on dry land such as sandbars, for brief spells.

Largest lizard
Komodo dragons (*Varanus komodoensis*) live on a handful of Indonesian islands, the majority on Komodo itself. Males average 2.59 m (8 ft 6 in) long and weigh 79–91 kg (174–200 lb).

Newest species of crocodile
The New Guinea crocodile (*Crocodylus novaeguineae*) was formally described in 1928, although some biologists argued that it represented two species. By studying factors such as bodily structure, egg-laying habits and distribution, scientists finally confirmed Hall's New Guinea crocodile (*C. halli*) as a distinct species in the journal *Copeia* in Sep 2019.

The **most widely distributed snake** overall is the pelagic sea snake (*Hydrophis platurus*) – see p.57.

– see p.57.

Longest reptile
The reticulated python (*Malayopython reticulatus*) of south-east Asia, Indonesia and the Philippines may exceed 6.25 m (20 ft 6 in).

The **shortest reptiles** are three species of Madagascan minute leaf chameleon: *Brookesia minima*, *B. micra* and *B. tuberculata*. Adult males may measure 14 mm (0.5 in) from snout to cloaca.

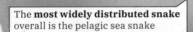

Most widely distributed terrestrial snake
The largest natural range for a land-based snake is that of the northern, or European, adder (*Vipera berus*). Its east-to-west range is some 8,000 km (5,000 mi), from the UK to Sakhalin Island off eastern Russia. This venomous snake lives as far north as Scandinavia and Russia's Kola Peninsula, 200 km (124 mi) north of the Arctic Circle, and as far south as the Balkans.

Most trafficked wild mammals
The scales of pangolins, aka scaly anteaters (family Manidae), are keratin-based – the same material that forms hair and horn. They serve as an effective defence against predators; when under threat, they protect their underbelly by curling into a ball, so their back faces outwards.

Sadly, their defence has also been the cause of their downfall. According to the International Union for Conservation of Nature, more than 1 million pangolins were illegally traded between 2000 and 2013. In some cultures, the scales are prized for traditional medicine, and the easily captured animals are also hunted for meat.

Anatomy of... reptile skin
Scale-covered skin offers armour and a watertight layer that enables reptiles to survive in arid conditions. However, scales aren't exclusive to reptiles: a number of mammals, amphibians and insects have also evolved this feature in various forms.

1. **Scale:** Stiff exterior plate that provides protection and helps the animal to retain moisture

2. **Hinge:** Flexible region between scales in the epidermis

3. **Chromatophores:** Pigment-containing cells that lend reptiles their varied colouration

4. **Osteoderm:** Bony deposits that reinforce keratinized scales in many lizards, turtles and crocodilians

5. **Dermis:** Muscular layer of skin below the scales supplied with nerves and blood vessels

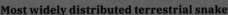

The name "pangolin" derives from the Malay word *pengguling*, which roughly translates as "one who rolls up".

Slowest insect wing-beat
The wings of the European swallowtail butterfly (*Papilio machaon*) flap 300 times per minute – just five times a second. The "dust" on the wings of butterflies and moths is actually a latticework of tiny scales (see inset) made from glucose-based chitin; it is nature's second-most common polymer after cellulose, found in plants.

The **heaviest reptile** is the saltwater crocodile (*Crocodylus porosus*) of south-east Asia and northern Australia. Large males can weigh as much as 1,200 kg (2,645 lb).

Largest family of moths
With a worldwide distribution, there are currently more than 35,000 species of owlet moth (family Noctuidae) known to science. However, given the cryptic colouration and patterning of their upper forewings, which makes them difficult to spot, there may be numerous more species – possibly as many as 65,000 – that are still awaiting formal discovery.

Recent research suggests that scales on moth wings may act as a defence mechanism, absorbing sound frequencies used by bats for echolocation.

Largest gecko
The New Caledonian giant gecko (*Rhacodactylus leachianus*) can reach 36 cm (1 ft 2 in) long including its tail.
The **smallest geckos** are the dwarf geckos of the genus *Sphaerodactylus*. Measurements of 16–18 mm (0.62–0.7 in) from snout to vent have been recorded for the Jaragua dwarf gecko (*S. ariasae*) from the Dominican Republic and the Virgin Islands dwarf gecko (*S. parthenopion*).

Most efficient thermoregulating lizard
The lava iguana (*Liolaemus multiformis*) is a black-scaled species native to the Peruvian Andes. After an hour basking in the sun in near-freezing external conditions of only 1.5°C (34.7°F), it can raise its body temperature to 33°C (91.4°F).

100%

Smallest chelonian
The speckled cape tortoise (*Chersobius signatus*) of South Africa has a shell length of 6–9.6 cm (2.3–3.7 in); it's small enough to hide between the cracks in rocks. As with all chelonians, this tiny tortoise features two types of scales: small epidermal scales on its skin and hard, keratin-covered scutes that encase its shell.

Largest lizard genus
As of 8 Feb 2020, there were 436 known species in the genus *Anolis*. Native to the Americas, anoles are arboreal (tree-dwelling) lizards. Males have large, species-specific coloured dewlaps for displaying to females.

With 143 species as of the same date, the **largest snake genus** is *Atractus*, or arrow ground snakes. They range from Panama south to Argentina.

This snake's rattle is a series of interlocking, hollow keratin segments formed from dead skin.

Heaviest venomous snake
The eastern diamondback rattlesnake (*Crotalus adamanteus*, pictured) of south-eastern USA weighs up to 6.8 kg (15 lb) and may reach 1.83 m (6 ft) in length. The heaviest on record was 15 kg (33 lb) – about the same as four human babies – and was 2.36 m (7 ft 9 in) long. A rival species for this title is the gaboon viper (*Bitis gabonica*) of sub-Saharan Africa with an 11.3-kg (25-lb) specimen documented in 1973.

The **longest venomous snake**, meanwhile, is the king cobra (*Ophiophagus hannah*), native to India and south-east Asia. Adults typically grow between 3.7 and 4 m (12–13 ft) long.

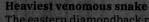

Scales (Aquatic)

Historically, European catfish (*Silurus glanis*) may have been the **largest freshwater fish**; yet another contender became extinct in 2020 (see pp.64–65).

The robust, armour-like scales of the arapaima can withstand even piranha attacks!

counting annual growth rings – similar to ageing a tree. A sample of 386 bigmouth buffalo revealed that, in multiple cases, as much as 90% of a population was aged 80 years or more, far exceeding the previously assumed age cap of 26 years for this species. Five specimens were confirmed to be centenarians, with the oldest aged 112 years.

Newest living shark
As noted in *Zootaxa* on 18 Jun 2019, the most recently described species of extant shark is the American pocket shark (*Mollisquama mississippiensis*), a type of kitefin shark. Caught in the Gulf of Mexico in Feb 2010, the 14.2-cm-long (5.6-in) juvenile male is only the second species of the genus found to date. As with all sharks, the skin of pocket sharks is almost fully covered in V-shaped placoid scales called denticles (see below left).

Largest freshwater fish
There are several species in the running for this title, depending on the criteria. The arapaima (*Arapaima gigas*, above) of South America's Amazon Basin grows to 4.5 m (14 ft 9 in) and weighs 200 kg (440 lb). The heavier Mekong giant catfish (*Pangasianodon gigas*, inset) and Chao Phraya giant catfish (*Pangasius sanitwongsei*) of Indochina both weigh in the region of 300 kg (660 lb) but grow to shorter lengths of 3 m (9 ft 10 in).

Largest mosasaurs
Mosasaurs were prehistoric aquatic lizards that sat at the top of the oceanic food chain towards the end of the Cretaceous era (94–66 million years ago). Estimates for the biggest specimens range from 15 m (49 ft) for *Hainosaurus bernardi*, up to 18 m (59 ft) for *Mosasaurus hoffmanni*. Like modern sea snakes, all mosasaurs are believed to have had scaly skin; small, keeled (ridged) scales possibly limited drag when swimming and also reduced shininess, helping with camouflage when hunting.

Oldest freshwater fish
As reported in *Communications Biology* in May 2019, the oldest age-authenticated freshwater fish is the bigmouth buffalo (*Ictiobus cyprinellus*), a member of the sucker family native to drainage waters of the Mississippi Basin and Hudson Bay in central USA and southern Canada. It's possible to calculate a specimen's age by extracting otoliths (earstones) and

Anatomy of... denticles

The skin of sharks, skates and rays has small placoid (plate-like) scales, giving it a texture similar to sandpaper. Known as "dermal denticles", these protective structures also help to reduce drag through the water in many cases.

1. **Dermal denticles:** V-shaped scales with a tooth-like structure

2. **Enamel:** A hard outer layer

3. **Dentine:** Tough, calcified tissue situated underneath the enamel

4. **Pulp cavity:** The centre of the scale, containing blood vessels, nerves and tissue

5. **Basal plate:** A bony feature that anchors the denticle to the skin with collagen fibres

Most diverse bioluminescent vertebrates
Up to 80% of ray-finned fish (class Actinopterygii) living in open water can produce their own light. Amazingly, the ability evolved independently within that group at least 27 times! Many such fish, including the deep-sea hatchetfish (family Sternoptychidae) pictured here, inhabit the ocean's mesopelagic ("twilight") zone, at depths of 200–1,500 m (650–4,920 ft).

The scales of hatchetfish scatter light, rather than reflecting it, making it harder for predators to spot them in the murky deep.

Longest dive by a chelonian
An adult female loggerhead turtle (*Caretta caretta*, example pictured) was submerged for 10 hr 14 min in the Mediterranean Sea, off the coast of Tunisia, in Feb 2003. The time was recorded by researchers led by Dr Annette Broderick of the University of Exeter (UK).

Sea turtles have tough, scaly skin on their bodies, while their shells are lined with hard, horn-covered scales known as "scutes".

Although pelagic sea snakes spend most of their lives in the open ocean, they do occasionally get washed on to the shore.

Most widely distributed snake

No species of snake has a greater range than the pelagic sea snake (*Hydrophis platurus*), aka the yellow-bellied sea snake. ("Pelagic" relates to the surface of the sea.) It lives in tropical regions of the Pacific and Indian oceans, from south-east Asia and Australia to California, USA, and Ecuador in South America. Its scales do not overlap, to reduce sites where marine ectoparasites may adhere. It also sheds its skin more often than terrestrial snakes – another means of removing these unwanted guests.

Largest predatory fish

Great white sharks (*Carcharodon carcharias*) measure 4.3–4.6 m (14–15 ft) in length, and generally weigh 520–770 kg (1,150–1,700 lb). Circumstantial evidence suggests that some great whites can exceed 6 m (20 ft), which is longer than a pick-up truck.

The internal structure of coelacanth scales has been likened to a "smart material" as it can reconfigure itself when placed under pressure.

Most recently described species of living coelacanth

Latimeria menadoensis was formally recognized in 1999. Until then, the only known extant coelacanth was *L. chalumnae*, described in 1938. Prior to this, these primitive fish had been thought to have become extinct more than 65 million years ago. Coelacanths boast bone-hard scales that have been rated to be about 10 times tougher than window-pane glass!

Largest anadromous fish

Fish that are born in fresh water, migrate to the sea as juveniles and return to fresh water to spawn are termed "anadromous". The biggest such fish, the beluga sturgeon (*Huso huso*), averages 2.3 m (7 ft 6 in) long and weighs 65–130 kg (143–286 lb). Sturgeon have diamond-shaped ganoid scales with an enamel-like coating.

Largest salmon

Native to the northern Pacific and Arctic oceans, chinook salmon (*Oncorhynchus tshawytscha*) can reach 1.5 m (4 ft 11 in) long. Like most soft-fin-rayed fish, salmon have smooth, overlapping cycloid scales, a layout that affords them a greater degree of flexible movement.

Heaviest bony fish

Adult sunfish (genus *Mola*) average 1.8 m (6 ft) long and weigh *c.* 1,000 kg (2,200 lb). The heftiest specimen was a bump-head sunfish (*M. alexandrini*) caught off Kamogawa in Chiba, Japan, in 1996. It weighed 2,300 kg (5,070 lb) and was 2.72 m (8 ft 11 in) between fin tips. Sunfish have ctenoid scales with a comb-like edge.

Longest duration flight by a flying fish

In May 2008, a film crew travelling between Honshu and Yakushima Island in Kagoshima, Japan, recorded a 45-sec flight by a flying fish (family Exocoetidae).

Largest parrotfish

The green humphead parrotfish (*Bolbometopon muricatum*) reaches 1.5 m (4 ft 11 in) long and weighs up to 75 kg (165 lb 5 oz). The sole member of its genus, it is indigenous to reefs in the Indian and Pacific oceans, where it is the largest herbivorous fish. Parrotfish are known for their bright colours and fused teeth that form a parrot-like "beak".

Largest fish

The plankton-feeding whale shark (*Rhincodon typus*) is found in warmer areas of the Atlantic, Pacific and Indian oceans. Those assessed to date typically measure 4–12 m (13 ft 1 in–39 ft 4 in) long, with sexual maturity generally agreed to be reached at 9 m (29 ft 6 in). However, evaluations of these elusive fish vary drastically from study to study. The largest documented specimen is a female caught in the Arabian Sea off Gujarat, India, on 8 May 2001; she was reported to measure 18.8 m (61 ft 8 in) – the length of a bowling alley!

The pattern of white stripes and spots across the upper half of a whale shark is unique to each fish.

Skin

Despite their name, mole-rats are not fully "naked", as they have whiskers and tiny sensory hairs distributed over their body.

liver and gut can be seen. Combined with typically lime-green colouration on their backs, the translucent skin offers highly effective camouflage when resting on leaves. Many species of glass frog also have green bones.

Largest frog
One key difference between frogs and toads lies in their skin. Frogs typically have moist, smooth skin, while toad skin is usually dry and bumpy. With an average length of 30 cm (11.8 in), the African goliath frog (*Conraua goliath*) is the biggest frog species.

The marine or cane toad (*Rhinella marina*) of South America and Australia (introduced) is the **largest toad**. In 1991, one specimen measured 38 cm (1 ft 3 in) from snout to vent.

▶ Longest-lived rodent
Africa's naked mole-rat (*Heterocephalus glaber*) can live up to 31 years in captivity. In the wild, they inhabit underground burrow systems below East Africa's arid grasslands. As this habitat is so warm, the rodents do not need fur. If they do become cold, they huddle together for warmth.

Most venomous cephalopod
Certain species of blue-ringed octopus (genus *Hapalochlaena*) carry a potent neurotoxin called tetrodotoxin (TTX). Each individual carries sufficient venom in their salivary glands alone to paralyse, or even kill, an adult human. Although they can bite, they are not aggressive, preferring to warn away threats by making the patterns on their skin glow. They are found around the coasts of Australia, Japan and parts of south-east Asia.

Thickest skin
Reaching up to 10 cm (4 in), the skin on the back of the whale shark (*Rhincodon typus*), below its scales (see p.57), has a rubber-like texture to deter predators such as orcas. They can make their skin tougher still by clenching dorsal muscles.

Certain marine mammals have been said to have thicker skin, but that includes fatty tissue beneath the dermis. The animal with the **thickest blubber** is the bowhead whale (*Balaena mysticetus*); in places, it can be 40 cm (1 ft 3.7 in) thick.

Most transparent amphibians
Some glass frogs (family Centrolenidae), native to the rainforests of Central and South America, have partly transparent abdomens, through which their heart,

100%

Most poisonous fish
All pufferfish (Tetraodontidae) contain TTX neurotoxin (also see above left), although potency varies across species. If ingested, a mere 16 mg can kill a 70-kg (154-lb) human, and less than 2 mg if injected. When threatened, the fish inflate and erect spines to ward off attackers.

The **smallest pufferfish** is the Malabar puffer, aka the pea puffer (*Carinotetraodon travancoricus*, inset) of south-west India, which measures no more than 3.5 cm (1.4 in) long.

Anatomy of... frog skin
All vertebrates have skin, though it may be covered by fur, spines, feathers or scales. It provides protection, helps to regulate body temperature and acts as a sensory organ. In amphibians, such as frogs, the skin is naked and semi-permeable, allowing for the exchange of air and water. Some amphibians are toxic, as they sequester toxins from the invertebrates that they feed on.

1. Epidermis: The outer layer of skin is highly permeable, allowing water and electrolytes to pass

2. Chromatophores: Cells that contain pigment and reflect light

3. Capillaries: Small vessels that transfer oxygen and nutrients from the blood to body tissues

4. Poison glands: While all frogs have these, in most they're not toxic enough to deter predators

5. Mucous glands: Mucus traps moisture, keeping the frog moist and helping it to absorb oxygen

Most poisonous frog
The toxic skin of the golden poison-dart frog (*Phyllobates terribilis*) has an LD_{50} (median lethal dose) of 0.2 micrograms (µg) per kg. Just 14 µg of its poison, called batrachotoxin, can be fatal to a 70-kg (154-lb) human. Endemic to the Pacific rainforest of western Colombia, the frog is 4–6 cm (1.6–2.4 in) long, also making it the **largest poison-dart frog**.

100%

Stickiest salamander
Native to woodland areas across much of the USA, the northern slimy salamander (*Plethodon glutinosus*) is named after the glue-like mucus that its skin secretes. This substance is so adhesive that predators often find they have bitten off more than they can chew, as the mucus effectively seals the attacker's mouth shut.

100%

Scientists wear surgical gloves when handling frogs and toads, as soap and chemicals on our bare skin can harm them.

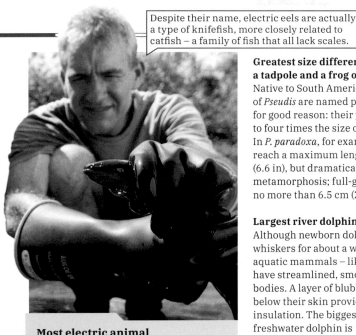

Despite their name, electric eels are actually a type of knifefish, more closely related to catfish – a family of fish that all lack scales.

Greatest size difference between a tadpole and a frog of the same species
Native to South America, the seven species of *Pseudis* are named paradoxical frogs for good reason: their young are three to four times the size of their parents! In *P. paradoxa*, for example, tadpoles reach a maximum length of 16.8 cm (6.6 in), but dramatically shrink during metamorphosis; full-grown frogs measure no more than 6.5 cm (2.5 in), and often less.

Largest river dolphin
Although newborn dolphins sport a few whiskers for about a week after birth, these aquatic mammals – like all cetaceans – have streamlined, smooth-skinned bodies. A layer of blubber below their skin provides insulation. The biggest freshwater dolphin is

Farthest-gliding amphibians
Some species of flying frog have been reported to glide as far as 15 m (50 ft) between trees using the extensive webbed skin on their feet. Pictured here is a Wallace's flying frog (*Rhacophorus nigropalmatus*), which also has oversized pads on its toes that help it to climb and to land softly.

Most electric animal
The electric eel, or poraquê (genus *Electrophorus*), is native to river systems in the tropics of South America and Central America. According to a Sep 2019 study in *Nature Communications*, of the three known living species, *E. voltai* generates the most electricity – up to 860 V, in the case of one 1.2-m-long (4-ft) female (above). The fish produce electricity via three paired organs along their bodies. Dr William Crampton (above), one of the paper's lead authors, told GWR that size and electrical potential are unrelated. "Electric eels can reach huge sizes – up to at least 2 m [6 ft 6 in] – but these monsters often have lower voltage than ones that are much smaller."

Largest gliding mammal
Found in the forests of Asia, giant flying squirrels (genus *Petaurista*) grow to 1.1 m (3 ft 7 in) long, including the tail. They glide using parachute-like, fur-coated skin between their limbs and chest. One specimen is recorded covering 450 m (1,476 ft) – around the same length as four soccer fields!

the boto (*Inia geoffrensis*) of the Amazon and Orinoco rivers in South America. This species' distinct pink colouring comes from blood vessels close to the skin's surface.

Most common New World vulture
Some animals have evolved patches of bare skin for strategic purposes. There are *c.* 4.5 million turkey vultures (*Cathartes aura*) worldwide; their bald heads and necks prevent them from soiling their feathers when eating bloody carcasses. The lack of plumage also helps control body temperature.

The gelada (*Theropithecus gelada*) of Ethiopia, a close relative of the baboon, has a hairless chest patch known as a "bleeding heart". When vivid red, it signals sexual receptiveness in females and dominance in males. The gelada boasts huge upper canine teeth but it is actually a grazer, with grass constituting up to 90% of its diet, making it the **most herbivorous monkey**.

Deepest-living octopus
Dumbo octopuses (genus *Grimpoteuthis*) live close to the ocean floor, some 4,865 m (16,000 ft) below sea level – more than two-and-a-half times the depth of the Grand Canyon. Their body, roughly 20 cm (7.8 in) long, is soft and semi-gelatinous, and two ear-like fins give them their common name. The eight limbs are joined by a web of skin, which can lend these octopuses an umbrella-like appearance.

Smallest rhinoceros
The Sumatran rhino (*Dicerorhinus sumatrensis*) has a head-and-body length of 2.3–3.2 m (7 ft 6 in–10 ft 6 in), a shoulder height of 1.1–1.5 m (3 ft 7 in–4 ft 11 in) and weighs up to 2 tonnes (4,400 lb). In 2019, it became extinct in Malaysia owing to deforestation to make way for palm-oil plantations. Along with elephants and hippos, rhinos were formerly classed as pachyderms (from the Greek *pachydermos* – meaning "thick skinned"). Their wrinkles trap moisture, helping these animals to moderate their body temperature in the tropics.

Below, the Sumatran rhino is compared with the white rhino (*Ceratotherium simum simum*), the **largest rhinoceros** at 4.2 m (13 ft 9 in) long and 1.85 m (6 ft) tall at the shoulder. It weighs approximately 3.6 tonnes (7,930 lb).

Exoskeletons

The majority of gastropod shells are spirally coiled in a "dextral" (i.e., right-handed) pattern.

Earliest exoskeletons

The oldest animals in the fossil record, dating to around 558 million years ago, were all soft-bodied marine organisms, such as *Dickinsonia*. It was not until around 8 million years later that some creatures began to develop a tough exterior for extra protection.

The first-known animals to exhibit this evolutionary advantage were *Cloudina*, sea-dwellers from the late Ediacaran period that are known collectively with other, later life forms as ESFs (early skeletal fossils). Loosely described as an exoskeleton or a shell, the outer, mineralized portion of their bodies resembled a tall nest of cones, one inside another, composed of calcite. *Cloudina*'s soft body form is presently unknown, as such tissues do not readily fossilize. Its remains have been found in many parts of the world, including Spain, Namibia, Uruguay, the USA, China, Antarctica and Russia.

Earliest trilobites

Taking the "outer skeleton" strategy of ESF life-forms to another level was Arthropoda. This phylum includes insects, arachnids and crustaceans, all of which boast an exoskeleton of some form.

One of the first arthropod groups to emerge were trilobites (Trilobita), some 520–540 million years ago. Now extinct, their closest living relatives are horseshoe crabs. The **earliest arachnid**, by comparison, was the scorpion *Parioscorpio venator*, dating from *c.* 436 million years ago. Described in *Scientific Reports* in Jan 2020, it's unknown whether the scorpion led a terrestrial, marine or amphibious lifestyle.

Largest land snail

Collected in Sierra Leone in Jun 1976, a specimen of the African giant snail (*Achatina achatina*) measured 39.3 cm (1 ft 3.4 in) from snout to tail when fully extended, with a shell length of 27.3 cm (10.75 in). It weighed exactly 900 g (2 lb). The supersized snail, named Gee Geronimo, was owned by Christopher Hudson of East Sussex, UK.

Smallest scorpion

Scorpions are one of the most well-known animals today to sport an exoskeleton. The smallest of their kind is *Microbuthus pusillus*, with a total length of around 1.3 cm (0.5 in). It is found on the Red Sea coast.

100%

The **heaviest scorpion** is the emperor scorpion (*Pandinus imperator*) of West Africa, which can weigh up to 60 g (2 oz) – more than a tennis ball. It measures between 13 and 18 cm (5–7 in) long. Scorpions give off a bright blue-green glow when placed under ultraviolet light. This is

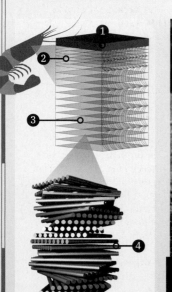

Anatomy of... exoskeletons

Animals can sport total or partial exoskeletons. In the latter case, e.g. arthropods, they are often called "shells". Exoskeletons are formed from the fibrous natural polymer chitin.

1. Epicuticle: Waxy protective outer layer

2. Exocuticle: Intermediate layer

3. Endocuticle: Highly chitinized inner layer

4. Helical nanofibres: Exoskeletons derive their toughness from their internal arrangement, a twisting stack of chitin and protein layers which resembles the grain in plywood.

Most dangerous sea urchin

The flower urchin (*Toxopneustes pileolus*) of the Indo-Pacific may look delicate, but it packs a punch. Its hard shell ("test") is covered in spines and pedicellaria (claw-like organs) that deliver a venom containing Contractin A. As well as causing severe pain, the toxin seems to affect smooth muscle, which can lead to respiratory problems and even paralysis.

Highest density of crabs

At the last population count in 2015, a total of 38 million Christmas Island red crabs (*Gecarcoidea natalis*) lived on the 135-km² (52-sq-mi) Christmas Island and nearby Cocos (Keeling) Islands in the Indian Ocean. That's around 280,000 crabs per km² (730,000 per sq mi). Numbers have plummeted since the invasion of the yellow crazy ant (*Anoplolepis gracilipes*). In 2017, researchers tried to arrest the decline by introducing a "biocontrol agent": Malaysian wasps, which eat the crazy ants' primary food source.

Once a year, the Christmas Island red crabs embark on a spectacular migration to the shore to mate.

Newest seadragon

As reported in the journal *Royal Society Open Science*, the ruby seadragon (*Phyllopteryx dewysea*) was formally described in 2015. Although similar in body shape to the common seadragon (see left), it is most readily distinguished in live specimens by its colouration: red with pink vertical bars. Ruby seadragons are only known to live off Western Australia.

Smallest horseshoe crab

The mangrove horseshoe crab (*Carcinoscorpius rotundicauda*) has a circular shell, or carapace, whose diameter measures up to 15 cm (5.9 in). It inhabits

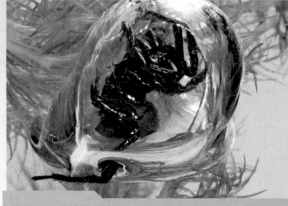

Most aquatic spider

The diving bell spider (*Argyroneta aquatica*) spends almost its entire life submerged. It builds a "diving bell" by collecting air bubbles with hydrophobic (water-repellent) hairs on its legs. It then deposits the bubbles between the strands of its underwater web until it becomes big enough to reside in.

Largest seadragon

The common or weedy seadragon (*Phyllopteryx taeniolatus*) can grow to a length of 45 cm (1 ft 5 in) from snout to tail tip. Unlike many other fish, seadragons and seahorses do not have scales. They are covered instead in a bony exoskeleton made up of hard rings.

owing to fluorescent chemicals present in the outer layer of their exoskeletons. Scientists are unsure as to the exact purpose of this luminescence. Theories include that it lures or confuses prey, or helps to locate other scorpions in the dark.

Largest spider

While spiders are covered in elongated hairs known as trichobothria, they too have an outer skeleton. When spiders outgrow their exoskeletons, they shed them in a process known as moulting.

The biggest spider is the goliath bird-eating tarantula (*Theraphosa blondi*), an ambush hunter with a leg span of up to 28 cm (11 in). It is found mainly in the coastal rainforests of Suriname, Guyana and French Guiana, and, despite its name, most commonly eats insects and toads.

Greatest sexual dimorphism for a beetle

Among trilobite beetles (genus *Platerodrilus*) of India and south-east Asia, there is a huge size difference between the sexes. The males, which look like typical beetles, can be as little as 5 mm (0.2 in) long, whereas the females can measure up to 60 mm (2.4 in) – an incredible 12-fold disparity. Females are neotenous, resembling worm-like beetle larvae their entire life, even as adults. Also unlike the males, the females bear armoured, spine-edged plates, most prominently upon the head, which lends them a resemblance to prehistoric trilobites (see opposite), hence this insect's common name.

coastal forests, mudflats and shores throughout India and south-east Asia. Horseshoe crabs are the last surviving members of an ancient arthropod lineage known as the xiphosurans, most closely related to prehistoric sea scorpions (eurypterids).

Most legs on an animal

Despite their name, millipedes do not have 1,000 legs. They usually have around 300 pairs, although the species *Illacme plenipes* – native to California, USA – can grow 375 pairs (i.e., 750 legs). Millipedes have a segmented armoured exoskeleton. Some species protect themselves by rolling into a ball when threatened.

Oldest animal (non-colonial)

A quahog clam (*Arctica islandica*) found off Iceland in 2006 was estimated to be between 405 and 410 years old. Sclerochronologists from Bangor University in Wales, UK, studied annual growth rings in the shell to determine its longevity; in 2013, a follow-up study using more advanced ageing techniques revised it to 507 years.

Largest ammonite

An incomplete fossil of a *Parapuzosia seppenradensis* ammonite discovered in Germany in 1895 measured 1.95 m (6 ft 4 in) across, with the complete shell estimated at 2.55 m (8 ft 4 in). Ammonites were related to squids and octopuses but lived inside coiled shells. Their most similar-looking relatives today are nautiluses (family Nautilidae, inset), sometimes called "living fossils".

Longest beetle

Dwelling in the rainforests of Central and South America, Hercules beetles (*Dynastes hercules*) range from 44 to 172 mm (1.7–6.7 in) long, a large proportion of which is taken up by their horn-like pincers. This super-strong bug is aptly named: during resistance experiments, they have been shown to be able to withstand a force of 850 times their own weight!

100%

The elytra (hardened wing covers) of Hercules beetles change colour from yellow/green to black with increased humidity as they absorb moisture.

Pets & Livestock

Longest human tunnel travelled through by a dog on a skateboard
A five-year-old bulldog named Dai-chan, owned by Marie Saito (JPN), skateboarded through the legs of 33 people on 17 Sep 2017 in Tokyo, Japan.
The same record for a **cat** is 13 people, by Boomer – a Bengal owned by Robert Dollwet (USA/AUS) – on 9 Feb 2017 in Coolangatta, Queensland, Australia.

Fastest time to perform 10 vaults off a human by a dog
On 12 May 2019, Jack Russell Little Joe bounced off Rachael Grylls (UK) 10 times in 9.843 sec at the DogFest canine show in Knebworth, Hertfordshire, UK.
At the same event, Nala performed the **most "sits" by a dog in one minute** – 35, guided by her owner, Nicci Hindson (UK).

Shortest horse (male)
Bombel measures 56.7 cm (1 ft 10 in; 5.3 hands) to the shoulders, as verified on 24 Apr 2018 at Kaskada Stable in Łódź, Poland. The miniature Appaloosa is owned by Katarzyna Zielińska (POL), who named him after the Polish word for "bubble", in reference to his rather rotund body.

Longest domestic cat
Barivel – a Maine Coon owned by Cinzia Tinnirello and Edgar Scandurra (both ITA) – was 120 cm (3 ft 11.2 in) from nose to tail tip on 22 May 2018. As ratified on 28 Aug 2010, the **longest domestic cat ever** was also a Maine Coon: the 123-cm-long (4-ft) "Stewie" belonged to Robin Hendrickson and Erik Brandsness (both USA).

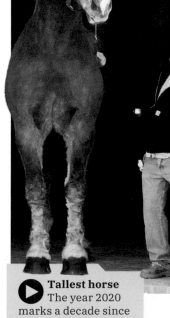

Farthest dock-jump by a dog
On 22 Sep 2019, four-year-old whippet Sounders, owned by Laurel Behnke (USA), leapt 11.02 m (36 ft 2 in) from a platform into a pool of water at The Michael Ellis School in Santa Rosa, California, USA. This beat his own record by 21 cm (8.2 in) and is more than 2 m (6 ft 6 in) farther than the human long jump record! North America Diving Dogs verified the feat.

Tallest horse
The year 2020 marks a decade since GWR first met Big Jake. On 19 Jan 2010, the then-nine-year-old Belgian gelding measured 210 cm (6 ft 10 in; 20.3 hands), without shoes, at Smokey Hollow Farm in Poynette, Wisconsin, USA. At his peak, Big Jake consumed a bale of hay and two full buckets of grain a day. He is currently enjoying retirement.

Most dance moves by a bird
Researchers analysing videos of Snowball, a sulphur-crested cockatoo who can strut his stuff in time to pop songs, have identified 14 different "dance movements". These include head banging, head shaking and foot lifting (above). Owned by Irena Schulz (USA), Snowball has favoured tunes to jive to, including Cyndi Lauper's "Girls Just Want to Have Fun" and Queen's "Another One Bites the Dust".

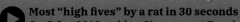

Most "high fives" by a rat in 30 seconds
On 5 Oct 2019, golden Siamese rat Frankie (inset right) completed 28 alternating paw tricks in half a minute with Luke Roberts (UK) in Watford, Hertfordshire, UK. Not to be outdone, Frankie's brother Freddie (a wheaten rex, inset left) completed the **O most hoop jumps by a rat in 30 seconds** – eight – on 5 Jan 2020. With 2020 being the Year of the Rat, Luke, who himself is a record holder, has plans to set further records with his rodents.

▶ Most dogs in a conga line

On 8 Dec 2019, Alexa Lauenburger (DEU) led a conga line with eight of her four-legged friends – Emma, Jennifer, Katy, Maya, Nala, Sabrina, Sally and Specki – in Todenbüttel, Germany. It was one of five dog-trick records broken by Alexa and her father Wolfgang on that day (see below). At just 12 years old, talented trainer Alexa has appeared on TV in Germany, the UK and the USA, debuting on *America's Got Talent* in 2020. She started to work with dogs at the age of five. "It's really important to find a trick that suits the dog," she advises.

Not satisfied with merely mastering canine conga, Alexa and her father Wolfgang Lauenburger – who comes from a circus background – set four further dog-trick records with their talented pack of pooches on 8 Dec 2019:
- ❯ **Fastest time to walk 10 m on hind legs by a dog**: 3.05 sec by Emma with Wolfgang.
- ❯ **Fastest 5 m backwards by a dog**: 6.73 sec by Jennifer with Alexa.
- ❯ **Most spins by a dog in 30 seconds**: 43 by Maya with Wolfgang.
- ❯ **Fastest five hurdles cleared by a dog on hind legs**: 5.66 sec by Emma with Alexa.

Largest goat yoga class

On 14 Sep 2019, Debbie and Rob Canton (both USA) held a yoga class for 501 people alongside the caprine inhabitants of Grady Goat Farm in Thonotosassa, Florida, USA. The record attempt was part of a charity campaign against child trafficking.

The **largest dog yoga class** featured 270 participants and was organized by Link Asset Management Limited (HKG) on 17 Jan 2016 in Hong Kong, China.

Largest parade of alpacas

On 14 Jun 2019, a herd of 1,048 alpacas took to the streets of the Peruvian city of Juliaca to celebrate the 58th anniversary of the Puno region's Southern Cattle Fair. Both breeds of alpaca were present: the *huacaya* (identifiable by its spongelike hair) and the *suri* (notable for its long hair and lustrous coat).

Highest bar jump by a llama

Caspa leapt over a 1.13-m-high (3-ft 8.5-in) bar on 14 Jun 2015 at DogFest held at Arley Hall, Cheshire, UK. He is owned by Sue Williams (UK).

Most bottlecaps removed by a parrot in one minute

Way ahead of the "bottlecap challenge" that went viral in 2019 was Gordon the hyacinth macaw. On 1 Nov 2014, he removed 12 tops from soda bottles in Los Altos, California, USA, under the supervision of his trainer, Julie Cardoza (USA).

Fastest time to complete five jumps by a rabbit

On 18 Jan 2020, Penelope cleared five hurdles in 4.816 sec. She saw off fellow leporine leapers Bullseye and Big Ben – all owned by rabbit showjumper Nicole Barrett (UK) – to claim the title at the Bradford Premier Small Animal Show in Doncaster, South Yorkshire, UK.

▶ Largest horn spread on a steer

A seven-year-old Texas longhorn named Poncho Via has horns that stretch 3.23 m (10 ft 7 in) from tip to tip. Poncho Via lives on a ranch in Goodwater, Alabama, USA – where he has been raised by the Pope family. Described as a "big, gentle character", he likes to eat apples, carrots and marshmallows.

As of 2019, the largest horn spread on a cow was 2.65 m (8 ft 8 in) for "3S Danica" in Texas, USA.

Longest horns on a yak

The curly horns belonging to Jericho, a 20-year-old Tibetan native trim yak, were a combined 3.23 m (10 ft 7 in) on 23 Dec 2018. Jericho is owned by Hugh and Melodee Smith (both USA) and lives in Welch, Minnesota, USA. Melodee (pictured) describes him as gentle and rideable. His horns have continued to grow throughout his life, becoming so heavy that they have curled forward and then back down around his neck.

Round-Up

Most recent fish extinction

The Chinese paddlefish (*Psephurus gladius*) was one of the largest freshwater fish (see p.56), growing to at least 3 m (9 ft 10 in) long and up to 300 kg (660 lb). The species was characterized by its elongated, sword-like rostrum (i.e., snout). In Jan 2020, it was formally declared extinct by the Chinese Academy of Fishery Sciences and sturgeon experts of the International Union for Conservation of Nature. It probably died out sometime between 2005 and 2010, owing to overfishing and habitat loss. Keen to avoid more records like this, Guinness World Records has partnered with The Lion's Share (see pp.10–11).

Sheepdogs, livestock and thoroughbred horses are still sold in guineas at many traditional rural auctions in the UK.

Most expensive sheepdog

Two-and-a-half-year-old border collie Megan, reared by shepherdess Emma Gray (UK), achieved an unprecedented hammer price of 18,000 guineas (£18,900; $24,361) at Skipton Auction Mart in North Yorkshire, UK, on 21 Feb 2020. The buyer was Brian Stamps, a rancher from Oklahoma, USA.

▶ Oldest sloth in captivity

A Linne's two-toed sloth (*Choloepus didactylus*) named Paula has lived at Halle Zoo in Germany since 25 Sep 1971 – a duration of 48 years 16 days as of 11 Oct 2019. She was thought to have been at least two years old on arrival, so the zoo nominated 14 Jun 2019 as her 50th birthday. The species has a typical lifespan of 20 years in the wild.

Fastest-running ant

The Saharan silver ant (*Cataglyphis bombycina*) of northern Africa can reach speeds of 85.5 cm/s (2 ft 9 in/s) – or 108 times its own body length – when running at full pelt. By way of comparison, Usain Bolt (JAM) ran at "just" 5.35 times his body height per second when he achieved the **fastest 100 m** – 9.58 sec – in Berlin, Germany, in 2009.

Fastest muscle in a mammal

A study of Daubenton's bats (*Myotis daubentonii*) revealed that superfast muscles in their throats contract and relax 200 times per second (200 Hertz). That's around 20 times faster than the muscle that controls blinking in our eyes, the orbicularis oculi – the **fastest human muscle**. This high oscillation in the bats' larynx produces a barrage of calls, referred to as "terminal buzz", which helps them to home in on prey through echolocation when hunting.

Oldest gorilla in captivity

Fatou, a western lowland gorilla (*Gorilla gorilla gorilla*), has lived at Zoo Berlin in Germany since May 1959. She marked her 63rd year on 13 Apr 2020, the date the zoo has allocated as her birthday. She had a rival for this title in another western lowland gorilla called Trudy (thought to have been born in Jun 1956) of Little Rock Zoo in Arkansas, USA. Sadly, Trudy passed away on 23 Jul 2019.

Longest recorded solitary dolphin

An Atlantic bottlenose dolphin (*Tursiops truncatus*) called Fungie has lived alone off Dingle in County Kerry, Ireland, for at least 37 years. According to a 2019 report reviewing the world's independent-living whales and dolphins by cetacean charity Marine Connection, he first appeared in 1983. The study sought to shed more light on the "lone rangers" among these typically social group animals. Fungie has become a much-loved symbol of the region among both locals and tourists.

The oldest gorilla that can be aged precisely was Colo, who was born in Columbus Zoo in Ohio, USA, on 22 Dec 1956 and died on 17 Jan 2017, aged 60 years 26 days. She was the **first gorilla born in captivity**.

The piercing cry of the white bellbird can be heard from around a mile (1.6 km) away and is on a sound-level equivalent to the hammering of a pile driver!

an additional pair of "pseudothumbs", giving it a total of 12 digits. They were previously thought to be fleshy protrusions, but closer analysis revealed that they are composed of bone and cartilage. The results of the study were published in the *American Journal of Physical Anthropology* on 21 Oct 2019.

Largest *Tyrannosaurus rex* skeleton

In Mar 2019, a new contender for this title emerged in the shape of "Scotty" (above, and in silhouette below). This *T. rex* may have been 13 m (42 ft 7 in) long and weighed some 8,870 kg (19,555 lb) according to the University of Alberta's Dr W Scott Persons (also above), who led a study into Scotty's size. Scotty is only 65% complete, however. The **most complete *T. rex* skeleton** is "Sue", found in 1990 and of similar proportions to Scotty. As the debate over their relative sizes is ongoing, GWR currently accords this title to both specimens.

Most expensive pigeon

On 17 Mar 2019, a bird named Armando – lauded as the "Lewis Hamilton of pigeons" – sold for

Loudest bird call

Native to rainforest in the Guianas, Venezuela and northern Brazil, male white bellbirds (*Procnias albus*) have been recorded making calls of 125.4 dBA at a distance of 1 m (3 ft 3 in) in courtship displays. The louder the calls, the shorter they tend to be – which is just as well for the females, as the males perform right next to them! The findings appeared in the journal *Current Biology* on 21 Oct 2019.

▶ First set of twin pandas born to a captive mother and a wild father

On 25 Jul 2018, He He ("Harmony") and Mei Mei ("Beautiful") were born to 16-year-old Cao Cao at the Hetaoping Base of China Conservation and Research Center for the Giant Panda in Sichuan, China. The twins were sired by a wild giant panda (*Ailuropoda melanoleuca*) whom Cao Cao met during a temporary release – a practice that aims to expand the species' limited gene pool.

€1,252,000 ($1,417,650; £1,065,870) via the PIPA online auction house. He was one of a group sold by Belgian pigeon fancier Joël Verschoot. Although he had recently retired, the five-year-old Armando came with an impeccable competitive pedigree, having won his last three events.

Most tricks performed by a dog in one minute

Daiquiri the Australian shepherd pulled off 60 tricks in 60 sec with owner Jennifer Fraser (CAN) in Calgary, Alberta, Canada, on 12 Dec 2019. The feat was equalled by fellow Canadian Sara Carson Devine with Hero the Super Collie in Lancaster, California, USA, on 11 Apr 2020.

Largest freshwater turtle ever

Stupendemys geographicus lived some 13 million–7 million years ago during the Miocene period. The largest specimens were the same size as a sedan car, reaching 4 m (13 ft) long and weighing 1.25 tonnes (1.37 US tons); that is five times heavier than today's **largest freshwater turtle**,

the critically endangered Yangtze giant softshell turtle (*Rafetus swinhoei*). *S. geographicus* inhabited lakes and rivers in what is now Colombia and Venezuela.

Most digits for a primate

The aye-aye (*Daubentonia madagascariensis*), a nocturnal lemur endemic to Madagascar, has

Largest camera-trap wildlife survey

In 2018–19, the fourth iteration of a nationwide survey of tigers (*Panthera tigris tigris*) took place in India. Cameras were placed in 26,838 locations across 141 different sites, covering an effective area of 121,337 km² (46,848 sq mi) – three times the size of Switzerland. They recorded 34,858,626 images of wildlife, 76,651 of which were of tigers. The project was overseen by the National Tiger Conservation Authority, the Wildlife Institute of India, state forestry staff and conservation NGOs.

The final tiger count from the 2018 census was 2,967 – encouragingly up 33% on 2014. However, experts warned the rise may partly reflect improved counting methods.

He He and Mei Mei now live at Shenshuping Panda Base, part of the China Conservation and Research Center for the Giant Panda. Above, they are pictured with Feng Li, Head of Animal Management at the facility's kindergarten.

ANIMALS

○ HALL OF FAME

Jane **Goodall**

Primatologist and conservationist Dr Jane Goodall (UK) has devoted her life to the study of chimpanzees and has devoted her life to the study of Peace for the United Nations. A Messenger voice on global ecological matters. she remains a touchstone voice on global matters.

On 14 Jul 2020, the project Jane began at Tanzania's Gombe Stream Chimpanzee Reserve (now just Gombe National Park) celebrated its 60th anniversary – making it the ● **longest-running wild-primate study**. Jane was just 26 when she first set up camp among the steep mountains and forested valleys near Lake Tanganyika. She says that she was "born loving animals", and grew up on tales of the jungle in stories such as *Tarzan* and *Dr Dolittle*. Having saved up for a dream trip to Kenya to assist him. It was then that she conceived a plan to study chimpanzees in their natural surroundings. Jane met the anthropologist Louis Leakey and began to assist him. It was then in Tanzania, in the hope of learning more about early human behaviour.

Once installed at Gombe Reserve, it took Jane months to earn the chimpanzees' trust and make her observations up-close. "Only when animals know you're there and aren't concerned can you be sure they're behaving normally," she says. She gave the chimps names, such as Goliath and Flo (a practice that ruffled a few feathers in the scientific community), and carefully studied their individual characters. Jane was amazed to witness them using the idea that twigs to help hunt for food such as termites. She told us that we still have much to only humans could make and use tools. Jane highlights, forever dispelling the idea that learn about chimps, especially with regard to their paternal relationships, both

Human population growth poses grave threats to chimpanzees, the through deforestation and the COVID-19 pandemic. As Jane highlights, if we latter driven home by the future – we must do all we can to better want to safeguard the future – we needs of the human **closest-living relatives**, as well as their territory.

"Mr H" is Jane's faithful companion and has understand them, as well as their territory. communities that share their territory.

"Mr H" is Jane's faithful companion and has travelled the world to more than 60 countries. was given Gary The original plush toy (seen below) was given travelled the world to almost 30 years ago by her friend Gary to her almost 30 years ago of your own, or to Haun. If you'd like a "Mr H" of valuable work make a contribution towards a shop to her you can find a shop of the Jane Goodall Institute, you can donate at **janegoodall.org**. and details of how to donate at **janegoodall.org**.

Sisters Golden and Glitter (b. 13–14 Jul 1998, pictured here as babies with their mother's) live in Gombe and are the world's Gremlin) live in Gombe and are the world's **oldest chimpanzee twins** – aged 20 years 117 days as of 8 Nov 2018.

Find out more about Jane in the Hall of Fame section at **www. guinnessworldrecords.com/2021**

1: The Jane Goodall Institute's Roots & Shoots programme educates young people – from preschool to university – about conservation. Founded in 1991 by Jane in Tanzania, the initiative now covers nearly 100 countries. along with 12 teenagers.

2: On 23 Jul 2019, Prince Harry, Duke of Sussex, met with Jane and Roots & Shoots members at Windsor Castle. He interviewed Jane for the September issue of *Vogue* and described her as "a woman of kindness".

3: Jane's interactions with the chimps of Gombe have shown that humans have more warmth and immense knowledge described and immense with them than just genetics. in common with them than just genetics.

Upon first arriving at Gombe, Jane had to make observations remotely from a perch high up above Lake Tanganyika – the world's **longest lake** at 673 km (413 mi). She described the time that she was first allowed to get up-close with a group of grooming apes as "the proudest moment of my life".

Humans

Largest gape

PAC-Man has nothing on Isaac Johnson (USA), whose mouth can stretch to 9.34 cm (3.67 in) – easily big enough to accommodate a baseball. His gape – the distance between the upper and lower incisors – was measured in Bloomington, Minnesota, USA, on 15 Apr 2019. Isaac was only 14 years old when he claimed his jaw-dropping record, last set in 2015 by Bernd Schmidt (DEU) with his 8.8-cm (3.4-in) gape. Discover more about Isaac, and further *maw*-some records, on pp.74–75.

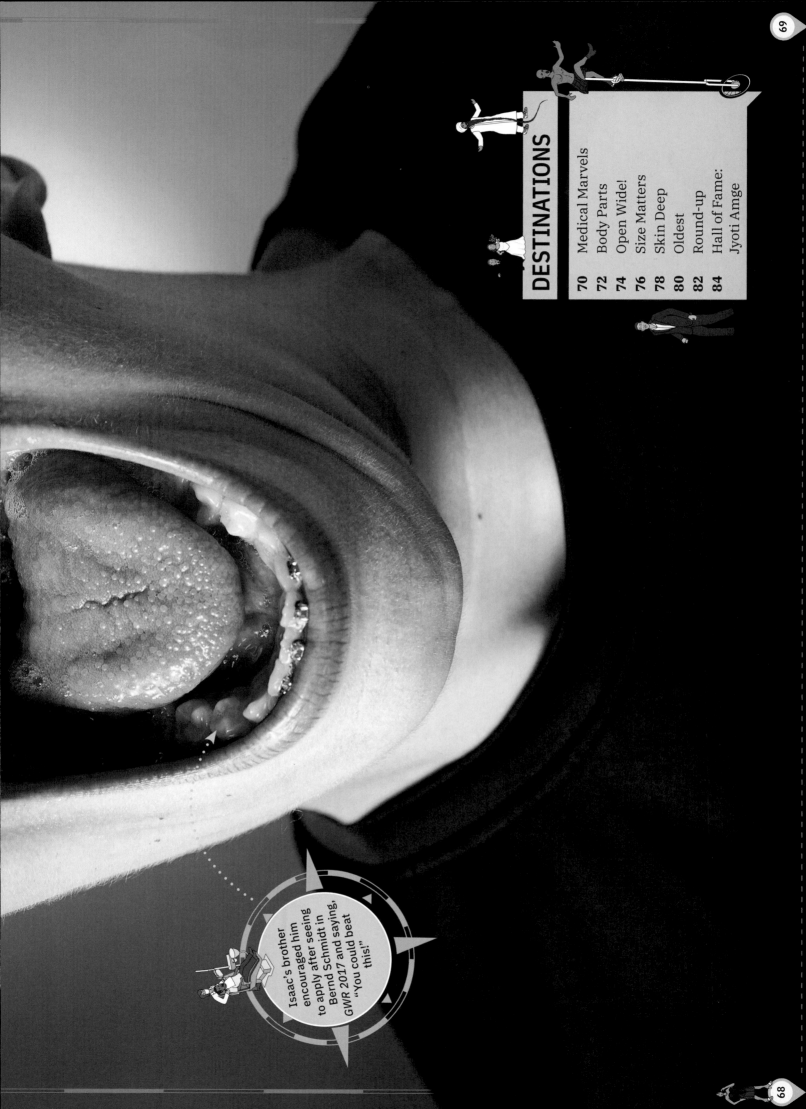

Isaac's brother encouraged him to apply after seeing Bernd Schmidt in GWR 2017 and saying, "You could beat this!"

Medical Marvels

Heaviest woman to give birth
Donna Simpson of New Jersey, USA, weighed 532 lb (241 kg; 38 st) when she delivered daughter Jacqueline in Feb 2007. At 8 lb 7 oz (3.8 kg), Jacqueline was around 1/60th of her mother's weight. She was born at Akron City Hospital in Ohio, USA, attended by a team of 30 medical professionals.

Shortest woman to give birth
Stacey Herald (USA), who stood 72.39 cm (2 ft 4.5 in) tall, delivered her first child on 21 Oct 2006 in Dry Ridge, Kentucky, USA.

Most operations endured
Charles Jensen (USA) had 970 operations to remove the tumours associated with basal cell nevus syndrome from 22 Jul 1954 to the end of 1994. This rare genetic condition increases the risk of certain cancers.

Youngest transplant patient
On 8 Nov 1996, aged just 1 hr, Cheyenne Pyle (USA) received a donor heart at the Jackson Children's Hospital in Miami, Florida, USA.

Longest-surviving quadruple heart-bypass patient
As of 19 Sep 2019, Tom E Diffenbach (USA) had lived for 42 years 284 days after his bypass on 9 Dec 1976 in Cleveland, Ohio, USA.

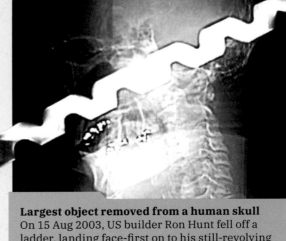

Largest object removed from a human skull
On 15 Aug 2003, US builder Ron Hunt fell off a ladder, landing face-first on to his still-revolving 46-cm (1-ft 6-in) drill bit. It passed through his right eye and exited through his skull above his right ear. Hunt's brain had been pushed aside rather than penetrated, which saved his life.

The **longest-surviving heart-transplant patient**, Ted Nowakowski (USA), lived for 34 years 261 days after his operation on 25 Apr 1983. He passed away on 11 Jan 2018.

Heaviest object removed from the stomach
A trichobezoar (hair ball) weighing 4.5 kg (10 lb) was surgically removed from the stomach of an unnamed 18-year-old woman in Nov 2007 at Rush University Medical Center in Chicago, Illinois, USA. The condition, known as Rapunzel syndrome, results from trichophagia – a compulsion to eat hair, usually one's own.

Youngest person to have gallstones and gall bladder removed
Ishani Choudhary (IND, b. 9 Feb 2019) was 217 days old when she underwent surgery on 14 Sep 2019 in Rajasthan, India.

Most extensive face transplant
Richard Lee Norris (USA) underwent 36 hr of surgery, completed on 20 Mar 2012, at the University of Maryland Medical Center in Baltimore, Maryland, USA. The operation gave him a new face from his scalp to the base of his neck, including jaws, teeth and part of his tongue. He had been disfigured in a gun accident in 1997 in which he lost his lips, nose and much of his lower and upper jaws. On 16 Oct 2012, the university reported that he was able to smile, eat, smell and taste.

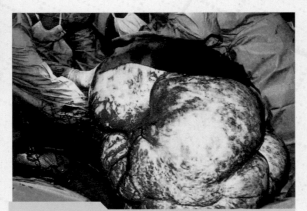

Largest tumour removed intact
In Oct 1991, a multicystic mass of the right ovary weighing 138.7 kg (306 lb, or nearly 22 st) was extracted from an unnamed woman at Stanford University Medical Center, California, USA. The tumour – as heavy as a giant panda – was 91 cm (3 ft) wide. The surgery took more than six hours.

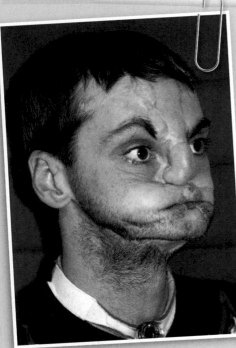

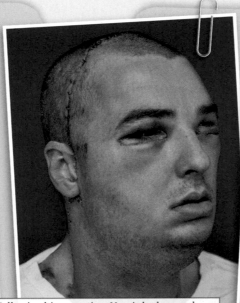

Following his operation, Norris had around 80% normal motor function on the right side of his face and around 40% on the left.

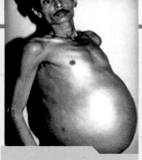

Most worms removed
In May 1990, a total of 56 white, thread-like worms were taken from the stomach of a 58-year-old woman in Isogaki Gastro-Entero-Surgical Clinic in Shizuoka, Japan. They were the larvae of *Anisakis simplex* and measured up to 17.27 mm (0.67 in) long.

Fastest car crash survived
On 17 Nov 1966, US land-speed-record racer Art Arfons was piloting his jet-powered car *Green Monster* at around 981 km/h (610 mph) when the bearings on the right front wheel seized. His vehicle tumbled for more than a mile across the Bonneville Salt Flats, near Salt Lake City in Utah, USA, yet he suffered only cuts, bruises and friction burns.

In 2008, Jason McVicar (CAN) was riding his Suzuki Hayabusa 1300 bike at 391 km/h (243 mph), also at Bonneville, when he lost control. He was taken to hospital with a broken kneecap and friction burns but was discharged that day, after the **fastest motorcycle crash survived**.

Oldest parasitic (undiscovered) twin
Sanju Bhagat (IND) lived for 36 years with a distended stomach. In Jun 1999, the enlarged abdomen began to crush his diaphragm, leaving him breathless. An operation revealed the 4-kg (9-lb) body of his unborn twin, which had been growing inside him.

First skull-and-scalp transplant
Treatment for a rare form of cancer known as leiomyosarcoma left James Boysen (USA) without the top of his skull. On 22 May 2015, he received partial skull and scalp grafts during a 15-hr operation at Houston Methodist Hospital in Texas, USA, with assistance from the MD Anderson Cancer Center.

Largest collection of foreign bodies surgically removed
In a 75-year career, Chevalier Quixote Jackson (USA) removed 2,374 objects from the throats, oesophaguses and lungs of his patients. The mementos are stored in the Chevalier Jackson Foreign Body Collection at the Mütter Museum of The College of Physicians of Philadelphia in Pennsylvania, USA. As well as the items shown here, they include a child's opera glasses, a padlock and a miniature trumpet.

Most bee stings survived
Johannes Relleke (ZWE) sustained 2,443 bee stings at the Kamativi tin mine in Gwaii River, Wankie District, Zimbabwe (then Rhodesia), on 28 Jan 1962. All the stings were removed and counted.

Longest time to survive with a bullet in the head
William Lawlis Pace (USA) was accidentally shot in Oct 1917, at the age of eight, in Wheeler, Texas, USA. The gunshot caused Pace a facial disfigurement, total hearing loss in his right ear and near blindness in his right eye. By the time he died on 23 Apr 2012, at the age of 103, the bullet had remained lodged in his head for 94 years and (at least) 175 days.

First recorded use of mouth-to-mouth resuscitation
The earliest documented instance of a person being revived by mouth-to-mouth resuscitation (also known as "expired-air respiration") took place on 3 Dec 1732 in the Clackmannanshire town of Alloa in Scotland, UK. The incident was described by surgeon William Trossach in *Medical Essays and Observations*, published in 1744.

The **first recorded use of mouth-to-mouth resuscitation to revive a victim of electric shock** took place in 1749 in Philadelphia, USA. American inventor and scientist Benjamin Franklin used a powerful electric shock to kill a chicken, then revived it by "repeatedly blowing into its lungs". He described this experiment in a letter to the British Royal Society, published the following year.

Longest-lasting hip replacement
As of 28 Jun 2019, Norman Sharp's (UK) left hip replacement was still going strong after 70 years 209 days. He was admitted to hospital in 1930 with septic arthritis and spent five years there having his hips fused and learning to walk again. His left hip was replaced on 1 Dec 1948 and he had the same operation on his right hip 21 days later.

More than 300,000 hip-replacement surgeries take place in the USA each year. The artificial joints are expected to last for at least 15 years.

THE DROP ZONE: HIGHEST FALL SURVIVED...

Without a parachute
Yugoslavian air hostess Vesna Vulović fell 10,160 m (33,333 ft) over Srbská Kamenice in Czechoslovakia (now Czech Republic) on 26 Jan 1972. According to the official accident report, an explosion tore the DC-9 she was working on to pieces.

In a skiing competition
In Apr 1997, while competing in the World Extreme Skiing Championships in Valdez, Alaska, USA, Bridget Mead (NZ) fell a vertical distance of nearly 400 m (1,312 ft). She suffered only bruises and concussion.

In an elevator
Betty Lou Oliver (USA) fell 75 storeys – more than 300 m (984 ft) – in a lift when a B-25 bomber struck the Empire State Building in thick fog in New York City, USA, on 28 Jul 1945.

Down an elevator shaft
Stuart Jones (NZ) fell 23 storeys, or 70 m (229 ft), down a lift shaft at the Midland Park building in Wellington, New Zealand, in May 1998.

By an infant
Garry Augur (CAN, b. Garry O'Neil) was just 21 months old when he fell from an eighth-floor window in Toronto, Ontario, Canada, on 27 Mar 1971. He survived the drop of 25.44 m (83 ft 6 in) despite landing on a grass-and-flagstone surface.

Body Parts

Most fingers and toes
On 11 Nov 2014, Devendra Suthar (IND) was verified as having a total of 28 digits (14 fingers and 14 toes) in Himatnagar, Gujarat, India. Devendra says that polydactylism doesn't affect his work as a carpenter, though he takes extra care when sawing wood.

In early 2020, another Indian contender for this title emerged: Kumari Nayak reportedly has at least 17 toes and 12 fingers, but she has yet to be investigated medically.

Longest fingernails on a pair of hands (female)
Professional manicurist Ayanna Williams (USA) grew her fingernails to a combined length of 576.4 cm (18 ft 10 in), as measured on 7 Feb 2017. It takes Ayanna up to 20 hours and two bottles of polish to paint her nails, which she protects by sleeping with them resting on a pillow.

Longest earlobes (stretched)
Monte Pierce (USA) can elongate his earlobes to a length of 12.7 cm (5 in) for his left and 11.4 cm (4.5 in) for his right. When not stretched, his earlobes measure just under 2.5 cm (1 in).

Longest beard (female)
Vivian Wheeler (USA, above right) grew her beard to a length of 25.5 cm (10 in) from the follicle to the tip, as measured on 8 Apr 2011 in Milan, Italy. This is still short of the **longest beard ever (female)** – 36 cm (1 ft 2 in), as grown by "Madame Devere", aka Janice Devere (USA, above left), in 1884.

The **youngest female with a full beard** is Harnaam Kaur (UK, below right, b. 29 Nov 1990). She was aged 24 years 282 days when her facial hair was verified on 7 Sep 2015.

Longest nose
The nose belonging to Mehmet Özyürek (TUR) measured 8.8 cm (3.46 in) from the bridge to the tip on 18 Mar 2010.

The **longest nose ever** is believed to have belonged to Thomas Wedders (UK), an 18th-century circus performer whose prominent proboscis reached 19 cm (7.5 in). On 19 Mar 2008, Lloyd's of London, UK, reported that Ilja Gort (NLD) had the **highest-insured nose**. Ilja – the owner of a vineyard in Bordeaux, France – insured his nose for €5 m (£3.9 m; $7.8 m) in order to protect his livelihood as a wine-maker.

Largest foot rotation
Maxwell Day (UK) can rotate his right foot through 157°, as verified on 23 Sep 2015 in London, UK. He can also twist his left foot 143°. Maxwell stepped forward at the *Minecraft* conference Minecon 2015, where he saw a picture of then-record holder Moses Lanham and told GWR staff that he could do even better. He feels no pain when rotating his feet.

Farthest eyeball pop
Kim Goodman (USA) can protrude her eyeballs out from their sockets by 12 mm (0.47 in), as verified on 2 Nov 2007 in Istanbul, Turkey. The extent of the "pop" was measured by an optometrist using a device known as a proptometer.

On average, toenails grow around 1.6 mm (0.06 in) a month; fingernails grow around 3.5 mm (0.13 in).

Longest toenails
Between 1982 and 1991, Louise Hollis (USA) grew her toenails to a combined length of 220.98 cm (7 ft 3 in). Louise embarked upon her unusual beauty regime having been inspired by a TV programme on long fingernails. She could only wear open-toed shoes with 7-cm-thick (3-in) soles, to prevent her nails from dragging on the ground.

▶ Longest legs (female)

Maci Currin of Cedar Park, Texas, USA, had a 135.2-cm-long (4-ft 5.2-in) left leg and a 134.3-cm (4-ft 4.8-in) right leg, as of 21 Feb 2020. Standing 205.7 cm (6 ft 9 in) tall, Maci hopes to follow in the footsteps of her predecessor Ekaterina Lisina (RUS), who at 205.16 cm (6 ft 8.7 in) is still the **○ tallest model**.

AMAZING ANATOMY: THE HUMAN BODY BY RECORDS

The six eye muscles move more than 100,000 times a day, making them the **most active muscles**; the orbicularis oculi, which closes the eyelid in just 0.1 sec, is the **fastest muscle**.

The stirrup, or stapes, in the middle ear is the **smallest bone**, at an average length of just 3 mm (0.12 in).

The **largest vein** is the inferior vena cava, which carries deoxygenated blood from the lower half of the body to the heart. Its average diameter in an adult is around 2 cm (0.78 in).

The **largest internal organ** is the liver, which can reach 1.5 kg (3 lb 5 oz) in weight and 22 cm (8 in) long. The **largest organ** is the skin. An average adult male has 1.5–2 m² (16–21.5 sq ft) of skin.

The **fastest turnover of body cells** occurs in the lining of the alimentary tract (gut), where cells are shed every 3–4 days.

Largest chest ever (male)

Robert Earl Hughes (USA) had a chest measurement of 315 cm (10 ft 4 in). For a period during his lifetime (1926–58), Robert was the world's **heaviest person** at 484 kg (1,067 lb; 76 st 3 lb).

The **widest waist ever** belonged to Walter Hudson (USA, inset). At his peak girth of 302 cm (9 ft 11 in), Walter was more than three times the circumference of an average middle-aged American male.

▶ Largest feet (female)

On 23 Mar 2019, the feet of Julie Felton (UK) were measured at 32.9 cm (1 ft 0.9 in – right foot) and 32.73 cm (1 ft 0.8 in – left foot) in Ellesmere, Shropshire, UK. Julie is 195 cm (6 ft 5 in) tall, and says her feet reached their current size around the age of 16–17. Her right foot has a tattoo of a daisy, her favourite flower.

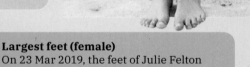

The fingertips are the **most touch-sensitive part of the body**. They can distinguish between two points of contact just 2 mm (0.07 in) apart.

The femur, or thigh bone, is the **longest bone**. It can reach 50 cm (1 ft 7 in) in a 180-cm-tall (6-ft) human.

The calf is the **least touch-sensitive part of the body**. It is 22.5 times less sensitive than the fingertips – see above.

At up to 60 cm (1 ft 11 in) in length, the sartorius is the **longest muscle**, running from the hip to below the knee.

For her wedding in 2019, Julie had a pair of size-15 shoes (US 15.5; Europe 49.5) custom-made for her.

DNA is the **largest molecule in human cells**. Unwound, it could reach 2 m (6 ft 6 in) in length.

The **rarest blood group** has only been reported in three people. It is a sub-type (h-h) of the Bombay blood group.

73

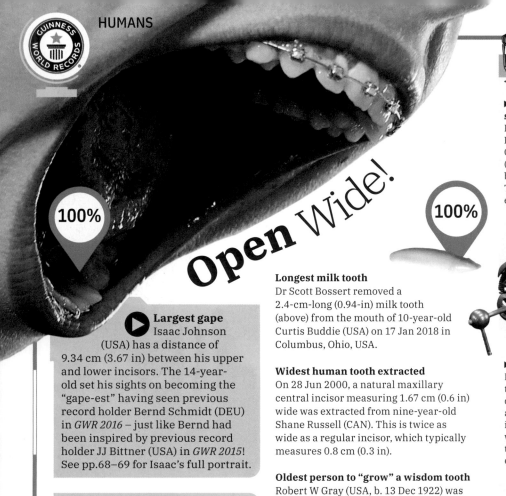

Open Wide!

100%

100%

▶ **Most expensive false teeth sold at auction**
Dentures used by wartime British prime minister Winston Churchill sold for £15,200 ($23,703) to an anonymous bidder on 29 Jul 2010. This was three times the estimated price.

◀ **Highest-insured dentures**
A set of false teeth that once belonged to US president George Washington (1732–99) are insured for $10 m (£7 m). They are currently on display at Mount Vernon, Washington's estate in Virginia, USA.

▶ **Oldest false teeth**
Discoveries made in Etruscan tombs suggest partial dentures were being worn as early as 700 BCE in what is now Tuscany, Italy. Some were permanently attached to existing teeth, while others were removable.

◀ **Youngest person to wear a full set of dentures**
A condition called hypohidrotic ectodermal dysplasia left Daniel Sanchez-Ruiz (UK) with complete anodontia – i.e., no teeth at all. He was given a full set of dentures aged 3 years 301 days on 25 Feb 2005.

▶ **Largest gape**
Isaac Johnson (USA) has a distance of 9.34 cm (3.67 in) between his upper and lower incisors. The 14-year-old set his sights on becoming the "gape-est" having seen previous record holder Bernd Schmidt (DEU) in *GWR 2016* – just like Bernd had been inspired by previous record holder JJ Bittner (USA) in *GWR 2015*! See pp.68–69 for Isaac's full portrait.

▶ **Longest tongue**
The tongue of Nick Stoeberl (USA) is 10.1 cm (3.97 in) from its tip to the middle of the closed top lip. Stoeberl, an artist, declared: "I'm not only able to lick my nose, but also my elbow!" The only downside is the extra time he has to spend brushing his tongue every day!

Longest milk tooth
Dr Scott Bossert removed a 2.4-cm-long (0.94-in) milk tooth (above) from the mouth of 10-year-old Curtis Buddie (USA) on 17 Jan 2018 in Columbus, Ohio, USA.

Widest human tooth extracted
On 28 Jun 2000, a natural maxillary central incisor measuring 1.67 cm (0.6 in) wide was extracted from nine-year-old Shane Russell (CAN). This is twice as wide as a regular incisor, which typically measures 0.8 cm (0.3 in).

Oldest person to "grow" a wisdom tooth
Robert W Gray (USA, b. 13 Dec 1922) was aged 94 years 253 days when his third molar (tooth #1) was confirmed to have erupted on 23 Aug 2017 in San Jose, California, USA.

The **youngest person to have a wisdom tooth extracted** is Matthew Adams (USA, b. 19 Nov 1992), who had his lower two wisdom teeth (#17 and #32) removed in Midland, Michigan, USA, on 24 Oct 2002 when he was aged 9 years 339 days.

Strongest human bite
In Aug 1986, Richard Hofmann (USA) achieved a bite strength of 442 kg (975 lb) for two seconds in a research test using a gnathodynamometer (an instrument for measuring bite force) at the University of Florida, USA. This is more than six times the normal biting strength.

First use of forensic odontology
The earliest recorded example of a corpse being identified from its teeth occurred in 66 CE. Having ordered the death of her rival Lollia Paulina, Roman Empress Agrippina had the head brought to her. Lollia's features had decomposed beyond recognition but Agrippina identified her by her distinctive teeth.

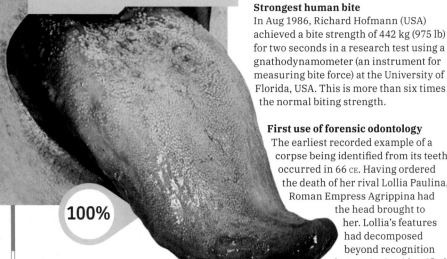

▲ **Most valuable grill jewellery**
In her music video for "Dark Horse", pop megastar Katy Perry wore a dental decoration valued at $1 m (£758,282) on 11 Oct 2017 in Los Angeles, California, USA. The gem-laden grill was the creation of cosmetic dentist Dr William Dorfman, with help from DaVinci Labs and XIV Karat jewellers (all USA).

ORAL HISTORY

2600 BCE
First dentist
An inscription on the tomb of physician Hesy-Re includes the title "the greatest of those who deal with teeth"

1700–1500 BCE
First treatise on dentistry
The Ebers Papyrus is the oldest known description of diseases of the teeth and toothache remedies

700 BCE
First false teeth
The Etruscans, an ancient civilization in modern-day Italy, make false teeth from human and animal remains (see above right)

1530
First book of dentistry
The Little Medicinal Book for All Kinds of Diseases and Infirmities of the Teeth is written by Artzney Büchlein

1780
First toothbrush
William Addis (UK) manufactures the first modern toothbrush; he had constructed the first prototype from pig bristles and bone while in prison for inciting a riot

1790
First dentist's chair
Josiah Flagg (USA) builds the first chair specifically for dental patients; the Wilkerson chair, the **first pump-type hydraulic dental chair**, is introduced in 1877

1880
First tube of toothpaste
The collapsible metal tube is invented by dental surgeon Dr Washington Sheffield (USA)

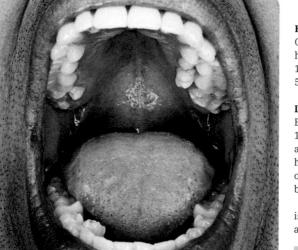

Widest tongue (male)
Measured on 30 Jul 2018 in La Cañada, California, USA, Brian Thompson's (USA) tongue has a maximum width of 8.88 cm (3.49 in). "My tongue has been an amusement to my friends and family for years," says Brian.

The **widest tongue (female)** is 7.33 cm (2.89 in) at its broadest point and belongs to Emily Schlenker of New York, USA.

100%

Largest model tooth
On 3 Feb 2019, a giant model tooth measuring 10.13 m (33 ft 2 in) tall and 5.86 m (19 ft 2 in) wide was unveiled at Pudukkottai in Tamil Nadu, India. The mandibular molar, made from plaster of Paris, was the work of Dr G Rajesh Kannan (pictured), Dental Primary and Thank You Dentist (all IND).

Most people brushing their teeth (single venue)
On 7 Nov 2019, a total of 26,382 people brushed their teeth simultaneously in Bhubaneswar, Odisha, India. The attempt was organized by the Indian Association of Public Health Dentistry, the Kalinga Institute of Social Sciences and Colgate-Palmolive India (all IND) to promote dental hygiene.

Heaviest weight balanced on teeth
Frank Simon (USA) supported a refrigerator weighing 63.5 kg (140 lb) on his teeth for 10 sec on 17 May 2007 in Rome, Italy.

Most expensive tooth sold at auction
A molar belonging to ex-Beatle John Lennon was bought by Canadian dentist Dr Michael Zuk for £23,010 ($36,857) on 5 Nov 2011. Lennon had apparently given the tooth – described as "browny with a cavity" – to his housekeeper as a gift.

Most teeth in a mouth
Vijay Kumar VA (IND) has 37 teeth in his mouth, as verified on 20 Sep 2014 in Bangalore, India. This is five more teeth than the average human. Vijay is proud of his GWR title, although he admits there are some disadvantages – he bites his tongue more often because of it...

Heaviest road vehicle pulled with teeth
On 7 Jan 2015, Igor Zaripov (RUS) used his jaws of steel to move a bus weighing 13.71 tonnes (15.11 US tons) a distance of 5 m (16 ft 4 in) in Jiangyin, Jiangsu, China.

Largest collection of human teeth
By 1903, Giovanni Battista Orsenigo (1837–1904), an Italian monk and dentist, had accumulated 2,000,744 human teeth during his 36-year career. Given the sheer number of teeth, it's unlikely that all were extracted by Brother Orsenigo personally.

The **largest collection of toothbrushes** is 1,320, amassed by Grigori Fleicher (RUS) as of 5 Nov 2008.

Widest mouth
"Chiquinho", aka Francisco Domingo Joaquim (AGO), has a 17-cm-wide (6.69-in) mouth – enough to squeeze in a drinks can sideways! First spotted by GWR researchers online, it took a further two years to track Chiquinho down to a marketplace in Angola.

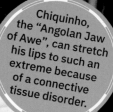

Chiquinho, the "Angolan Jaw of Awe", can stretch his lips to such an extreme because of a connective tissue disorder.

Size Matters: Tallest...

Twins ever (male)
The identical Lanier twins (USA, b. 1969) – Michael (d. 2018) and James – each measured 223.5 cm (7 ft 3 in) tall. Michael made a brief but memorably chilling appearance as the "Giant Man" in the horror movie *It Follows* (USA, 2015).

Teenager ever (female)
Anna Haining Swan (CAN, 1846–88) reached a height of 241.3 cm (7 ft 11 in) by the age of 17. At six years old, she was reportedly taller than her 165.1-cm (5-ft 5-in) mother.

On 17 Jun 1871, Anna married the "Kentucky Giant", aka Martin van Buren Bates (USA, 1837–1919), who stood 236.22 cm (7 ft 9 in) tall. They were the **tallest married couple ever**, with a combined height of 477.52 cm (15 ft 8 in).

Woman ever
At the time of her death, Zeng Jinlian (CHN, 1964–82) measured 246.3 cm (8 ft 1 in). Her growth accelerated from the age of four months and she stood 217 cm (7 ft 1 in) tall aged 13, though neither of her parents were very tall. She lived in Yujiang village in the Bright Moon Commune, Hunan Province.

Politician
Jon Godfread (USA) measures 210.76 cm (6 ft 10 in), as verified on 4 Oct 2019 in Bismarck, North Dakota, USA. After graduating from college, he played professional basketball in Germany for six months before returning to North Dakota. He was elected state insurance commissioner in 2016.

▶ Man
Turkey's Sultan Kösen measured 251 cm (8 ft 2.8 in) on 8 Feb 2011 in Ankara, Turkey. He owes his giant frame to a tumour on his pituitary gland, which was brought under control by a life-saving operation in 2008. Sultan is the third-tallest person to have ever lived – see right for the tallest.

The **tallest woman** is Siddiqa Parveen (IND). She is unable to stand upright, but a doctor estimated her height to be at least 233.6 cm (7 ft 8 in) in Dec 2012.

Family
The Zegwaards – father Sjoerd, mother Janneke van Loo and sons Dirk, Rinze and Sjoerd H (all NLD) – average 201.18 cm (6 ft 7.2 in). The family, most of whom must duck to pass through doorways, was measured in Weesp, Netherlands, on 13 Oct 2019.

▶ Married couple
Sun Mingming and his wife Xu Yan (both CHN) measure 236.17 cm (7 ft 8.98 in) and 187.3 cm (6 ft 1.74 in) respectively: a combined height of 423.47 cm (13 ft 10.72 in). Sun – a basketball player – met Xu – a handball player – at the National Games of China in 2009, and they married in Beijing, China, on 4 Aug 2013.

Man ever
Robert Pershing Wadlow (USA, 1918–40) was found to be 272 cm (8 ft 11.1 in) tall when last measured on 27 Jun 1940. His unprecedented stature was the result of an overactive pituitary gland. Robert's peak daily food consumption was 8,000 calories and his greatest recorded weight, at the age of 21, was 222.71 kg (35 st 1 lb).

Robert was 2.45 m (8 ft 0.5 in) tall by the age of 17, making him the **tallest teenager ever**.

Aged nine, Robert was able to carry his father – who stood 180 cm (5 ft 11 in) tall and weighed 77 kg (170 lb) – up the stairs of their family home.

Shortest…

Person ever
Chandra Bahadur Dangi (NPL, 1939–2015) stood 54.6 cm (1 ft 9.5 in) tall when measured on 26 Feb 2012 at CIWEC Clinic in Lainchaur, Kathmandu, Nepal.

Woman

Jyoti Amge (IND) had a height of 62.8 cm (2 ft 0.7 in) when measured on 16 Dec 2011 in Nagpur, India. Find out more about Jyoti on p.84.

The **shortest woman ever** is "Princess" Pauline Musters (NLD, 1876–95). She measured 30 cm (1 ft) at birth, and by nine years of age was 55 cm (1 ft 9.6 in) tall and weighed only 1.5 kg (3 lb 5 oz). She died of pneumonia with meningitis in New York City, USA, at the age of 19; a post-mortem examination showed her to be exactly 61 cm (2 ft).

Twins ever
Born in Budapest, Hungary, in 1901, the Matina twins — Matyus (d. 1954) and Béla (fl. 1957) — each grew to 76 cm (2 ft 6 in). They became naturalized US citizens in 1924 and worked in circuses as Mike and Ike Rogers. They also appeared as Munchkin villagers in *The Wizard of Oz* (USA, 1939).

Married couple
When measured in Itapeva, São Paulo, Brazil, on 3 Nov 2016, Paulo Gabriel da Silva Barros and Katyucia Lie Hoshino (both BRA) reached a combined height of 181.41 cm (5 ft 11.42 in). The couple met via social media in Dec 2008; Katyucia initially blocked Paulo, but he eventually won her over and they married on 17 Sep 2016.

Man (mobile)
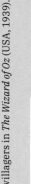
Edward Niño Hernández (COL, right) measured 72.1 cm (2 ft 4.3 in) tall on 29 Feb 2020 in Bogotá, Colombia. The 33-year-old reclaimed the record he had last held in 2010, following the death of Khagendra Thapa Magar (NPL, inset above) on 17 Jan 2020. Khagendra sadly succumbed to pneumonia at the age of 27.

The **shortest man (non-mobile)** is currently Junrey Balawing (PHL, b. 12 Jun 1993), who measured 59.93 cm (1 ft 11.5 in) tall on 12 Jun 2011 in Sindangan, Zamboanga del Norte, Philippines.

Frank's height is the result of a condition called achondroplasia, a common form of dwarfism.

Nationalities
According to the journal *elife* on 26 Jul 2016, the women of Guatemala had an average height of 149.4 cm (4 ft 10 in). The men of East Timor had an average height of c. 160 cm (5 ft 3 in).

Stuntperson
Kiran Shah (UK, b. KEN) has appeared in more than 50 movies since 1976. On account of his short stature – he measured 126.3 cm (4 ft 1.7 in) on 20 Oct 2003 – Kiran is often hired as a stunt-double for child actors. He also doubled for Elijah Wood in the *Lord of the Rings* trilogy (NZ/USA, 2001–03).

Professional pianist ever

Michel Petrucciani (FRA, 1962–99) was an acclaimed 91-cm-tall (2-ft 11.8-in) jazz pianist. Despite hundreds of bone fractures caused by osteogenesis imperfecta, Michel became a much-sought-after performer and refused to let his condition limit his ambitions. He counted the prestigious French Prix Django Reinhardt among his awards.

Bus driver
On 5 Feb 2018, Frank Faeek Hachem (UK, b. IRQ) was measured at 136.2 cm (4 ft 5.6 in) in Chichester, West Sussex, UK. He moved to the UK over 20 years ago and has been working as a driver since 2017. His bus requires no alterations, although Frank has to make sure that the seat is pulled forward and the steering wheel is adjusted.

Skin Deep

Known as the "Mexican Vampire Lady", Maria José Cristerna (MEX) is a lawyer-turned-tattooist and mother of four whose extreme body makeover resulted in her travelling the world to tell her story.

Maria got her first tattoo at the age of 14 and now has the ◯ **most body modifications (female)** – 49. She embarked upon a campaign of self-transformation to present herself as a warrior and strong female role model. Referring to her skin as "carpet", Maria uses her tattoos as a kind of graphic autobiography – e.g., the stars on her face refer to her late mother.

Subdermal forehead implants. According to Maria, they represent a queen's crown

Exposed titanium horn implants

Four upper-nose bars

Right eyebrow has nine piercings

Left eyebrow has 10 piercings

Eyes coloured powder blue

Nose ring chained to left earring

Both earlobes have been expanded

Dental fang implants complete vampyric look

Three piercings in lower lip

Total tattoo coverage of 96%

Subdermal (i.e., under the skin) implants

Subdermal horn implants

A total of 37 piercings across both eyebrows

A total of 111 piercings around lips and mouth

R olf Buchholz (DEU) is the reigning king of body modifications. The IT consultant is a relatively late starter: he received his first tattoo and piercing on the same day, aged 40. He went on to transform himself from head to toe.

Rolf now sports 481 piercings plus 35 implants and other mods. This total of 516 – the **most body modifications (male)** – was verified on 12 Dec 2012. The most painful? The tattoos on his palms.

After two decades of relentless body modding, Rolf is still looking out for new challenges and ways to reinvent himself. In recent years, he has adopted a stringent fitness regime and has completed four marathons in two years.

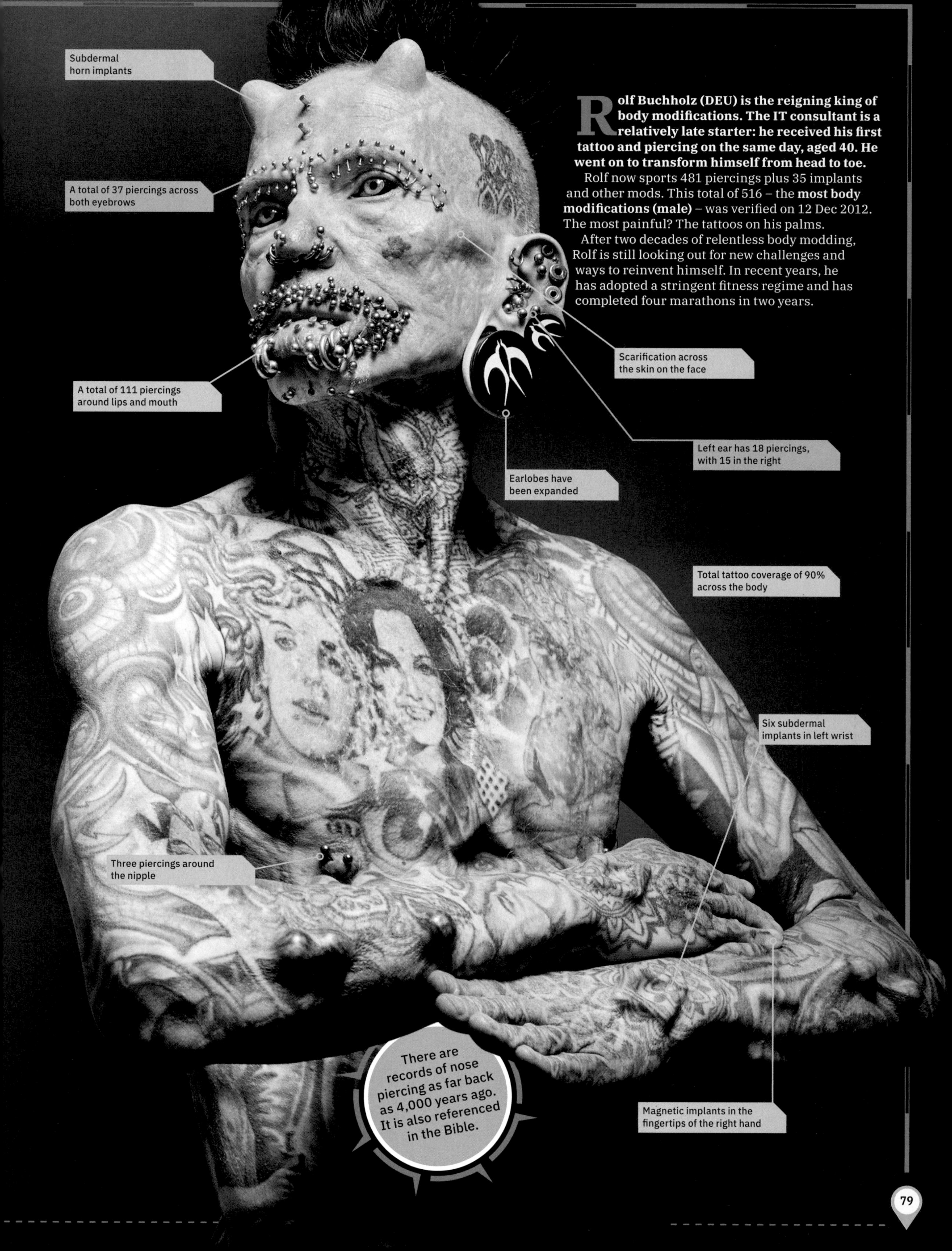

Scarification across the skin on the face

Left ear has 18 piercings, with 15 in the right

Earlobes have been expanded

Total tattoo coverage of 90% across the body

Six subdermal implants in left wrist

Three piercings around the nipple

There are records of nose piercing as far back as 4,000 years ago. It is also referenced in the Bible.

Magnetic implants in the fingertips of the right hand

Oldest...

Person to release a debut album
Colin Thackery (UK, b. 9 Mar 1930) was 89 years 195 days old when his first album, *Love Changes Everything*, was released on 20 Sep 2019. The singing octogenarian was the winner of the 13th series of the TV show *Britain's Got Talent* (ITV, UK).

Person to row across an ocean solo
Graham Walters (UK, b. 17 Jul 1947) was aged 72 years 192 days when he set out from the Canary Islands to row the Atlantic, arriving in Antigua on 29 Apr 2020. He made his voyage in the *George Geary*, which was named after his grandfather. It was the fifth time that Graham had rowed the Atlantic, and his third solo effort.

YouTube gamer
As of 25 Nov 2019, Hamako Mori (JPN, b. 18 Feb 1930) was posting clips to her "Gamer Grandma" YouTube channel at the age of 89 years 280 days. Hamako, who counts *Call of Duty*, *Resident Evil* and *Grand Theft Auto* among her gaming repertoire, has amassed more than 150,000 subscribers and 8 million views.

Serving monarch
Her Majesty Queen Elizabeth II (UK, b. 21 Apr 1926) celebrated her 94th birthday in 2020. She had succeeded to the throne on 6 Feb 1952, making her the **longest-reigning queen**, having ruled for 68 years 75 days as of her birthday. She became the oldest monarch on 23 Jan 2015, aged 88 years 277 days, after the death of Saudi Arabia's King Abdullah.

Person to reach No.1 on the UK's Official Singles Chart
On 30 Apr 2020, "Captain Tom" Moore (UK, b. 30 Apr 1920) debuted at No.1 at the age of exactly 100 with "You'll Never Walk Alone", featuring Michael Ball and The NHS Voices of Care Choir (both UK). The former British Army officer rose to prominence when he set himself the challenge of making 100 laps of his 25-m-long (82-ft) garden during the COVID-19 pandemic. The same day saw the end of his campaign, which generated over £32.79 m ($40.82 m) for the NHS – the **most money raised by a charity walk (individual)**.

Tandem parachute jump (female)
On 15 Aug 2019, Kathryn "Kitty" Hodges (USA, b. 9 Apr 1916) leapt out of a plane 10,000 ft (3,048 m) above Snohomish in Washington, USA, at the age of 103 years 128 days. The intrepid centenarian was inspired by her son, Walter – himself a keen skydiver. Kitty claimed not to be nervous before being strapped up with a diving instructor. "It's fun," she declared, "so why not have some fun? Hallelujah!"

Conductor
Frank Emond (USA, b. 21 May 1918) was aged 101 years 6 days when he conducted "The Stars and Stripes Forever" at the Pensacola Civic Band's Memorial Day Concert on 27 May 2019 in Florida, USA. A Navy Band horn player and conductor from 1938 to 1968, Frank was on board the USS *Pennsylvania* during the attack on Pearl Harbor in 1941. He began conducting the Pensacola Civic Band in 2011.

Beauty advisor
A beauty director at the Rijyo shop in Hiroshima, Japan, Kikue Fukuhara (JPN, b. 31 Mar 1920) was still working aged 99 years 171 days as of 18 Sep 2019. She survived the atomic bombing of the city on 6 Aug 1945 and in 1960 joined the POLA cosmetics firm. "For make-up, there's no day that I slack off out of 365 days," she said. It's always important to keep up personal appearances."

"It's normal for Kitty to do unusual things!" said a friend who witnessed the jump.

Person to cycle from Land's End to John o' Groats (female)
Mavis Margaret Paterson (UK, b. 24 May 1938; left) was aged 81 years 29 days when she reached John o' Groats in northern Scotland on 22 Jun 2019. She had set out from the Cornish coast in south-west England on 30 May. Her friend Heather Curley accompanied her on the ride.

Competitive footbag player
Ken Moller (USA, b. 14 Jul 1947) competed in the 2019 US Open Footbag Championships in Boston, Massachusetts, USA, aged 72 years 34 days. He was introduced to the game in his 40s, when his son brought it back from university, and competed in his first hacky-sack competition in 2009 at the age of 61. Ken practises for up to an hour most days.

▶ Woman
Kane Tanaka (JPN, b. 2 Jan 1903) was aged 117 years 131 days as of 12 May 2020 in Fukuoka, Japan. In Jan 2020, she celebrated her 117th birthday at a nursing home with friends, family and "tasty" birthday cake. She is currently also the **oldest living person**. The **oldest person ever**, Jeanne Louise Calment (FRA, b. 21 Feb 1875), died on 4 Aug 1997, aged 122 years 164 days.

Qualifier for a National Hot Rod Association (NHRA) elimination round
Drag racer Chris Karamesines (USA, b. 11 Nov 1931) was 87 years 335 days when he made it to the elimination round of the NHRA Carolina Nationals on 12 Oct 2019. His top race speed is 504.54 km/h (313.51 mph), which he set in 2015 aged 83.

Pair of siblings (male)
Portugal's Andrade brothers – Albano (b. 14 Dec 1909) and Alberto (b. 2 Dec 1911, both PRT) – had an aggregate age of 216 years 230 days, as verified on 2 Apr 2019 in Santa Maria da Feira, Aveiro, Portugal. Albano is the oldest living man in Portugal. The brothers still live together in the family home in which they were born.

▶ Married couple
As of 27 Dec 2019, John Henderson (b. 24 Dec 1912) and his wife Charlotte (b. 8 Nov 1914) of Austin, Texas, USA, had a combined age of 212 years 52 days. They met in 1934 and married in 1939. On 22 Dec 2019, Charlotte and John celebrated their oak (80th) wedding anniversary, aged 105 and 106 years respectively.

Band
As of their gig on 27 Oct 2019, the Golden Senior Trio (JPN, formed 2008) had an average age of 87 years 132 days: Naoteru Nabeshima on vibraphone (93 years 166 days), Zensho Otsuka on piano (85 years 254 days) and Naosuke Miyamoto on bass (82 years 348 days).

Vogue cover model
Actress Dame Judi Dench (UK, b. 9 Dec 1934) appeared on the front of the June 2020 edition of British *Vogue* – published on 7 May – at the age of 85 years 150 days. Dame Judi also holds the overall record for **most Laurence Olivier Awards won** (8).

Heli-skier
Heli-skiers are taken up mountains by helicopter before skiing down them. On 28 Mar 2019, Gordon Precious (CAN, b. 26 May 1924) skied down the Cariboo Mountains in British Columbia, Canada, aged 94 years 306 days.

▶ Man
Robert Weighton (UK, b. 29 Mar 1908) was 112 years 1 day old when verified on 30 Mar 2020 in Alton, Hampshire, UK. He spent World War II in Canada and the USA – where he worked with the American Secret Service – before returning to the UK. Robert became the oldest man following the passing of Chitetsu Watanabe (JPN, b. 5 Mar 1907, below) on 23 Feb 2020.

The **oldest man ever**, Jiroemon Kimura (JPN, b. 19 Apr 1897), passed away on 12 Jun 2013 aged 116 years 54 days.

Dentist
As of 26 Feb 2020, Seiji Sakanashi (JPN, b. 24 May 1923) was receiving patients five days a week aged 96 years 278 days in Suginami, Tokyo, Japan. Seiji still has some way to go to match the **oldest doctor ever** – Dr Leila Denmark (USA, 1898–2012), who retired in May 2001 at the age of 103!

As we went to press, the oldest known patient to have survived COVID-19 was 113-year-old María Branyas (b. 4 Mar 1907) of Girona, Spain.

Top 10 oldest living people		
# Name	Date of birth	Age
1 Kane Tanaka (JPN)	2 Jan 1903	117 y 131 d
2 Lucile Randon (FRA)	22 Feb 1904	116 y 91 d
3 Jeanne Bot (FRA)	14 Jan 1905	115 y 119 d
4 Shigeyo Nakachi (JPN)	1 Feb 1905	115 y 101 d
5 Hester Ford (USA)	15 Aug 1905	114 y 271 d
6 Iris Westman (USA)	28 Aug 1905	114 y 258 d
7 Mina Kitagawa (JPN)	3 Nov 1905	114 y 191 d
8 Tekla Juniewicz (UKR)	10 Jun 1906	113 y 337 d
=9 Anne Brasz-Later (NLD)	16 Jul 1906	113 y 301 d
=9 Irene Dutton (USA)	16 Jul 1906	113 y 301 d

Source: Gerontology Research Group, as of 12 May 2020; all female

Robert was born on the same day as 112-year-old Joan Hocquard, currently the oldest woman in Britain.

Round-Up

Most generations born on the same day

Six families have members of four generations with the same birthday. The youngest record-breaker in this category is Lori Peeler (USA), who was born on 13 Aug 2017. She shares her birthday with her mother (1980), grandfather (1950) and great-grandmother (1926), all shown above.

Most consecutive boy/girl births in a family

The Ewers family from Chicago, Illinois, USA, experienced a sequence of 11 births in which a boy was followed by a girl between 1955 and 1975. The run was verified on 23 Feb 2018.

First mother-child supercentenarians

Supercentenarians are people who have reached, or passed, the age of 110. Mary P Romero Zielke Cota (USA, b. 1870) died in 1982 aged 112 years 17 days. Her daughter, Rosabell Zielke Champion Fenstermaker (USA, b. 1893), was equally long-lived, eventually passing away in 2005 at the age of 111 years 344 days.

First successful separation of conjoined twins

Swiss surgeon Johannes Fatio separated two conjoined twins in Basel, Switzerland, in a three-stage operation ending on 3 Dec 1689. The patients were a pair of girls named Elisabet and Catherina who were joined at the sternum. Both siblings recovered fully from the surgery and were soon feeding normally.

Most premature baby

James Elgin Gill was born to Brenda and James Gill (all CAN) on 20 May 1987 in Ottawa, Ontario, Canada. He was 128 days premature and weighed 624 g (1 lb 6 oz), nearly six times lighter than the average birth weight.

Shortest competitive bodybuilder

Vince Brasco (USA) stands 127 cm (4 ft 2 in) tall. He was born with achondroplasia, a condition that gives rise to shortened limbs. Vince endured 15 major surgical operations during his childhood, after which he turned to weightlifting as a way to build up his muscles. Known as "Mini Hulk", he made his debut in the bantamweight category at the 2014 NPC (National Physique Committee) Pittsburgh Championships in Pennsylvania, USA.

Vince occasionally volunteers at his local fire station in Greensburg, Pennsylvania, also making him the **shortest firefighter**.

Vince began bodybuilding partly to give himself greater control over his body mass. Extra weight can result in back and joint problems for those with dwarfism.

Most premature twins

Kambry and Keeley Ewoldt (left to right, both USA) were born on 24 Nov 2018 at the University of Iowa Hospitals & Clinics in Iowa City, USA. The twins shared a gestational age of 22 weeks 1 day, or 155 days, meaning that they were 125 days premature. The estimated delivery date for the baby girls had been 29 Mar 2019.

Loudest burp

Paul Hunn (UK) has reigned for 20 years as the "Burper King", having first set a record for his deafening eructations in May 2000. His last official burp, measured on 23 Aug 2009 in Bognor Regis, in West Sussex, UK, reached 109.9 decibels.

Longest tattoo session

Tattoo artist Aleksandr Pakostin (RUS) carried out a 60-hr 30-min session at his studio in Vologda, Russia, ending on 12 Sep 2019. In that time, he inked 15 tattoos on 12 people.

Most tattoos of the same cartoon character

Nikolay Belyanskiy (RUS) had 52 tattoos of Rick, from *Rick and Morty* (Adult Swim, USA), inked on to his body in a single nine-and-a-half-hour sitting in Moscow, Russia. The count was confirmed on 31 Aug 2019.

Lightest birth

As ratified by the Tiniest Babies Registry, the lowest known birth weight for a surviving infant is 245 g (8.6 oz) in the case of "Saybie" (USA; real name protected for privacy reasons). Weighing only about the same as a cooking apple, she was delivered by emergency Caesarian section in Dec 2018 at Sharp Mary Birch Hospital in San Diego, California, USA. She had had a gestation of just 23 weeks 3 days.

Longest-lived quadriplegic

At the age of 19 in 1959, while on his way home from a Thanksgiving trip, Walter Lewis (USA, b. 17 Sep 1940) was involved in a car crash that left him paralysed. In 2019, Lewis – now a resident of Gautier, Mississippi, USA – celebrated his 79th birthday, and on 23 Mar 2020, he was confirmed as the longest-lived quadriplegic – a total of 60 years 115 days after his accident took place.

Tallest NBA player

Tacko Fall (SEN, below) made his National Basketball Association debut for the Boston Celtics on 26 Oct 2019. He is 226 cm (7 ft 5 in) tall with a standing reach of 311 cm (10 ft 2.4 in), meaning he can dunk a basketball without jumping!

The title of **tallest NBA player ever** is tied between Gheorghe Mureşan (ROM) and Manute Bol (USA, b. SDN). Both stood at 231 cm (7 ft 7 in).

Largest hands on a teenager

The humongous hands of 17-year-old Lars Motza (DEU) each span 23.3 cm (9.1 in) from the wrist to the tip of the middle finger. They were measured in Berlin, Germany, on 12 Dec 2019. Lars also boasts the **largest feet on a teenager**. His left foot is 35.05 cm (1 ft 1.8 in) long and his right is 34.9 cm (1 ft 1.7 in), as verified on 19 Nov 2018. His shoes are size 57 (EUR), which is 20 (UK) or 21 (US).

Longest colour sequence memorized

Subhash Mogili (IND) committed to memory a series of 170 colours in Hyderabad, India, on 12 Jun 2019. The test requires the competitor to recall a sequence of four colours – generated by a software package – that are displayed randomly within a set time. For more feats of remarkable recall, don't forget to see the table, right.

Longest hair

The locks of Xie Qiuping (CHN) measured 5.627 m (18 ft 5.5 in) on 8 May 2004. She has been growing her hair since 1973, when she was aged 13. Beyond the scalp, though, there are other lengthy individual hairs to be lauded, including:
• **Ear**: 18.1 cm (7.1 in), Anthony Victor (IND) as of 26 Aug 2007.
• **Leg**: 22.5 cm (8.8 in), Jason Allen (USA) as of 25 May 2015.
• **Chest**: 28.2 cm (11.1 in), Vittorio Lullo (ITA) as of 6 Sep 2019.

▶ **Largest afro (female)**
On 31 Mar 2012, the afro belonging to Aevin Dugas (USA) was measured at 16 cm (6.3 in) high from the crown of the head, with a total circumference of 1.39 m (4 ft 7 in). You can see Aevin on p.84, alongside the **shortest woman**.

World Memory Sports Council

Since 1991, the WMSC has overseen the competitive World Memory Championships. Participants are tested on their ability to memorize various categories of information within a limited time frame.

Most spoken numbers memorized at a rate of one per second	547	Ryu Song I (PRK)
Most decimal digits memorized in five minutes	616	Wei Qinru (CHN)
Most decimal digits memorized in one hour	4,620	Ryu Song I
Most binary digits memorized in 30 minutes	7,485	Ryu Song I
Most playing cards memorized in one hour	2,530	Kim Surim (PRK)
Fastest time to memorize and recall a deck of playing cards	13.96 sec	Zou Lujian (CHN)
Most historical dates recalled in five minutes	154	Prateek Yadav Imm Igm (IND)
Most names and faces memorized in 15 minutes	187	Yanjindulam Altansuh (SWE)
Most abstract images memorized in 15 minutes	804	Hu Jiabao (CHN)
Most random words memorized in 15 minutes	335	Prateek Yadav Imm Igm

Tallest Mohican

Joseph Grisamore (USA) has grown a 108.2-cm-tall (3-ft 6.5-in) Mohawk, as verified on 20 Sep 2019 at the Family Hair Affair salon in Park Rapids, Minnesota, USA. The gravity-defying 'do was sculpted by hair stylist Kay Jettman (far right) – assisted by Joseph's mother Kay (near right) and wife Laura – using half a can of his favourite hairspray!

Fall has a two-way contract with the Boston Celtics and the Maine Red Claws. He's seen here with 178-cm-tall (5-ft 10-in) Red Claws teammate Tremont Waters.

All of Jyoti's clothes – and much of her jewellery – have to be custom-made.

GUINNESS WORLD RECORDS

○ HALL OF FAME

Jyoti Amge

A small girl with big dreams, Jyoti Amge has grown into one of the brightest stars in the GWR universe.

O nce a small girl with big dreams, Jyoti Amge has grown into one of the brightest stars in the GWR universe.

She was born on 16 Dec 1993 in Nagpur, India. According to her mother, Jyoti was of average stature until she reached the age of five. But her growth had stalled, and it soon became evident that her own it soon became subsequently provided with her own Jyoti was diagnosed with her own dwarfism. At school, she was and Jyoti was subsequently provided with her own special-sized desk and chair.

On her 18th birthday – 16 Dec 2011 – Jyoti visited the Wockhardt Super Speciality Hospital in Nagpur, where she was measured by orthopaedic consultant Dr Manoj Pahukar. She was found to be 62.8 cm (2 ft 0.7 in) tall, making her the world's ○ **shortest woman**.

62.8 cm (2 ft 0.7 in)

As one of the most famous faces in the world, Jyoti has been able to realize her the world (see below).

As one of the most famous faces in the world, Jyoti has been able to realize her ambition to travel the world – where Jyoti was a crowd GWR family. Jyoti has been able to realize her ambition to travel the world, USA – where she drew a crowd wherever she went. In 2014, she fulfilled her dream her ambition to travel the world – making In New York City, USA – where Jyoti was the hit US show shorter than Ma Petite, she joined Ma Petite – making wherever she went. In 2014, she fulfilled her dream of becoming an actress by joining the role of Ma Petite in *American Horror Story* in the world's **shortest actress**.

Find out more about Jyoti in the Hall of Fame section at **www.guinnessworldrecords.com/2021**

1: A hair-raising meeting with Aevin Dugas (USA), owner of the ❯ **largest afro**.

2: Sharing the spotlight with the former ❯ **shortest man (mobile)**, Nepal's Khagendra Thapa Magar (see p.83).

3: Seeing the sights at the Giza pyramids in Egypt with Sultan Kösen (TUR), the ❯ **tallest man** at 251 cm (8 ft 2.8 in).

4: Measuring up to Venezuela's Jeison Orlando Rodríguez Hernández, who has the ❯ **largest feet**.

Jyoti Amge is almost exactly a quarter of the height of Turkish titan Sultan Kösen (see **3**), and only 1.5 times taller than Jeison Hernández's right foot (**4**)! She's 40.55-cm (1-ft 3.96-in) right foot that taller than Jeison Hernández's (1-ft 3.96-in) right foot that just over twice as tall as the *GWR* book that you're reading right now.

100%

Most cones hit with flying discs in one minute

On 11 Oct 2017, trick-shot maestro Brodie Smith (USA) struck 13 cones with flying discs in 60 sec in Brooklyn, New York City, USA. The same event saw the YouTube star (his channel has 2.2 million-plus subscribers) register the **most drink cans hit with flying discs in one minute** – 31 – and secure the **longest flying disc target throw**, passing it into a basketball hoop from 46.33 m (152 ft) away.

Of course, a strong arm and an aptitude for judging distances are vital to anyone striving to top Brodie's achievements. But competing within a timeframe adds an extra dimension of tension. In this chapter, you'll meet a range of record holders who know how to keep a cool head when the seconds are ticking down. You'll also hear from our adjudicators, who've picked out five challenges that you can try at home. Are *you* Officially Amazing? It's time to find out, as you pit yourself against the clock...

I'd rather be poor and do what I love than rich and hate what I do.

IN **30 SECONDS**

Italy's Silvio Sabba is a serial record-breaker (he's even got a Guinness World Records tattoo on his arm to prove it!) and he loves nothing more than a challenge against the clock. He holds a host of 30-second record titles, including the **most dice stacked into a tower** (38) and **most pencils stood on end** (23). Lightning-fast reactions and a steady hand have helped Silvio, a personal trainer, become a familiar face in the *GWR* books. If you want to try to match his records, you've got a long way to go – one way to start is by trying your hand at the **most tins stacked in 30 seconds**: see right to find out how...

> *For me, breaking records means working to become the very best in the world in whatever I do. Record-breaking is not a hobby for me, but a job.*

Most dominoes stacked in 30 seconds
On 28 Apr 2013, Silvio stacked 48 dominoes in half a minute in Milan, Italy. This was equalled by Rocco Mercurio (ITA) on 25 Feb 2019. Silvio is also responsible for the **fastest time to build a five-level domino pyramid** (pictured) – 18.40 sec, on 11 Dec 2012 in Pioltello, Italy.

Most sticky notes stuck on the face in 30 seconds
On 18 Apr 2018, Silvio affixed 38 sticky notes to his face in half a minute. Each note had to be placed one at a time, with the adhesive strips placed directly on to the skin. The notes had to stay stuck for a further 10 sec after the time limit had ended to count.

00:30

MOST CANS STACKED INTO A PYRAMID IN 30 SECONDS

You have half a minute to build the highest possible pyramid formation of tins. Can you hold your nerve – and keep your hand steady – as the clock ticks round? If you want your effort to count, be careful to follow adjudicator Adam's guidelines below. With the right "can-do" attitude, a GWR title could be yours!

• A can pyramid is a formation in which cans are stacked in layers and each layer has fewer cans than the one below – e.g., 4, 3, 2, 1 – to form a structure with sloping sides and a single-can point at the top.

• Cans used for this record must be commercially available and with their lids intact. The diameter must not be less than 12 cm (4.7 in) and the height must not be less than 16 cm (6.2 in).

• Any number of cans may be used during the attempt.

• You can only use one hand for this record attempt. The other is to remain behind your back for the duration of the attempt.

• Ahead of the attempt starting, all cans must be placed on their side on the ground or table upon which the attempt is being performed.

• Start with your chosen hand flat next to the cans. Only one can at a time is to be stacked.

• All the cans must be stacked facing the right way up – i.e., with the base of the first can on the building surface, and the base of each subsequent can touching the top of the one below it.

• The pyramid must be made so there is a single can on the top layer at the end of the 30 seconds.

• The pyramid needs to be stable enough to stand alone for 5 sec once the clock has stopped. If any can falls from the pyramid in that time, the attempt will be disqualified.

• You may take a pause or break during the attempt, but the clock must not be stopped under any circumstance.

For the full set of official GWR guidelines, go to **guinnessworldrecords. com/2021**.

Steady as you go!
Although stacking as quickly as possible is the name of the game, remember that your tower has to stay upright for 5 sec after the time limit to count. With practice and preparation, you can work out the best way to keep your structure of tins stable. Remember – you only have half a minute, so make sure that every second counts!

HALF-A-MINUTE HEROES: RECORDS SET IN 30 SECONDS

Most socks put on one foot
On 10 Oct 2017, Slovakia's Pavol Durdik slipped on 28 socks over his right foot in 30 sec in Púchov, Slovakia. He beat the previous record – which he shared with Mr Cherry, aka Cherry Yoshitake (JPN) – by two. All socks had to be pulled up above the ankle joint to count towards the final total.

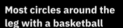

Most skips on rollerskates
On 19 May 2019, Zorawar Singh (IND) jumped a rope 135 times in half a minute in Delhi, India. He beat his own record, set the previous year, by three. Zorawar is the proud owner of two GWR titles, having also achieved the **most double-under frogs in 30 seconds** – 14 – on 19 May 2019, also in Delhi.

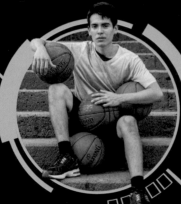

Most circles around the leg with a basketball
Luis Diego Soto Villa (MEX) circled a basketball around his leg 70 times in 30 sec on 16 May 2018 in Nicolás Romero, Mexico. Luis is the holder of several freestyle basketball GWR titles, including **longest time spinning three basketballs** – 17.8 sec.

Most popcorn moved by a straw
On 24 Jul 2019, using just lung power and a drinking straw, Ruby Fothergill (UK, left, with GWR's Anna Orford) transferred 25 pieces of popcorn through a 3-cm-wide (1.1-in) hole and into a receptacle. Her 30-sec record was equalled by Taya Frearson (UK) two days later – also in Blackpool, Lancashire, UK.

Most mustard drunk from a tube
André Ortolf (DEU) guzzled down 416 g (14.7 oz) of mustard from a tube in 30 sec on 5 Jan 2015 in Schwarzach, Germany. The serial record-breaker has a taste for the hot stuff: on 8 Aug 2019, he reclaimed his GWR title for **fastest time to drink 200 ml of mustard** – 11.79 sec.

IN A **MINUTE**

You can do a lot in a minute. Take Eli Bishop (USA), who can clap his hands 1,103 times. Then there's Daisuke Mimura (JPN), who skipped over a rope 348 times, while Gaber Kahlwai Gaber Ali (EGY) did 67 cartwheels. Taekwondo instructors Chris and Lisa Pitman (both UK, pictured) prefer to smash things with their fists of steel. Their pine-board-breaking exploits below might only have taken 60 seconds, but they required years of dedicated training to achieve. If you want to attempt a record with slightly fewer physical demands, how about the **most cocktail sticks snapped in one minute**? See right for more...

> *We're not average people that get up, put a suit on and go to work... We get up and smash things!*

▶ Most pine boards broken in one minute with one hand

On 9 Apr 2018, Chris Pitman broke 315 pine boards in 60 sec in Bromley, Kent, UK, while his wife Lisa took the **female** title with 230. Both Pitmans are experienced taekwondo practitioners and already held GWR titles for smashing roof tiles. "But breaking wood is a different experience," according to Lisa and Chris, "as the edges can be sharp. You have to train to condition the bones in your hands – and we have the scars to prove it!"

MOST COCKTAIL STICKS SNAPPED IN ONE MINUTE

Could your 60-second skills earn you a place in the GWR annals? Find out by taking a crack (or should that be snap?) at this brand-new record. You have one minute to snap as many cocktail sticks as possible – but if you want your effort to count, make sure you listen to adjudicator Lou's guidelines:

• The cocktail sticks used must be commercially available. Details regarding the size and type of cocktail sticks must be submitted along with the claim.

• Each cocktail stick must be laid out on a table or similar flat surface prior to the start of the attempt.

• Your hands must be placed on the table, palms down, prior to the attempt. The first cocktail stick cannot be handled until the clock has started.

• A digital stopwatch must be used.

• The time will start after a 3, 2, 1 countdown.

• Only one cocktail stick may be snapped at a time.

• Each cocktail stick must be snapped in two (with a clean break, and the sticks in two separate pieces), using only your hands and fingers.

• Only cocktail sticks clearly broken into two separate pieces within the one-minute timeframe will count towards the final total.

• Make sure you film your record attempt from start to finish. The camera must be focused on the attempt at all times and preferably kept static.

• A predetermined loud start and finish signal recognized by all participants must be used.

• There must be two independent witnesses present to oversee the record attempt.

If you've read this far, you should be ready to get snapping! To receive the full set of official GWR guidelines, register your application now at **guinnessworldrecords.com/2021**

Watch out!

The key thing to remember when attempting this record is that the cocktail sticks MUST be snapped cleanly in two – any that remain threaded together will be discounted from your final total. If you need to pause or take a break during the attempt then that is fine (though we don't recommend it!), but once the clock has started it cannot be stopped. Good luck, and happy snapping!

ONE-MINUTE WONDERS

Most dominoes stacked on one vertical domino

On 16 Jan 2019, Silvio Sabba (ITA) balanced 52 dominoes on top of a vertical domino in Rodano, Milan, Italy. Silvio, one of GWR's most prolific record-breakers (see pp.88–89), surpassed his own mark of 45, set in Dec 2017, by seven. The stack had to stand unsupported for 5 sec after the time limit for the record to count.

Most magic tricks performed blindfolded

Magician Martin Rees (UK) performed 24 tricks unsighted in 60 sec on 29 May 2019 at GWR HQ in London, UK. The intrepid illusionist currently holds four GWR titles, including **most magic tricks performed in a single skydive** – 11.

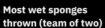

Most wet sponges thrown (team of two)

Bipin Larkin threw 76 wet sponges at Ashrita Furman (both USA) on 5 Feb 2019 in Nusa Dua, Bali, Indonesia. Each sponge had to be hurled 3 m (9 ft 10 in) to hit Ashrita in the face. Bipin and Ashrita are one of the great duos of record-breaking, with more than 40 team GWR titles to their names. Find out more about Ashrita overleaf.

Most diabolo spins around arm

On 2 May 2019, Niels Duinker (NLD) completed 71 diabolo spins around the arm in Gatlinburg, Tennessee, USA. Only 360° spins of the diabolo that went both under and over the arm counted towards the total. Niels is a comedy juggler whose GWR titles include **most shaker cups juggled** – 14.

Most triple "around the world" ball-control tricks (male)

Freestyle footballer Tobias Becs, aka Tobias Brandal Busæt (NOR), performed 13 triple "around the world" tricks in Oslo, Norway, on 30 Sep 2018. Tobias is a multiple Norwegian, European and world champion freestyler.

IN AN **HOUR**

Performing any challenge for an hour requires not only physical stamina but great powers of concentration. Just ask Ashrita Furman (USA). A veteran record-breaker with more than 200 GWR titles to his name at any time, Ashrita devotes countless hours to physical and mental training. The results – whether it's the **most balloons inflated by the nose in one hour** (380), or the **most underwater SCUBA rope jumps in one hour** (1,608) – speak for themselves. Follow his example and look right to see if you can claim your first world record.

Attempting records has become part of my spiritual journey. I get joy not only in practising the activity itself, but also in seeing my progress towards achieving a once-daunting goal.

Most tennis balls caught in one hour
On 21 Jul 2015, Ashrita Furman caught 1,307 tennis balls in 60 min in New York City, USA. The attempt required great dexterity and concentration, as each projectile was fired at a speed of 100 km/h (61 mph) by a tennis-ball machine just 6 m (19 ft 8 in) away from Ashrita. He smashed the previous best of 904, set by Anthony Kelly (AUS) on 13 Nov 2011.

01 HOUR

MOST DOMINOES TOPPLED IN ONE HOUR BY A TEAM

Toppling dominoes is child's play – but not when the clock is ticking and a GWR title is on the line! Can you and up to 11 other team-mates keep your cool and set up an awesome arrangement of the classic rectangular game tiles? Make sure you follow adjudicator Christelle's guidelines:

• The record is to be attempted by a team of up to 12 people.

• Any commercially available dominoes can be used, on the condition that they are equal to or larger than the following dimensions: 39 x 19 x 7 mm (1.53 x 0.74 x 0.27 in).

• The dominoes must be laid out flat on any surface before the attempt starts.

• A predetermined loud start and finish signal recognized by all participants must be used.

• During the attempt, the dominoes must all be stacked on their smallest edge. The line can be serpentine or straight.

• The setting up of the dominoes must be completed within the one-hour time frame; the toppling should then take place once the hour is complete.

• If any dominoes fall during the one-hour set-up, the challengers are permitted to re-stack these at any time before the clock stops.

• Challengers may pause or take a break during the attempt but the clock must not stop under any circumstance.

If you've read this far, it's time to get toppling! To receive the full set of official GWR guidelines, register your application now at **guinnessworldrecords. com/2021**.

Toppling records
Knocking over objects in a domino fashion is proving a popular challenge for would-be record holders. On 3 Dec 2017, H. Frank Carey High School (USA) achieved the **most cereal boxes toppled** – 3,416 (right) – while confectionary manufacturer Perfetti Van Melle (UK) were behind the **most mint dispensers toppled in 3 min (team of 100)** – 1,365 – on 26 Jan 2018 (above left). The **most laptops toppled** is 520, by Lenovo BT/IT (CHN) on 27 Apr 2018 (below).

HEROES OF THE HOUR: RECORDS SET IN 60 MIN

Most caber tosses
On 8 Sep 2018, Reverend Kevin Fast (CAN) tossed a caber 122 times at Warkworth Fair in Ontario, Canada. The powerlifting priest has a host of Herculean GWR titles, including the **heaviest aircraft pulled** – 188.83 tonnes (416,299 lb) – set on 17 Sep 2009 in Trenton, Ontario, Canada.

Farthest distance on a penny farthing bicycle (no hands)
Neil Laughton (UK) covered a distance of 26 km (16.15 mi) in 60 min on 14 Nov 2019 at the Preston Park velodrome in Brighton, East Sussex, UK. Neil completed almost 45 laps of the track without touching the handlebars with his hands. It was one of three world records he attempted for GWR Day.

Most books toppled in a domino fashion
Kmart Australia took an hour to set up 3,000 copies of *Guinness World Records* – before knocking them all over – at their annual conference on 31 Oct 2018 in Queenstown, New Zealand. A total of 334 employees took part, beating the previous best of 2,500, set by Aconex (AUS) on 20 Jul 2017.

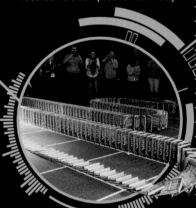

Most stairs descended in a wheelchair
Haki Achille Doku (ITA, b. ALB) went down 2,917 steps in 60 min on 27 Mar 2019 in Seoul, South Korea. It was the third time he had improved on his own world record. Haki is a Paralympian who represented Albania at the 2012 Games in London, UK.

Most pots thrown (individual)
On 14 Nov 2019, Michael Weber (USA) shaped 212 flowerpots on the potter's wheel in 60 min at Sunset Hill Stoneware in Neenah, Wisconsin, USA. He had to fashion each pot from a lump of clay weighing at least 600 g (1 lb 5 oz) using his hands, water, tools and wheel.

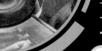

IN A **DAY**

Australia's Eva Clarke is a formidable fitness icon who overcame the legacy of a challenging childhood by dedicating herself to rigorous workouts and body conditioning. The results speak for themselves. Eva's determination has secured her a range of endurance records, including the **most pull-ups in 24 hours (female)** – 3,737 – and the **most burpees in 24 hours** – 12,003. The latter is nearly 2,000 more than the **male** record, held by the UK's Lee Ryan. Out of all the categories she's attempted, it's these day-long feats that Eva finds the most demanding. "They really start to mess with your mindset about eight hours into the challenge," she told GWR.

Whether they realize it or not, women inspire each other to achieve greatness [...] For any girl doubting herself – stop thinking and start making an action plan to be your best. Records are meant to be broken, so go out there and break them!

Most chest-to-ground push-up burpees in 24 hours (female)
On 23 Feb 2018, Eva completed 5,555 of these exacting exercises at New York University Abu Dhabi in UAE. The attempt took place during a fitness challenge, and she credits the crowds and other participants from NYUAD – some of whom performed 1,000 burpees themselves at the event – for encouraging her.

Most knuckle push-ups in 24 hours
On 1 Feb 2014, Eva completed her favourite GWR achievement: 9,241 knuckle push-ups at Al Wahda Mall in Abu Dhabi, UAE. "It was the first time I had the courage to take on such a physical feat," she admits, "and it has led to so many more Guinness World Records titles." Eva has Kienböck's disease in her right wrist, which affects the bone tissue, so she does push-ups and burpees on her knuckles.

01 DAY

LONGEST PAPER CHAIN MADE IN 24 HOURS BY A TEAM

Even if you don't have Eva's athletic physique, there are plenty of other 24-hr records that you can take on. What about assembling a string of paper loops? This requires dextrous fingers and heaps of stamina. Just be sure to stick to adjudicator Tripp's rules:

• This is a record for a team of unlimited size, so you can enlist the help of friends and family.

• The chain is to consist of single strips of paper with maximum dimensions of 46 cm (1 ft 6 in) long and 4.5 cm (1.77 in) wide.

• Challengers must form each paper strip into a link using a hand-held stapler, double-sided sticky tape or glue. Another strip is then be put through this link, and the ends of this second strip must be stapled/taped/glued together to

make a chain. These paper links in turn must all be joined to make a continuous paper chain.

• The strips of paper can be pre-cut in advance but not pre-linked: the entirety of the chain must be formed within the 24-hr period. Because this is a team record, participants can create their own shorter chains and join them together, as long as the chains are all made and joined within 24 hr and at the same venue.

• Measures must be taken to guarantee that all challengers can be monitored by the independent witnesses (e.g., by assigning independent stewards, restricting the attempt area, etc.) during the day of the attempt.

• The full length of the chain must be measured and not merely calculated by multiplying the length of a smaller section.

Go to **guinnessworld records.com/2021** to get the full GWR guidelines and register your application.

Thinking of linking?
If time's *not* against you, it's incredible what lengths you can go to... Ben Mooney (UK, above) set a new record for the **longest paperclip chain** back in 2017, although the current record holder is Imran Sharif (BGD) with a 2,527-m-long (8,290-ft 8-in) chain. And the Davies family (UK, brothers Edward, below left, and James are shown) strung together the **longest chain of conkers**, from 16,847 nuts, as ratified on 1 Dec 2018.

ALL IN A DAY'S WORK: 24-HOUR RECORD-BREAKERS

Greatest vertical distance ascended on a pogo stick
On 23 Mar 2019, Lee Griggs (NZ) bounced his way into the record books when he pogo-sticked 1,602 m (5,255 ft 10 in) up Mount Fyffe in Kaikoura, New Zealand. Lee – a pogo novice – made the attempt in aid of the Mental Health Foundation of New Zealand.

Most consecutive Scrabble games
Craig Beevers (UK) played 30 games of Scrabble in a row on 13–14 Apr 2015 in Plymouth, UK. The event took place on National Scrabble Day and was organized by Scrabble, Mattel UK and Mindsports International. Craig won 29 of his 30 games, only losing out to fellow competitive Scrabble player Jesse Matthews from Canada.

Most hair braided by an individual
Vasugi Manivannan (IND) added braids to 167 heads of hair in Chennai, India, from 7 to 8 Jun 2019. She washed and dried the hair of each model before braiding it, leaving less than an inch of hair at the end of each braid.

Longest individual wheelchair push
Graham Inchley (UK) pushed a succession of people in a wheelchair for 161.61 km (100.4 mi), finishing on 29 Jun 2014. The distance represented 44 laps of Thruxton Race Circuit in Hampshire, UK. Graham's goal was to raise funds and publicity for the Association of Young People with ME and the National Autistic Society.

Greatest virtual distance ridden on a static cycle (male)
On 22–23 Oct 2019, Canada's Ed Veal covered a relative distance of 952.12 km (591.62 mi) on a static cycle, in an event sponsored by Splunk (USA). The attempt took place in Las Vegas, Nevada, USA. He used the virtual cycling platform Zwift for the attempt.

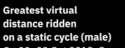

ROUND-UP

In certain rare cases, we monitor records that are attempted outside of our standard time increments, stretching from two minutes to a year to an entire lifetime. Whatever your talent – whether you can pluck paintballs from the air, pull on underpants in the blink of an eye or braid hair in a blur – why not test it against the clock and see if you too can be officially amazing? If you're unsure where to begin, we've got the perfect suggestion for you: see right for more...

Most participants in an underwater clean-up in 24 hours (single venue)
On 15 Jun 2019, Dixie Divers (USA) organized a clean-up of Deerfield Beach Pier in Florida, USA, that involved 633 people. More than 544 kg (1,200 lb) of rubbish – largely consisting of fishing line and lead weights – was removed from the water by the eco-minded SCUBA divers.

Greatest distance cycled in a year (WUCA-approved)
Between 15 May 2016 and 14 May 2017, Amanda Coker (USA) rode 139,326 km (86,573.2 mi). The record was verified by the World UltraCycling Association. Amanda also set the **fastest time to cycle 100,000 miles (WUCA-approved)** – 423 days, between 15 May 2016 and 11 Jul 2017 – breaking a 77-year-old record.

Most items washed up in eight hours
On 10 Jan 2011, Louise Dooey (UK) travelled to the Guinness World Records head office in London, UK, where she washed up 2,250 items in 8 hr. As stated in the guidelines, Louise had to organize the dirty dishes to ensure that she washed the same amount of each item. She cleaned 450 individual dinner plates, bowls, pans, cups and pieces of cutlery.

Most bones broken in a lifetime
Evel Knievel (USA, b. Robert Craig Knievel), the pioneer of motorcycle long-jumping exhibitions, had suffered 433 bone fractures by the end of 1975. In the winter of 1976, he was seriously injured during a televised attempt to jump over a tank full of sharks at the Chicago Amphitheater. The stunt rider decided to retire from major performances as a result.

MOST BALLOONS BLOWN UP IN THREE MINUTES

Take a deep breath: it's your turn to attempt a GWR title. Have you got the lung power to inflate as many balloons as possible in 180 seconds? If you don't want to blow your chances, follow adjudicator Chris's guidelines:

• The record is to be attempted by individuals only.

• Commercially available, standard-sized balloons must be used, details of which must be submitted with the claim. The balloons must have a minimum diameter of 20 cm (7.8 in) when inflated.

• All balloons must be inflated by mouth. Artificial means such as gas pumps or compressors may not be used.

• Inflated and tied-off balloons that explode or deflate during the three minutes will still count towards the total, provided they met the minimum size requirement when tied.

• The attempt must be overseen by two independent witnesses.

• Witnesses should count and measure the balloons as soon as they are tied off, in case they do explode or deflate later on.

• Participants may take a break during the attempt but the clock must not stop under any circumstances.

• A loud start and finish signal recognized by all participants must be used.

Enough about the rules – it's time to get blowing. To receive the full set of official GWR guidelines, register your application now at **guinnessworldrecords. com/2021**.

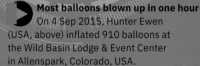

Most balloons blown up in one hour
On 4 Sep 2015, Hunter Ewen (USA, above) inflated 910 balloons at the Wild Basin Lodge & Event Center in Allenspark, Colorado, USA.

There are lots of different ways to try a balloon-related GWR title. The **most balloons inflated by the nose in one minute** is nine, by Ashrita Furman (USA) on 6 Jun 2016 in New York City, USA. Or, if blowing them up isn't your thing, try the **most balloons popped using a pogo stick in one minute** – 57, by Mark Aldridge (UK) on 1 Apr 2010 in Rome, Italy.

Be sure to use biodegradable balloons – and dispose of them responsibly when you're done.

TIME-HONOURED FEATS

Most Christmas trees chopped in two minutes
Erin Lavoie (USA) axed 27 Christmas trees in 120 sec on 19 Dec 2008 in a televised challenge in Cologne, Germany. "I love trees, but I love to kill them too," she said afterwards. Erin is a CrossFit athlete and one of the world's top lumberjills. She has won multiple titles at the Lumberjack World Championships.

Most sticky notes on the body in five minutes
With the help of 22 children and one TV presenter, Japanese comedian Tetsurō Degawa affixed 674 sticky notes to himself on 2 Feb 2014 on the set of *Grand Whiz-Kids TV* (NHK) in Tokyo, Japan. Tetsurō smashed the previous record of 454, set three years earlier.

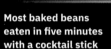

Most baked beans eaten in five minutes with a cocktail stick
David Rush (USA) gobbled down 275 baked beans using a cocktail stick on 6 Dec 2018 in Boise, Idaho, USA. Each bean had to be spiked individually. David also set the **three-minute** (178) and **one-minute** (68) records.

Most films seen in cinemas in one year
Vincent Krohn (FRA) watched 715 films at the cinema in Paris, France, from 23 Mar 2017 to 21 Mar 2018. He saw an average of 14 films a week – everything from *Casablanca* (USA, 1943) to *My Little Pony: The Movie* (USA/CAN, 2017). Vincent's favourite flick was *Back to the Future* (USA, 1985).

Most bhut jolokia chilli peppers eaten in two minutes
On 4 Feb 2018, "Jack Pepper" – aka Giancarlo Gasparotto (ITA) – munched his way through 146.27 g (5.15 oz) of the fearsomely fiery chilli pepper in Tarquinia, Italy. Giancarlo attempted the record during the ArgenPic chilli festival.

Longest gum-wrapper chain

Gary Duschl (USA) has patiently linked together a 32.55-km-long (20.22-mi) string of gum wrappers, as confirmed on 10 Jan 2020 in Virginia Beach, Virginia, USA. Gary has devoted more than 42,000 hours to creating his colossal chain, which incorporates 2,583,335 separate wrappers. It's so long that it could be wrapped 23 times around the Pentagon in Washington, DC, USA.

Every wrapper in the chain comes from a stick of Wrigley's gum. Gary has devoted part of his house to memorabilia connected with the company, including one pack from 1895.

DESTINATIONS

At an average speed, it would take some six-and-a-half hours to walk the length of Gary's chain!

Big Fruit & Veg

Longest gourd
On 21 Sep 2019, a gourd of the Kikinda variety was measured to be 3.954 m (12 ft 11 in) in Mozirje, Slovenia, with the achievement verified by the Great Pumpkin Commonwealth. The gourd was cultivated by Goran Lazic (SRB).

Longest parsnip
Champion grower Joe Atherton (UK, see **longest turnip** below) presented a 6.55-m-long (21-ft 5-in) parsnip at the UK National Giant Vegetables Championship on 23–24 Sep 2017 in Malvern, Worcestershire.

At the same show, Atherton unveiled the **longest radish**, measuring 6.7 m (21 ft 11 in). His green fingers have also been behind the **longest beetroot** (7.95 m; 26 ft 1 in) and the **longest carrot** (6.24 m; 20 ft 5 in).

Heaviest red cabbage
On 29 Sep 2018, a red cabbage weighing 23.7 kg (52 lb 4 oz) was ratified at the CANNA UK National Giant Vegetables Championship in Malvern, Worcestershire, UK. The colossal brassica – more than three times the weight of a bowling ball – was grown by Tim Saint (UK), a veteran of growing competitions.

Largest orange by circumference
An orange measuring 63.5 cm (2 ft 1 in) around its widest point was ratified on 22 Jan 2006. The 2.27-kg (5-lb) specimen grew in the garden of Patrick and Joanne Fiedler in Fresno, California, USA.

Largest bunch of bananas
A cluster of 473 individual bananas weighed in at 130 kg (286 lb 9 oz) on 11 Jul 2001, on the island of El Hierro in the Canary Islands, Spain. Grown by Kabana SA and Tecorone SL (both ESP), it was harvested at the Finca Experimental de las Calmas. The bonanza bunch was the result of a 30-year project by farmers to develop a desert area of the island into a tropical fruit farm.

Heaviest grapefruit
A white grapefruit grown by Douglas and Mary Beth Meyer (both USA) tipped the scales at 3.59 kg (7 lb 14 oz), as verified on 19 Jan 2019 in Slidell, Louisiana, USA. The Meyers' six grandchildren helped tend to the giant citrus fruit, which was so heavy it required a purpose-built hammock for support while it grew on the tree.

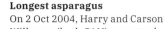

Heaviest jack o'lantern
The Cosumnes Community Services District (USA) presented a jack o'lantern weighing 942.11 kg (2,076 lb 15 oz) on 6 Oct 2018 at the 24th annual Elk Grove Giant Pumpkin Festival in California, USA. The pumpkin, which was weighed before carving, was grown by Josiah Brandt and carved by Mike Brown, Deane Arnold and Brandy Davis.

Longest asparagus
On 2 Oct 2004, Harry and Carson Willemse (both CAN) presented a 3.51-m-long (11-ft 6-in) spear of asparagus at the Port Elgin Pumpkinfest in Ontario, Canada.

Longest courgette (zucchini)
A courgette measuring 2.52 m (8 ft 3.2 in) long – more than twice the length of a baseball bat – was grown by Giovanni Batista Scozzafava (ITA) and measured on 28 Aug 2014 in Niagara Falls, Ontario, Canada. Giovanni claimed not to have used fertilizer or manure, but he did give the plant plenty of water.

Tallest Brussels sprout plant
A Brussels sprout plant growing in the garden of Patrice and Steve Allison (USA) reached a height of 2.8 m (9 ft 2 in) in Newport Beach, California, USA. It was measured on 17 Nov 2001.

GARDEN GOLIATHS

Longest turnip
4.064 m (13 ft 4 in), grown by Joe Atherton (UK) and ratified in Malvern, Worcestershire, UK, on 28 Sep 2019

Heaviest gooseberry
64.83 g (2.28 oz), grown by Graeme Watson (UK) and ratified in Egton Bridge, North Yorkshire, UK, on 6 Aug 2019

Heaviest tomato
4.377 kg (9 lb 10 oz), grown by Steve and Jeanne Marley (both USA) and weighed on 20 Sep 2019 in Clinton, New York, USA

Heaviest bell pepper
720 g (1 lb 9 oz), grown by Ian Neale (UK) and ratified in Malvern, Worcestershire, UK, on 29 Sep 2018

Heaviest beetroot
23.995 kg (52 lb 14 oz), grown by Jamie Courtney-Fortey and Gareth, Marjorie and Kevin Fortey (all UK) in Gwent, UK, on 23 May 2019

Horticultural heavyweights

Fruit/vegetable	Weight	Grower	Date
Apple	1.84 kg (4 lb 1 oz)	Chisato Iwasaki (JPN)	24 Oct 2005
Aubergine	3.06 kg (6 lb 11 oz)	Ian Neale (UK)	29 Sep 2018
Blueberry	15 g (0.5 oz)	Agricola Santa Azul SAC (PER)	19 Jul 2018
Cantaloupe melon	30.47 kg (67 lb 1.8 oz)	William N McCaslin (USA)	5 Aug 2019
Carrot	10.17 kg (22 lb 6 oz)	Christopher Qualley (USA)	9 Sep 2017
Cauliflower	27.48 kg (60 lb 9 oz)	Peter Glazebrook (UK)	21 Apr 2014
Cherry	23.93 g (0.8 oz)	Frutícola Patagonia (CHL)	1 Feb 2019
Cucumber	12.9 kg (28 lb 7 oz)	David Thomas (UK)	26 Sep 2015
Fig	295 g (10.4 oz)	Lloyd Cole (UK)	28 Aug 2015
Gourd	174.41 kg (384 lb 8 oz)	Jeremy Terry (USA)	6 Oct 2018
Green cabbage	62.71 kg (138 lb 4 oz)	Scott Robb (USA)	31 Aug 2012
Jicama	21 kg (46 lb 4 oz)	Leo Sutisna (IDN)	25 Jan 2008
Kale	48.04 kg (105 lb 14 oz)	Scott Robb (USA)	29 Aug 2007
Kohlrabi	43.98 kg (96 lb 15 oz)	Scott Robb (USA)	30 Aug 2006
Leek	10.7 kg (23 lb 9 oz)	Paul Rochester (UK)	29 Sep 2018
Lemon	5.26 kg (11 lb 9 oz)	Aharon Shemoel (ISR)	8 Jan 2003
Mango	3.43 kg (7 lb 9 oz)	Sergio and Maria Socorro Bodiongan (both PHL)	27 Aug 2009
Marrow	93.7 kg (206 lb 9 oz)	Bradley Wursten (NLD)	26 Sep 2009
Onion	8.5 kg (18 lb 11 oz)	Tony Glover (UK)	12 Sep 2014
Parsnip	7.85 kg (17 lb 4 oz)	David Thomas (UK)	23 Sep 2011
Pear	2.94 kg (6 lb 8 oz)	JA Aichi Toyota Nashi Bukai (JPN)	11 Nov 2011
Pineapple	8.28 kg (18 lb 4 oz)	Christine McCallum (AUS)	29 Nov 2011
Plum	323.77 g (11.4 oz)	Minami-Alps City JA Komano Section Kiyo (JPN)	24 Jul 2012
Pomegranate	2.60 kg (5 lb 11 oz)	Zhang Yuanpeng (CHN)	27 Nov 2017
Potato	4.98 kg (10 lb 15 oz)	Peter Glazebrook (UK)	4 Sep 2011
Pumpkin	1,190.49 kg (2,624 lb 9 oz)	Mathias Willemijns (BEL)	9 Oct 2016
Quince	2.34 kg (5 lb 2 oz)	Edward Harold McKinney (USA)	Jan 2002
Radish	31.1 kg (68 lb 9 oz)	Manabu Oono (JPN)	9 Feb 2003
Squash	960.70 kg (2,117 lb 15 oz)	Joe Jutras (USA)	7 Oct 2017
Strawberry	250 g (8.8 oz)	Koji Nakao (JPN)	28 Jan 2015
Swede	54 kg (119 lb)	Ian Neale (UK)	28 Sep 2013
Sweet potato	37 kg (81 lb 9 oz)	Manuel Pérez Pérez (ESP)	8 Mar 2004
Taro	3.19 kg (7 lb)	Fuding Tailao Mountain Admin Committee (CHN)	13 Oct 2009
Turnip	17.78 kg (39 lb 3 oz)	Scott and Mardie Robb (both USA)	1 Sep 2004
Watermelon	159 kg (350 lb 8 oz)	Chris Kent (USA)	4 Oct 2013

All figures correct as of 12 Jan 2020

Largest bunch of grapes
On 4 Aug 2018, a bunch of grapes weighing 10.12 kg (22 lb 4 oz) – about the same as 20 soccer balls – was verified in Los Palacios y Villafranca, Spain. It was grown by Sebastián Gómez Falcón (pictured right) and the Delegación de Agricultura del Ayuntamiento de Los Palacios y Villafranca (both ESP). The previous record of 9.4 kg (20 lb 11 oz) had stood since 1984.

100%

Tallest sweetcorn plant
Jason Karl (USA) produced a sweetcorn plant that stretched up to 10.74 m (35 ft 3 in) – almost twice the height of an adult male giraffe. It was measured on 22 Dec 2011.

Tallest tomato plant
A tomato plant grown by Nutriculture Ltd in Mawdesley, Lancashire, UK, reached 19.8 m (64 ft 11 in) on 11 May 2000.

Heaviest nectarine
Eleni Ploutarchou (CYP) grew a smooth-skinned peach weighing 500 g (1 lb 1 oz), as verified on 30 Jun 2018 in Ayioi Vavatsinias, Cyprus. Eleni had been farming for more than 65 years before producing the huge nectarine, which is more than three times heavier than average.

Heaviest celery
42 kg (92 lb 9 oz), grown by Gary Heeks (UK) and ratified in Malvern, Worcestershire, UK, on 29 Sep 2018

Heaviest avocado
2.55 kg (5 lb 9 oz), grown by Mark, Juliane and Loihi Pokini (all USA) in Kahului, Hawaii, USA, and confirmed on 14 Dec 2018

Longest chilli pepper
50.5 cm (1 ft 7.8 in), grown by Jürg Wiesli (CHE) and measured in Jona, St Gallen, Switzerland, on 30 Sep 2018

Heaviest chilli pepper
420 g (14.8 oz), grown by Dale Toten (UK) and ratified in Malvern, Worcestershire, UK, on 29 Sep 2018

Food Feats

LARGEST...

• Artichoke salad: On 15 Sep 2019, Universidad San Ignacio de Loyola and Danper (both PER) served an artichoke salad weighing 784.53 kg (1,729 lb 9 oz) – heavier than a Holstein cow – in Trujillo, Peru.

• Falafel: A 101.5-kg (223-lb 12-oz) patty made of chickpeas, spices and herbs was prepared by Hilton Dead Sea Resort & Spa (JOR) in Sweimeh, Jordan, on 31 May 2019.

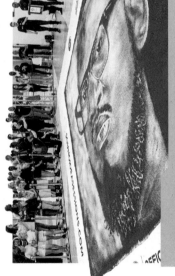

Largest coffee-grounds mosaic (image)

On 12 Sep 2019, BrainFarm (PTY) and artist Percy Maimela (both ZAF) produced an artwork from coffee grounds measuring 25.96 m² (279 sq ft). The portrait, of record producer DJ Black Coffee, was created by Maimela in just four hours at the Sandton City mall in Johannesburg, South Africa.

Tallest chocolate fountain

On 11 Apr 2019, *maître chocolatier* Helmut Wenschitz (AUT) put Willy Wonka to shame by building a 12.27-m-tall (40-ft 3-in) chocolate fountain. The three-storey confection celebrated the opening of Helmut's Pralinenwelt ("Praline World") chocolate factory in Allhaming, Austria.

The fountain supports cascades of liquid chocolate weighing around 1 tonne (2,200 lb).

• Gazpacho: On 9 Jun 2019, Unica Group (ESP) produced a cold vegetable soup measuring 9,800 litres (2,588 US gal) in Almería, Spain. That is enough to fill 30 bath tubs.

• Mille-feuille: On 23 Feb 2019, a French pastry slice that tipped the scales at 673.5 kg (1,484 lb 13 oz) was prepared in Trieste, Italy. It was the work of shopping centre Torri D'Europa, in collaboration with Tess and Pasticceria Bom Bom (all ITA).

• Green-bean casserole: Frozen vegetable brand Green Giant (USA) produced a 457-kg (1,009-lb) helping of this classic Thanksgiving dish on 20 Nov 2019 in New York City, USA. Afterwards, it was donated to Citymeals on Wheels.

• Serving of mango sticky rice: The Tourism Authority of Thailand prepared 4.5 tonnes (9,920 lb) of the traditional dessert *khao neeo mamuang* in Bangkok, Thailand, on 20 Jan 2019. The prodigious pudding weighed the same as three pick-up trucks!

• Serving of profiteroles: On 15 Sep 2019, a mound of chocolate-drizzled profiteroles weighing 430 kg (947 lb 15 oz) was served up by Consorzio Centro Commerciale Latinafiori (ITA) in Latina, Italy.

◆ Longest egg noodle (hand-made)

Japanese chef Hiroshi Kuroda created an egg noodle with a length of 183.72 m (602 ft 9 in) – about the same as Seattle's Space Needle stands tall – on 20 May 2019 in Tokyo, Japan. The noodle, which had to be made as a single continuous strand from dough, required an hour of cooking in a hot wok.

Longest baguette

On 16 Jun 2019, a baguette measuring 132.62 m (435 ft 1 in) was unveiled in Como, Italy. Stood on end, it would be more than twice the height of the Leaning Tower of Pisa. The baguette was created by Croce Rossa Italiana – Comitato della Provincia di Como (ITA) as part of a fundraising event.

Largest cream-tea party

In 2019, the world went cream-tea crazy! On 23 Oct, a total of 1,054 people celebrated the National Lottery's 25th birthday with scones, jam, clotted cream and tea at the Sage Gateshead in Gateshead, UK (main picture). This was promptly beaten on 29 Nov, when Beijing Mercedes-Benz Sales Service (CHN) served a cream tea for 1,088 people (inset) in Xiamen, Fujian, China.

Longest cooking marathon

Chef Lata Tandon (IND) cooked a range of Indian dishes for 87 hr 45 min on 3–7 Sep 2019 in Rewa, India. She more than doubled the previous record.

Longest tiramisu

On 16 Mar 2019, culinary school students together with Galbani Santa Lucia (ITA) prepared a 273.5-m-long (897-ft 3-in) coffee dessert in Milan, Italy. The students were directed by chef and *Masterchef Italia* winner Stefano Callegaro.

Most blueberries stuffed in the mouth

Serial record-breaker David Rush (USA) found room in his mouth for 124 blueberries on 16 Jun 2019 in Boise, Idaho, USA. He beat his own record by just a single blueberry.

Most people eating breakfast in bed

A total of 574 people ate breakfast in bed on 30 Mar 2019 in Johannesburg, South Africa. The event was organized by juice brand Cappy (ZAF).

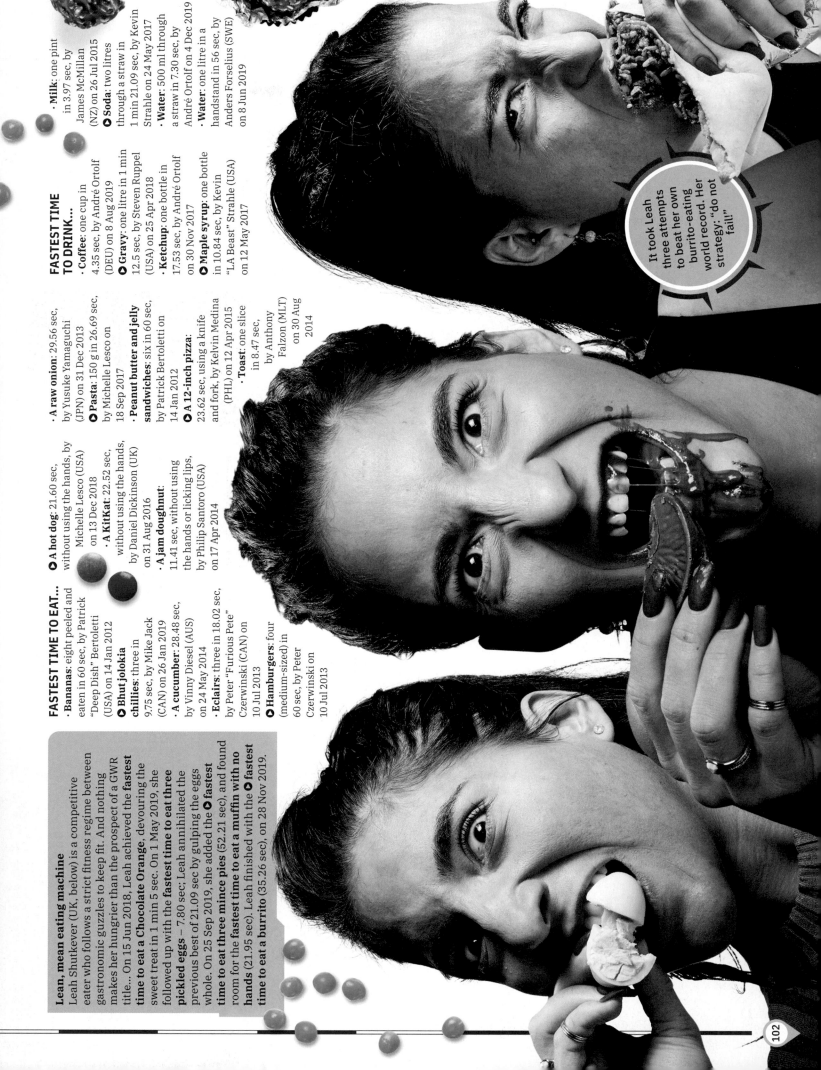

Lean, mean eating machine
Leah Shutkever (UK, below) is a competitive eater who follows a strict fitness regime between gastronomic guzzles to keep fit. And nothing makes her hungrier than the prospect of a GWR title… On 15 Jun 2018, Leah achieved the **fastest time to eat a Chocolate Orange**, devouring the sweet treat in 1 min 5 sec. On 1 May 2019, she followed up with the **fastest time to eat three pickled eggs** – 7.80 sec; Leah annihilated the previous best of 21.09 sec by gulping the eggs whole. On 25 Sep 2019, she added the ❍ **fastest time to eat three mince pies** (52.21 sec), and found room for the **fastest time to eat a muffin with no hands** (21.95 sec). Leah finished with the ❍ **fastest time to eat a burrito** (35.26 sec), on 28 Nov 2019.

FASTEST TIME TO EAT…
· **Bananas:** eight peeled and eaten in 60 sec, by Patrick "Deep Dish" Bertoletti (USA) on 14 Jan 2012
❍ **Bhut jolokia chillies:** three in 9.75 sec, by Mike Jack (CAN) on 26 Jan 2019
· **A cucumber:** 28.48 sec, by Vinny Diesel (AUS) on 24 May 2014
· **Eclairs:** three in 18.02 sec, by Peter "Furious Pete" Czerwinski (CAN) on 10 Jul 2013
❍ **Hamburgers:** four (medium-sized) in 60 sec, by Peter Czerwinski on 10 Jul 2013

❍ **A hot dog:** 21.60 sec, without using the hands, by Michelle Lesco (USA) on 13 Dec 2018
· **A KitKat:** 22.52 sec, without using the hands, by Daniel Dickinson (UK) on 31 Aug 2016
· **A jam doughnut:** 11.41 sec, without using the hands or licking lips, by Philip Santoro (USA) on 17 Apr 2014

· **A raw onion:** 29.56 sec, by Yusuke Yamaguchi (JPN) on 31 Dec 2013
· **Pasta:** 150 g in 26.69 sec, by Michelle Lesco on 18 Sep 2017
· **Peanut butter and jelly sandwiches:** six in 60 sec, by Patrick Bertoletti on 14 Jan 2012
❍ **A 12-inch pizza:** 23.62 sec, using a knife and fork, by Kelvin Medina (PHL) on 12 Apr 2015
· **Toast:** one slice in 8.47 sec, by Anthony Falzon (MLT) on 30 Aug 2014

FASTEST TIME TO DRINK…
· **Coffee:** one cup in 4.35 sec, by André Ortolf (DEU) on 8 Aug 2019
❍ **Gravy:** one litre in 1 min 12.5 sec, by Steven Ruppel (USA) on 25 Apr 2018
· **Ketchup:** one bottle in 17.53 sec, by André Ortolf on 30 Nov 2017
❍ **Maple syrup:** one bottle in 10.84 sec, by Kevin "LA Beast" Strahle (USA) on 12 May 2017

· **Milk:** one pint in 3.97 sec, by James McMillan (NZ) on 26 Jul 2015
❍ **Soda:** two litres through a straw in 1 min 21.09 sec, by Kevin Strahle on 24 May 2017
· **Water:** 500 ml through a straw in 7.30 sec, by André Ortolf on 4 Dec 2019
· **Water:** one litre in a handstand in 56 sec, by Anders Forselius (SWE) on 8 Jun 2019

It took Leah three attempts to beat her own burrito-eating world record. Her strategy: "do not fail!"

EXPENSIVE TA$TES

Savour GWR's ritzy *à la carte* menu – strictly for epicureans with deep pockets!

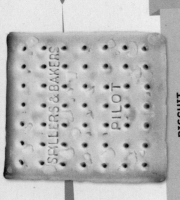

BISCUIT

A bittersweet taste of history. Part of a survival kit in a lifeboat from the ill-fated ocean liner RMS *Titanic*, which sank in Apr 1912. The "Pilot" cracker was salvaged by a passenger on the rescue vessel, the RMS *Carpathia*. Auctioned at Henry Aldridge & Son in Devizes, Wiltshire, UK, in Oct 2015. One to be savoured for its poignance rather than consumed.
£15,000 ($23,064)

SOUFFLÉ

Lighter-than-air egg soufflé, filled with delicate quail eggs and royal reserve caviar, flambéd with Hennessy Richard and decorated with gold leaf. Prepared by executive chef Richard Farnabe and Alexandre Petrossian (both USA) at Petrossian in New York City, USA.
$2,500 (£1,889)

HOT DOG

~ *"The Juuni Ban"* ~
Tempting smoked-cheese bratwurst with butter-teriyaki grilled onions, maitake mushrooms, wagyu beef, foie gras, shaved black truffle, caviar and Japanese mayonnaise, nestling in a brioche bun. From Tokyo Dog in Seattle, Washington, USA.
$169 (£101)

Chocolate
~ *"La Chuorsa"* ~
Saffron, crystallized orange crisps and 68% Chuao chocolate from Venezuela combine in a confectioner's dream. Sold by Attimo Chocolate Zurich (CHE) in Switzerland.
£6,268.50 per kg ($8,072.69)

Crab cake
~ *"The Platinum Crab Cake"* ~
A peerless patty of black truffle, platinum leaves, platinum dust, king crab meat, lump crab meat, butter and herbs. Prepared by Lazarius Leysath by Lazarius Leysath Walker (USA) at the Twist Walker (USA) at the Twist restaurant in Columbia, South Carolina, USA.
$310 (£243)

Cocktail
~ *"The Winston"* ~
Class in a glass: Croizet 1858 cognac, Grand Marnier liqueur, Chartreuse and Angostura bitters, mixed at Club 23 in Melbourne, Australia.
£8,583 ($13,438)

Dim sum dumpling
Each delicate parcel houses black bone chicken, saffron, truffle, caterpillar fungus, truffle and blueberry powder. Made by Hongmei Zhang (CHN) and Kevin Brück (DEU).
€448 (£399; $523)

SANDWICH

~ *"The Quintessential Grilled Cheese"* ~
Delicious French Pullman bread made with Dom Perignon champagne and gold flakes, glistening with white truffle butter and rare Caciocavallo Podolico cheese. Served with a velvety dipping sauce of South African lobster tomato bisque. As sold by Serendipity 3 in New York City, USA.
$214 (£132)

BENTO (MEAL IN A BOX)

Ten choice cuts of tender beef accompanied by a palate-pleasing array of rice, citrus, fresh wasabi and pear sauce. Made by Star Festival Inc. (JPN) in Shibuya, Tokyo, Japan.
292,929 yen (£1,960; $2,739)

DURIAN FRUIT

A rare kanyao durian, hand-picked just a day before its sale by Maliwan Han Chai Thai, Pa Toi Lung Mu farm and the King of Durian festival (all THA) in Nonthaburi, Thailand. Painstakingly cultivated, if distinctively offensive to the nose. Discover for yourself why the durian is known as "The King of Fruit".

1.5 million Thai baht (£37,635; $47,784)

CHEESECAKE

Decadence *par excellence*, this sumptuous dessert comprises buffalo ricotta, 200-year-old cognac, Madagascan vanilla, Italian white truffles, ground hazelnuts, velvet-like melted chocolate, gold leaf and a fresh block of honeycomb. Its creator is chef Raffaele Ronca (ITA/USA) of Ristorante Rafele in New York City, USA.

$4,592 (£3,496)

PIZZA

~ *"The 24K"* ~

The crust of this international taste sensation is infused with Indian black-squid ink and sprinkled with Ecuadorian gold flakes. Its heavenly topping features white Stilton cheese from the UK, French foie gras and black truffles, ossetra and almas caviar from the Caspian Sea and 24-karat gold leaf. Orders should be placed two days ahead (as the exclusive ingredients are imported) at Industry Kitchen in New York City, USA.

$2,700 (£2,106)

MILKSHAKE

~ *The "LUXE"* ~

Indulge yourself with this heavenly blend of Jersey cream, Tahitian vanilla ice-cream, Devonshire luxury clotted cream, Madagascan vanilla beans, 23-karat edible gold, whipped cream, *le cremose baldizzone* (donkey caramel sauce) and Luxardo gourmet maraschino cherries. Sold at Serendipity 3 and made in partnership with Swarovski® and the Crystal Ninja in New York City, USA.

$100 (£75)

TRUFFLE

A to-die-for white truffle (*Tuber magnatum pico*), weighing *c.* 1.3 kg (2 lb 13 oz), unearthed in Pisa, Italy, on 23 Nov 2007 by Cristiano and Luciano Savini (both ITA). Bought by Stanley Ho, bidding by phone via his wife, Angela Leong (both CHN), in a simultaneous auction at the Grand Lisboa Hotel in Macau, China.

$330,000 (£159,977)

LEG OF HAM

~ *Iberian "Manchado de Jabugo"* ~

Exclusive joint taken from pigs reared for three years and then placed in a traditional curing cellar for a further six years. May be purchased in its entirety, boned and in pieces, or in vacuum-packed slices. Presented in a box made by a local artisan from oaks grown in the same region. Sold by Dehesa Maladúa (ESP).

€4,100 (£3,192; $4,620)

Mass Participation

Largest music lesson
A total of 2,869 primary school students attended a beginner's lesson on how to play the ukulele on 15 May 2019 at SJKC Kuo Kuang 2 in Johor, Malaysia. With the help of instructor Ric Cho, they learned how to hold their instrument and strum a chord or two. The 33-min class finished with a group performance of the popular children's song "Baby Shark".

Music & dance: Largest...

Record	People	Location	Date
Bharatanatyam dance	10,176	Chennai, Tamil Nadu, India	8 Feb 2020
Bharatanatyam dance lesson	416	Chennai, Tamil Nadu, India	2 Feb 2020
Drum crescendo	556	St Petersburg, Russia	26 May 2019
Ladakhi dance	408	Hemis, Ladakh, India	20 Sep 2019
Matouqin ensemble	2,019	Qianguo, Songyuan, Jilin, China	13 Jul 2019
Samba dance lesson	643	Hong Kong, China	19 May 2019
Schuhplattler dance	1,312	Antdorf, Bavaria, Germany	30 May 2019
Singing relay (multiple songs)	384	Sheffield, South Yorkshire, UK	7 Nov 2019

Most people dressed as Smurfs
On 16 Feb 2019, a total of 2,762 fans of the famous Belgian comic characters gathered in Lauchringen, Germany, to paint the town blue. To qualify for the record, participants had to wear blue body paint or blue clothing, while classic red or white Smurf hats were an essential accessory. Many came dressed as specific characters, such as Papa Smurf or Smurfette. The event was organized by Dä Traditionsverein (DEU).

Most people scuba diving simultaneously
On 3 Aug 2019, the Indonesia Women's Organisation held a mass scuba dive with 3,131 participants in Manado, North Sulawesi, Indonesia. They followed up by producing the **largest flag unfurled underwater** – 1,014 m² (10,914 sq ft). This was their third GWR title, having formed the **longest human chain underwater** – 578 people – two days earlier. They had spent a year preparing for the event.

Largest human image of a...

Record	People	Location	Date
Bicycle	2,620	Moscow, Russia	13 Jul 2019
Burger	1,047	Madrid, Spain	14 Oct 2019
Cloud	1,207	Qingdao, Shandong, China	8 Jul 2019
Fingerprint	800	Hebron, Palestine	14 Oct 2019
Maple leaf	3,942	Quinte West, Ontario, Canada	29 Jun 2019
Peace sign	1,076	Thiruvananthapuram, Kerala, India	2 Oct 2019
Pencil	761	Rydalmere, New South Wales, Australia	20 Aug 2019

Hazza al Mansouri flew to the *International Space Station* on 25 Sep 2019. He returned eight days later.

Largest human image of a rocket
To celebrate the achievements of Hazza al Mansouri, the first Emirati to go into space, the PACE Group (UAE) arranged a human image of a rocket with 11,443 school children and staff members on 28 Nov 2019 in Sharjah, UAE. The children were drawn from five schools and represented 21 different nations.

Largest gathering of people dressed...

Record	People	Location	Date
As brides	1,347	Petrer, Alicante, Spain	29 Jun 2019
As Ji Gong	339	Hong Kong, China	9 Nov 2019
As scarecrows	2,495	Ilagan, Isabela, Philippines	25 Jan 2019
As wizards	440	National Harbor, Maryland, USA	5 Jan 2019
In tartan	1,359	Kenora, Ontario, Canada	27 Jul 2019

Most people...

Record	People	Location	Date
Making bouquets simultaneously	339	Newport, New Hampshire, USA	7 Sep 2019
Performing the chair pose (yoga) simultaneously	623	Shanghai, China	23 Jun 2019
Picking tea leaves simultaneously	576	Kamo, Gifu, Japan	7 Jul 2019
Using manual mowing tools	564	Cerkno, Slovenia	12 Aug 2019
Wearing sock puppets (single venue)	628	Birmingham, West Midlands, UK	3 Jun 2019

Most contributors to a...

Record	People	Location	Date
Colour by numbers	2,462	Dubai, UAE	17 Oct 2019
LEGO®-brick miniature city in eight hours	1,025	Shanghai, China	22 Sep 2019
Rubik's Cube mosaic	308	London, UK	30 Sep–2 Oct 2019

Largest lesson in...

Record	People	Location	Date
Archaeology	299	Ostroh, Rivne, Ukraine	10 Oct 2019
Artificial intelligence programming	846	Dallas, Texas, USA	17 Apr 2019
Biology	5,019	São Paulo, Brazil	30 Oct 2019
Calligraphy	2,671	Macau, China	13 Oct 2019
Employability skills	330	London, UK	30 Oct 2019
Football (soccer)	835	Melbourne, Victoria, Australia	26 Oct 2019
Gardening	286	Kuwait City, Kuwait	16 Nov 2019
Laundry	400	Mumbai, Maharashtra, India	17 May 2019
Software	775	Guadalajara, Jalisco, Mexico	23 Apr 2019

Largest...

Record	People	Location	Date
Coffee tasting	2,133	Moscow, Russia	7 Sep 2019
Game of freeze tag	2,172	Phoenix, Arizona, USA	13 Nov 2019
Human knot	123	Jeju, South Korea	21 Jun 2019
Laser tag winner-stays-on tournament	978	Farmington, Michigan, USA	25 Aug 2019
Paper ball fight	653	Morgantown, Kentucky, USA	4 Jul 2019

Longest line of human mattress dominoes
Globo Comunicação e Participações and Ortobom (both BRA) organized a giant game of human mattress dominoes with 2,019 people on 6 Aug 2019 at Riocentro in Rio de Janeiro, Brazil. They beat the previous record by three people. The topple took 11 min 13 sec, with the mattresses donated to charity afterwards.

Largest orchestra
A total of 8,097 musicians came together to perform the Russian national anthem on 1 Sep 2019 in St Petersburg, Russia. The event, organized by Gazprom's Fund for Supporting Social Initiatives (RUS), drew performers from 181 orchestras and 200 choirs from across the country. The performance was followed by a live screening of a Russian football match.

Largest Mexican folk dance
On 24 Aug 2019, a total of 882 participants dressed in traditional charro and caporal costumes took part in a Jalisco dance for 6 min 50 sec on the Plaza de la Liberación in Guadalajara, Jalisco, Mexico. The record attempt, which almost doubled the previous best of 457, was organized by Cámara de Comercio and Servicios y Turismo de Guadalajara (both MEX).

The PACE Group's image depicted a space shuttle mounted on three giant rockets.

Big Stuff

POSTCARD from *Casey* Illinois

The small town with a big appetite for records!

Wish you were here!

Largest golf club

Largest key

Largest mailbox

Largest rocking chair and largest clogs

Largest pitchfork

Largest golf tee

Largest barber's pole

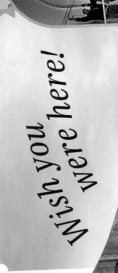

FIRST CLASS

To...

Guinness World Records, London

from...

Casey, Illinois, USA, 62420

Largest golf tee

Here in Casey, Illinois, USA, our small town has some very BIG attractions. We currently hold 11 GWR titles, all for super-sized objects created by local businessman Jim Bolin (USA). Down at the Country Club, our giant golf tee measures 9.37 m (30 ft 9 in) long, has a head diameter of 1.91 m (6 ft 3 in) and a shaft width of 64 cm (2 ft 1 in). It was shaped from a block of yellow pine boards using chainsaws.

Largest mailbox

Take a trip to the downtown business district, where our large letter-holder measures 11.09 m long by 4.41 m high (36 ft 4 in x 14 ft 5 in). Like all of our super-sized creations, it's fully functional! Find the hidden stairway located in the post stand to climb up inside. The opening is operated on a cable winch, and looks out over a giant birdcage across the street.

Largest golf club

If you've got time to play nine holes, don't forget your Casey-sized club, measuring 13.95 m (45 ft 9 in). It's guaranteed to add some distance to your drives – if you can pick it up, that is!

Largest key

A replica of the key to Jim Bolin's Chevy Silverado truck stands 8.58 m (28 ft 1 in) tall – that's nearly twice the height of a double-decker bus! It also has a maximum width of 3.47 m (11 ft 4 in). If Jim's truck were scaled up to the same size, it would be the length of the *Queen Elizabeth 2* ocean liner.

Largest rocking chair

Towering over Main Street is a 17.09-m-tall (56-ft 1-in) wood-and-steel rocking chair. It's 9.99 m (32 ft 9.5 in) wide and weighs 20.9 tonnes (46,200 lb). A "dove of hope" is carved into the head rest. And while you're there, don't miss (as if you could!) the **largest clogs**. They measure 3.5 m (11 ft 5 in) long – which is a shoe size of about 390!

Largest pitchfork

At Casey, we're proud of our agricultural heritage. Nothing illustrates this better than our mighty farm tool, which measures 2.56 m (8 ft 5 in) wide and 18.65 m (61 ft 1 in) long. This is 10 times the size of a normal pitchfork, and about the length of a bowling alley! You'll find it displayed outside Richard's Farm Restaurant – and if you've got a big, Casey-sized appetite, be sure to try the pie!

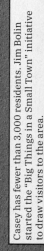

Largest barber's pole

In need of a trim? At 4.46 m (14 ft 7 in), our barber's pole will point you in the right direction. It was dreamed up by our "Big Things in a Small Town" initiative, which offers residents and city officials the chance to decide what outsized object to create next.

Casey has fewer than 3,000 residents. Jim Bolin started the "Big Things in a Small Town" initiative to draw visitors to the area.

Shoes

Footwear feats

Fastest...	Time	Holder
100 m in clogs	13.16 sec	André Ortolf (DEU)
100 m in high heels	13.55 sec	Majken Sichlau (DNK)
100 m in ski boots	13.85 sec	André Ortolf (DEU)
100 m in ski boots (female)	16.86 sec	Emma Kirk-Odunubi (UK)
100 m on high-heeled roller skates	26.10 sec	Marawa Ibrahim (AUS)
Half marathon in flip-flops	1 hr 30 min 23 sec	Rakshith Shetty (IND)
Half marathon in ski boots	3 hr 7 min 35 sec	Emilie Cruz (FRA)
Marathon in Wellington boots	3 hr 21 min 27 sec	Damian Thacker (UK)
Marathon in flip-flops	3 hr 42 min 29 sec	Pardip Singh Minhas (UK)
Marathon in ski boots	5 hr 30 min 27 sec	Paul Harnett (UK)

Correct as of 5 Dec 2019

Largest collection of...
◗ **Shoes**: at the last count on 20 Mar 2012, Darlene Flynn (USA, above) owned 15,665 shoes and shoe-related items.
◗ **Sneakers**: as of 17 May 2012, Jordy Geller (USA) had amassed a total of 2,388 pairs of trainers (above right).
Converse: at the last inventory, on 8 Mar 2012, Joshua Mueller (USA, right) owned 1,546 different pairs of the classic sports shoe. They were archived in Lakewood, Washington, USA.

1. Largest hiking boot
On 30 Sep 2006, Schuh Marke (DEU) presented a walking boot 7.14 m (23 ft 5 in) long, 2.5 m (8 ft 2 in) wide and 4.2 m (13 ft 9 in) tall in Hauenstein, Germany. It's twice as long as a Mini Cooper, wider than a London TX4 taxi and almost as tall as a Routemaster bus! The giant-sized footwear weighs in at some 1,500 kg (3,306 lb), or around the same as a forklift truck, while the 35-m-long (114-ft 9-in) lace is nearly four times longer than a typical stretch limo.

2. Largest cowboy boot
On 24 Jan 2008, Belachew Tola Buta (ETH) presented a black leather cowboy boot measuring 2.5 m (8 ft 2 in) tall and 2.38 m (7 ft 9 in) long in Addis Ababa, Ethiopia.

3. Largest shoe
Electric sekki (HKG) displayed a trainer 6.4 m (20 ft 11 in) long, 2.39 m (7 ft 10 in) wide and 1.65 m (5 ft 4 in) tall on 12 Apr 2013 in Hong Kong, China. It was modelled on a Superga 2750 shoe.

4. Largest high-heeled shoe
A high-heeled shoe measuring 3.96 m (12 ft 11 in) long and 2.82 m

(9 ft 3 in) tall was unveiled in Sfax, Tunisia, on 20 Apr 2019. The shoe was the result of a collaboration between the Tunisian fashion designer Ahmed Gargouri, the Dido Fashion Club, Complexe des Jeunes de Sfax, CNCC (Tunisia's National Leather and Shoe Centre) and UTICA Sfax (the country's industry, trade and handicraft union).

While this Tunisian shoe is a one-off, the **highest-heeled shoes commercially available** went on sale to the public at boldnbootiful.com in Feb 2004. Produced by James Syiemiong (IND), the extreme footwear boasted platforms measuring 43 cm (1 ft 5 in) high and heels reaching 51 cm (1 ft 8 in) – taller than a bowling pin!

Most valuable boots
In Dec 2013, Antwerp diamond company Diarough/UNI-Design and fashion house AF Vandevorst (both BEL) unveiled a pair of size-6 ankle boots. Made with 4.73 kg (10 lb 7 oz) of gold and covered in 39,083 natural fancy coloured diamonds weighing a total of 1,550 carats, they were valued at $3.1 m (£1.8 m).

Oldest leather shoe
In 2008, archaeologists discovered a 5,500-year-old leather shoe inside the Areni-1 cave in the south-eastern Vayots Dzor province of Armenia. The shoe is 24.5 cm (9.6 in) long, made from a single piece of hide leather and shaped to fit the wearer's foot. It is complete and well preserved thanks to the thick layer of sheep dung in which it was covered and the cool, dry conditions inside the cave.

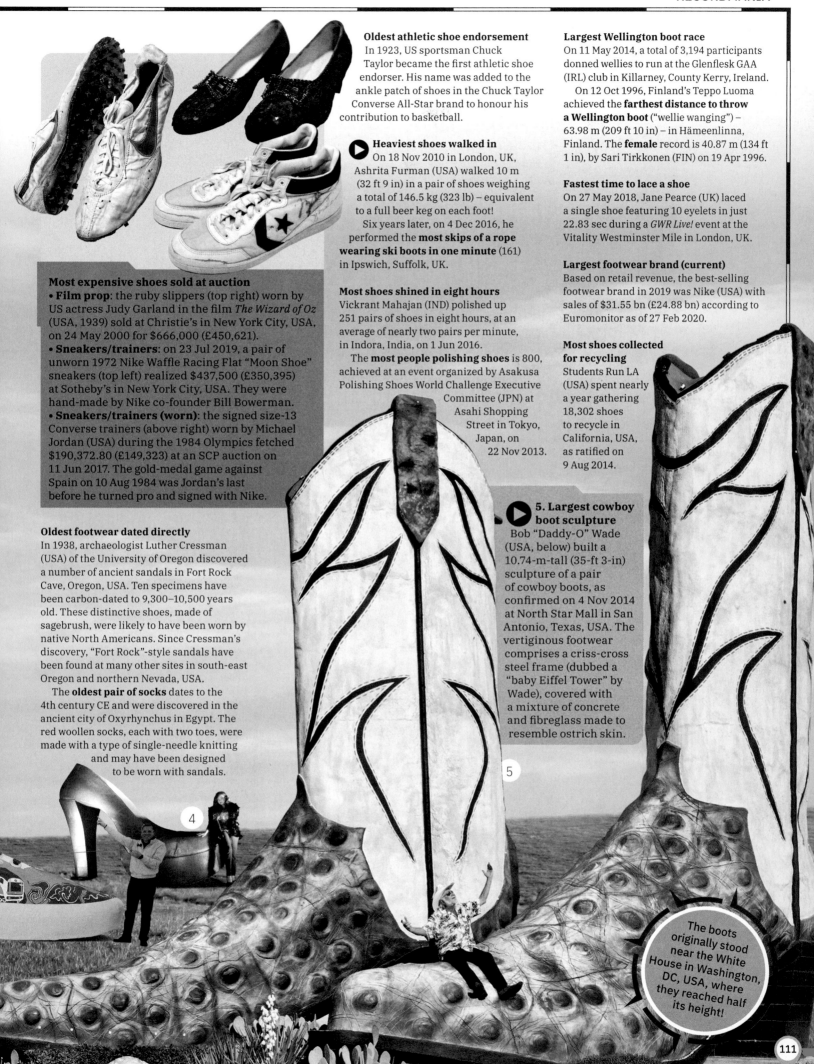

Oldest athletic shoe endorsement

In 1923, US sportsman Chuck Taylor became the first athletic shoe endorser. His name was added to the ankle patch of shoes in the Chuck Taylor Converse All-Star brand to honour his contribution to basketball.

▶ Heaviest shoes walked in

On 18 Nov 2010 in London, UK, Ashrita Furman (USA) walked 10 m (32 ft 9 in) in a pair of shoes weighing a total of 146.5 kg (323 lb) – equivalent to a full beer keg on each foot!

Six years later, on 4 Dec 2016, he performed the **most skips of a rope wearing ski boots in one minute** (161) in Ipswich, Suffolk, UK.

Most shoes shined in eight hours

Vickrant Mahajan (IND) polished up 251 pairs of shoes in eight hours, at an average of nearly two pairs per minute, in Indora, India, on 1 Jun 2016.

The **most people polishing shoes** is 800, achieved at an event organized by Asakusa Polishing Shoes World Challenge Executive Committee (JPN) at Asahi Shopping Street in Tokyo, Japan, on 22 Nov 2013.

Largest Wellington boot race

On 11 May 2014, a total of 3,194 participants donned wellies to run at the Glenflesk GAA (IRL) club in Killarney, County Kerry, Ireland.

On 12 Oct 1996, Finland's Teppo Luoma achieved the **farthest distance to throw a Wellington boot** ("wellie wanging") – 63.98 m (209 ft 10 in) – in Hämeenlinna, Finland. The **female** record is 40.87 m (134 ft 1 in), by Sari Tirkkonen (FIN) on 19 Apr 1996.

Fastest time to lace a shoe

On 27 May 2018, Jane Pearce (UK) laced a single shoe featuring 10 eyelets in just 22.83 sec during a *GWR Live!* event at the Vitality Westminster Mile in London, UK.

Largest footwear brand (current)

Based on retail revenue, the best-selling footwear brand in 2019 was Nike (USA) with sales of $31.55 bn (£24.88 bn) according to Euromonitor as of 27 Feb 2020.

Most shoes collected for recycling

Students Run LA (USA) spent nearly a year gathering 18,302 shoes to recycle in California, USA, as ratified on 9 Aug 2014.

Most expensive shoes sold at auction

- **Film prop**: the ruby slippers (top right) worn by US actress Judy Garland in the film *The Wizard of Oz* (USA, 1939) sold at Christie's in New York City, USA, on 24 May 2000 for $666,000 (£450,621).
- **Sneakers/trainers**: on 23 Jul 2019, a pair of unworn 1972 Nike Waffle Racing Flat "Moon Shoe" sneakers (top left) realized $437,500 (£350,395) at Sotheby's in New York City, USA. They were hand-made by Nike co-founder Bill Bowerman.
- **Sneakers/trainers (worn)**: the signed size-13 Converse trainers (above right) worn by Michael Jordan (USA) during the 1984 Olympics fetched $190,372.80 (£149,323) at an SCP auction on 11 Jun 2017. The gold-medal game against Spain on 10 Aug 1984 was Jordan's last before he turned pro and signed with Nike.

Oldest footwear dated directly

In 1938, archaeologist Luther Cressman (USA) of the University of Oregon discovered a number of ancient sandals in Fort Rock Cave, Oregon, USA. Ten specimens have been carbon-dated to 9,300–10,500 years old. These distinctive shoes, made of sagebrush, were likely to have been worn by native North Americans. Since Cressman's discovery, "Fort Rock"-style sandals have been found at many other sites in south-east Oregon and northern Nevada, USA.

The **oldest pair of socks** dates to the 4th century CE and were discovered in the ancient city of Oxyrhynchus in Egypt. The red woollen socks, each with two toes, were made with a type of single-needle knitting and may have been designed to be worn with sandals.

▶ 5. Largest cowboy boot sculpture

Bob "Daddy-O" Wade (USA, below) built a 10.74-m-tall (35-ft 3-in) sculpture of a pair of cowboy boots, as confirmed on 4 Nov 2014 at North Star Mall in San Antonio, Texas, USA. The vertiginous footwear comprises a criss-cross steel frame (dubbed a "baby Eiffel Tower" by Wade), covered with a mixture of concrete and fibreglass made to resemble ostrich skin.

4

5

The boots originally stood near the White House in Washington, DC, USA, where they reached half its height!

Collections

Assassin's Creed memorabilia
As of 10 Feb 2019, Carlo Prisco (ITA) had 1,030 items related to the award-winning action game in Pozzuoli, Naples, Italy.

Pikachu memorabilia
Lisa Courtney (UK) has amassed a 1,293-strong archive based on the *Pokémon* star. Her hoard was ratified in Welwyn Garden City, Hertfordshire, UK, on 7 Aug 2019. Lisa also had the **largest collection of *Pokémon* memorabilia** – 17,127 items – as of 10 Aug 2016.

Whale-related items
As verified on 24 May 2019, Cynde McInnis (USA) had acquired 1,347 pieces related to these marine mammals – from postcards and clothing to magnets and jewellery – stored in Topsfield, Massachusetts, USA.

The **largest collection of dolphin-related items** numbers 3,516, and is the property of Ausra Saltenyte (LTU) in Vilnius, Lithuania, as counted on 31 Jan 2019.

Sunglasses
Lori-Ann Keenan (CAN) owned 2,174 sets of shades in Vancouver, British Columbia, Canada, as ratified on 29 Jun 2019.

Rolling Stones memorabilia
Matthew Lee (UK) has amassed 2,789 pieces of ephemera related to the veteran rockers, as verified on 14 Nov 2019 in London, UK.

Valid credit cards
Zheng Xiangchen (CHN) had 1,562 credit cards as of 28 Aug 2019 in Shenzhen, Guangdong, China. Following GWR guidelines, each card had a spending limit of at least $500 (£407). Overall, the collection would have offered a minimum credit availability of $781,000 (£637,010, as of the date above).

LEGO® Minifigures
Fabio Bertini (ITA) owned 3,310 LEGO Minifigures, as verified on 1 Dec 2018 in the republic of San Marino. Every item in the collection, which dates back to the 1970s, is part of an original LEGO set and has at least one detail that distinguishes it from the others. Shown above with Fabio are Banana Guy, Chicken Suit Guy and President Business.

Top Trumps
Mark Maggs (UK) owns 300 uniquely themed sets of the card game Top Trumps, as ratified in London, UK, on 8 Jul 2019. He began amassing the "Collectible, Competitive, Compulsive!" cards in 2002. Subjects include "Barbie", "The Mary Rose" and his favourite, "Sports Cars". Top Trumps first appeared in the UK in 1978.

Spider-Man memorabilia
As of 27 Apr 2019, Tristan Mathews (USA) possessed 3,089 items related to the world-famous web-slinger, as confirmed in Burbank, California, USA. Aside from comics, Tristan's Marvel-ous archive includes action figures, lamps, lunch trays, videogames, clothing and even themed tins of spaghetti.

Tristan has been a devoted Spidey fan since the age of 11, when he read *Web of Spider-Man* #126.

Fortune-cookie fortunes
By 1 Aug 2019, Kris L Duke (USA) had collected 4,350 of these "prophetic" notes in Bolton Valley, Vermont, USA.

Perfume bottles
As of 13 Sep 2019, Anna Leventeri (GRC) had sniffed out 5,410 scent bottles, which she keeps stored in Neo Psychiko, Greece.

One Piece memorabilia
Yoshikazu Sanada (JPN) has an archive of 5,656 items connected to the popular manga series in Kawasaki, Kanagawa, Japan, as verified on 17 Jul 2019.

Dragon Ball memorabilia
Hitoshi Uchida (JPN) has two rooms dedicated to this manga/anime classic, accommodating 10,098 items. They were counted in Tokyo, Japan, on 18 Jun 2019.

▶ Funko Pop! figurines
At the last count on 5 Mar 2020, Paul Scardino (USA) had 5,306 Funko Pop! figurines in his basement in Winchester City, Virginia, USA. The stylized vinyl models depict licensed characters from comic books, movies and games. Paul's collection began with a two-pack set featuring Marvel's Hawkeye and Spider-Man (above). A colleague bought it for him as a birthday present, kick-starting his obsession.

Largest guitar collection sold at a charity auction
On 20 Jun 2019, the "David Gilmour Guitar Collection" sale saw 123 guitars owned by the Pink Floyd member auctioned by Christie's in New York City, USA. They realized $21,198,250 (£16,823,500), with proceeds going to environmental charity ClientEarth. The Fender Stratocaster shown below bears the coveted serial number 0001.

Banknotes
Wissam Ali Youssef (LBN) had saved up 12,282 unique banknotes by 2 Oct 2019, with a total face value of c. $294,408 (£239,713).

Postcards
As of 28 Jul 2019, Michael Schefers (DEU) had 15,553 unique postcards in Hannover, Germany; each depicts a bridge. Michael specializes in bridge construction.

***Digimon* memorabilia**
Ng Tze Ying (HKG) owned 18,264 pieces inspired by this Japanese digital-monster franchise at the last count on 3 May 2019 in Osaka, Japan.

▶ Videogames
Antonio Romero Monteiro of Richmond, Texas, USA, owned 20,139 items of videogame ephemera as of 2 Feb 2019.

Teddy bears
There were 20,367 bears in the archive of arctophile Istvánné Arnóczki (HUN) in Harsány, Hungary, as of 27 Apr 2019.

▶ *God of War* memorabilia
Emmanuel Mojica Rosas (MEX) owned 570 items relating to the *God of War* videogame franchise, as confirmed on 3 Mar 2019 in Xalisco, Mexico. He was presented with his GWR certificate while on a tour of the developers' studio, where he was also given the disc on which *God of War* was first burned.

The pick of the auction was "The Black Strat", heard on several classic Pink Floyd albums, including *The Dark Side of the Moon* (1973) and *Wish You Were Here* (1975).

Fitness

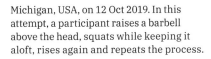

Most skips over a rope in 24 hours

Sella Rosa Rega (USA) skipped a rope 168,394 times in 24 hr in Boiceville, New York, USA, on 30 Mar 2019.

On the way to this record, Sella also achieved the **most skips over a rope in eight hours** (70,030), and also in **12 hours** (100,364). Her superlative skipping ability was honed as part of her mixed martial arts training.

Longest time to hold a tree pose (yoga)

M Kavitha (IND) held a yogic tree pose for 55 min in Chennai, India, on 19 Jun 2019. The position requires the practitioner to balance on one leg, with the foot of the other leg pressed against it. The hands may be raised or held, palms together, at the chest.

Most people holding an abdominal plank position

On 26 Jan 2020, Bajaj Allianz Life Insurance (IND) brought together 2,471 people to sustain an abdominal plank pose for 60 sec in Mumbai, India.

Heaviest deadlift in 24 hours

On 26–27 Oct 2019, Chris Dack (UK) lifted an aggregate weight of 480,000 kg (1,058,218 lb) in Norwich, Norfolk, UK. That's heavier than an Airbus A380, the **heaviest passenger aircraft**.

The **most weight lifted by overhead squats in one minute** is 2,125 kg (4,684 lb), by Casey Lambert (USA) in Owosso,

Michigan, USA, on 12 Oct 2019. In this attempt, a participant raises a barbell above the head, squats while keeping it aloft, rises again and repeats the process.

Farthest distance pushing a car in 24 hours (individual)

On 27–28 Apr 2019, Croatian fitness coach Tomislav Lubenjak pushed a 740-kg (1,630-lb) car with driver for 106.93 km (66.44 mi). He completed 33 lengths of a road in Zagreb, Croatia's capital city.

FASTEST...

100 m hula hooping

Thomas Gallant (USA) hula-hooped a distance of 100 m (328 ft) in 15.97 sec in St Johns, Florida, USA, on 18 May 2019. During the attempt, he also achieved the **fastest 50 m hula hooping** – 8.08 sec.

Farthest distance rolled on Swiss balls

Nicholas Smith (AUS) travelled for 95.17 m (312 ft 2 in) along a row of Swiss balls in Cubberla Creek Reserve, Queensland, Australia, on 14 Aug 2018.

The **most headers of a Swiss ball in 30 seconds** is 53, and was achieved by Josh Horton (USA) in Malibu, California, USA, on 16 May 2017.

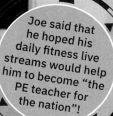

Most live streams of a fitness workout on YouTube

Following the coronavirus outbreak in early 2020, Joe "The Body Coach" Wicks (UK) began streaming daily workouts from his home. On 24 Mar 2020, a total of 955,185 households joined Joe as he ran, jumped and bunny-hopped around his living room.

On 5 Jul 2017, Joe oversaw the **largest high-intensity interval training class**, putting 3,804 participants through a rigorous exercise session at the British Summer Time Festival in Hyde Park, London, UK.

Joe said that he hoped his daily fitness live streams would help him to become "the PE teacher for the nation"!

Most lunges in one minute (female)

Sandra Hickson (IRL) executed 80 lunges in 60 sec in Castleisland, Kerry, Ireland, on 25 Jul 2019.

Between them, the super-fit Hickson family have achieved 10 GWR titles. On the same day, siblings Sandra and Jason joined legs to run the **fastest three-legged mile** in 6 min 52.12 sec.

Most one-arm, one-leg push-ups in one minute
Thounaojam Niranjoy Singh (IND) performed 36 push-ups supporting himself on one arm and one leg in Imphal, India, on 14 Aug 2019.

The **most one-arm push-ups carrying a 100-lb pack in one minute** is 20, and was achieved by Patrick Murray (USA) in Hoboken, New Jersey, USA, on 30 Mar 2019.

200 m backwards
Christian Roberto López Rodríguez (ESP) completed a 200-m (656-ft) reverse run in 30.99 sec in Toledo, Spain, on 30 Jul 2019.

The previous month, Christian had juggled and jogged to set the record for the **fastest 200 m joggling backwards with three objects** (in 48.83 sec) and then repeated this over **400 m** (in 1 min 48 sec).

Time to box-jump the height of Everest
Jamie Alderton (UK) took 22 hr 18 min 38 sec to scale the equivalent of the **highest mountain** (8,848 m; 29,029 ft) by jumping on to a box. The attempt took

place in Bognor Regis, West Sussex, UK, on 29–30 Nov 2019. Jamie's attempt raised a total of £21,000 ($27,119) for a local hospice.

MOST...

Handstand push-ups in three minutes (male)
On 27 Jun 2019, Armenian bodybuilder Manvel Mamoyan performed 73 push-ups – a rate of one every 2.5 sec – in Moscow, Russia.

Parallel bar dips with a 100-lb pack in one minute
Denys Havrikov (UKR) carried out 38 dips on parallel bars while weighed down by a 100-lb (45-kg) pack on 8 Jun 2019 in Miami, Florida, USA.

Pull-ups with an 80-lb pack in one minute
On 8 Mar 2020, Anthony Robles (USA) carried out 23 pull-ups in 60 sec while bearing 80 lb (36.2 kg) of weights in Phoenix, Arizona, USA.

▶ **Jumping jacks in 30 seconds**
On 14 Nov 2019, Simon Idio (UK) completed 68 jumping jacks, or star jumps, in half a minute in London, UK.

Longest abdominal plank (female)
Canada's Dana Glowacka held herself in this demanding position for 4 hr 19 min 55 sec in Naperville, Illinois, USA, on 18 May 2019.

The outright ○ **longest abdominal plank** lasted for 8 hr 15 min 15 sec, by former Marine George Hood (USA) at the same location on 15 Feb 2020. He planned his attempt to serve as a tribute to veterans of the armed forces. Dana and George are good friends and he helped her prepare for her record.

Farthest distance on a penny farthing in one hour (indoor)
On 17 Sep 2019, Chris Opie (UK) rode 34.547 km (21.466 mi) on a high-wheeler at the Derby Arena velodrome, UK. He narrowly broke Mark Beaumont's record of 33.865 km (21.042 mi), set shortly before at the same venue. Afterwards, Chris described the ride as "very painful". The attempt was organized by the Global Cycling Network.

Fastest time to run 100 miles on a treadmill
Sri Lanka-born Suresh Joachim Arulanantham (CAN) covered 100 mi (160 km) on a treadmill in 13 hr 42 min 33 sec at the Square One shopping centre in Mississauga, Ontario, Canada, on 28 Nov 2004.

Suresh is shown below with his GWR certificate for the **longest escalator ride**. From 25 to 31 May 1998, he covered the equivalent of 225.44 km (140.08 mi) travelling up and down a moving staircase at Westfield Burwood shopping centre in New South Wales, Australia.

Another of Suresh's off-kilter endurance feats is the **longest time rocking a rocking chair**: 75 hr 3 min.

Odd Talents

Fastest speed on a motorcycle while performing a headstand
Marco George (UK) achieved a speed of 122.59 km/h (76.17 mph) while balancing upside down on a motorbike. He performed the daredevil stunt at Elvington airfield in North Yorkshire, UK, on 17 Aug 2019. Marco has been a competition stunt rider for five years and practised for this attempt for seven months.

Highest jump-pot of a billiard ball
Theo Mihellis (USA) pocketed a billiard ball by chipping it over a bar set at 63.5 cm (2 ft 1 in) in Parkersburg, West Virginia, USA, on 13 Oct 2019.

Highest standing jump
Brett Williams (USA) jumped to a height of 1.65 m (5 ft 5 in) from a standing start in Fort Worth, Texas, USA, on 2 Sep 2019.

Farthest distance walked on toe knuckles
On 20 Sep 2019, Narayan Acharya (NPL) walked 31.5 m (103 ft 4 in) on his metatarsal phalangeal joints in Birgunj, Nepal.

Farthest distance walked balancing a hand-push lawnmower on the chin
James "Jay" Rawlings (UK, see right) covered 279.1 m (915 ft 8 in) with a manual lawnmower balanced upside down on his chin at the Glastonbury Festival in Somerset, UK, on 27 Jun 2019.

Farthest trampette dive-roll by a mascot
On 12 Sep 2019, Pierre the Pelican – the costumed mascot of the New Orleans Pelicans NBA team – used a small trampoline to launch himself 4.26 m (14 ft) over a line of cheerleaders while performing a front flip in Louisiana, USA.

Most layers in a bed-of-nails sandwich
On 23 Oct 2019, nine hardy people stacked themselves on top of each other, separated by beds of nails. The participants were Vispy Kharadi, Jecky Patel, Bhavesh Panwala, Khushru Kadwa, Jamshid Bhathena, Manan Patel, Abubakar Kadodia, Daraius Cooper and Rameez Virani (all IND). The feat took place in Surat, Gujarat, India.

MOST...

Drinks cans placed on the head using air suction
On 1 Sep 2019, Shunichi Kanno (JPN) suctioned nine cans on to his face and head in Tokyo, Japan. He beat the previous record, by Jamie "Canhead" Keeton in 2016, by one.

Eggs balanced on the back of the hand
Konok Karmakar (BGD) held 15 eggs on the back of his hand in Noakhali, Chittagong, Bangladesh, on 11 Aug 2019. Fakhrul Islam (BNG), Rocco Mercurio and Silvio Sabba (both ITA) all matched his feat within the year.

Most baubles in a beard
On 7 Dec 2019, Joel Strasser (USA) clipped 302 festive baubles into his voluminous beard in Olympia, Washington, USA.
Joel holds current records for the **most chopsticks in a beard** (520, pictured below right), the **most golf tees** (607) and the ❍ **most toothpicks** (3,500). He is currently in training for jabbing the most forks into his facial hair...

Joel also held the record for the **most plastic straws in a beard** (312) before the category was discontinued by GWR.

Baked beans eaten with chopsticks in one minute

Chisato Tanaka (JPN) ate 72 baked beans – one at a time – in 60 sec with a pair of chopsticks in Shibuya, Tokyo, Japan, on 8 Nov 2019.

Consecutive eye-to-eye soccer ball rolls

Yuuki Yoshinaga (JPN) rolled a football from one eye to the other 776 times in Kōtō, Tokyo, Japan, on 18 May 2019. On 9 Oct 2017, he recorded the **most soccer ball touches with the shoulders in one minute** – 230.

FASTEST TIME TO...

Fold and throw a paper aircraft

On 3 Aug 2019, Akimichi Hattori (JPN) folded and launched a paper plane in 7.03 sec in Kōtō, Tokyo, Japan. The guidelines for this record required Akimichi to craft a sharply pointed seven-fold aircraft and then launch it on a flight of at least 2 m (6 ft 6 in).

Heaviest car balanced on the head

John Evans (UK) balanced a gutted original Mini Cooper car weighing 159.6 kg (352 lb) on his head for 33 sec at The London Studios, UK, on 24 May 1999.

Two years earlier, John recorded the **greatest weight balanced on the head** – 188.7 kg (416 lb) – in the form of 101 bricks, also in London, UK.

Most pineapples on heads sliced in 30 seconds

On 15 Dec 2019, martial-arts instructor Harikrishnan S (IND) used a samurai sword to bisect 61 pineapples balanced on volunteers' heads in half a minute in Kerala, India. After the event, the fruit was cleaned and distributed to the participants and witnesses.

▶ Iron bars bent with the neck in one minute

Using his bare hands, Indian martial-arts expert Vispy Kharadi – a layer in the record-breaking bed of nails opposite – folded 21 iron bars, each measuring 1 m (3 ft 3 in) in length, across the back of his neck in 60 sec in Surat, India, on 23 Oct 2019. Each bar had to bend to a minimum of 90°.

Countries identified from their outline in one minute

On 8 Oct 2019, Aima'az Ali Abro (PAK) correctly recognized 57 countries from just their borders in 60 sec in Karachi, Pakistan.

Fastest mile on crutches on one leg

Michael Quintanilla (USA) completed one mile (1.6 km) hopping on crutches in 11 min 17 sec at his high-school sports track in Portland, Texas, USA, on 6 Aug 2019. Michael is a keen cross-country runner but had broken his foot. Eager to get back on the running track again, he began training for this GWR title with help from his team and coaches.

James achieved his record at the first attempt. He certainly impressed the BGT judges: they gave him four yesses.

Most chairs balanced on the chin

James "Jay" Rawlings kept 11 metal chairs on his chin for 10 sec on the set of *Britain's Got Talent* (ITV). His balancing act took place at the UK's London Palladium on 23 Jan 2019.

The **longest duration balancing a chair on the chin** is 35 min 10 sec, by Konok Karmakar (see left) on 19 Oct 2019 in Noakhali, Chittagong, Bangladesh.

Hit two soccer goalposts and the crossbar

Going against his footballing instincts, Ryan Sessegnon (UK) intentionally struck all three sides of the woodwork in 7.75 sec at St George's Park in Burton upon Trent, UK, on 27 May 2019. Ryan plays for Premier League team Tottenham Hotspur as well as the England Under-21 national side. Balls had been lined up along the edge of the penalty area for Ryan to kick, but he hit the left and right posts with his first two shots and clipped the crossbar with his fourth.

Arrange a chess set

Nakul Ramaswamy (USA) set up a chess board in 31.55 sec in Simsbury, Connecticut, USA, on 1 Aug 2019.

Arrange all elements of the periodic table

On 27 Sep 2019, Meenakshi Agrawal (IND) sorted the 118 elements of the periodic table in 2 min 49 sec in Delhi, India. He assembled the table from printed index cards, as the actual elements would have exposed him to a great deal of radiation!

Juggling Acts

Most consecutive chainsaw-juggling catches

Ian Stewart (CAN) completed 105 straight catches of a running chainsaw on 6 Sep 2019 in Truro, Nova Scotia, Canada. In 2017, he set the **greatest distance travelled while juggling three chainsaws** – 50.9 m (167 ft). Ian says that one of the greatest challenges of his death-defying act is the sheer weight of the chainsaws.

Fastest 100 m joggling with five objects (male)

In Jul 1988, Owen Morse (USA) ran 100 m in 13.8 sec while juggling five objects at the International Jugglers' Association festival in Denver, Colorado, USA. A year later, Owen set the **three objects** record in 11.68 sec – that's only 2.1 sec off Usain Bolt's 100-m record.

The **fastest 100 m joggling with three objects (female)** is 17.2 sec, by Sandy Brown (USA) in Jul 1990 in Los Angeles, California, USA.

Fastest half marathon joggling with three objects (male)

On 21 Oct 2018, Michael Lucien Bergeron (CAN) crossed the finish line of the Scotiabank Toronto Waterfront Marathon in 1 hr 17 min 9.4 sec in Ontario, Canada. He managed to finish the race two seconds quicker than a rival who had been attempting to claim the same record.

Most consecutive overhead juggling catches with seven objects

Michael Ferreri (ESP) achieved 71 consecutive catches with seven balls on 30 May 2019 in Laguna Hills, California, USA. To qualify for the record, he had to juggle with his forearms higher than his upper arms, with all catches and throws performed above the shoulders. See opposite page for more of Michael's records.

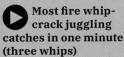

▶ Most fire whip-crack juggling catches in one minute (three whips)

On 7 Sep 2019, Aaron Bonk (USA) cracked a trio of blazing whips 82 times while juggling them in 60 sec. He achieved the record at his fourth and final show of the day at the New York Renaissance Faire in Tuxedo Park, New York City, USA.

Farthest distance travelled on inline skates while juggling three objects

On 3 Aug 2019, David Rush (USA) covered 1.2 km (0.7 mi) on inline skates while juggling a trio of e8 Pro Gballz in Boise, Idaho, USA. It took David 7 min 55 sec to complete three laps of a local high-school track juggling in a left-right-left-right pattern. He has earned more than 100 GWR titles.

MOST...

Individual juggling rotations in 30 seconds (five clubs)

Circus artist Victor Krachinov (RUS) completed 508 individual rotations of a quintet of clubs in half a minute on 12 Jul 2019. He was performing at the Obhur Festival in Jeddah, Saudi Arabia. To qualify for the record, all patterns used had to alternate right-left-right-left, while "multiplexing" (i.e., throwing more than one object at the same time) was not allowed.

▶ Consecutive samurai-sword juggling catches (three swords)

On 25 Jan 2019, fearless Marcos Ruiz Ceballos (ESP) completed 191 juggling catches of samurai swords in San Fernando, Cádiz, Spain.

Slightly safer – but no less impressive – is the **most hats juggled on to the head in one minute**. Marcos placed one of a trio of hats on his head 71 times in the course of juggling them for 60 sec on 7 Jul 2015.

Footballs juggled

Victor Rubilar (ARG) juggled five soccer balls at the same time on 4 Nov 2006 at the Gallerian shopping centre in Stockholm, Sweden. This equals the record held by a number of jugglers, including Enrico Rastelli (RUS), Toni Störzenbach (DEU), Eddy Carello Jr (CHE) and Andreas Wessels (DEU).

Farthest distance skied while juggling three objects

On 16 Mar 2019, Lukas Pichler (AUT) skied 569.2 m (1,867 ft) while juggling three balls in Kirchbach, Austria. Lukas is a passionate skier and wanted to break this record on the Skiing Lift Kirchbach slope.

Aaron also juggles with flaming axes and chainsaws, and even with a sword balanced on his head.

Images of women juggling have been found on the walls of a tomb in Beni Hasan in Egypt dating from 2000 BCE.

Torches juggled on a balance board

Josh Horton (USA) juggled five torches while standing on a balance board on 3 Nov 2017 at Art Factory in Paterson, New Jersey, USA. Josh set the record for **most samurai swords juggled** – four – on the same day.

360° spins while juggling three objects in three minutes

On 7 Nov 2019, Michael Ferreri (ESP, see left) completed 102 spins in 180 sec while juggling three objects. This took place in Lakewood, California, USA.

Michael has also achieved the **most consecutive backcross juggling catches (three objects)** – 433, on 2 Sep 2019.

Juggling catches in one minute while hanging suspended by the teeth (three objects)

On 4 Jul 2019, Leonardo Costache (ROM) completed 195 juggling catches of three clubs in 60 sec. The iron-jawed performer was hanging suspended by the teeth above a circus ring in Gilleleje, Denmark.

▶ Juggling tricks in one minute (three balls)

Taylor Glenn (USA) performed 39 tricks – including behind-the-back and under-the-leg throws – with a trio of balls in 60 sec on 16 Dec 2018. The attempt took place at SkillCon in Las Vegas, Nevada, USA.

Most juggling catches in three minutes (three balls)

Mark Hanson (USA) made 1,320 catches of a trio of juggling balls in 180 sec – seven every second – on 2 Jun 2019 in Garner, Iowa, USA. Mark used the "shower" juggling pattern, where the balls are transferred in a circular motion. He kept count with a metronome.

Fastest mile bounce-juggling three basketballs

Bob Evans (USA) ran a mile bounce-juggling three basketballs in 6 min 23.97 sec on 31 Aug 2019 in Warrenton, Oregon, USA. Bounce jugglers transfer objects from hand to hand by bouncing them off the ground or another hard surface. Bob and his wife Trish are juggling acrobats.

Most items juggled

Prop		Number	Juggler(s)	Date
Balls	Juggled	11	Alex Barron (UK, pictured above)	3 Apr 2012
	Flashed*	14	Alex Barron	19 Apr 2017
	Passed (duo)	15	Chris & Andrew Hodge (both USA)	Feb 2011
Clubs	Juggled	8	Anthony Gatto (USA)	30 Aug 2006
	Flashed	9	Bruce Tiemann; Scott Sorensen; Chris Fowler; Daniel Eaker (all USA)	various
	Passed (duo)	13	Wes Peden (USA) & Patrik Elmnert (SWE)	2009
Rings	Juggled	10	Anthony Gatto	2005
	Flashed	13	Albert Lucas (USA)	28 Jun 2002
	Passed (duo)	15	Tony Pezzo (USA) & Patrik Elmnert (SWE)	Aug 2010

*A "flash" is an exercise that focuses on throwing form. Jugglers throw the objects in a juggling pattern, then catch them without repeating the pattern. The aim is to get the most objects possible in the air at the same time.

EUROPEAN JUGGLING CONVENTION

First staged in 1978, the European Juggling Convention is the largest of its kind in the world. The 2019 edition was held on 3–11 Aug in Newark, Nottinghamshire, UK. Always on the lookout for exciting new talent, GWR was in attendance to adjudicate a number of record attempts. Find out how the jugglers and performers got on below...

▶ Most somersaults on a Korean cradle in one minute

The team of Roisin Morris (IRL) and Massimiliano Rossetti (ITA) completed 16 somersaults on a Korean cradle in 60 sec. They improved their own world record by two. Thrower Massimiliano stood upright on a raised platform, catching acrobat Roisin between somersaults. A Korean cradle is a piece of aerial circus equipment that allows a standing performer (the "thrower") to swing and toss another performer (the "flyer") high above their head.

▶ Most juggling catches while blindfolded on a balance board

"Jack Flash", aka Simon West (NZ), completed 74 juggling catches, beating the previous mark set by David Rush (see opposite page) by 23.

▶ Longest duration performing a five-hula-hoop split

Eve Everard (AUS) spun five hula hoops around separate parts of her body for 5 min 2.34 sec. Circus artist Eve has performed all around the world.

Urban Sports

Highest jump on a pogo stick
On 20 Nov 2018, Dmitry Arsenyev (RUS) bounced his way into the record books, clearing a bar set at 3.40 m (11 ft 1 in) on his pogo stick in Rome, Italy. The **longest jump on a pogo stick** is 5.52 m (18 ft 1 in), by multiple world champion Dalton Smith (USA) on 18 May 2019 in Tokyo, Japan.

Most parkour backward somersaults against a wall in 30 seconds
On 14 Jan 2018, Dinesh Sunar (NPL) completed 16 backward somersaults kicking off a wall in half a minute in Kathmandu, Nepal. Dinesh is a police officer, stuntman and parkour enthusiast. On 11 Mar 2019, he achieved the **most parkour twisting backflips off a wall in 30 seconds** – 12.

Longest parkour side flip
Jacob Major (USA) executed a 5.71-m-long (18-ft 8-in) side flip in Indian River, Florida, USA, on 13 May 2015.

The **male record** – 79.94 m (262 ft 3 in), by Sertan Aydın (TUR) – is almost 2 m (6 ft 6 in) shorter than Bilge's.

Longest underwater walk with one breath
On 25 Mar 2019, freediver Bilge Çingigiray (TUR) walked 81.60 m (267 ft 8 in) along the bottom of a swimming pool on a single breath in Istanbul, Turkey. That's four times the length of a tenpin bowling alley. Bilge spent almost two-and-a-half minutes underwater, carrying a dumbbell to prevent her from floating to the surface. She reclaimed the record, having last held it in 2017.

Highest bicycle bunny hop
Rick Koekoek (NLD) bunny-hopped over a bar set at 1.45 m (4 ft 9 in) at Prudential RideLondon FreeCycle on 29 Jul 2017 in London, UK. The **highest bicycle forward step-up** – 1.79 m (5 ft 10 in) by László Hegedűs (HUN) – and the **longest bar-to-bar bicycle jump** – 2.81 m (9 ft 2 in) by Andrei Burton (UK) – were also set at the same event.

Fastest 50 m hand skating
Mirko Hanßen (DEU) inline skated 50 m (164 ft) on his hands in 8.55 sec on 16 Nov 2017 in Bocholt, North Rhine-Westphalia, Germany. He trained for four years to perfect the art of skating upside down, and can perform skills including slaloming, front and back flips and even a ramp jump.

Highest unicycle platform high jump (male)
On 3 Aug 2018, unicyclist Mike Taylor (UK) jumped up on to a 1.48-m-tall (4-ft 10-in) pallet platform at Unicon XIX in Ansan, South Korea. For his record to count, Mike had to remain mounted for three seconds on top of the pallet – as per International Unicycling Federation guidelines.

Longest highline walk with harness (ISA-verified)
On 24 Jul 2019, Lukas Irmler (DEU) and Mia Noblet (CAN) crossed a 1,975-m-long (6,479-ft) highline at Slackfest in Asbestos, Quebec, Canada. It took Lukas 58 min to complete his walk; Mia finished in 2 hr 10 min. The line was stretched 250 m (820 ft) above the ground.

Longest longline walk without harness (female, ISA-verified)
Annalisa Casiraghi (ITA) traversed a 305-m (1,000-ft) slackline across a field near Bern, Switzerland, on 17 Sep 2019.

Most skateboard ollies in one minute
On 25 Aug 2018, Adam Żaczek (POL) landed 82 skateboard jumps in 60 sec in Andrespol, Łódzkie Wschodnie, Poland. The **most consecutive skateboard ollies** is 302, by Nicholas Drachman (USA) on 14 Oct 2018 in Providence, Rhode Island, USA.

Longest urban downhill bicycle race
On 2 Dec 2018, a group of 26 daredevil bikers took to the steep streets of Medellín's Commune 13 in Colombia to compete on a demanding 2.274-km-long (1.412-mi) course. The Downhill Challenge Medellín 2018, staged by PX Sports (MEX), featured stairs, hairpin corners and even an escalator. Pedro Ferreira won the race in 3 min 49 sec.

Colombia also hosts the **longest downhill bicycle stair race**. The "Devotos de Monserrate" in Bogotá measured 2.40 km (1.49 mi) on 16 Feb 2019.

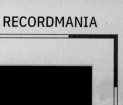

To celebrate their GWR title, the slackliners also took to the highline at night.

Highest urban highline walk with harness (ISA-verified)

On 8 Sep 2019, in an event organized by Anna Vlasova of Slackline Tribe and Moscow Seasons (RUS), a line of flat webbing was stretched at a height of 350 m (1,148 ft) between the OKO Tower and Neva Towers in Moscow, Russia. Seven fearless slackliners – Alexander Gribanov (pictured), Maxim Kagin, Vladimir Murzaev, Gennady Skripko (all RUS), Mia Noblet (CAN), Friedi Kuhne (DEU) and Nathan Pauling (FRA) – made it across the 216-m-long (708-ft) highline. Their feat was ratified by the International Slackline Association (ISA).

Slacklining was invented in the early 1980s by climbers Adam Grosowsky and Jeff Ellington in Yosemite National Park in California, USA.

Round-Up

Longest duration pole-sitting in a barrel
Vernon Kruger (ZAF) remained atop a 25-m (82-ft) pole for 75 days in Dullstroom, Mpumalanga, South Africa, from Oct to Dec 2019. In doing so, he surpassed his own record of 67 days 14 min, set in Dullstroom in 1997. Vernon planned both feats as fundraising events and donated all proceeds to charity.

▶ Largest model train set
Miniatur Wunderland (DEU) is home to a model train set with 15.7 km (9.7 mi) of track, as ratified in Hamburg, Germany, on 14 Aug 2019. Built to a ratio of 1:87, it's also the ◉ **largest model train set (scale length)**, with an equivalent real-world extent of 1,367.2 km (849.5 mi) – the distance from Madrid in Spain to Rome, Italy.

Farthest distance fire-walking
Csaba Kerekes (HUN) walked 200 m (656 ft) on red-hot embers in Szalafő, Vas, Hungary, on 27 Sep 2019.

Largest firework phrase
Sheikh Zayed Festival (UAE) spelled "HAPPY NEW YEAR 2020" with 320 fireworks in Al Wathba, Abu Dhabi, UAE, on 1 Jan 2020. Each word was displayed at an interval of one second to celebrate the start of the new year.

Largest Christmas snowflake ornament
On 28 Oct 2019, Universal Studios Japan unveiled a snowflake decoration that measured 3.196 m (10 ft 5 in) on its longest axis in Osaka, Japan.

Maintaining the festive theme, at the same event the company also presented the **most lights on an artificial Christmas tree** – 591,840.

Largest lightsaber battle
On 2 Nov 2019, Kalamazoo Wings (USA) brought together 3,889 combatants wielding *Star Wars*-inspired lightsabers in Kalamazoo, Michigan, USA.

Highest launch of an effervescent tablet rocket
BYU Rocketry (USA) sent a tablet rocket fizzing 269.13 m (883 ft) skywards at the Kennedy Space Center Visitor Complex in Florida, USA, on 12 Dec 2018.

Longest bra chain
Jennifer Jolicoeur, Athena's Home Novelties and The Athena's Cup (all USA) linked up 196,564 brassieres in Woonsocket, Rhode Island, USA, on 16 Oct 2019.

Longest duration...
• **On a slackline between two moving cars**: On 14 Dec 2019, Lu Anmin, backed by Chevrolet (both CHN), balanced for 1 min 57.28 sec between two moving vehicles in Beijing, China.
• **Spinning a frying pan on one finger**: Fayis Nazer (IND) spun a pan on a finger for a digitally demanding 1 hr 12 sec in Kerala, India, on 13 Sep 2019.
• **Live-stream (video)**: From 13 to 20 May 2019, three people in Hulu's (USA) social team plus guests took turns to watch a 161-hr 11-min 32-sec stream of *Game of Thrones* in its entirety – twice. The venue was Hulu's Santa Monica HQ in California, USA.

Most fire-breathing backflips in one minute
Ryan Luney (UK) blew 17 flames while performing backflips in 60 sec on 21 Jun 2019 in Antrim, UK. On the same day, he also achieved the even trickier **most fire-breathing full corkscrew flips in one minute** – 11 flames blown, but with a full 360° twist incorporated into each backflip.

Thinking big on a small scale: this mini marvel is the work of German twins Frederik and Gerrit Braun.

FASTEST...

100 m zorbing
James Duggan (IRL) covered 100 m (328 ft) in 23.21 sec while inside an inflatable ball in Dunmanway, Cork, Ireland, on 8 Sep 2019.

Marathon wearing *geta*
Hirokazu Fukunami (JPN) ran a marathon in 3 hr 58 min 43 sec in traditional Japanese platform sandals at the Osaka Marathon in Japan on 1 Dec 2019.

MOST...

Monster trucks jumped in a monster truck
Colton Eichelberger (USA) launched his big-wheeled behemoth over seven others in Orlando, Florida, USA, on 11 May 2019.

Sword swallows in three minutes
On 22 Dec 2019, Wang Lei (CHN) swallowed a 44-cm (1-ft 7.3-in) sword 22 times in Dezhou, Shandong, China.

Consecutive books identified from their first sentence
Schoolboy Montgomery-Everard Lord (UK) named 129 successive books from their opening lines on 12 Dec 2019 in Bolton, UK.
On 13 Feb 2020, he also set the **fastest time to identify 10 books by main character** – 11.15 sec.

People unboxing simultaneously
Xiaomi Inc (USA) brought together 703 individuals to unwrap items in New York City, USA, on 21 Dec 2019.

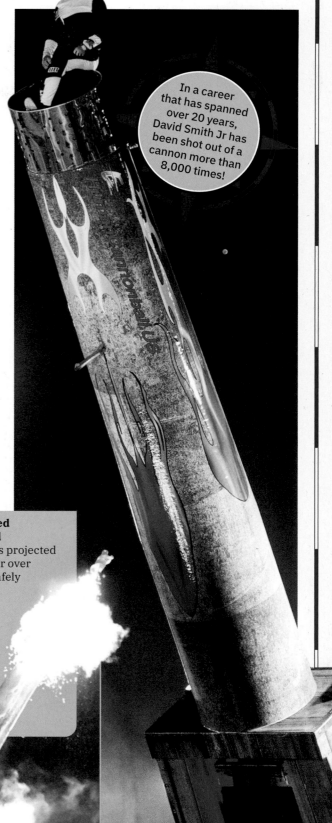

In a career that has spanned over 20 years, David Smith Jr has been shot out of a cannon more than 8,000 times!

Fastest half marathon wearing high heels
On 8 Sep 2019, Holly Ferguson (UK) completed a half marathon in 3 hr 35 min 52 sec as part of the Great North Run in Newcastle upon Tyne, Tyne and Wear, UK. Sporting 10-cm (4-in) heels (inset), Holly ran with her firefighter colleagues, all dressed as superheroes and villains. As part of her preparation, she ran 28.9 km (18 mi) in conventional sneakers.

Marathon distance in a robotic walking device (male)
Adam Gorlitsky (USA) battled pain, exhaustion and micro-blackouts to complete the Charleston Marathon in 33 hr 16 min 28 sec on 11 Jan 2020 in North Carolina, USA. Gorlitsky had competed in more than 40 races in his ReWalk Robotic Exoskeleton as part of his nonprofit "I Got Legs" initiative. But this was only the second marathon he had attempted – and the first that he had completed.

Greatest height achieved by a human cannonball
David Smith Jr (USA) was projected 27.12 m (89 ft) into the air over a Ferris wheel, to land safely on an airbed, in Riyadh, Saudi Arabia, on 26 Nov 2019. The previous year, on 13 Mar, David travelled the **farthest distance by a human cannonball** – 59.43 m (195 ft) – on behalf of Xbox and *Sea of Thieves* in Tampa, Florida, USA.

Most diamonds set on a toilet
Aaron Shum Jewelry Ltd (HKG), in collaboration with its Swiss signature brand Coronet, decorated a toilet seat with 40,815 diamonds, as verified on 22 Oct 2019 in Hong Kong, China. The gold-plated, 334.68-carat convenience was valued at $1,288,000 (£994,000).

Possibly to provide an additional level of security, the diamonds in the seat are embedded within bullet-proof glass.

GUINNESS WORLD RECORDS®

○ HALL OF FAME

Aaron Fotheringham

Outrageous skills. Steely determination. Guts. No doubt about it: Fotheringham's daredevil feats have made him an icon.

○ Aaron "Wheelz" Fotheringham (USA) is a sportsman whose daredevil feats have made him an icon.

Aaron was born with spina bifida, a condition that left him unable to use his legs. When he was aged eight, he was encouraged to try riding his wheelchair at skate parks by his BMX-crazy brother, Brian. Inevitably, he fell over. Inevitably, being Aaron, he tried again until he improved. Soon, he was winning BMX freestyle contests, nailing tricky mid-air 180° turns, and earned himself his first GWR title with the **first landed wheelchair backflip** in 2008 (see right).

In 2012, Aaron achieved the **longest duration balancing a side wheelie in a manual wheelchair** – 18.22 sec – in Rome, Italy. On 20 Jul 2018, he nailed the ○ **highest wheelchair hand plant** – 8.40 m (27 ft 6.7 in) – at Woodward West in Tehachapi, California, USA.

Aaron worked with Box Wheelchairs to design a lightweight vehicle tough enough to withstand serious punishment. He uses it on his stunt-packed ramp jump during the Rio opening ceremony and rode it for his 2016 Paralympic Games jaw-dropping ramp jump (see below right). Aaron has even inspired a Hot Wheels toy (inset), based on his high-spec chair.

Today, he's pioneering wheelchair motocross, aka "WCMX". The sport held its first world championships in Germany in 2019 and now devotees want to see it formally accepted into the Paralympics. Aaron's vision and stellar feats have made him an inspiration to countless fans, whether wheelchair users or not.

"You know, you're on a wheelchair. It's not a prison."

1

1: Captured halfway to achieving the ○ **farthest wheelchair ramp jump** – 21.35 m (70 ft 0.5 in) – on 20 Jul 2018.

2: Aaron showing off his daredevil skills on tour with action-sports company Nitro Circus in Nov 2013.

3: Performing on 25 Oct 2008 at Doc Romeo skate park in Las Vegas, Nevada, USA. Aaron takes the plunge for the ○ **tallest backflip on a wheelchair**.

4: Aaron's wheelchair **first landed wheelchair quarter-pipe drop-in on a wheelchair** (27 ft 6.7 in).

5: Opening the Rio 2016 Paralympic Games in style with a spectacular ramp jump – 8.40 m on 20 Jul 2018.

2

3

Find out more about Aaron in the Hall of Fame section at **www.guinnessworldrecords.com/2021**

Aaron's bespoke vehicle, made by Box Wheelchairs, has a reinforced frame, special wheels, and front and back suspension.

5

4

GUINNESS WORLD RECORDS

CERTIFICATE

OFFICIALLY AMAZING

RECORD HOLDER

The highest wheelchair hand plant (WCMX) was achieved by Aaron Fotheringham (USA) in Los Angeles, California on 20 July 2018

Aside from sheer determination, Aaron owes his success to relentless practice. To keep himself safe, he wears protective padding, a naturally safe, he wears protective padding, a helmet and neck brace.

Culture & Society

Largest cemetery
The Wadi al-Salam ("Valley of Peace") in the city of Najaf, Iraq, is a burial ground covering 9.17 km² (3.54 sq mi) – larger than Gibraltar – and has been in continuous use since the seventh century. Shi'ite Muslims from across Iraq, Iran and, more recently, the wider world, choose to be buried in the heart of the holy city, with funeral prayers at the nearby Imam Ali Mosque. The latter contains the tomb of Ali ibn Abi Talib, the first Shi'ite imam (religious leader). In Shi'ite Islam, only the Great Mosque of Mecca and the Prophet's Mosque in Medina, both in Saudi Arabia, are considered more important than this shrine as a pilgrimage destination.

The graveyard incorporates tens of thousands of crypts, mausoleums and catacombs. Some may hold as many as 50 sets of human remains.

DESTINATIONS

Archaeology

Largest pyramid
The Great Pyramid of Cholula – aka Tlachihualtepetl ("man-made mountain") – in Puebla, Mexico, stands 66 m (216 ft) tall and its base covers an area of 16 ha (39.5 acres). The total volume has been estimated at 3.3 million m³ (166 million cu ft) – almost 1 million m³ more than Giza's Pyramid of Khufu in Egypt.

Highest-altitude archaeological site
On 16 Mar 1999, three Incan mummies were discovered at 6,736 m (22,100 ft) above sea level at the peak of the Llullaillaco mountain in Argentina. The frozen remains belonged to child-sacrifice victims who had died *c.* 500 years ago. The archaeological team was led by Dr Johan Reinhard (USA) and Dr Constanza Ceruti (ARG) and funded by the National Geographic Society.

The **lowest-altitude archaeological site**, meanwhile, is the Byzantine monastery

Largest amphitheatre
The iconic Flavian amphitheatre – or Colosseum – in Rome, Italy, covers 2 ha (5 acres) and measures 187 m (613 ft) long and 157 m (515 ft) wide. Completed in 80 CE, the Colosseum staged gladiatorial contests, animal hunts and dramas for up to 87,000 spectators. Earthquakes and stone robbers have left it partially ruined.

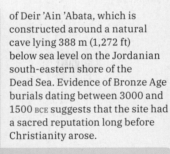

of Deir 'Ain 'Abata, which is constructed around a natural cave lying 388 m (1,272 ft) below sea level on the Jordanian south-eastern shore of the Dead Sea. Evidence of Bronze Age burials dating between 3000 and 1500 BCE suggests that the site had a sacred reputation long before Christianity arose.

Oldest mummies
The earliest examples of artificial mummification have been traced to the Chinchorro, a coastal tribe that lived on the fringes of the Atacama Desert (in modern-day Peru and Chile) between *c.* 7020 and 1110 BCE. (By comparison, the earliest-known Egyptian mummies date to *c.* 4500 BCE.) Initially, the Chinchorro culture took advantage of the arid conditions in this region to naturally preserve their dead, before developing more complex techniques. These involved removing the skin, muscles and organs of the deceased before "reupholstering" the body with wood, plants and clay. The skin would then be replaced and smothered with a paste made from substances such as manganese, red ochre or mud. Often, the face would be covered with a clay mask (see inset) painted in the same style.

MOST HISTORIC SHIPWRECKS VISITED

Marine archaeologist Alejandro Mirabal (CUB) explored the remains of 243 shipwrecks in seas all over the world between Dec 1986 and Aug 2017.

How did you get into marine archaeology?
I started free diving at eight years old and made my first SCUBA immersion at 14. I didn't know about archaeology, I just wanted to dive. Then I joined the excavation team for the *Nuestra Señora de las Mercedes*, a galleon in the 1698 Tierra Firme treasure fleet that sank off the western coast of Cuba. I got hooked, and did my specialization in Maritime Archaeology a year later.

What is the most valuable artefact you have found?
For an archaeologist, all artefacts are valuable! Our team has recovered items estimated at $220 m [£178 m]. Only 108 astrolabes [navigational instruments] are known to exist, and I have been lucky enough to find six of them.

Which wrecks are still on your must-dive list?
I would love to find the remains of any of Christopher Columbus's ships during his trips to America, such as the *Santa María* or the *Vizcaína*. Or the lead coffin where Sir Francis Drake was buried at sea off Panama.

Any tips for would-be shipwreck divers?
Do it responsibly, ethically and respectfully. Underwater Cultural Heritage sites are non-renewable resources and we often have only one chance to recover the history contained in them.

A TASTE OF ANCIENT HISTORY: OLDEST...

Leftovers
400,000–200,000 BCE
Marrow-rich deer bones discovered in Qesem Cave near Tel Aviv, Israel. They had been stored for future use by drying the outer layer of skin and bone

Bread
c. 12,380 BCE
Charred flatbread aged 14,400 years old; unearthed at a dig site in the Black Desert, Jordan, by archaeologists from the University of Copenhagen (DNK)

Plants cultivated for food
9500 BCE
Eight species of Neolithic "founder" crop domesticated by early Holocene farming communities in south-west Asia's Fertile Crescent region

Alcoholic beverage
7000 BCE
Chemical evidence found inside pottery jars excavated at the early Neolithic village of Jiahu in the Yellow River Valley, Henan, China

Wine
6000–5800 BCE
Residues of tartaric acid – evidence of early wine-making – in ancient pottery excavated in Gadachrili Gora and Shulaveris Gora, Georgia

Beer
3500 BCE
Detected in remains of a jug found at Godin Tepe, Iran, in 1973 during a Royal Ontario Museum (CAN) expedition

Chocolate
c. 3280 BCE
Evidence of early cacao processing from 5,300–5,450 years ago was found at the Amazon site of Santa Ana-La Florida in Ecuador, as revealed on 29 Oct 2018

Newest human species

On 10 Apr 2019, a new species of human from the Late Pleistocene era (*c.* 67,000–50,000 years ago) was described in *Nature*. Named *Homo luzonensis*, the discovery is based on remains excavated on the island of Luzon in the Philippines. *H. luzonensis* has curved finger bones, which could indicate arboreal (tree-dwelling) behaviour.

Longest-surviving hominin

Fossil evidence of *Homo erectus* dated as recently as 108,000–117,000 years ago has been found in a bone bed (deposit of bones) in Central Java, Indonesia, according to a study published in *Nature* in Dec 2019. The earliest *H. erectus* remains, unearthed in Africa, have been aged at *c.* 1.9 million years old. This means that *H. erectus* lived on Earth roughly nine times longer than our own species – *H. sapiens* – has to date.

Longest continuous excavation

The Roman city of Pompeii, located south of Naples in Italy, was buried under volcanic ash and pumice when Mount Vesuvius erupted in 79 CE. In 1748, a full-scale excavation began under Spain's King Charles III. Pompeii was formally identified in 1763, and work on the site has been ongoing in some form ever since.

Oldest figurative art

On 11 Dec 2019, a paper in *Nature* described a 4.5-m-long (nearly-15-ft) cave art panel on the Indonesian island of Sulawesi. The artwork depicts a scene of four small buffalo (most likely anoa) and two wild pigs being hunted by weapon-wielding human-like figures. Uranium-series dating on overlying deposits of calcium carbonate suggests that elements of the painting are at least 43,900 years old. Even older examples of stencilled art, such as hand prints, have been discovered.

Largest trove of Iron Age coins

In 2012, a hoard of 69,347 coins dating from 50 BCE to 10 CE was discovered by metal detectorists Richard Miles and Reg Mead (both UK, the latter pictured) in Grouville, Jersey, UK. The coins – found at a depth of 1 m (3 ft) – are believed to have been buried by the Celtic Coriosolitae tribe. The value of the cache has been estimated at £10 m ($16.1 m).

OLDEST...

Shipwreck site

All that remains of the Early Bronze Age "Dokos shipwreck" is a pair of stone anchors and collection of clay pottery, found 20 m (65 ft) below the sea – dated to *c.* 2,200 BCE. The remnants were found in the Aegean Sea off the Greek island of Dokos by Peter Throckmorton of the Hellenic Institute of Marine Archaeology in 1975.

Surviving wooden building

The Hōryū-ji temple in Ikaruga, Nara, Japan, was constructed in 607 CE and is one of 48 buildings in the area protected by UNESCO. Analysis of the central pillar of the temple's five-storey pagoda suggests that the wood was initially felled in 594 CE.

Bog body

Naturally mummified corpses found in peat bogs can be incredibly well preserved, owing to a lack of oxygen and microbes in this environment. The so-called "Koelbjerg Man" was discovered in 1941 in a bog near Odense in Denmark. Carbon dating indicates that he died aged 25 years around 8000 BCE, during the time of the Maglemosian culture in northern Europe.

"Chewing gum"

Birch pitch is a blackish-brown, gum-like substance that was widely used as a form of adhesive throughout the Neolithic era. Teeth impressions show that it was also chewed – probably to make it more pliable for manipulation, but also for its antiseptic qualities and ability to relieve toothache. On 15 May 2019, the journal *Communications Biology* reported that birch pitch aged at 9,540–9,880 years old had been excavated in western Sweden.

Oldest pyramid

The Djoser Step Pyramid at Saqqara in Egypt was designed *c.* 2630 BCE by Pharaoh Djoser's royal architect, Imhotep. It began as a flat-roofed *mastaba* or tomb, with additional levels added on top of it. Recent evidence also suggests that an ancient city featuring up to 20 pyramids was constructed at Caral in Peru around the same time, perhaps as early as 2700–2600 BCE.

Cake
2200 BCE
Found sealed and vacuum-packed in the grave of Egyptian prince Pepionkh. Currently displayed in the Alimentarium Food Museum in Vevey, Switzerland

Bowl of noodles
c. 2050 BCE
Noodles made from millet preserved under an upturned bowl, found 3 m (10 ft) below the ground at the Lajia site in Qinghai, China

Cheese
1300–1201 BCE
Sealed within the tomb of Ptahmes, the mayor of the city of Memphis in Egypt; the results were published on 25 Jul 2018 in Analytical Chemistry

Wanderlust

The **female** trans-America record is 69 days 2 hr 40 min, by Mavis Hutchison (ZAF) from 12 Mar to 21 May 1978.

New Zealand
Between 1 Jan and 5 Feb 2020, Menna Evans (UK) ran the 2,090-km (1,300-mi) distance between Cape Reinga on North Island and Bluff on South Island – a total of 35 days 27 min. Evans, who ran on behalf of mental-health charities Mind and Save the Brave, said a GWR title was "the absolute cherry on top of a… once-in-a-lifetime experience".

Iceland
Tom Whittle (UK) ran some 700 km (435 mi) across Iceland, north to south, in 10 days 13 hr 14 min between 4 and 14 Oct 2018.

Qatar
Jad Hamdan (FRA) crossed the Middle Eastern state from Al Ruwais to Salwa in 1 day 23 hr 56 min between 6 and 8 Dec 2019.

Lebanon
It took Ali Wehbi (LBN) 1 day 15 hr 49 min to cross Lebanon, from 31 Mar to 2 Apr 2018. Ali began in Arida and ended in Naqoura.

▶ Fastest time to visit all sovereign countries
Taylor Demonbreun (USA) toured the globe in 1 year 189 days, from 1 Jun 2017 to 7 Dec 2018. She visited the 195 countries stated in GWR guidelines, comprising the 193 UN member states, Vatican City and Chinese Taipei. Taylor began in the Dominican Republic and ended in Canada; above, she is at Machu Picchu in Peru, the **most-visited Inca site.**

Longest ongoing pilgrimage
As of 24 Apr 2013, evangelist Arthur Blessitt (USA) had roamed 64,752 km (40,235 mi) across all seven continents, including Antarctica, since first setting out on 25 Dec 1969. He has borne a 3.7-m-tall (12-ft) wooden cross throughout his pilgrimage and preaches from the Bible as he goes.

FASTEST CROSSING BY FOOT

Canada
Al Howie (UK) ran from St John's in Newfoundland to the British Columbian capital of Victoria in 72 days 10 hr 23 min. He began on 21 Jun and ended on 1 Sep 1991, having covered 7,295.5 km (4,533.2 mi).

Between 17 Apr and 8 Sep 2002, Ann Keane (CAN) achieved the **female** record, going from St John's to Tofino, British Columbia, in 143 days. Her route covered 7,831 km (4,866 mi).

USA
On 12 Sep 2016, Pete Kostelnick (USA) set out from San Francisco City Hall in California and reached New York City Hall by 24 Oct 2016. His trek lasted 42 days 6 hr 30 min.

Fastest time to visit all NFL stadiums
It took Jacob Blangsted-Barnor (UK, right) 84 days 3 hr 24 min to watch a game in all of the USA's 31 National Football League stadiums between 5 Sep and 28 Nov 2019.

The **fastest time to visit all Major League Baseball parks** is 29 days, by Michael Wenz and Jacob Lindhorst (both USA) from 12 Jun to 10 Jul 2005. They were also required to watch a full game at each of the 30 venues.

Fastest time to visit all Munich U-Bahn stations
It took friends Alessandro Di Sano (left) and Nils Schmalbuch (both DEU) 4 hr 55 min 34 sec to pass through all 96 U-Bahn metro stations in Munich, Germany, on 17 Sep 2019.

This was surpassed just over a month later by Adham Fisher (UK), who completed the challenge in 4 hr 48 min 53 sec on 23 Oct 2019.

Fastest completion of the Pieterpad trail by foot
Wouter Huitzing (NLD) took 4 days 2 hr 16 min to navigate the 492-km (306-mi) Pieterpad trail in the Netherlands, finishing on 23 Apr 2019. The path begins in Pieterburen in the northern part of Groningen and travels south via forests, farmland, villages and cities to end just south of Maastricht, on Mount Saint Peter (aka Sint-Pietersberg).

FASTEST TIME TO VISIT…

All countries by public surface transport
Graham Hughes (UK) visited every sovereign country without flying in 4 years 30 days between 1 Jan 2009 and 31 Jan 2013.

All Disney theme parks
Lindsay Nemeth (CAN) completed her 75-hr 6-min survey of the world's 12 Disney theme parks on 6 Dec 2017 at Tokyo DisneySea in Urayasu, Chiba, Japan.

All London Underground stations
On 21 May 2015, Steve Wilson (UK) and AJ (full name and nationality withheld) called at all 270 London Tube stations in a whistlestop tour of 15 hr 45 min 38 sec.

All Paris Métro stations
On 23 Feb 2016, Clive Burgess and Simon Ford (both UK) completed a 13-hr 23-min 33-sec jaunt through the 303 Métro stops in the French capital.

Every location on the London Monopoly board by foot
Alex Radford (UK) walked between the 28 sites on the famous board game in 1 hr 45 min 35 sec in London, UK, on 5 Aug 2018.

There are 32 NFL teams but only 31 stadiums, as the New York Giants and New York Jets share MetLife Stadium.

MOST...

Continents visited in one day

On 29 Apr 2017, Thor Mikalsen and his son Sondre Moan Mikalsen (both NOR) flew between countries on five different continents: Turkey (Asia), Morocco (Africa), Portugal (Europe), the USA (North America) and Colombia (South America). This equalled the feat of Gunnar Garfors (NOR) and Adrian Butterworth (UK), who travelled between Istanbul, Turkey, and Caracas, Venezuela, on 18 Jun 2012.

▶ Most sovereign capital cities visited in 24 hours by scheduled transport

On 25–26 Nov 2018, Adam Leyton (left) and Chris Fletcher (both UK) journeyed to nine capital cities on planes, trains and buses, starting in London, UK, and ending in Budapest. The duo arrived in the Hungarian capital with 10 min to spare!

Countries visited by bicycle in 24 hours

Dávid Kővári (HUN) rode through seven countries on 23–24 Aug 2017: Poland, the Czech Republic, Slovakia, Austria, Hungary, Slovenia and Croatia.

Hungary's Maja Tóth holds the **female** record. She cycled between five countries – Slovakia, Austria, Hungary, Slovenia and Croatia – on 14 Jun 2018.

The **team** record is also seven countries. On 1–2 Oct 2016, James van der Hoorn and Thomas Reynolds (both UK) toured Croatia, Slovenia, Hungary, Austria, Slovakia and the Czech Republic before ending in Poland.

Countries visited by electric car (single charge)

On 7–8 Jul 2016, Frederik Van Overloop (BEL) drove a Tesla Model S across seven nations: Switzerland, Liechtenstein, Austria, Germany, Italy, Slovenia and Croatia.

Mar 2019 found Lexie roasting marshmallows by the Darvaza Crater – itself a record-breaker (see p.40).

Youngest person to visit all sovereign countries

Lexie Alford (USA, b. 10 Apr 1998) was aged 21 years 177 days when she arrived in the final country on her list – Mozambique – on 4 Oct 2019. Helpfully, she'd travelled widely with her parents as a youngster: aged 18, she'd already been to around 70 countries.

The **male** record holder is James Asquith (UK, b. 30 Dec 1988). He was 24 years 190 days old on 8 Jul 2013 when he completed his globe-trotting odyssey, terminating in the Federated States of Micronesia in the Pacific Ocean.

Countries visited by train in 24 hours

Alison Bailey, Ian Bailey, John English and David Kellie (all UK) rode through 11 countries on 1–2 May 1993. Departing from Hungary, it took them 22 hr 10 min to reach their final stop, the Netherlands.

UNESCO World Heritage Sites visited in 24 hours

On 14–15 Nov 2019, Adam Leyton and Chris Fletcher (see above left) visited 20 UNESCO cultural sites in a day. Their 1,930-km (1,200-mi) trip took in the Neolithic flint mines of Spiennes in Belgium, the Tower of London and Blenheim Palace (birthplace of Sir Winston Churchill) near Oxford, UK.

Music festivals visited in 30 days

From 24 Jun to 23 Jul 2011, Greg Parmley (UK) attended 26 music festivals, including Glastonbury, Montreux Jazz and Balaton Sound. His musical pilgrimage took in Germany, the Czech Republic, Hungary, Slovenia and Italy, among other countries.

Embassies visited in 24 hours

On 26 Mar 2019, Morocco's Omar Oualili visited 32 foreign embassies in London, UK. He began his diplomatic dash at the Embassy of the Republic of Poland and ended the day at the Guatemalan embassy.

Zoos visited

As of 6 Feb 2020, Jonas Livet (FRA) had been to 1,215 zoos, as well as 232 aquaria. He has worked as a zoological consultant for more than 30 years. His "zo-odyssey" began in 1987 at Tierpark Berlin in Germany.

Most countries visited by bicycle in seven days

Marek Dzienisiuk (POL) cycled through 14 countries – from Promachonas in Greece to Cieszyn in Poland – between 16 and 23 Sep 2018. He passed through Greece, Bulgaria, North Macedonia, Albania, Montenegro (above), Serbia, Bosnia and Herzegovina, Croatia, Slovenia, Hungary, Austria, Slovakia, the Czech Republic and Poland.

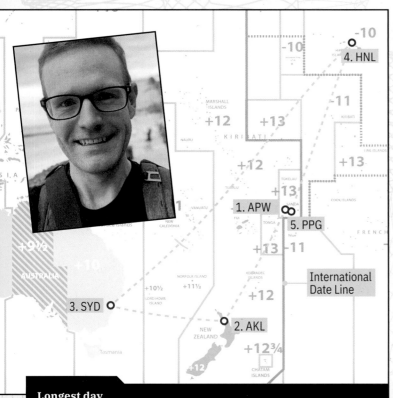

4. HNL
1. APW
5. PPG
3. SYD
2. AKL

International Date Line

Longest day

Taking advantage of closely grouped time zones bordering the International Date Line, Julian O'Shea (AUS, inset) lived through a single calendar day lasting 49 hr on 14 Feb 2019. Starting in Apia, Samoa, he journeyed to Auckland (New Zealand), Sydney (Australia) and Honolulu (Hawaii, USA), ending in Pago Pago (American Samoa). This matched the record of Mariusz Majewski (POL), who completed a 49-hr day on 13 Mar 2017.

Owing to the number of territories it governs beyond Europe, France is the **country with the most time zones**: 12 (and for a period of the year, 13).

Maps

First interactive 3D map
The Aspen Movie Map was created between Oct 1977 and Sep 1980 by a team at the MIT Media Lab in Cambridge, Massachusetts, USA. It comprised a 3D reconstruction of the town of Aspen in Colorado, USA, texture-mapped using photographs taken by stop-motion cameras mounted on a vehicle. Users could navigate around the virtual town using a touch-screen display.

OLDEST...

Clay tablet map
Maps inscribed on clay tablets dating to approximately 2300 BCE were excavated in the 1920s at Nuzi in present-day northern Iraq. They depict hills, streams and rivers, including the Euphrates, as well as various settlements.

Silk maps
In 1973–74, a pair of silk maps were recovered from tombs believed to date from the 2nd century BCE in Hunan, China. Scholars believe that the maps were created by cartographers in the court of the King of Ch'ang-sha, whose realm included Hunan.

Oldest surviving terrestrial globe
The Erdapfel ("Earth Apple") is a globe created in 1492 by German cosmographer and explorer Martin Behaim. The map was painted on to linen by Georg Glockendon just a few months before news of Columbus' voyage to the Americas reached Europe. The Erdapfel is currently housed in the German National Museum in Nuremburg.

The Erdapfel globe features Saint Brendan's Isle, a phantom medieval island once believed to exist in the North Atlantic.

Tourist guide
The *Itinerarium Burdigalense* is a guide for Christian pilgrims making the journey from the French city of Bordeaux to Jerusalem in the Holy Land. Composed by an anonymous traveller in 330 CE, it described the locations of hostels and places where pilgrims could take water and exchange horses and donkeys.

Periplus
A periplus is a navigational guide for sailors listing the ports and landmarks along a route. The Periplus of Hanno the Navigator records a sea journey to West Africa made by Carthaginian seafarer Hanno in the early-to-mid fifth century BCE. The oldest edition of the text as it survives today is a 9th-century-CE Byzantine manuscript.

Map of the New World
A chart drawn by Juan de la Cosa (ESP) in 1500 shows the Americas as a large green mass that extends to the left-hand margin

Largest surviving medieval world map
The *Hereford Mappa Mundi* measures 1.58 x 1.33 m (5 ft 2 in x 4 ft 4 in). The vellum map was created in England around 1300 and shows the world as it was known to scholars in medieval Europe. It includes 500 illustrations of people, locations and creatures, as well as events from history and classical mythology. The Garden of Eden is pictured inset, as an island ringed with fire.

of the map. De la Cosa was the captain of the *Santa María*, one of three ships to sail with Christopher Columbus in search of the New World in 1492.

MISCELLANEOUS...

Oldest surviving star chart on paper
Dating back to *c.* 649–684 CE, the Dunhuang Star Chart comprises a sequence of drawings of sky maps on rolls of vellum and depicts the constellations visible from the Northern Hemisphere. The atlas was discovered in 1907 by Hungarian-born archaeologist Aurel Stein in the Mogao Caves, Dunhuang, Gansu, China.

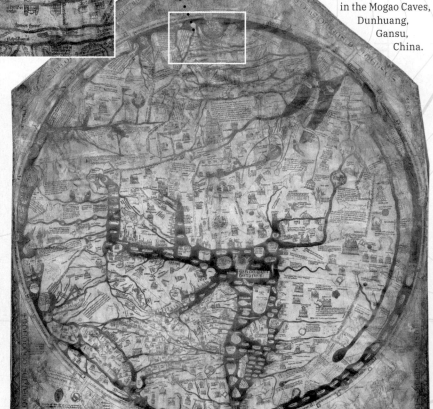

Youngest drone cartographer
On 15 Apr 2019, Nathan Lu (USA, b. 25 Sep 2004) made his first upload to US digital mapping service Soar aged 14 years 202 days. He had taken pictures of a soccer field in Rossmoor, California, USA, from a height of 113.8 m (373 ft 4 in) using his DJI Mavic Air FC2103 drone. Nathan has been mapping his neighbourhood and the surrounding environs with drones since he was 11 years old.

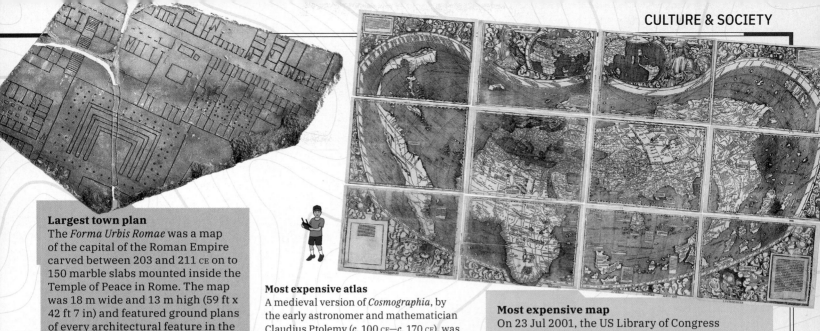

Largest town plan
The *Forma Urbis Romae* was a map of the capital of the Roman Empire carved between 203 and 211 CE on to 150 marble slabs mounted inside the Temple of Peace in Rome. The map was 18 m wide and 13 m high (59 ft x 42 ft 7 in) and featured ground plans of every architectural feature in the city, including small shops, rooms and staircases. Only fragments of the *Forma Urbis Romae* have survived.

Longest-lived phantom island
Reportedly located north-west of the Yucatán Peninsula in the Gulf of Mexico, the island of Bermeja was first described by Spanish cartographer Alonzo de Santa Cruz in 1539. The last significant map to include a depiction of Bermeja was the 1921 edition of the *Atlas of the Mexican Republic*, some 382 years later. Its invention is probably the result of early cartographical error, but Bermeja could possibly have disappeared beneath rising sea levels.

Most expensive atlas
A medieval version of *Cosmographia*, by the early astronomer and mathematician Claudius Ptolemy (*c*. 100 CE–*c*. 170 CE), was sold for £2,136,000 ($3,990,010) at Sotheby's in London, UK, on 10 Oct 2006. The atlas was printed in 1477 in Bologna, Italy, and covers the known world from the Canary Islands in the west to parts of south-east Asia. Longitudes and latitudes are provided for more than 8,000 locations.

Smallest map
In 1992, Dr Jonathon Mamin of IBM's Zürich laboratory used electrical pulses to create a map of the Western Hemisphere from atoms. The map has a scale of one trillion to one and a diameter of about one micron (one millionth of a metre) – about one hundredth of the diameter of a human hair.

Most expensive map
On 23 Jul 2001, the US Library of Congress purchased the only surviving copy of the *Universalis Cosmographia* for $10,000,000 (£7,005,500). Created by German cartographer Martin Waldseemüller in 1507, the printed wall map of the world is the first to use the name "America" to describe the New World.

Largest engraved atlas
The *Klencke Atlas* is 1.78 m high, 1.05 m wide and 11 cm thick when closed (5 ft 10 in x 3 ft 5 in x 4 in), and 2.31 m wide (7 ft 6 in) when open. Each of the atlas's 41 maps was printed from hand-drawn copperplate engravings. The *Klencke Atlas* was commissioned by a group of Dutch merchants and presented to King Charles II of England upon the restoration of the monarchy in 1660.

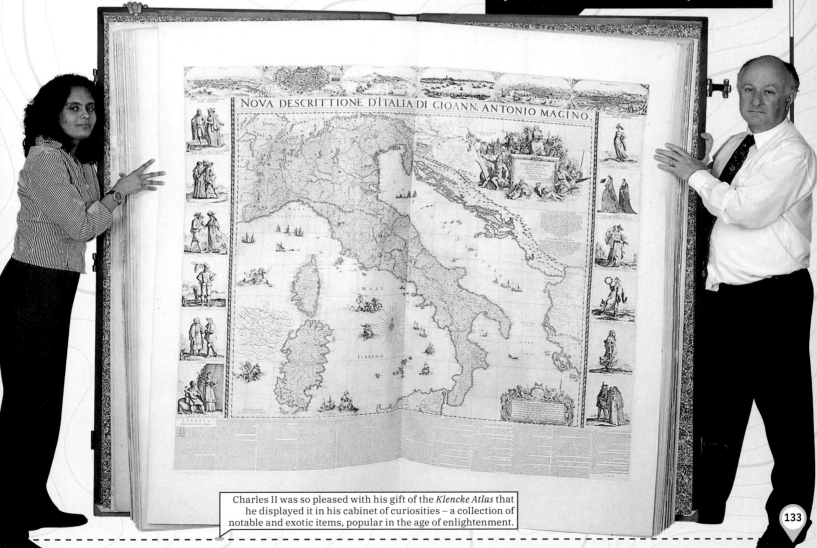

Charles II was so pleased with his gift of the *Klencke Atlas* that he displayed it in his cabinet of curiosities – a collection of notable and exotic items, popular in the age of enlightenment.

Young Achievers

▶ Fastest time to solve a Rubik's Cube on a pogo stick

Twelve-year-old George Turner (UK) finished a 3x3x3 puzzle cube in 22.89 sec on 29 Mar 2019, while pogo-sticking in Gerrards Cross, Buckinghamshire, UK. George was inspired to take up cubing by his father. "I was in such awe of my dad when he solved it... I just really wanted that ability," he revealed.

MOST...

▶ Times to fold a piece of paper

Aged 16, Britney Gallivan (USA) folded a 1,219-m-long (4,000-ft) piece of tissue paper in half 12 times at her school in Pomona, California, USA, on 27 Jan 2002. Eight times was thought to be the maximum until then.

Decimal digits memorized in five minutes

Wei Qinru (CHN) recalled 616 digits at the ASEAN Junior Memory Open championships in Nanning, China, held on 28–30 Aug 2019.

▶ Finger snaps in one minute

On 13 Sep 2018, Niclas Nadasdy (DEU) – aged 14 – snapped his fingers 334 times in 60 sec in Weissenohe, Germany.

Fastest 3-6-3 sport stacking

Aged 13, Chan Keng Ian (MYS) set up a 3-6-3 cup stack in 1.713 sec in Nilai, Malaysia, on 23 Aug 2018. He went on to set the **fastest individual cycle stack** – 4.753 sec – in Subang Jaya, Malaysia, on 19 May 2019, and the **fastest doubles cycle stack** – 5.798 sec – with Wong Jun Xian (MYS) on 9 Jun 2019.

Largest water rocket

On 10 Jun 2017, a 4-m-tall (13-ft 3-in) water rocket soared 22.8 m (75 ft) off the ground in Toronto, Ontario, Canada. The water-powered projectile was created by sibling scientists Aidan and Keeley Aird (both CAN), who are founders of the not-for-profit educational group STEM Kids Rock, which encourages other youngsters to engage with the wonders of science and technology. The rocket was made for TV series *Furze World Wonders*, which is presented by fellow record-setting amateur inventor Colin Furze (see p.172).

▶ Youngest club DJ

Archie Norbury (UK, b. 20 Nov 2014) was aged just 4 years 130 days when he played at Bungalow in Hong Kong, China, on 30 Mar 2019. He delighted the crowd with more than an hour's worth of classic house music, although his preferred genre is drum and bass.

Most consecutive football touches in one minute with a ball on the head
On 14 Nov 2019, Eche Chinoso (NGA) kept a soccer ball aloft for 60 sec with his feet and knees, making 111 touches, all the while balancing another ball on his head. Eche performed his skills showcase in Warri, Nigeria.

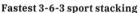

In 2017, Shristi stooped to new lows on ice, achieving the **lowest 10-m limbo ice skate**: 17.8 cm (7 in).

▶ Lowest limbo-skating over 25 m

Aged 11, Shristi Sharma (IND, pictured) skated 25 m (82 ft) under bars set at a height of just 17 cm (6.7 in) in Nagpur, Maharashtra, India, on 7 Oct 2015.
The ▶ **farthest distance limbo-skating under cars** is 115.6 m (379 ft 3 in), by 10-year-old G Devisri Prasad (IND) on 31 Aug 2017 in Amaravathi, Andhra Pradesh, India.

Youngest winner of a professional golf tournament (male)

Josh Hill (UK, b. 27 Mar 2004, above left) was aged 15 years 210 days on 23 Oct 2019 when he won the Al Ain Open on the MENA Tour in the UAE. Unfortunately, as an amateur, Josh wasn't allowed to claim the £10,477 ($13,553) winner's prize. He's shown here with five-time European Tour winner Tommy Fleetwood.

YOUNGEST...

Professional film director

Saugat Bista (NPL, b. 6 Jan 2007) was 7 years 340 days old when *Love You Baba* (NPL) was released on 12 Dec 2014. It claimed two prizes at Nepal's National Film Awards.

Chess grandmaster

• **Male**: On 12 Aug 2002, Sergey Karjakin (UKR, b. 12 Jan 1990) reached the game's top rank at the age of 12 years 212 days.
• **Female**: Hou Yifan (CHN, b. 27 Feb 1994) became a grandmaster at the age of 14 years 184 days on 29 Aug 2008.

Magazine editor

Eight-year-old Roxanne Downs (AUS) took on the role of editor for *It GiRL* magazine in early 2017. The first issue under her tenure hit the shelves in Australia and New Zealand on 6 Apr 2017. On the perks of the job, Roxanne said, "I love coming up with ideas, quizzes and getting to interview people... The freebies are great too!"

Professional music producer

Konomi Yamasaki (JPN, b. 18 Aug 2008) was 10 years 234 days old when her debut album *Burgmüller 25 Etudes* was released on 9 Apr 2019. The album comprises 25 instrumental compositions, all arranged by Konomi.

Nobel Prize laureate

Malala Yousafzai (PAK, b. 12 Jul 1997) was awarded the Nobel Peace Prize on 10 Oct 2014 at the age of 17 years 90 days. She shared the plaudit with India's Kailash Satyarthi. In Mar 2020, Malala met with fellow young trailblazer Greta Thunberg (SWE), who in 2019 became the **youngest *TIME* Person of the Year** (see pp.142–43).

Most Scripps National Spelling Bee winners

Established in 1925, the US-based Scripps National Spelling Bee has never had more than two co-winners at one of its contests. That was shattered on 30 May 2019 when eight competitors correctly spelled every word given to them by the organizers. All hailing from the USA, the so-called "Octochamps" were: Rishik Gandhasri (aged 13), Erin Howard (14), Abhijay Kodali (the youngest of the octet, aged 12), Shruthika Padhy (13), Rohan Raja (13), Christopher Serrao (13), Sohum Sukhatankar (13) and Saketh Sundar (13).

▶ Youngest person to achieve nuclear fusion

In nuclear fusion, two or more atoms are brought together to form a larger atom, also producing energy. Hours before his 13th birthday in 2018, Jackson Oswalt (USA, b. 19 Jan 2005) fused two deuterium atoms using a reactor he had built in the playroom of his family home in Memphis, Tennessee, USA. Jackson's passion for building things stems from an early age. He told GWR: "When I was younger, I worked in my grandfather's wood shop, building figurines and stuff like that... All that creativity eventually led to building something like this."

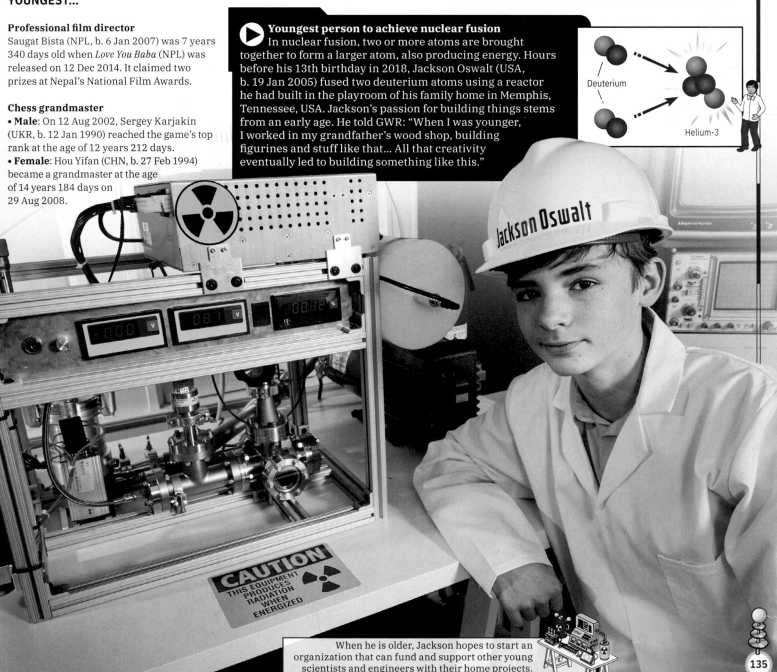

When he is older, Jackson hopes to start an organization that can fund and support other young scientists and engineers with their home projects.

Espionage

By their very nature, spying and subterfuge take place in a secretive, hidden world. Often, we only hear about covert operations and advanced surveillance technology ███████████████ long after they have been abandoned. And Official Secrets Acts hide politically sensitive and ███████████ material from the public, sometimes in perpetuity. Given which, the records that appear on these pages can offer only a partial glimpse into the organizations, extraordinary characters and ███████████ that act on behalf of secretive ██████████ and shadowy government agencies. Then again, perhaps it's best if we don't know too much…

First photo-reconnaissance satellite
On 16 Sep 1960, a US Air Force C-119 "Flying Boxcar" snatched a cannister of film out of the air as it descended under a parachute near Hawaii, USA. The cannister had been ejected from the *Discoverer 14* research probe (which was secretly a spy satellite called *Corona C-9*). This was the first successful mission of the Corona programme, which returned pictures of nuclear sites, ██████ and military bases in the Soviet Union.

ROBERT PHILIP HANSSEN
DOB 04-18-1944
65A-WF-220648

Highest sum paid for a piece of intelligence
The FBI paid $7 m (£4.8 m) to former KGB agent Aleksandr Shcherbakov (RUS) for a dossier on the mole known as "Ramon Garcia" (later identified as FBI agent Robert Hanssen; see left). The dossier was handed over to US intelligence in Moscow on 4 Nov 2000; Shcherbakov and his family were smuggled to the USA 10 days later.

Highest-ranked US officer charged with espionage
On 14 Jun 2001, retired Army Reserve colonel George Trofimoff (USA) was found guilty of spying for the USSR and Russia, including the sale of classified material. He had done so while serving as the civilian chief of the US Army Element of the Nuremberg Joint Interrogation Center, an intelligence unit in Germany, from 1969 to 1994. On 28 Sep 2001, he was sentenced to life imprisonment.

FIRST…

Official state cryptographer
Cicco Simonetta (1410–80) was a state secretary in the Duchy of Milan (in what is now Italy), one of the most meticulously informed cities in the late medieval period. In the second half of the 15th century, he was responsible for the Milanese secret chancery and its ciphers. In 1474, he published his *Regulae extraendis litteras zifferatas sive exempio* ("Rules for deciphering enciphered documents without a key").

Longest prison sentence served for espionage
Ronald Pelton (USA), a former National Security Agency analyst, served 28 years 343 days from his conviction on 16 Dec 1986 to 24 Nov 2015. Arrested by the FBI on 25 Nov 1985, he confessed to having provided the Soviet Union with details of US intelligence-gathering activities. He received three concurrent life sentences. Including the time he served on remand before his trial, Pelton was incarcerated for one day shy of 30 years.

Longest prison sentence for espionage
On 10 May 2002, FBI agent and Russian mole Robert Hanssen (USA) was given 15 consecutive life sentences with no possibility of parole. He had been passing information to the Soviet Union (and later Russia) since 1979. This unlikely double agent was an ultra-conservative Catholic and devoted career officer with a spotless disciplinary record.

Largest espionage museum
The International Spy Museum in Washington, D.C., USA, houses a collection of 9,241 espionage-related artefacts. The tools of the intelligence trade are displayed in galleries themed around stealing secrets, intelligence analysis and covert action. A considerable number of the museum's exhibits come from the **largest private collection of espionage-related items** – a hoard of more than 7,000 artefacts, documents and photographs amassed by espionage historian H Keith Melton (USA; pictured left).

Many figures involved in the US-backed struggle against the Soviet invaders became notorious terrorist leaders, including Mohammed Omar (of the Taliban) and Osama bin Laden (of al-Qaeda).

Passive listening device

"The Thing" was a microphone with no active electronic parts; it only became active when energized by an external radio signal. It comprised a metal cylinder with a thin membrane at one end and a long metal rod extending from the side. US counter-intelligence officers found it inside a huge carving of the Great Seal of the United States within the US embassy in Moscow in 1951. It's also known as the "Great Seal Bug".

Spy satellite

Launched on 22 Jun 1960, *SOLRAD 1* (aka *GRAB 1*) was a beach-ball-sized satellite designed by ██████ ████████ at the US Navy's Naval Research Laboratory. Ostensibly, it was a solar observatory. While it did produce scientific data about the Sun's X-ray emissions, its main purpose was to map the Soviet Union's air-defence radar network.

Incident of cyber-espionage

Between Sep 1986 and Jun 1987, a group of German computer hackers accessed the networks of US defence contractors, universities and military bases, then sold on the information – which included details of ██████ ██████ – to the Soviet KGB. The lead hacker, Markus Hess, was arrested on 29 Jun 1987 and convicted of espionage, along with two confederates, on 15 Feb 1990.

Longest-undetected spy

Known to Soviet intelligence as "Agent Hola", Melita Norwood (née Sirnis; UK) began passing classified information to the NKVD (the predecessor of the Soviet KGB) in 1935, becoming a full agent in 1937. She provided intelligence to her KGB handlers until retiring in 1972, around 37 years after initial contact. Norwood was a secretary at the British Non-Ferrous Metals Research Association, which oversaw research related to defence projects including the British nuclear weapons programme and ██████

Most expensive covert action

Operation Cyclone was the CIA's programme to arm and train Islamist insurgent groups (known as *mujahideen*) fighting the Soviet Red Army in Afghanistan. From 1979 to 1989, the CIA channelled some $2 bn (£1.3 bn) in weapons, logistical support and training to them. The operation was the brainchild of President Jimmy Carter's National Security Adviser, Zbigniew Brzezinski. He believed that arming the *mujahideen* would draw the Soviet Union or its proxies into a protracted, inconclusive anti-insurgency campaign (referred to as "their Vietnam"). Taken on 25 Feb 1987, the image above shows Afghan *mujahideen* with Congressman Charles "Charlie" Wilson (front, centre), a leading proponent of the project.

First robotic flying insect

The insectothopter was an artificial dragonfly capable of flying up to 200 m (656 ft). It was designed for the CIA by ██████ ██████ at the Vought Corp Advanced Technology Center in Dallas, Texas, USA. Work began on the project in the early 1970s and ended sometime after 1974. It was hoped that agents in the field would be able to pilot the insectothopter up to persons of interest, then use the reflectors in its eyes as the aim-point for a laser microphone (which detected sound from the distortion in the returned beam). It proved too fragile to use, though: even slight breezes sent it tumbling to the ground.

100%

First permanent state-run intelligence organization

There is evidence that a dedicated intelligence-gathering organization was in place in Venice from the mid-15th century. Its roots lie in the Council of Ten, formed in 1310 to assist the Doge – the republic's ruler – in matters of state security. Its remit expanded to include clandestine operations, intelligence analysis and cryptography. In time, its networks of casual informants were replaced by a professional workforce – based in the Doge's Palace (pictured) – that coordinated surveillance efforts.

Disasters

Highest-altitude mid-air collision
In the early hours of 5 Feb 1958, a US Air Force B-47 bomber collided with an F-86 fighter on a training flight over Georgia, USA, at a height of 11,582 m (38,000 ft). Remarkably – especially given that the B-47 was carrying a 3,450-kg (7,600-lb) nuclear bomb – there were no fatalities.

Costliest year for natural disasters
According to a report issued by *The Economist* on 31 Mar 2012 and based on figures from insurers Swiss Re, there was a global loss of $362 bn (£234.2 bn) in 2011 from natural disasters. The most costly single event was an earthquake off the Pacific coast of Japan on 11 Mar (see opposite).

FIRST...

Rail fatality
On 5 Dec 1821, a carpenter named David Brook (UK) was walking home from Leeds in Yorkshire, UK, along the Middleton Railway in a blinding sleet storm. He was struck and fatally injured by an oncoming train of coal wagons.

Worst damage toll from a hailstorm
On 10 Apr 2001, the Tristate Hailstorm ranged over Kansas, Missouri and Illinois, USA. It spawned a few small tornadoes and minor floods, but the worst damage was caused by hailstones, some 7 cm (2.75 in) in diameter – about the same as a cricket ball – causing $1.5 bn (£1 bn) in insured losses.

Highest death toll in a terror attack
The year 2021 marks the 20th anniversary of an event that shocked the world. According to the official count, 2,753 individuals died as a result of the attack on the World Trade Center in New York City, USA, on 11 Sep 2001. A hijacked American Airlines 767 (Flight 11) was flown into the North Tower at 8:46 a.m. Eastern Standard Time (EST). Terrorists had also seized a second 767, United Airlines (Flight 175), which struck the South Tower at 9:02 a.m. EST. On the same day, a hijacked aircraft struck the Pentagon in Washington, DC, USA, with the loss of 189 lives, and another seized plane crashed in a field in Pennsylvania, killing 44 people.

Road fatality
On 31 Aug 1869, scientist Mary Ward (IRL) was killed in an accident involving an experimental steam car on the streets of Birr in County Offaly, Ireland. The vehicle, built by her cousin, the astronomer William Parsons, was jolted by the rough road and Mary was thrown under the wheels.

Deadliest airship disaster
At around 1 a.m. on 4 Apr 1933, the USS *Akron* (ZRS-4) broke up in bad weather off the coast of New Jersey, USA. Of the 76 crew, 73 died. As with most large airships, the *Akron* (inset, seen over downtown New York City, USA) had awkward controls and was vulnerable in high winds. The most famous airships were the British *R100* and *R101*; the American *Akron* and *Macon*; and the German *Graf Zeppelin II* and *Hindenburg*. The last two remain the **largest airships**, at 213.9 tonnes (471,570 lb). Four of these six were destroyed in accidents, with 111 lives lost.

Fatal aeroplane crash
Thomas E Selfridge (USA) died on 17 Sep 1908 when the *Wright Military Flyer* (piloted by Orville Wright), on which he was a passenger, crashed during a test flight at Fort Myer in Virginia, USA.

Satellite collision
On 10 Feb 2009, the active commercial satellite *Iridium 33* was struck by the derelict Russian military satellite *Kosmos-2251*. The impact, which occurred at a relative speed of 42,120 km/h (26,172 mph), scattered some 10,000 pieces of debris in Low Earth Orbit.

Costliest natural disaster

According to estimates by *The Economist*, the earthquake and related tsunami that struck off the Pacific coast of Tōhoku in Japan on 11 Mar 2011 resulted in an economic loss to the country of $210 bn (£130 bn). Of that figure, only $35 bn (£21.6 bn) was insured. Two-thirds of the global death toll from natural disasters in 2011 was brought about by the quake and its aftermath.

Largest accidental marine oil spill

On 20 Apr 2010, around 779 million litres (205.7 million US gal) of crude oil entered the ocean after an explosion on the *Deepwater Horizon* oil-drilling rig in the Gulf of Mexico.

Elastec/American Marine, Inc. (USA) deliberately set fire to the oil on 19 May 2010 in an effort to clear it. This initiated the **longest continuous burn of an oil spill**, lasting for 11 hr 48 min.

DEADLIEST...

Spaceflight disaster

Seven crew members died on each occasion when the space shuttles *Challenger* and *Columbia* broke apart on 28 Jan 1986 and 1 Feb 2003 respectively.

Mountaineering disaster

On 13 Jul 1990, a minor earthquake initiated a devastating ice-and-snow avalanche near Lenin Peak, on the border between present-day Kyrgyzstan and Tajikistan. It killed 43 out of 45 climbers at a local base camp.

Avalanche

At 5:30 a.m. on 13 Dec 1916, a massive avalanche struck wooden army barracks on the slopes near the Gran Poz summit of Italy's Monte Marmolada. At least 332 people,

Deadliest wartime maritime disaster

On 30 Jan 1945, at least 7,000 people died when the German liner MV *Wilhelm Gustloff* – pictured above in 1938 – was torpedoed off Danzig (now Gdańsk, Poland) by the Soviet submarine *S-13*. There were only around 900 survivors. The ship was transporting civilian refugees and military personnel at the time of the attack.

including Austro-Hungarian mountain infantry and a Bosnian support company, were camped there. Figures for the eventual death toll vary from 270 to 330.

Pandemic

Peaking between 1347 and 1351, the Black Death killed some 75 million people worldwide. Approximately a quarter of the then-population of Europe perished. The disease still affects 1,000 to 3,000 people a year, but can now be cured.

At the time of going to press, the World Health Organization (WHO) was monitoring the spread of coronavirus disease 2019 (COVID-19). On 11 Mar 2020, it was classified by WHO as a global pandemic, with cases on every populated continent.

Worst nuclear reactor disaster

On 26 Apr 1986, an explosion at the Chernobyl Nuclear Power Plant in northern Kiev Oblast, Ukraine, killed 31 people – either from injuries sustained in the initial detonation or as a result of radiation poisoning. Some studies suggest that by 2065 there will have been around 30,000 premature fatalities attributable to the effects of the radiation released, while others propose that the death toll may already have reached 50,000.

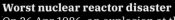

At around 2,600 km² (1,000 sq mi), the Chernobyl Nuclear Power Plant Zone of Alienation surrounding the site of the failed reactor is the **largest radioactive exclusion zone**. Shown above are vignettes from the evacuated landscape.

Round-Up

Youngest serving prime minister

Sanna Marin (FIN, b. 16 Nov 1985) was aged 34 years 24 days when she assumed the office of Prime Minister of Finland on 10 Dec 2019. Previously the transport minister for the Social Democratic Party of Finland, Marin leads a notably youthful five-party coalition government, with four of the party leaders still in their 30s.

Country with the most languages

Papua New Guinea is home to speakers of a total of 840 living languages, according to the 22nd edition of *Ethnologue: Languages of the World*, published in 2019. These languages include Tok Pisin, Motu and English.

Most Blue Flag beaches

The Blue Flag is an international certification awarded to sites that meet strict environmental, safety and accessibility criteria. Spain had 566 Blue Flag beaches as of 30 Aug 2019.

The **most Blue Flag marinas** is 122, in the Netherlands.

Largest stairwell mural

"Around the World in 50 Floors" is an artwork that covers 2,980.59 m² (32,082 sq ft) of the walls of the Allianz Tower in Milan, Italy. Actually spread across 53 floors, it depicts iconic city skylines. The project was conceived by the Italian branch of insurance company Allianz, in conjunction with street artists Orticanoodles, and verified on 5 Mar 2019.

Most people breaking bread

On 4 Oct 2019, homelessness action group The Journey Home (USA) hosted an event at which 478 people came together to share bread in Baltimore, Maryland, USA.

Most habitable city

The Austrian capital of Vienna was awarded the title of Most Liveable City for the second year running in 2019, scoring 99.1 points out of 100 on *The Economist*'s Global Liveability Index. The report assesses more than 30 factors across five key areas: stability, healthcare, culture and environment, education, and infrastructure.

Most valuable dreidel

Dreidels are four-sided spinning tops traditionally played with on the Jewish holiday of Hanukkah. A custom-designed piece by Estate Diamond Jewelry (USA) was valued at $70,000 (£54,375) on 27 Nov 2019 in New York City, USA. Its Hebrew letters are made of white gold and encrusted with 222 diamonds.

Most living figures in a nativity scene

On 20 Dec 2019, a total of 2,101 people participated in a nativity scene organized by the city government of San Jose del Monte in Bulacan in the Philippines. This smashed the previous total of 1,254.

Oldest continuously staffed operating fire station

The City of Manistee Fire Department in Michigan, USA, celebrated its 130th anniversary on 17 Jun 2019. Driver engineer/medic Fred LaPoint trawled through the local archives to prove that the fire station had been staffed 24 hours a day, 365 days a year since it first opened in 1889. A new sign honouring its GWR title now hangs outside.

Largest prayer wheel

Prayer wheels are hollow cylinders containing replicas of Buddhist mantras wrapped around a spindle. The action of turning the wheel serves to multiply the number of prayers expressed. The Nyingma Temple in Gansu, China, has a prayer wheel measuring 35.81 m (117 ft 5 in) in height and a diameter of 12.43 m (40 ft 9 in), as verified on 31 Aug 2018. There are 11,000 Buddhist scriptures stored inside.

Most expensive cardigan sold at auction

On 26 Oct 2019, the grey mohair five-button cardigan once worn by Nirvana frontman Kurt Cobain sold for $334,000 (£260,230) at auction in New York City, USA. Cobain famously sported the item during his band's acoustic set on *MTV Unplugged* (pictured). The cardigan bears all the scars of the rock 'n' roll lifestyle, with a missing button, cigarette burns and a mysterious crunchy brown stain around the right front pocket.

Most expensive artwork by a living artist sold at auction

Rabbit (1986) sold for $91,075,000 (£70,408,300) on 15 May 2019 at Christie's in New York City, USA. The stainless-steel sculpture, one of a set of three, is the work of artist Jeff Koons (USA). The **most expensive artwork** is *Salvator Mundi* (*c.* 1500) by Leonardo da Vinci (ITA), which sold for $450,312,500 (£343,033,000) on 15 Nov 2017.

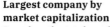

100%

Most diamonds set in one ring

Lakshikaa Jewels (IND) presented a ring adorned with 7,777 diamonds on 7 May 2019 in Mumbai, India. The jewels are set on an 18-karat-gold base and the ring is designed to replicate the Lotus Temple in Delhi. A team of 12 crafters, a jeweller and a designer worked on the project for 18 months.

Largest merengue dance

The merengue is a dance originating in the Dominican Republic. On 3 Nov 2019, a total of 844 participants (422 couples) took to the Plaza España in the country's capital, Santo Domingo, to dance for 5 min 18 sec. The attempt was organized by AZ Films Producciones (DOM).

Most people dancing with swords

As part of the coronation celebrations of honorary monarch HH Thakore Saheb Mandhatasinhji Jadeja of Rajkot, 2,126 sword dancers performed on 28 Jan 2020. The Rajkot Rajya and Bhagini Seva Foundations and Rani Saheb Kadambaridevi Jadeja (all IND) helped to organize the record. For more large-scale dancing displays, turn to p.106.

Oldest ruling house

Emperor Naruhito (JPN), who acceded to Japan's Chrysanthemum Throne on 1 May 2019, is the 126th descendant of the country's first ruler, Jimmu, whose reign is believed to have begun in 660 BCE. Naruhito took the place of his father, Akihito, who is the first Japanese monarch to abdicate the throne. As per tradition, a new imperial era was also coined to mark the transition: Reiwa (meaning "beautiful harmony").

Longest career in the same company

As of 12 Apr 2019, sales manager Walter Orthmann (BRA) had been working at textile company RenauxView for 81 years 85 days in Brusque, Santa Catarina, Brazil. His first day was on 17 Jan 1938. He has collected pay in nine different currencies.

Largest display of origami...

• **Butterflies**: 29,416, by Juanne-Pierre De Abreu (ZAF) on 5 Dec 2019 in Cape Town, South Africa.
• **Fish**: 10,879, by Boek.be (BEL) on 11 Nov 2019 in Antwerp, Belgium.
• **Frogs**: 3,542, by Japan Hospital Clown Association on 16 Sep 2019 in Yokohama, Kanagawa, Japan.

Largest company by market capitalization

Based on the total market value of a company's shares and stocks, tech giant Microsoft (USA) had a value of $905 bn (£693.8 bn) as of 31 Mar 2019, according to the annual *Global Top 100 Companies* report produced by PricewaterhouseCoopers.

First little person on the cover of *Vogue*

Activist and broadcaster Sinéad Burke (IRL) appeared on the front of the Sep 2019 edition of British *Vogue* magazine. The cover choice was made by the guest editor, Meghan, Duchess of Sussex, who selected Burke alongside 13 other "trailblazing changemakers" in Britain and Ireland. Burke was born with achondroplasia, a form of dwarfism. The term "little person" (or "LP") is the language that Sinéad prefers, but some people favour the term "dwarf", "person of short stature" or "person of restricted growth" to describe themselves. As Burke points out in her advocacy, it is important that the personal preference of the individual is respected.

Sinéad said of her *Vogue* cover appearance: "The response I've received has been overwhelmingly supportive, uplifting and really quite emotional."

In a stand against air travel, Greta sailed to several summits on zero-emission yachts in 2019.

CULTURE & SOCIETY

○ HALL OF FAME

Greta **Thunberg**

Swedish climate-change activist Greta Thunberg may only have risen to prominence in mid-2018, but in a very short time this dauntless teenager has made a huge impact on the world stage.

Born on 3 Jan 2003, Greta first became aware of climate change at the age of eight. Wanting to be proactive, she started her activism at home, encouraging her own family to reduce its carbon footprint.

Unimpressed with a global lack of ambition when it came to environmental policy, in 2018 Greta embarked on a month-long school strike after Sweden's hottest summer in 250-plus years. This grew into the now-worldwide "Fridays for Future" protest movement. Since her campaign began, Greta has convinced dozens of countries to pledge to cut greenhouse gases to zero by 2050.

During her crusade, Greta has met with many political and religious leaders. She has gained the approval of Pope Francis, US Democratic presidential candidate Bernie Sanders and the Dalai Lama. But she has notably not always seen eye to eye with politicians, having locked horns with President Donald Trump – among others – on several occasions.

She has had numerous honours bestowed upon her, but hasn't accepted them all: she rejected the Nordic Council Environment Prize in 2019 on the grounds that "the climate movement does not need any more awards". Greta did, however, become the **youngest TIME Person of the Year** on 23 Dec 2019, aged 16 years 354 days old.

In early 2020, Greta warned that we only have eight years. "This is not the time for dreams," she insisted. "climate catastrophe". "This is not the time for dreams," she insisted. "This is a moment in history where we need to be wide awake."

Making regular appearances since Greta first rose to fame, her yellow rain jacket has become one of the activist's most enduring symbols.

Find out more about Greta in the Hall of Fame section at **www. guinnessworldrecords.com/2021**

1: Greta and former US president Barack Obama meeting in Washington, DC. Obama – writing on Twitter's greatest advocates". is a great supporter of Greta, is "already one of our planet's greatest advocates".

2: One of many "Fridays for Future" protests led by Greta in the Swedish capital, Stockholm. On 15 Mar 2019 alone, took more than 2,200 climate-change events worldwide. a total of 125 countries with more than place across participating person ever 1 million people worldwide.

Greta is now the youngest person ever to receive the annual *TIME* accolade.

3: Greta is now the youngest person impact on to have received the industry's pioneer Rather aptly, given 25 years the planet, she surpassed aviation (USA); he was 25 years Charles Lindbergh became the **first *TIME* Person of the Year** in 1927. old when he became the first *TIME* Person

4: Greta has said that American civil-rights activist Rosa Parks was one of the first people to inspire her. In an interview with *Rolling Stone* magazine, the teen revealed, "Parks] taught me one person can make such a huge difference."

5: At the Climate Change Conference in Madrid, Spain), Greta delivered a speech to UN COP25 (relocated from Chile to dignitaries on 11 Dec 2019.

Greta was nominated for a Nobel Peace Prize in 2019, but lost out to Ethiopian PM the Abiy Ahmed.

In Oct 2019, a tiny new beetle – *Nelloptodes gretae* – was named after Greta by Dr Michael Darby. The beetle belongs to some of the family, which includes the Ptiliidae smallest beetles in the world. Its antennae are said to resemble the campaigner's iconic pigtails.

100%

COP25 CHILE MADRID 2019

PERSON *of the* YEAR
TIME
GRETA THUNBERG
THE POWER OF YOUTH

Adventurers

Stop 1: TSE Airport
Nur-Sultan, Kazakhstan

Start/end point:
Kennedy Space Center, USA

Stop 2: MRU Airport
Port Louis, Mauritius

Stop 3: PUQ Airport
Punta Arenas, Chile

Fastest circumnavigation via both Poles by aeroplane
Setting out on 9 Jul 2019, Captain Hamish Harding (UK, third from right below) and crew flew a Qatar Executive Gulfstream G650ER jet around the globe via the geographic Poles in 46 hr 40 min 22 sec. Their attempt was verified on 11 Jul at Kennedy Space Center in Florida, USA.

Dubbed "One More Orbit", the attempt was organized to mark 50 years since NASA's historic Moon landings and the 500th anniversary of the **first circumnavigation** (see overleaf). Captain Harding is also shown in the inset photo, along with Akbar Al Baker (centre), CEO of Qatar Airways, who were a partner in the project.

Film-maker Jannicke Mikkelsen (right) oversaw a live on-board stream of the attempt.

Shown here are the triumphant crew of circumnavigators.
Left to right: Magdalena Starowicz (Pol/USA; flight attendant), Yevgen Vasylenko (UKR; pilot), Jacob Ove Bech (DNK; pilot), Jeremy Ascough (ZAF; pilot), Colonel Terry Virts (USA; astronaut and film-maker), Hamish Harding (pilot), Benjamin Rueger (DEU; lead engineer) and Jannicke Mikkelsen (NOR; film-maker).

First Circumnavigation

The year 2019 marked the quincentenary since Portuguese explorer Ferdinand Magellan (illustrated right) embarked on what would become the first round-the-world voyage. Many of the 239 men (including Magellan) who set sail from Spain would never return to Europe, but a single ship did make it back in 1522. Five hundred years later, GWR celebrates the overlooked pioneers behind the first circumnavigation, including Magellan's dauntless replacement and the handful of crew (see table below) who went the full distance – though a few were delayed...

Leaving Sanlúcar de Barrameda in Andalucía, Spain, on 20 Sep 1519 **(1)**, the five-ship expedition endured mutiny and scurvy to reach a strait in southern Chile, later named after Magellan, on 21 Oct 1520 **(2)**. One vessel was wrecked; another returned to Spain following a second uprising.

The rest successfully crossed the Pacific Ocean, but on 27 Apr 1521 disaster struck: Magellan and many of his crew were killed (or fled) during a skirmish on Mactan Island, now in the Philippines **(3)**. Finding themselves short-handed, the decision was taken to scuttle the *Concepción*, with the crew consolidating on to the two remaining vessels.

Finally reaching their intended destination – Indonesia's Maluku Islands (aka Spice Islands) on 8 Nov **(4)** – the company stocked up on spices and began the return trip; however, the flagship *Trinidad* sprang a leak and its crew had to be left behind. Spanish navigator Juan Sebastián de Elcano ("Elkano" in Basque) led the depleted force back to Europe in the *Victoria*, rounding Africa's Cape of Good Hope on 19 May 1522 **(5)**.

However, after the ship arrived in the Cape Verde archipelago on 9 Jul **(6)**, a group of 12 sailors were taken prisoner. (Once released months later, they too completed the trip, so also deserve recognition.) Just 18 crew members went on to Spain, reaching Seville on 8 Sep 1522 **(7)**, rounding off the voyage that had begun almost three years previously.

The Elkano Foundation is currently celebrating the 500th anniversary of this feat as well as the multinational diversity of the crew. Its website features a timeline tracing the stops on that historic journey, mirroring the expedition's progress in real time. Find out more at **elkanofundazioa.eus/en**.

First circumnavigators NAME	NATIONALITY	PROFESSION
Juan Sebastián de Elcano	Basque Country	Navigator/captain
Francisco Albo	Greece	Pilot
Miguel de Rodas	Greece	Countermaster/master
Juan de Acurio	Basque Country	Pilot
Martín de Judicibus	Italy	Chief steward
Hernando de Bustamante	Spain	Barber
Hans aus Aachen	Germany	Gunner
Diego Gallego	Spain	Leading seaman
Nicolás el Griego	Greece	Leading seaman
Miguel Sánchez de Rodas	Greece	Leading seaman
Francisco Rodrigues	Portugal	Leading seaman
Juan Rodríguez	Spain	Leading seaman
Antonio Hernández Colmenero	Spain	Leading seaman
Juan de Arratia	Basque Country	Ordinary seaman
Juan de Santandrés	Spain	Ordinary seaman
Vasco Gomes Galego	Portugal	Ordinary seaman
Juan de Zubileta	Basque Country	Page
Antonio Pigafetta Lombardo	Italy	Supernumerary (and chronicler of the voyage)
Martín Méndez	Spain	Notary/accountant
Pedro de Tolosa	Basque Country	Seaman/steward
Ricarte de Normandía	France	Carpenter
Roldán de Argote	Belgium	Gunner
Felipe de Rodas	Greece	Leading seaman
Gómez Hernández	Spain	Leading seaman
Ocacio (Socacio) Alonso	Spain	Leading seaman
Pedro de Chindurza	Basque Country	Page
Vasquito Gallego	Spain	Page
Juan Martín(ez)	Spain	Supernumerary
Maestre Pedro	Spain	Supernumerary
Simón de Burgos	Portugal	Supernumerary

The last 12 names are those of crew members captured and imprisoned in Cape Verde in Jul 1522. They were only able to complete the voyage upon their release.

Henrique de Malaca (aka "Panglima Awang") – a slave Magellan acquired in what is now Malaysia *c.* 1511 – could have been the first person to circle the world. But his movements after 1 May 1521 in the Philippines are unknown.

The 381 sacks of cloves brought back on the *Victoria* were worth more than twice the total cost of the entire five-ship expedition!

The crew spoke of meeting "giants" in Patagonia – most likely members of the statuesque Tehuelche (Aónikenk) tribe.

The voyage was undertaken using rudimentary instruments such as astrolabes, which use celestial bodies to determine latitude.

Magellan was the first to coin the name *Mar Pacifico* ("Peaceful Sea").

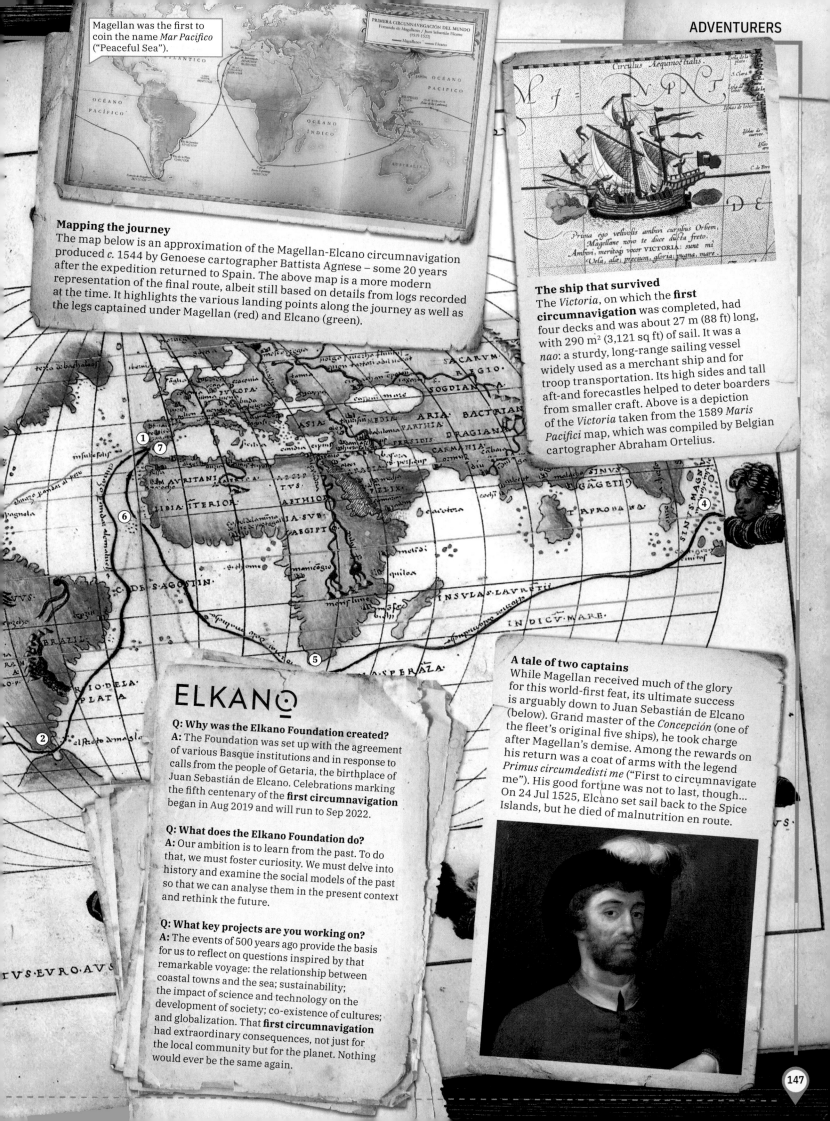

PRIMERA CIRCUNNAVEGACIÓN DEL MUNDO
Fernando de Magallanes / Juan Sebastián Elcano
(1519-1522)

Mapping the journey

The map below is an approximation of the Magellan-Elcano circumnavigation produced *c.* 1544 by Genoese cartographer Battista Agnese – some 20 years after the expedition returned to Spain. The above map is a more modern representation of the final route, albeit still based on details from logs recorded at the time. It highlights the various landing points along the journey as well as the legs captained under Magellan (red) and Elcano (green).

The ship that survived

The *Victoria*, on which the **first circumnavigation** was completed, had four decks and was about 27 m (88 ft) long, with 290 m² (3,121 sq ft) of sail. It was a *nao*: a sturdy, long-range sailing vessel widely used as a merchant ship and for troop transportation. Its high sides and tall aft-and-forecastles helped to deter boarders from smaller craft. Above is a depiction of the *Victoria* taken from the 1589 *Maris Pacifici* map, which was compiled by Belgian cartographer Abraham Ortelius.

ELKANO

Q: Why was the Elkano Foundation created?
A: The Foundation was set up with the agreement of various Basque institutions and in response to calls from the people of Getaria, the birthplace of Juan Sebastián de Elcano. Celebrations marking the fifth centenary of the **first circumnavigation** began in Aug 2019 and will run to Sep 2022.

Q: What does the Elkano Foundation do?
A: Our ambition is to learn from the past. To do that, we must foster curiosity. We must delve into history and examine the social models of the past so that we can analyse them in the present context and rethink the future.

Q: What key projects are you working on?
A: The events of 500 years ago provide the basis for us to reflect on questions inspired by that remarkable voyage: the relationship between coastal towns and the sea; sustainability; the impact of science and technology on the development of society; co-existence of cultures; and globalization. That **first circumnavigation** had extraordinary consequences, not just for the local community but for the planet. Nothing would ever be the same again.

A tale of two captains

While Magellan received much of the glory for this world-first feat, its ultimate success is arguably down to Juan Sebastián de Elcano (below). Grand master of the *Concepción* (one of the fleet's original five ships), he took charge after Magellan's demise. Among the rewards on his return was a coat of arms with the legend *Primus circumdedisti me* ("First to circumnavigate me"). His good fortune was not to last, though... On 24 Jul 1525, Elcano set sail back to the Spice Islands, but he died of malnutrition en route.

Mountaineering

All climbs made with bottled oxygen unless stated otherwise

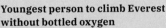

Youngest person to climb Everest without bottled oxygen

Tashi Lakpa Sherpa (NPL, b. 18 Nov 1985) topped Everest – at 8,848 m (29,029 ft), the **highest mountain** – on 31 May 2005, aged 19 years 194 days.

Fastest time to climb Everest twice (female)

Anshu Jamsenpa (IND) climbed Everest from the south side – base to summit and back – twice within five days between 16 and 21 May 2017. Jamsenpa is not the **first woman to climb Everest twice in a season** – Chhurim Dolma Sherpa (NPL) achieved that feat in 2011 – but she is the fastest to do so.

Fastest climb of Everest by a married couple

Pasang Phuti Sherpa and her husband Ang Dawa Sherpa (both NPL) started climbing Everest at 3 a.m. on 14 May 2019 and reached the top on 16 May at 10.36 a.m. – completing the feat in 2 days 7 hr 36 min.

Fastest time to climb Everest and K2

Mingma Gyabu "David" Sherpa (NPL, see right) topped Everest on 21 May 2018 and K2 – at 8,611 m (28,251 ft), the second-highest mountain – on 21 Jul 2018, a total time of 61 days 55 min.

Most ascents of K2 in one season

During the 2018 climbing season on K2, a total of 64 ascents were made, up from 51 in 2004, the previous busiest season.

Fastest climb of Everest (female)

During the 2018 season, Phunjo Jhangmu Lama (NPL) climbed Everest in a record time of 39 hr 6 min. She left basecamp at 3.20 p.m. on 15 May and reached the top at 6.26 a.m. on 17 May. Lama grew up in the Gorkha District of Nepal, where she used to work as a yak and dzo herder before becoming a mountain guide.

Youngest person to climb all 8,000ers

Mingma Gyabu "David" Sherpa (NPL, b. 16 May 1989) climbed all 14 mountains over 8,000 m (26,246 ft) by the age of 30 years 166 days. His first ascent was Everest on 23 May 2010 and his last was Shisha Pangma (8,027 m; 26,335 ft) on 29 Oct 2019. The project took him 9 years 159 days. He is pictured here just below the summit of Manaslu (see right).

Fastest ascent of Manaslu without bottled oxygen

François Cazzanelli (ITA) climbed from basecamp to the top of Manaslu – at 8,163 m (26,781 ft), the eighth-highest mountain – in exactly 13 hr on 25–26 Sep 2019. He started his journey at 9 p.m. on 25 Sep and reached the apex at 10 a.m. the next morning. He was part of a group, but as an experienced mountaineer was able to climb more quickly than the others.

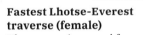

Fastest Lhotse-Everest traverse (female)

The women's record for crossing from the top of Lhotse (8,516 m; 27,939 ft) to the top of nearby Everest is just 21 hr 30 min, by Qu Jiao-Jiao (CHN, left) between 20 and 21 May 2018. The reverse record – **fastest Everest-Lhotse traverse (female)** – is 22 hr 40 min and was achieved by Élisabeth Marie Bernadette Revol (FRA), who completed her climbs on 23–24 May 2019.

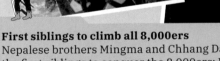

First siblings to climb all 8,000ers

Nepalese brothers Mingma and Chhang Dawa Sherpa are the first siblings to conquer the 8,000ers: Mingma between 2000 and 2011, and Dawa between 2001 and 2013. Both used supplementary oxygen for only the four highest mountains. The brothers now operate the expedition firm Seven Summit Treks, organizing supported climbs and treks throughout Nepal, Pakistan and China.

A BRIEF HISTORY OF ADVENTURE

1522

First circumnavigation of the world
On 8 Sep, the Spanish vessel Victoria, under Basque captain Juan Sebastián de Elcano, reaches Seville in Spain. It had set out from Spain on 20 Sep 1519, under Ferdinand Magellan (see p.146).

1775

First female circumnavigator
Disguised as a man, Jeanne Baret serves as an assistant botanist on the first French round-the-world voyage in 1766–69. She settles in Mauritius but returns to France in 1775, completing her circumnavigation.

1903

First powered flight
On 17 Dec, Orville Wright flies the 9-kW (12-hp) chain-driven Flyer I – built with his brother Wilbur (both USA) – for 36.5 m (120 ft). Orville maintains an altitude of 2.5–3.5 m (8–12 ft) for about 12 seconds.

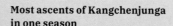

Above 8,000 m, the amount of oxygen available, and the lungs' functionality, decreases. Climbers often use bottled oxygen for such ascents. Well-oxygenated tissue is less prone to frostbite.

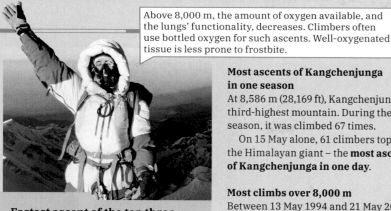

Fastest ascent of the top three highest mountains (female)

Viridiana Álvarez Chávez (MEX) climbed the world's three highest mountains in 729 days. She ascended Everest at 9.30 a.m. on 16 May 2017, K2 at 9 a.m. on 21 Jul 2018 and Kangchenjunga (above) at 4.44 a.m. on 15 May 2019. She beat the previous record by three days.

Most ascents of Kangchenjunga in one season

At 8,586 m (28,169 ft), Kangchenjunga is the third-highest mountain. During the 2019 season, it was climbed 67 times.

On 15 May alone, 61 climbers topped the Himalayan giant – the **most ascents of Kangchenjunga in one day**.

Most climbs over 8,000 m

Between 13 May 1994 and 21 May 2019, Kami Rita Sherpa (aka "Thapke", NPL) made 36 ascents of mountains higher than 8,000 m, including the **most ascents of Everest**. (Discover more about Kami Rita and his female Everest-climbing counterpart on pp.46–47.)

Fastest Everest-Lhotse traverse

Mingma Dorchi Sherpa (NPL) stood on the pinnacle of both Everest and Lhotse – the highest and fourth-highest mountains in the world – within a period of just 6 hr 1 min. He topped Everest on 27 May 2019 at 12.44 a.m. and traversed via the South Col to the top of Lhotse by 6.45 a.m. on the same day.

Fastest double-header of the "higher 8,000ers" without bottled oxygen

There is a large difference in altitude between the fifth- and sixth-highest mountains, reflected in the category "higher 8,000ers". Juan Pablo Mohr Prieto (CHL) reached the top of two higher 8,000ers in 6 days 20 hr. He conquered Lhotse at 3.30 p.m. on 16 May 2019 and then descended to camp II before ascending Everest (above), reaching the top at 11.30 a.m. on 23 May. Camp II serves Everest and neighbouring Lhotse.

The **most ascents of Everest in one season** is 872, achieved during the 2019 climbing season.

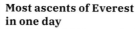

Fastest time to climb all 8,000ers

Nirmal "Nims" Purja (NPL) ascended all 14 of the 8,000ers in just 189 days, from Annapurna I (8,091 m; 26,545 ft) on 23 Apr 2019 to Shisha Pangma on 29 Oct 2019.

En route, he broke the record for the **fastest time to climb the "higher 8,000ers"** – 70 days. He topped Kangchenjunga on 15 May, Everest and Lhotse on 22 May, Makalu (8,485 m; 27,838 ft) on 24 May and K2 on 24 Jul.

Most ascents of Everest in one day

On 23 May 2019, a total of 354 climbers reached the highest point of Everest. The unprecedented – and some would say alarming – number of climbers during the 2019 spring season was highlighted in this photograph taken on 22 May by "Nims" Purja (see left). It shows a solid line of climbers along the Hillary Step. Around 100 people were attempting to descend while about 150 others pushed forward up the narrow ridge.

The most familiar name for the **highest mountain** is taken from that of a former Surveyor General of India, Sir George Everest. Its Nepali title is Sagarmāthā, while in Tibetan it is known as Chomolungma.

1911

First person to reach the South Pole

A five-strong Norwegian party led by Captain Roald Amundsen (left) reach the pole at 11 a.m. on 14 Dec. They had trekked for 53 days, with dog sledges, from the Bay of Whales.

1924

First circumnavigation by aircraft

Four US lieutenants circle the globe in two US Army Douglas DWC seaplanes, the Chicago and the New Orleans, from 6 Apr to 28 Sep. Two other planes that began the trip with them fail to complete the journey.

1929

First circumnavigation by car (female)

Racing driver Clärenore Stinnes (DEU, right) and film-maker Carl-Axel Söderström set out on 25 May 1927 from Frankfurt in Germany. They return two years later, arriving in Berlin on 24 Jun 1929.

Open-Water Swimming

Longest-distance ice swim
Hamza Bakırcıoğlu (TUR) swam 3.44 km (2.14 mi) at Sonthofersee in the Bavarian Alps, near Sonthofen in Germany, on 7 Feb 2018. The average water temperature during his swim was 4.13°C (39.43°F).

The **female** record is 3.30 km (2.05 mi), by Carmel Collins (IRL) in a freshwater outdoor pool at Wild Water in Armagh, Northern Ireland, UK, on 21 Feb 2016. The water for her swim averaged 4.63°C (40.33°F). Both records were approved by IISA.

Highest-altitude swim
On 4 Jan 2020, Australian adventurer Daniel Bull completed a swim at an altitude of 6,370 m (20,898 ft) in Copiapó, Chile. He'd spotted a lake on the eastern flank of the volcano Ojos del Salado ("Eyes of the Salty One") on 27 Apr 2017, during his successful bid to become the then-**youngest person to climb the Seven Summits and Seven Volcanic Summits**.

Longest-duration ocean swim (individual)
The longest-lasting non-stop swim in the open sea under WOWSA regulations is 76 hr 30 min, by Nejib Belhedi (TUN, below) on 15–18 Sep 2018. Belhedi swam some 120 km (75 mi) across Tunisia's Gulf of Gabès in the Mediterranean Sea, between Sfax and Djerba island.

The **longest-distance ocean swim** was set by Veljko Rogošić (HRV); he swam for 225 km (139.8 mi) across the Adriatic Sea off Italy on 29–31 Aug 2006.

Youngest person to swim the Oceans Seven
Inspired by the Seven Summits mountain-climbing challenge (see p.150), this open-water odyssey, overseen by WOWSA, requires individuals to traverse seven channels or straits around the world. Darren Miller (USA, b. 13 Apr 1983) swam his final strait – the North Channel between Northern Ireland and Scotland, UK – on 29 Aug 2013, aged 30 years 138 days.

Elizabeth Fry (USA, b. 28 Oct 1958) became the **oldest person to swim the Oceans Seven** after crossing the North Channel on 25 Aug 2019 (see p.9).

The North Channel is considered one of the toughest channel swims on Earth, owing to its cold water, powerful currents and numerous jellyfish. Michelle Macy (USA) swam the **fastest North Channel crossing** in 9 hr 34 min 39 sec on 15 Jul 2013.

Keith Garry (IRL) achieved the **male** record in 9 hr 57 min 28 sec on 14 Aug 2016. Both Macy and Garry's feats were ratified by officials from ILDSA.

Fastest time to complete six 10-km marathon swims on six continents (female)
It took ultraswimmer Jaimie Monahan (USA) just 15 days 8 hr 19 min to perform this truly global feat. Her first swim started in Cartagena, Colombia (South America) on 13 Aug 2018 and the last one ended in New York City (North America) on 28 Aug.

Monahan is also the **first person to complete the Ice Sevens Challenge**. Devised and administered by WOWSA and IISA, the Ice Sevens sees participants attempt a swim in waters sub 5°C (41°F) on each of the seven continents. On 2 Jul 2017, Monahan completed her seventh and

Fastest Ice Mile swim (female)
This challenge involves a 1-mi (1.6-km) swim in water below 5°C (41°F), following IISA rules. Julia Wittig (left) and Ines Hahn (both DEU) completed it in 21 min 33 sec on 20 Dec 2019 in Lake Wöhrsee in Burghausen, Bavaria, Germany.

The **fastest Ice Mile swim** is 20 min 29 sec, by Rostislav Vitek (CZE) in a flooded quarry in Blansko, Czech Republic, on 7 Mar 2015.

First swim beneath the Antarctic Ice Sheet
On 23 Jan 2020, endurance swimmer Lewis Pugh (UK) swam 1 km (0.6 mi) down a "subglacial river" in East Antarctica, in a bid to spotlight the rise of glacial melting on the frozen continent. Wearing just a pair of Speedos and a cap, he passed through a tunnel of ice, withstanding water temperatures of 0.1°C (32.1°F) for 10 min 17 sec.

As the UN's Patron of the Oceans, Pugh has taken on many never-before-attempted swims to raise awareness of climate change, including a 49-day English Channel crossing (inset; see table right).

Pugh is on a mission to gain global backing for a marine protected area around East Antarctica – something that he already helped to secure for the continent's Ross Sea in 2016.

A BRIEF HISTORY OF ADVENTURE

1947
First supersonic flight
On 14 Oct, Captain Charles "Chuck" Elwood Yeager (USA) reaches Mach 1.06 (1,127 km/h; 700 mph) in the Bell XS-1 rocket aircraft. The flight takes place over Rogers Dry Lake in California, USA.

1949
First commercial jet aircraft
The 36-seat British de Havilland Comet 1 takes to the skies on 27 Jul. It makes its first scheduled passenger-carrying flight, between London, UK, and Johannesburg, South Africa, on 2 May 1952.

1953
First ascent of Everest
Edmund Percival Hillary (NZ, far left) and Tenzing Norgay (IND/Tibet) top the world's **highest mountain** at 11:30 a.m. on 29 May. Their expedition is led by Henry Cecil John Hunt (UK). Hillary is later knighted and Norgay receives the George Medal.

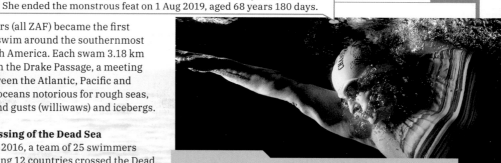

Gallant-Charette is also the **oldest to complete the Triple Crown of Lake Monster swims** (three lakes said to harbour a mythical beast). She ended the monstrous feat on 1 Aug 2019, aged 68 years 180 days.

Fastest stage swim around Kauai

Terence Bell (AUS) circled the fourth-largest island of Hawaii, USA, in 27 separate legs between 1 and 19 Jul 2019, clocking an aggregate time of 51 hr 57 min. In total, he swam a distance of 177.48 km (110.28 mi), and took 76,532 strokes, to complete the first-ever circumnavigation of the island. The average water temperature was a notably balmy 26°C (79°F).

final ice mile in the Beagle Channel, near Ushuaia, Argentina, in 29 min 5 sec. She wore neither a wetsuit nor a neoprene hat.

Fastest 5-km swim wearing leg irons

On 4 Oct 2019, during WOWSA's Ocean Fest event held at Redondo Beach in California, USA, Pablo Fernández Álvarez (ESP) swam 5 km (3.1 mi) with his feet shackled across Santa Monica Bay in just 1 hr 58 min.

FIRST...

Swim around Cape Horn

On 22 Feb 2011, Ram Barkai, Andrew Chin, Kieron Palframan, Ryan Stramrood and

Toks Viviers (all ZAF) became the first people to swim around the southernmost tip of South America. Each swam 3.18 km (1.97 mi) in the Drake Passage, a meeting point between the Atlantic, Pacific and Southern oceans notorious for rough seas, abrupt wind gusts (williwaws) and icebergs.

Swim crossing of the Dead Sea

On 15 Nov 2016, a team of 25 swimmers representing 12 countries crossed the Dead Sea to draw attention to the plight of the long-shrinking body of water. Starting in the Wadi Mujib river delta in Jordan, the group swam to Ein Gedi in Israel, covering 17.5 km (10.8 mi). The high salt content of the water, which could cause respiratory problems if swallowed, posed a particular challenge. The participants had to wear full-face snorkel masks and take regular breaks to drink and eat, without leaving the water.

Highest-altitude scuba dive

On 13 Dec 2019, Marcel Korkus (POL) dived in a lake that was 6,395 m (20,980 ft) above sea level. The location was the **highest active volcano** – Ojos del Salado (6,887 m; 22,595 ft), on the Chile-Argentina border (see also left).

Oldest person to complete the Triple Crown of Open Water Swimming

Pat Gallant-Charette (USA, b. 2 Feb 1951) was 67 years 148 days old when she completed the 20 Bridges Circumnavigation Swim of Manhattan – a distance of 28.5 mi (45.8 km) – on 30 Jun 2018. She'd swum the Catalina Channel (20.2 mi; 32.5 km) between Santa Catalina Island and the California mainland on 18 Oct 2011, and the English Channel (20.9 mi; 33.6 km) on 17 Jun 2017.

Relay swim crossing of the Bering Strait

The International Relay Swim Across the Bering Strait – a multinational project led by Russia – came to fruition on 5–11 Aug 2013. Setting out from Cape Dezhnev in Chukotka, mainland Russia, the six-day staged relay ended at Cape Prince of Wales in mainland Alaska, USA. In total, 65 swimmers hailing from 16 different countries participated, remaining in the icy water for 10–15 min at a time. The intended 86-km (53.4-mi) route ended up being 134 km (83.2 mi) as a result of tidal currents.

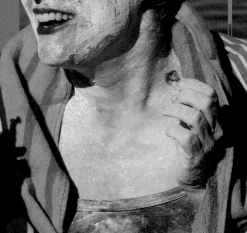

Swimming the English Channel: First...

Person*	24–25 Aug 1875	Matthew Webb (UK)**
Person (female)	6 Aug 1926	Gertrude Caroline Ederle (USA)
Double crossing by a two-person relay team	9 Jul 2018	Rugby for Heroes team: John Robert Myatt and Mark Leighton (both UK)
Double crossing by a three-person relay team	22 Jul 2018	Sportfanatic team: Dezider Pék, Ondrej Pék and Richard Nyáry (all SVK)
Medley relay	18 Sep 2010	Julie Bradshaw (butterfly), Susan Ratcliffe (backstroke), Peter May (breaststroke) and Kim Owen (front crawl) (all UK)
Person to swim it lengthways	12 Jul–29 Aug 2018	Lewis Pugh (UK; see opposite)

*No life jacket **Napoleonic soldier Giovan Maria Salati (ITA) may have escaped a prison barge off Dover and swum to Boulogne c. Jul/Aug 1815

Most consecutive swim crossings of the English Channel

On 15 Sep 2019, American ultraswimmer Sarah Thomas set out from Shakespeare Beach in Dover, Kent, UK, at just after midnight, swimming to Cap Gris-Nez in France. She swam back to Dover, then repeated the round trip. She arrived back in the UK at 6.30 a.m. (BST) two days after starting out, having been at the task for 54 hr 10 min. The **first quadruple English Channel crossing** was ratified by the CS&PF.

Sources: Channel Swimming Association, Channel Swimming & Piloting Federation (CS&PF), International Ice Swimming Association (IISA), Irish Long Distance Swimming Association (ILDSA) and World Open Water Swimming Association (WOWSA)

1958

First crossing of the Antarctic continent
Led by Vivian Ernest Fuchs (UK), a 12-strong party completes the trek at 1:47 p.m. on 2 Mar. Their journey of 3,473 km (2,158 mi) begins on 24 Nov 1957 and lasts 99 days.

1960

First dive to the Challenger Deep by a crewed vessel
*Jacques Piccard (CHE; left, rear) and Donald Walsh (USA) pilot the Swiss-built US Navy bathyscaphe Trieste to a depth of 10,911 m (35,797 ft) on 23 Jan. (Discover more about the Challenger Deep – the **deepest point in the sea** – as well as more recent expeditions to have explored it on pp.160–61.)*

1961

First person in space
Soviet cosmonaut Flight Major Yuri Gagarin performs the first manned spaceflight in Vostok 1 on 12 Apr. Gagarin completes a single orbit of Earth, covering 40,868 km (25,394 mi) in 1 hr 48 min, before landing in what is now Kazakhstan.

Ocean Rowing

First person to row across the South Pacific Ocean (west to east)
Between 6 Dec 2018 and 9 May 2019, Russian explorer Fyodor Konyukhov rowed from Port Chalmers in New Zealand to the Diego Ramírez Islands off Chile. He covered 4,036 nautical mi (7,475 km; 4,644 mi) in 154 days 13 hr 37 min. At the start of his trip, Konyukhov (b. 12 Dec 1951) was aged 66 years 359 days – the **oldest person to row solo across the Pacific**.

First person to row solo around Great Britain
On 4 Nov 2018, Andrew Hodgson (UK) arrived back at the Tower of London in the UK having rowed around the coast of Great Britain in 175 days 2 hr 51 min. He had departed on 13 May on board *Spirit of Ahab*. After 146 days at sea, Hodgson paused for 10 days in Grimsby, Lincolnshire – he resupplied food but did not disembark.

In the last few weeks of his journey, Hodgson frequently crossed paths with Ross Edgley (UK), who was completing the **first stage swim around Great Britain**.

First brother and sister team to row across an ocean
Anna (UK/USA) and Cameron McLean (UK) joined forces to take part in the 2019 Talisker Whisky Atlantic Challenge. "The Seablings" rowed *Lily* from east to west across the Atlantic Ocean, from La Gomera in the Canary Islands to Antigua. They crossed the finish line in 18th position, in a time of 43 days 15 hr 22 min.

Youngest person to row the Mid-Pacific (east to west)
Michael Prendergast (UK, b. 18 Apr 1995) was aged 23 years 50 days when he set out on 7 Jun 2018 for the annual Great Pacific Race. Together with his "Uniting Nations" teammates – Robert Behny, Evan Buckland and Jordan Godoy – Prendergast rowed *Isabel* from Monterey in California to Waikiki in Hawaii, USA. They arrived on 27 Jul 2018, winning the race in a time of 49 days 23 hr 15 min.

Youngest team of three to row any ocean
Megan Hoskin (UK, b. 25 Dec 1983), Caroline Lander (UK, b. 21 Aug 1989) and Eleanor Carey (AUS, b. 21 Aug 1989) had a combined age of 33,617 days (92 years 14 days) at the start of the Great Pacific Race on 7 Jun 2018. The team – "Pacific Terrific" – finished

Most solo ocean rows
On 14 Jun 2019, Emmanuel Coindre (FRA) completed his seventh solo ocean row when he arrived in *Onoff* at Dégrad des Cannes in French Guiana. It had taken him 58 days to cross the Atlantic from Dakar, Senegal – the fifth time he had crossed that ocean. Coindre has also rowed the Pacific and the Indian, and traversed the Atlantic a further time in a leg-powered hydrocycle.

First team of three brothers to row any ocean
Ewan, Jamie and Lachlan Maclean (all UK) took part in the 2019 Talisker Whisky Atlantic Challenge, rowing the Atlantic Ocean east to west from La Gomera to Antigua in *BROAR*. The Scottish siblings finished the race in third place in 35 days 9 hr 9 min. They were raising money for the Feedback Madagascar and Children 1st charities.

the race in second place in *Danielle*, after a journey lasting 62 days 18 hr 36 min. Along the way, they had to contend with 12-m (40-ft) waves, sharks and hurricanes. They became the **first team of three to row the Mid-Pacific (east to west)**.

First registered blind person to row the Mid-Pacific (east to west)
Former Royal Marine Steve Sparks (UK) suffered a dramatic loss of eyesight following a diving incident. He teamed up with Michael Dawson for the 2018 Great Pacific Race and the pair arrived in Waikiki in *Bojangles* on 28 Aug. Their journey had lasted 82 days 13 hr 54 min. Sparks could make out the sky and the sea but could not discern waves, making the journey all the more challenging. The **first registered-blind ocean rower** was Alan Lock (UK), who rowed the Atlantic in 2008.

A number of records have been set during the Talisker Whisky Atlantic Challenge – a (now-annual) race from the Canary Islands to the West Indies.

Oldest pair to row across any ocean	61 years 287 days (average age)	Peter Ketley and Neil Young (both UK)
Fastest row across the Atlantic	3.59 knots (6.64 km/h)	Stuart Watts, Richard Taylor, George Biggar and Peter Robinson (all UK)
Fastest pair	2.85 knots (5.27 km/h)	Max Thorpe and David Spelman (both UK)
Fastest trio (female)	2.14 knots (3.96 km/h)	Maureen O'Brien, Bridie "Bird" Watts and Claire Allinson (all UK)
Fastest team of five	2.96 knots (5.48 km/h)	Kevin Gaskell, William Hollingshead, Samuel Coxon, Christopher Hodgson and Matthew Gaskell (all UK)

Source: Ocean Rowing Society. All records in the open/classic category

A BRIEF HISTORY OF ADVENTURE

1963
First woman in space
On 16 Jun, Soviet cosmonaut Valentina Tereshkova takes off in Vostok 6 from the Baikonur Cosmodrome. She completes a flight of 2 days 22 hr 50 min and orbits Earth 48 times.

1965
First spacewalk
On 18 Mar, Soviet Lieutenant-Colonel Alexei Leonov spends 12 min 9 sec outside the Voskhod 2 spacecraft. His spacesuit inflates in the vacuum of space and he has to release a valve in order to return inside his capsule.

1969
First person to sail around the world (solo, non-stop)
On 22 Apr, Robin Knox-Johnston (UK) returns to Falmouth in Cornwall, UK, as the only remaining competitor in the Sunday Times Golden Globe Race. He had set out on 14 Jun 1968.

1969
First people on the Moon
On 20 Jul, NASA astronaut Neil Armstrong steps down from the Eagle module and walks on the lunar surface, closely followed by Buzz Aldrin (left, both USA). Crewmate Michael Collins remains in orbit around the Moon.

Longest time rowing non-stop solo across an ocean

On 8 Jun 2019, Jacob Adoram (USA) arrived at Trinity Beach in Queensland, Australia, after an epic solo row lasting 335 days 22 hr 30 min. The veteran fighter pilot had set out from Neah Bay in Washington, USA, on 7 Jul 2018, and rowed the Pacific from east to west in *Emerson*.

Fastest row across the Atlantic by a pair (female, east to west)

"Whale of a Time", comprising Jemma Rix and Lauren Woodwiss (both UK), spent 50 days 5 hr 53 min rowing in *Boudicea* from La Gomera in the Canary Islands to English Harbour in Antigua between 12 Dec 2018 and 31 Jan 2019. The pair, who met as students at the University of Reading's hockey club, were competing in the Talisker Whisky Atlantic Challenge race and beat the previous record by just over one hour.

Youngest person to row any ocean solo

Lukas Michael Haitzmann (UK/ITA/ AUT, b. 20 Apr 2000) was 18 years 236 days old at the start of his east-to-west row across the Atlantic. It took Haitzmann 59 days 8 hr 22 min to complete the journey from La Gomera to Antigua between 12 Dec 2018 and 9 Feb 2019 on board *Cosimo*.

Fastest to row the Mid-Pacific (east to west) in the Classic Pair category

The team "Sons of the Pacific" – Louis Bird (UK) and Erden Eruç (USA/TUR) – rowed 2,090 nautical mi (3,870 km; 2,405 mi) on board *Yves* from Monterey in California to O'ahu in Hawaii, USA, between 5 Jun and 29 Jul 2016, achieving an average speed over the 54 days of 1.61 knots (2.98 km/h; 1.85 mph). Louis is the son of Peter Bird (UK), who, in 1983, became the **first person to row solo across the Pacific**. Louis' row was in memory of his father, who died attempting another Pacific crossing in 1996.

More "Impossible Row" records		
First row on the Southern Ocean	13–25 Dec 2019	Fiann Paul (ISL), Colin O'Brady (USA), Andrew Towne (USA), Cameron Bellamy (ZAF), Jamie Douglas-Hamilton (UK) and John Petersen (USA)
First row to the Antarctic continent		
Most southerly start of a rowing expedition	56.96°S	
Most southerly latitude reached by a rowing vessel	64.21°S	
First person to row in the open waters of both polar regions	2017 & 2019	Fiann Paul
Most polar open water rows completed by a rower	3	

Source: Ocean Rowing Society

First Ocean Explorers Grand Slam

Fiann Paul (ISL) has rowed on the Atlantic (2011), Indian (2014), Mid-Pacific (2016), Arctic Ocean open waters (2017) and Antarctic Ocean (2019, see below). All bar the last of these comprise the **most ocean rowing speed records held simultaneously on different oceans** – four.

First row across the Drake Passage

On 25 Dec 2019, the "Impossible Row" team completed the first ever crossing by rowboat of the notoriously treacherous Drake Passage between Cape Horn in Chile and Charles Point on the Antarctic Peninsula. The crew – captain Fiann Paul (ISL, see above), first mate Colin O'Brady (USA), Andrew Towne (USA), Cameron Bellamy (ZAF), Jamie Douglas-Hamilton (UK) and John Petersen (USA) – are pictured above receiving their certificates at the GWR London offices.

1972
First woman to row an ocean
Between 26 Apr 1971 and 22 Apr 1972, Sylvia Cook and John Fairfax (both UK) complete the **first row across the Pacific** in Britannia II. Along the way, Cook saves Fairfax from a shark by hauling him back into the boat.

First solo expedition to the North Pole
Single-handedly, Naomi Uemura (JPN) completes a 770-km (478-mi) dog-sled journey to reach the North Pole on 29 Apr. He had set out on 5 Mar from Cape Edward on Ellesmere Island, northern Canada.
1978

First solo summit of Everest
After a three-day climb from his basecamp at 6,500 m (21,325 ft), Reinhold Messner (ITA) reaches the summit of Everest on 20 Aug. He does not use bottled oxygen, making the climb all the more impressive.
1980

Around the World

First circumnavigation
The earliest known voyage around the globe took place 500 years ago. Discover the full story on p.146.

First circumnavigation (female)
Jeanne Baret (aka Baré or Barret, FRA) joined the explorer Louis-Antoine de Bougainville on his round-the-world scientific expedition in 1766–69. Women were not allowed on French Navy ships at the time, so Baret travelled in disguise as the "male" valet of the expedition's naturalist Philibert Commerson.

First submarine circumnavigation
Between 24 Feb and 25 Apr 1960, the USS *Triton* made a submerged circuit of the world. Commanded by Capt. Edward L Beach, the nuclear-powered military submarine sailed 49,491 km (26,723 nautical mi; 30,752 mi) in 60 days 21 hr, starting and ending at the St Peter and Paul Rocks in the mid-Atlantic Ocean.

First surface circumnavigation via both Poles
Sir Ranulph Fiennes and Charles Burton (both UK) of the British Trans-Globe Expedition travelled south from Greenwich, London, UK, on 2 Sep 1979, crossing the South Pole on 15 Dec 1980 and the North Pole on 10 Apr 1982. They returned to Greenwich on 29 Aug 1982, having completed a 56,000-km (35,000-mi) journey.

GEORGE M. SCHILLING, FAMOUS AMERICAN ATHLETE, WHO HAS WALKED ROUND THE WORLD FOR A WAGER, and has walked 55,000 miles since August, 1897, having left New York in a newspaper suit and penniless, the only man living who has accomplished this extraordinary feat.

First circumnavigation walking
George Matthew Schilling (USA, left) is reputed to have walked around the world between 1897 and 1904, reportedly prompted by a wager, although his feat was not verified. The first verified circumnavigation on foot was by David Kunst (USA, right) between 20 Jun 1970 and 5 Oct 1974. He walked 23,250 km (14,450 mi), covering four continents. His brother John, who had set out with him on the trip, died en route in Afghanistan.

First solo circumnavigation by balloon
Between 19 Jun and 2 Jul 2002, Steve Fossett (USA) flew around the world in *Bud Light Spirit of Freedom*, a 42.6-m-tall (140-ft) mixed-gas balloon. He took off from Northam, Western Australia, and landed at Eromanga in Queensland, Australia, having flown a total distance of 33,195 km (20,627 mi).

First circumnavigation by aircraft
Two US Army Douglas DWC seaplanes circled the globe in 57 "hops" from 6 Apr to 28 Sep 1924. The *Chicago* was piloted by Lowell H Smith (below right, with co-pilot Leslie Arnold) and the *New Orleans* by Erik Nelson and co-pilot Jack Harding (all USA).

The flights started and finished in Seattle, Washington, USA, and covered 42,398 km (26,345 mi).

First circumnavigation by car
Racing driver Clara Eleonore "Clärenore" Stinnes (DEU, third from right), accompanied by Swedish film-maker Carl-Axel Söderström (far right), left Frankfurt, Germany, on 25 May 1927 in a three-speed, 50-hp Adler Standard 6 automobile. On 24 Jun 1929 – 2 years 30 days later – they arrived in Berlin, Germany, having driven 46,063 km (28,622 mi). They married a year later.

A BRIEF HISTORY OF ADVENTURE

1986
Patrick Morrow (CAN) summits Puncak Jaya on Indonesia and becomes the **first person to climb the Seven Summits**. These are the highest points on each continent, according to the list drawn up by alpinist Reinhold Messner (which identifies Oceania instead of Australia).

1986
The **first person to reach the North Pole solo** is Dr Jean-Louis Étienne (FRA), who – without help from dogs but with resupplies along the way – takes 63 days to ski to the Pole dragging a sled. He averages 20 km (12.4 mi) – or 8 hr of skiing – per day.

1987
On 2–3 Jul, Richard Branson (UK, pictured top) and Per Lindstrand (SWE, bottom) fly 4,947 km (3,074 mi) from Maine, USA, to Northern Ireland, UK, in the Virgin Atlantic Flyer: the **first crossing of the Atlantic by hot-air balloon**.

First circumnavigation by autogyro

On 22 Sep 2019, James Ketchell (UK) completed a 175-day flight around the world, having travelled approximately 44,450 km (27,620 mi) in a Magni M16C autogyro. His open-cockpit aircraft has a top speed of 129 km/h (80 mph), around half that of the average helicopter.

Fastest circumnavigation by bicycle

Mark Beaumont (UK) made his second – and fastest – transglobal cycle from 2 Jul to 18 Sep 2017. His 78-day 14-hr 40-min trip began and ended in Paris, France.

The ◗ female record is 124 days 11 hr, by fellow Scottish cyclist Jenny Graham (UK). She left Berlin, Germany, on 16 Jun 2018 and returned on 18 Oct.

Lloyd Edward Collier and Louis Paul Snellgrove (both UK) completed the ◗ fastest circumnavigation by tandem bicycle in 281 days 22 hr 20 min from 7 Aug 2018 to 16 May 2019. The start and end point was Adelaide, Australia.

Youngest person to circumnavigate the globe by motorcycle

Kane Avellano (UK, b. 20 Jan 1993) finished his epic round-the-world trip at the town hall in South Shields, Tyne and Wear, UK, on 19 Jan 2017 aged 23 years 365 days.

First circumnavigation by solar-powered boat

MS *TÛRANOR PlanetSolar* (CHE) circumnavigated the world in a westward direction from the principality of Monaco in 1 year 220 days from 27 Sep 2010 to 4 May 2012 on solar power only. The boat had accumulated 32,410 nautical mi (60,023 km; 37,296 mi) by the time it returned to Monaco.

Fastest circumnavigation by car

The record for the **first and fastest man and woman to have circumnavigated the Earth by car** covering six continents under the rules applicable in 1989 and 1991 embracing more than an equator's length of driving (24,901 road miles; 40,075 km), is held by Saloo Choudhury and his wife Neena Choudhury (both India). The journey took 69 days 19 hours 5 minutes from 9 September to 17 November 1989. The couple drove a 1989 Hindustan "Contessa Classic" starting and finishing in Delhi, India.

Fastest circumnavigation by helicopter (female)

Sixty-year-old Jennifer Murray (UK, b. USA) piloted her Robinson R44 helicopter around the world solo in 99 days from 31 May to 6 Sep 2000. The journey started and finished at Brooklands airfield in Surrey, UK, and crossed 30 countries.

First solo circumnavigation using human power

Erden Eruç (TUR) rowed, kayaked, hiked and cycled around the world between 10 Jul 2007 and 21 Jul 2012. His journey lasted 5 years 11 days 12 hr 22 min, starting and finishing at Bodega Bay in California, USA. He cycled across three continents (North America, Australia and Africa) and rowed three oceans (the Pacific, Indian and Atlantic).

Youngest person to complete a solo circumnavigation by aircraft

Mason Andrews (USA, b. 26 Apr 2000) was aged 18 years 163 days when he finished his round-the-world flight on 6 Oct 2018 at Monroe in Louisiana, USA. The journey took him 76 days.

The **oldest person** to achieve this feat is Fred Lasby (USA, b. 28 May 1912), who completed his solo trip around the globe aged 82 years 84 days. His journey lasted from 30 Jun to 20 Aug 1994, beginning and ending at Fort Myers in Florida, USA.

Kay Cottee (AUS) becomes the **first woman to sail around the world solo and non-stop**, making the 189-day voyage unassisted in her 11-m (36-ft) yacht First Lady. She had departed from Sydney, Australia, on 29 Nov 1987 and arrived back on 5 Jun the following year.

1988

On 17 Jan, Shirley Metz and Victoria "Tori" Murden (both USA) become the **first women to reach the South Pole by land**. They had departed from Hercules Inlet off the Ronne Ice Shelf on 27 Nov 1988, reaching the Pole using skis and snowmobiles.

1989

FROM THE SEA TO THE SUMMIT!

Tim Macartney-Snape (AUS) makes history by becoming the **first person to climb Everest from sea level**. Over a three-month period, he treks from the coast of India to the top of Everest – all without the use of bottled oxygen or Sherpas.

1990

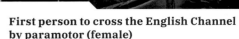

Epic Journeys

flying an electric helicopter a distance of 56.8 km (35.3 mi) on 7 Dec 2018. The flight took place in Los Alamitos, California, USA.

By cycle rickshaw/pedicab
Between 1 Jun and 17 Sep 2018, Len Collingwood (UK) travelled 6,248.28 km (3,882.50 mi) by rickshaw. Starting in Edinburgh, UK, he passed through 12 countries, ending in Istanbul, Turkey.

By electric vehicle (prototype)
Car-maker Aiways (CHN) drove their U5 electric SUV 15,022 km (9,334.24 mi) between Xi'an in Shaanxi, China, and Frankfurt in Germany from 17 Jul and 7 Sep 2019.

Longest journey by electric skateboard
Between 19 and 31 May 2019, Daniel Roduner (left) and Dwayne Kelly (both AUS) rode their battery-powered skateboards 1,036.42 km (644 mi) across Texas, USA. Their trip raised funds for Melanoma Patients Australia.

Most countries visited in 24 hours by kick scooter
Felix Frenzel (DEU) scooted through five countries on 3 Aug 2019. Beginning in Montespluga, Italy, he called by Switzerland, Liechtenstein and Austria, ending in Lindau, Germany. He covered some 160 km (100 mi).

Oldest person to cross Canada by bicycle (female)
Lynnea Salvo (USA, b. 21 Sep 1949) was 68 years 339 days old when she cycled into Lawrencetown Beach in Nova Scotia, Canada, on 26 Aug 2018. She'd set off from Tofino in British Columbia on 18 Jun.

FARTHEST JOURNEY...

By electric helicopter (prototype)
Martine Rothblatt, Lung Biotechnology, Tier 1 Engineering and Ric Webb (all USA) collaborated on

Fastest solo road 100 km by bicycle
As ratified by the World UltraCycling Association, Marcello Danese (ITA) cycled 100 km (62 mi) in 2 hr 45 min 35 sec on 23 Aug 2019. He beat the previous record by more than 8 min. The record-breaking ride took place in Verona, Italy.

First person to cross the English Channel by paramotor (female)
On 5 Dec 2016, Sacha Dench (UK) flew a powered paraglider across the English Channel. She set off at 11 a.m. from Saint-Inglevert in France, arriving at 12.38 p.m. in Dover, Kent, UK. It was part of a 7,000-km (4,350-mi) trip following endangered Bewick's swans (*Cygnus columbianus*) on their winter migration from Russia.

By 50-cc scooter
Michael Reid (USA) and Yonatan Belik (ISR) – founders of the Wheeling for the World (W4W) collective – rode a pair of 50-cc scooters 15,925.41 km (9,895.59 mi) through the 48 contiguous states of the USA. They started on 7 Sep 2019 and finished on 19 Nov, opting where possible to take backroads.

FASTEST TIME TO...

Travel the Thames by tandem stand-up paddleboard (SUP)
Mark Horne and James Smith (both UK) negotiated the Thames, the UK's second-longest river, in 2 days 9 hr 20 min. They set out on 15 Jul 2019 in Lechlade, Gloucestershire, reaching Teddington Lock in south-west London two days later.

Longest journey by scooter and sidecar
From 21 Jul 2017 to 20 Jan 2019, Matt Bishop (far left) and Reece Gilkes (both UK) rode for 54,962 km (34,151.8 mi) through 35 countries and five continents. The purpose of their trip was to generate awareness of modern slavery and raise funds for the charity Unseen UK. The pair – who had no biking experience prior to their trip – took turns in the driving seat.

A BRIEF HISTORY OF ADVENTURE

Fly from Land's End to John o' Groats by powered paramotor

James Du Pavey (UK) flew the length of the UK in 1 day 12 hr 19 min on 8–9 Jul 2019.

Cycle the length of...

• **Japan**: From 19 to 26 Jul 2018, Hiroki Nagaseki (JPN) cycled south from Cape Sōya on Hokkaidō to Cape Sata on Kyūshū in a time of 7 days 19 hr 37 min.

• **India**: Vikas Lnu (IND) cycled from Srinagar in northern India to Cape Comorin in the south in 10 days 3 hr 32 min. His ride lasted from 25 Oct to 4 Nov 2018.

Sufiya Khan (IND) covered the same distance by foot in 87 days 2 hr 17 min from 25 Apr to 21 Jul 2019 – the **fastest time to walk the length of India (female)**.

• **The Pan-American Highway**: Between 23 Jul and 16 Oct 2018, Michael Stresser (AUT) cycled from Prudhoe Bay in Alaska, USA, to Ushuaia in Argentina, covering the 22,642-km (14,069-mi) route in just 84 days 11 hr 50 min. En route, he also broke the **South America** record, crossing the continent north to south in 41 days 41 min.

Fastest crossing of Lake Baikal on foot

Michael Stevenson (UK) walked and skied the length of the frozen Lake Baikal in Siberia, Russia, in 11 days 14 hr 11 min. He embarked on his 652.3-km (405.3-mi) solo expedition from Kultuk in the south on 25 Feb 2020 and reached Nizhneangarsk in the north on 7 Mar, pulling a 66.3-kg (146-lb) pulk of supplies.

Fastest journey from Land's End to John o' Groats by triplet bicycle

Robert Fenwick, Alexander Lord and James Tyson (all UK, left to right) rode their three-person cycle the length of the UK in 6 days 9 hr 35 min. Their journey lasted from 16 to 22 Jun 2019. The three cyclists, who first met at school, surpassed the previous record by almost four hours, despite two lengthy setbacks caused by tyre punctures.

Fastest solo circumnavigation of Australia by sail boat (monohull)

As confirmed by the World Sailing Speed Record Council, the speediest single-handed, non-stop circumnavigation of Australia in a monohull vessel took 58 days 2 hr 25 min, by Lisa Blair (AUS). She set out from d'Albora Marinas Rushcutters Bay in Sydney Harbour on 20 Oct 2018 and returned there on 17 Dec.

On 25 Jul 2017, Lisa became the **first woman to sail around Antarctica**, taking 183 days 7 hr 21 min.

1999

First solo row across any ocean (female)

Victoria "Tori" Murden (USA) arrives at the Caribbean island of Guadeloupe on 3 Dec, having rowed across the Atlantic Ocean in 81 days 7 hr 31 min. She'd started out from Tenerife in the Canary Islands on 13 Sep.

2000

First non-motorized circumnavigation along the Equator

Mike Horn (ZAF) circles the Equator in 513 days between 2 Jun 1999 and 27 Oct 2000. Horn travels by bicycle, dugout canoe, sailing trimaran and on foot. He ends where he started, near Libreville in Gabon, on Africa's west coast.

First women to reach both poles

On 5 May, Catherine Hartley and Fiona Thornewill (both UK) reach the North Pole, having previously skied to the South Pole between 5 Nov 1999 and 4 Jan 2000. Fiona's husband Mike (UK) is also a member of both expeditions, making them the **first married couple to reach both poles**.

2001

Round-Up

Most climbs over 8,000 m without bottled oxygen
Denis Urubko (KAZ/RUS) has made 20 ascents of mountains higher than 8,000 m (26,246 ft) without supplementary oxygen. He began with Everest on 24 May 2000 and finished with Kangchenjunga on 19 May 2014. In 2019, he and Adam Bielecki were named National Geographic Adventurers of the Year after abandoning their expedition to K2 to aid stricken climbers nearby. Had they not done so, they would have made the first summit of K2 in winter.

Highest and lowest points visited on land
David Tait (UK) has visited two points on Earth separated by an elevation of 10,910 m (35,794 ft). He climbed Everest (8,848 m; 29,029 ft) five times, lastly in 2013. Then, on 18 Mar 2019, he descended to 2,062 m (6,765 ft) below sea level in the Mponeng gold mine in Gauteng, South Africa. (See the **first person to reach Earth's highest and lowest points** in the timeline below.)

Highest-altitude…
• **Dinner party**: 7,056 m (23,149 ft), at North Col in the Tibet Autonomous Region, China, on 30 Apr 2018. The diners included (left to right above) Nima Kanchha Sherpa (NPL), Jane Chynoweth (AUS), Sadie Whitelocks and Neil Laughton (both UK).
• **Harp recital**: 4,954 m (16,253 ft), by Siobhan Brady (IRL) with Desmond Gentle and Anna Ray (both UK) at Singla Pass, India, on 6 Sep 2018.
• **Dance party**: 5,892 m (19,330 ft), organized by an eight-person US team including Keith, Emma and JoJo Rinzler *et al*, at the top of Mount Kilimanjaro in Tanzania on 4 Aug 2019.

Oldest person to sail around the world solo and non-stop (female)
Jeanne Socrates (UK, b. 17 Aug 1942) was aged 76 years 47 days at the start of her successful circumnavigation under sail on 3 Oct 2018.
The **oldest** is Bill Hatfield (AUS, b. 14 Jan 1939). He was 80 years 145 days old when he sailed westabout, arriving back at The Spit in Gold Coast, Australia, on 22 Feb 2020, aged 81 years 39 days.

First person to walk the length of the Yangtze river
Ash Dykes (UK) walked the length of China's 6,437-km--long (3,999-mi) Yangtze from 26 Aug 2018 to 12 Aug 2019. The Yangtze is the world's third-longest river.

First skydive into the jet stream
High above the Earth's surface, at an altitude of 6,000–9,000 m (19,680–29,500 ft), is the jet stream (see p.38): meandering air currents that can travel at around 400 km/h (250 mph). Marc Hauser (CHE) became the first person to skydive into these fast-flowing winds near Forbes, Australia, on 30 Jun 2018. He dived from a hot-air balloon at an altitude of 7,400 m (24,270 ft).

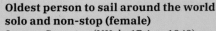

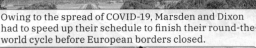

Owing to the spread of COVID-19, Marsden and Dixon had to speed up their schedule to finish their round-the-world cycle before European borders closed.

Fastest circumnavigation by tandem bicycle
Nurse consultant Rachael Marsden (near right) and her friend Catherine Dixon (both UK) cycled the world on a tandem bicycle in 263 days 8 hr 7 min from 29 Jun 2019 to 18 Mar 2020. They rode their pink two-seater, named *Alice*, across five continents, covering more than 28,960 km (18,000 mi). The ride raised £37,265 ($45,260) for Oxfam and the Motor Neurone Disease Association.

A BRIEF HISTORY OF ADVENTURE

First circumnavigation by balloon solo
Steve Fossett (USA) circles the globe in Bud Light Spirit of Freedom, *a 42.6-m-tall (140-ft) mixed-gas balloon, between 19 Jun and 2 Jul. He covers a distance of 33,195 km (20,626 mi).*
2002

2004
Fastest circumnavigation sailing non-stop, westbound, solo (male)
Jean-Luc Van Den Heede (FRA) sails the globe in 122 days 14 hr 3 min 49 sec in Adrien. *He crosses the Lizard Point-Ushant finishing line on 9 Mar, having set off on 7 Nov 2003.*

First person to complete the Explorers Grand Slam
Park Young-seok (KOR) reaches the North Pole on 30 Apr. He had previously reached the South Pole and climbed the Seven Summits (the highest point on each of the seven continents).

2005

2006
First circumnavigation sailing non-stop, westbound, solo (female)
Dee Caffari (UK) takes 178 days 3 hr 5 min 34 sec to circle the globe in her monohull Aviva. *She arrives into Portsmouth, UK, on 18 May, having left there on 20 Nov 2005.*

Oldest person to row an ocean (female)

On 12 Dec 2019, Sara Brewer (b. 12 Jan 1956) was 63 years 355 days old when she set off to cross the Atlantic with her 35-year-old rowing partner, Ann Prestidge (both UK). Their 86-day trip, as the "Row off the Wall" team, came during the Talisker Whisky Atlantic Challenge. Leaving from the Canary Islands, they reached Antigua in the Caribbean on 7 Mar 2020 – the eve of International Women's Day. (See p.80 for the **oldest person to row an ocean solo**.)

Swim 100 km in open water

On 29 Jul 2019, Pablo Fernández Álvarez (ESP) swam 100 km (62 mi) in 12 hr 21 min 14 sec in the waters off the coast of Jupiter in southern Florida, USA. He dedicated his feat to promoting the cause of ocean conservation. (For another of his extreme swims, see p.151.)

Ski solo, unsupported and unassisted to the South Pole

Anja Blacha (DEU) took 57 days 18 hr 50 min to ski from Berkner Island to the South Pole, arriving on 8 Jan 2020. At the end of the 1,400-km (870-mi) trek, she planted a flag at the pole bearing her provocative campaign slogan: "Not bad for a girl – almost impossible for everyone else".

Youngest person to reach the South Pole solo, unsupported and unassisted

Matthieu Tordeur (FRA, b. 4 Dec 1991) was 27 years 40 days old when he completed this feat of individual endurance. His trek from Hercules Inlet to the South Pole ended on 13 Jan 2019. Tordeur's most terrifying moment came on day one, when he fell into a hole up to his waist!

FASTEST TIME TO...

Become an "Iron Iceman"

Alexandre Fuzeau (FRA) was the first person to finish an Ice Mile swim and a full IRONMAN® triathlon in a calendar year. The feat took him 198 days. He swam an Ice Mile under International Ice Swimming Association regulations on 18 Jan 2019, at a 4.97°C (40.94°F) pool in Volendam, Netherlands. On 4 Aug 2019, he completed an IRONMAN triathlon in Hamburg, Germany.

Climb the highest points of Europe

Adam Stevenson (UK) scaled geographical Europe's highest peaks in 173 days 20 hr 45 min, from 2 Apr to 23 Sep 2019.

Visit all European capital cities by scheduled surface transport

Glen Burmeister (UK) took 24 days 22 hr 6 min to visit all 43 European capitals. He started in Valletta (Malta) on 9 Nov 2019 and finished in Reykjavík (Iceland) on 3 Dec. He covered 25,554 km (15,879 mi) using ground- and water-based public transport, and walked a further 145 km (90 mi).

Greatest distance skied in Antarctica solo, unsupported and unassisted

Richard Parks (UK) single-handedly skied 3,700 km (2,299 mi) during four Antarctic expeditions from Hercules Inlet to the Geographic South Pole between 18 Dec 2012 and 15 Jan 2020.

His quartet of expeditions to date also includes two visits to the South Pole and represents the **most solo, unsupported and unassisted journeys in Antarctica**. Parks is from Pontypridd in Wales, hence the Welsh national flag in the inset picture.

Prior to becoming an extreme endurance athlete, Parks played rugby union, appearing for the Barbarians and his home country (see right).

2006
First double amputee to climb Everest
Mark Inglis (NZ) reaches the summit from the north side and with the aid of bottled oxygen on 15 May. In 1982, his legs were amputated below the knees after they had become frostbitten.

2008
Fastest circumnavigation by helicopter
Edward Kasprowicz and co-pilot Steve Sheik (both USA) circle the globe in an AgustaWestland Grand helicopter in 11 days 7 hr 5 min, ending on 18 Aug. They begin and end in New York City, USA; their average speed is 136 km/h (84 mph).

2012

First circumnavigation using human power solo
From 10 Jul 2007 to 21 Jul 2012, Erden Eruç (TUR) rows, kayaks, hikes and cycles his way around the world. His trip takes 5 years 11 days 12 hr 22 min. He cycles North America, Australia and Africa, and rows the Pacific, Indian and Atlantic oceans.

2019

First person to reach Earth's highest and lowest points
On 28 Apr, Victor Vescovo (USA) reaches the Challenger Deep at the bottom of the Pacific Ocean in the deep-sea submersible Limiting Factor. He had climbed Everest on 24 May 2010. (To find out more, turn the page!)

HALL OF FAME

Victor Vescovo

We know more about the surface of Mars than Earth's ocean depths. Only a handful of explorers have ventured into these dark waters. Victor Vescovo (USA) is one of them.

The Challenger Deep is a valley found at the bottom of the Mariana Trench in the Pacific Ocean. At almost 11 km (6.8 mi) below the surface, it is Earth's **lowest known point**. It was first sounded using a weighted rope on 23 Mar 1875 by the British survey vessel HMS *Challenger*, from which it takes its name.

Only three submersibles with a human crew have ever made it to this remote region of the sea floor. The **first** was the *Challenger* club. Across two dives on 25 Mar 2012, piloted by film-maker James Cameron (CAN) – the most recent vessel to join this exclusive club. Across two dives *Factor* was the **first solo dive into the Challenger Deep**. Victor's *Limiting* Next was *DEEPSEA CHALLENGER* on 25 Mar 2012, piloted by film-maker James on 28 Apr and 1 May 2019, the former naval officer guided his sub solo to the *Limiting* region of the sea floor. The **first** was the *Trieste* in 1960 (see below).

Factor was the most recent submersible. The **first solo dive into the Challenger Deep** – the former naval officer guided his sub solo to an average depth of 10,925 m (35,843 ft) in a manned submersible. Cameron was *Factor* on 28 Apr and 1 May 2019, becoming the **deepest dive** on record with Victor's "Five Deeps Expedition" an average depth of 10,925 m (35,843 ft) in a manned submersible. this is the **deepest dive** on record with Victor's "Eastern Pool";

The descent was the fourth leg of Victor's five oceans. The mission began with the Puerto Rico Trench in the Atlantic, followed by to map the deepest point in Earth's five oceans. The mission began with the Puerto Rico Trench (Southern Ocean) and Java Trench the South Sandwich. It ended on 24 Aug 2019, when Victor reached the deepest point in Earth's five oceans. The descent was the fourth leg of Victor's the South Sandwich. It ended on 24 Aug 2019, Deep, becoming the began with the Puerto Rico Trench (Southern Ocean) and Java Trench (Indian Ocean). It ended on 24 Aug 2019's Molloy Deep, becoming the the bottom of the Arctic Ocean's **deepest point in each ocean**. **first person to visit the deepest point** in a point that is the the bottom of the Arctic Ocean **to visit the deepest point such** a feat, the real achievement of, and perhaps find a point such **first person** is scheduled to return to the Challenger Deep

In 2020, Victor is scheduled to return to the Challenger Deep deeper still. But for anyone intrepid enough to attempt such to ratify his 2019 readings, and perhaps find a point that is a feat, the real achievement is reaching, making it back again.

In 2020, Victor is scheduled to return to the Challenger Deep to ratify his 2019 readings. But for anyone intrepid enough to attempt such a feat, the real achievement is reaching such a rarely visited part of our world at all – and, of course, making it back again.

A polystyrene cup, which was positioned outside *Limiting Factor*, after its visit to the *Limiting Factor*. Submariners often take cups like this on Challenger Deep. Submariners deep dives to show the effect of pressure at extreme depths.

100%

CHALLENGER
DEEP
~10,900
APRIL
2019

CERTIFICATE

GUINNESS WORLD RECORDS

The deepest dive by a crewed vessel is 10,925 m (35,843 ft), achieved by explorer Victor Vescovo (USA) on reaching the bottom of the submersible Challenger Deep during two descents Limiting Factor on 28 Apr–1 May 2019

OFFICIALLY AMAZING

RECORD HOLDER

VICTOR

1: Victor and his team review diving sites. The "Five Deeps Expedition" was very much supported by a collaborative effort. He was supported by scientists, engineers and sonar specialists, among others. Standing to his left is Patrick Lahey, president of Triton Submarines. The company that built DSV Limiting Factor.

2: Victor is congratulated on his Challenger Deep dives by Jacques Piccard (CHE) – made along with Don Walsh (USA), who – company that built **dive to the Challenger Deep**. They piloted the Swiss-built US Navy the **first crewed dive to the Challenger** bathyscaphe Trieste on 23 Jan 1960, on the 8,848-m (29,029-ft) peak of Everest, the **Deep**. They piloted the Swiss-built US Navy a dive that lasted nearly five hours.

3: On 24 May 2010, proud Texan Victor tops the 8,848-m (29,029-ft) peak of Everest, the **highest mountain**, guided by fellow record-breaker Kami Rita Sherpa (see pp.46–47). This also makes Victor the **first person to reach Earth's highest and lowest points.**

4: A deep-sea creature filmed by Victor's team during a dive into the 7,450-m-deep Java Trench in the Indian Ocean (24,442-ft) Java Trench. His scientists believe it to on 16 Apr 2019. His scientists believe it to be a tunicate, or "sea squirt", although at present the be a tunicate, or "sea squirt", although its exact species remains a mystery at present.

5: Victor pilots Limiting Factor near the intense bottom of the Mariana Trench. The intense water pressure at such depths is more than 1,000 times that at sea level.

Find out more about Victor in the Hall of Fame section at www. **guinnessworldrecords.com/2021**

Formerly a US Navy submarine hunter, the DSSV Pressure Drop is now refitted as a state-of-the-art support ship. The inset shows Limiting Factor, the sub in which Victor visited the oceans' deepest points. Its features include a 9-cm-thick (3.5-in) titanium hull. In the event of a power cut on a dive, weight ballasts are released, enabling it to rise.

DSSV PRESSURE

Technology

▶ Fastest tractor (modified)

On 23 Oct 2019, ex-motorcycle racer and TV presenter Guy Martin (UK) drove a race-tuned JCB Fastrac at an average of 217.570 km/h (135.191 mph) over two runs at Elvington airfield in North Yorkshire, UK. The tractor had been transformed into a speed machine with the help of a smaller cab and light aluminium bodywork, as well as a new 1,000-hp (745-kW) JCB engine with an ice-tank cooler, turbocharger and 3D-printed manifold.

Guy pushed the first iteration of this tractor to 166.79 km/h (103.64 mph) on 20 Jun 2019.

DESTINATIONS

JCB
8000

WFT

RICARDO

WILLIAMS

Delphi
Technologies

BKT

DENSO

FEDERAL
MOGUL

ZF

GKN

Whatever the machine, Guy Martin will make it go
quickly. On 16 Oct 2014, he drove the **fastest soapbox**
to a speed of 137.78 km/h (85.61 mph).

163

Rollercoasters

Most visited theme park
Magic Kingdom at Walt Disney World in Florida, USA, had 20,859,000 visitors in 2018, according to the *2018 Global Attractions Attendance Report*. Magic Kingdom has four rollercoasters, including classics such as *Space Mountain*; a new *TRON*-inspired ride is due to open in 2021.

Most rollercoasters (country)
China had 1,518 rollercoasters of any kind, as of 21 Nov 2019. It had almost twice as many as the next-highest country, the USA, with 826. Japan was third with 244.

Asia is home to the **most rollercoasters (continent)**: 50.5%, a total of 2,549. By contrast, there are only 79 in all of Africa.

Longest inverted rollercoaster
Banshee at Kings Island in Mason, Ohio, USA, measures 1,257 m (4,124 ft). Like all inverted rollercoasters, passengers are seated below the track rather than above it. *Banshee* carries its passengers at speeds of up to 109 km/h (68 mph) through seven separate inversions, including a dive loop, a zero-gravity roll and a "pretzel knot".

Fastest flying rollercoaster
The cars on *Flying Dinosaur* are towed by an "out-of-control Pteranodon" at a top speed of 100 km/h (62 mph). The ride, at Universal Studios Japan in Konohana, Osaka, is also the **longest flying rollercoaster**, with a total track length of 1,124 m (3,687 ft). Flying rollercoasters simulate the sensation of flight by suspending passengers horizontally beneath the cars.

Oldest fully restored rollercoaster
Leap-the-Dips, a traditional wooden rollercoaster at Lakemont Park in Altoona, Pennsylvania, USA, was built by the Edward Joy Morris Company in 1902. It was closed to the public in 1985, seemingly at the end of its life, only to be restored and re-opened in 1999.

The **oldest rollercoaster operating continuously** is *The Great Scenic Railway* at Luna Park in Melbourne, Victoria, Australia. It opened to the public on 13 Dec 1912 and has remained in operation ever since.

Steepest steel rollercoaster
The *TMNT Shellraiser* – located at the Nickelodeon Universe Theme Park in East Rutherford, New Jersey, USA – features a 43-m (141-ft) vertical lift hill that descends on a slope curving to an angle of 121.5°. The ride opened to the public on 25 Oct 2019.

The **steepest wooden rollercoaster** is *Goliath*, which has a drop at an angle of 85.13°. The giant ride opened to the public on 19 Jun 2014 at Six Flags Great America in Gurnee, Illinois, USA.

Longest mountain coaster
Mountain coasters run on a track that follows the terrain of a hill or mountain, typically using one- or two-person sleds. *Tobotronc,* at the Naturlandia resort near Sant Julià de Lòria in Andorra, has a total track length of 5.3 km (3.2 mi). Its fast-descent stage measures 3.6 km (2.2 mi) long and drops a vertical distance of 400 m (1,312 ft).

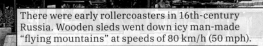
There were early rollercoasters in 16th-century Russia. Wooden sleds went down icy man-made "flying mountains" at speeds of 80 km/h (50 mph).

Fastest rollercoaster
Formula Rossa accelerates to 240 km/h (149.1 mph) in 4.9 sec and climbs to 52 m (170 ft). It opened in 2010 at Ferrari World in Abu Dhabi, UAE.

Fastest shuttle rollercoaster
A top speed of 161 km/h (100 mph) has been recorded by two shuttle rollercoasters: *Superman: The Escape* (later renamed *Superman: Escape from Krypton*) at Six Flags Magic Mountain in California, USA; and *Tower of Terror* at Dreamworld in Gold Coast, Australia. Both rides opened in 1997: on 23 Jan, *Tower of Terror* also became the **first rollercoaster to reach 100 mph**.

Longest rollercoaster
Steel Dragon 2000 has a total length of 2,480 m (8,136 ft). Found in Nagashima Spa Land in Mie, Japan, it has a top speed of 153 km/h (95 mph) and is steel-reinforced against earthquakes.

Longest shuttle rollercoaster
The 600-m-long (1,968-ft) *Fury* opened on 24 Jun 2019 at Bobbejaanland near Antwerp in Belgium. The tracks of shuttle rollercoasters do not form a continuous circuit – cars return to their start point in the opposite direction. Riders on *Fury* press buttons to vote on whether it launches forwards or backwards.

Largest drop on a steel rollercoaster
Kingda Ka at Six Flags Great Adventure near Jackson, New Jersey, USA, has a drop of 127.4 m (418 ft). The total height reaches a maximum of 139 m (456 ft) above ground level, making it the **tallest rollercoaster** (see below). It opened in 2005.

Most track inversions on a rollercoaster
There are 14 track inversions on *The Smiler* at Alton Towers Resort in Staffordshire, UK. The rollercoaster opened to the public on 31 May 2013. Riders whirl through the twists at speeds of up to 85 km/h (52.82 mph), with the highest drop reaching 30 m (98 ft). It takes just 165 sec to complete the 1,170-m-long (3,839-ft) track.

Most rollercoasters in one theme park
Situated in Valencia, California, USA, Six Flags Magic Mountain has 19 rollercoasters. This includes three record-breaking tall rides (see below).

Fastest floorless rollercoaster
Yukon Striker, found at Canada's Wonderland in Vaughan, Ontario, Canada, can reach speeds of 130 km/h (80.8 mph). Riders are seated within an open framework that allows them to see down past their feet. *Yukon Striker* opened on 3 May 2019, taking the record from its sister dive coaster, the 120.7-km/h (75-mph) *Valravn*.

Tallest wooden rollercoaster
Located in the Everland theme park in Yongin-si, South Korea, *T Express* rises to a height of 56 m (183 ft). The ride opened to the public on 14 Mar 2008, and claimed the record when the 66.4-m (218-ft) *Son of Beast* in Mason, Ohio, USA, closed in 2009. *T Express* carries thrillseekers at speeds of up to 104 km/h (64.6 mph).

Tallest rollercoasters

Type	Name	Location	Height
Steel	*Kingda Ka*	Jackson, New Jersey, USA	139 m (456 ft)
Shuttle	*Superman: Escape from Krypton*	Valencia, California, USA	126.5 m (415 ft)
Inverted	*Wicked Twister*	Sandusky, Ohio, USA	65.5 m (215 ft)
Flying	*Tatsu*	Valencia, California, USA	52 m (170 ft)
Stand-up	*Riddler's Revenge*	Valencia, California, USA	47.5 m (156 ft)
Indoor	*Mindbender*	Edmonton, Alberta, Canada	44 m (145 ft)
Suspended	*Vortex*	Vaughan, Ontario, Canada	27.7 m (91 ft)

On the Road

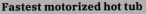

(19-mi) distance at an average speed of 26 km/h (16 mph). *La Marquise* has only had five owners since its creation. Its current owner bought the car for $4.62 m (£2,995,430) at an auction on 7 Oct 2011 in Hershey, Pennsylvania, USA.

Longest car
American Dream is a 26-wheeled limousine that measures 30.5 m (100 ft) in length – about three-and-a-half times that of a London Routemaster bus. Features include a swimming pool and a helipad, and it is hinged in the middle to aid cornering. The luxury limo was designed by Jay Ohrberg (USA), the "King of the Show Cars", who also created the DeLorean in *Back to the Future* (USA, 1985).

Largest loop-the-loop in a car
On 25 Nov 2019, Terry Grant (UK) drove a Jaguar F-Pace through a Hot Wheels loop with a diameter of 19.49 m (63 ft 11 in) in Riyadh, Saudi Arabia. He beat his own record of 19.08 m (62 ft 7 in) from 14 Sep 2015.
  In 2017, stunt driver Grant used a Jaguar E-Pace to set the **farthest barrel roll in a car** – 15.3 m (50 ft 2 in) – on 11 Jul in London, UK.

First passenger car
On 24 Dec 1801, inventor and mining engineer Richard Trevithick (UK) took seven passengers for a ride through Camborne in Cornwall, UK, in a steam-powered automobile named the *Puffing Devil*.

Oldest functioning car
La Marquise is a steam-powered, four-wheeled, four-seater vehicle manufactured by De Dion, Bouton et Trépardoux (FRA) in 1884. In 1887, it drove from Paris to Neuilly in France, covering the 30.5-km

Largest monster truck
Bigfoot 5 is 4.7 m (15 ft 6 in) tall and weighs 17.2 tonnes (38,000 lb). Built by Bob Chandler (USA) in 1986, it is one of 21 monster trucks in the *Bigfoot* line. Its gargantuan 3-m-high (10-ft) tyres were taken from an experimental land train used by the US Army. *Bigfoot 5 is* now permanently parked in St Louis, Missouri, USA.

Fastest motorized hot tub
Carpool DeVille averaged a speed of 84.14 km/h (52.28 mph) over two runs on 10 Aug 2014 in Wendover, Utah, USA. Creators Phillip Weicker and Duncan Forster (both CAN) took a 1969 Cadillac and fitted it with a fibreglass tank. A liquid-to-liquid heat exchanger with engine coolant warmed the water in the hot tub to 38.8°C (102°F).

Longest continuous car skid
On 15 Oct 1964, while decelerating after an attempt at the land-speed record at the Bonneville Salt Flats in Utah, USA, driver Craig Breedlove (USA) lost control of the jet-powered *Spirit of America*. The car skidded for around 10 km (6 mi) in the desert before clipping telegraph poles and crashing into a salt pond. Incredibly, Breedlove walked away unharmed.

Lowest roadworthy car
Mirai measures just 45.2 cm (1 ft 5.7 in) from the ground to the highest part of the car, as verified on 15 Nov 2010. It was created by students and teachers of the automobile engineering course at Okayama Sanyo High School in Asakuchi, Japan.

Hairiest car
Maria Lucia Mugno and Valentino Stassano (both ITA) sewed 120 kg (264 lb 8 oz) of human hair to the interior and exterior of Maria's Fiat 500. The coiffeured car was measured at a public weighbridge on 15 Mar 2014 in Salerno, Italy.

Demolition derby drivers can be disqualified for "sandbagging" – i.e., avoiding contact with other cars!

Largest demolition derby
On 3 Aug 2019, the Festival de la Galette de Sarrasin staged a motorized melee with 125 participants in Saint-Lazare-de-Bellechasse, Quebec, Canada. The event was organized by Nicolas Tremblay, Julien Fournier and Paul Morin (all CAN). Mathieu Langlois was declared the winner after 50 min of crashing and bashing; he was driving a 2001 Toyota Corolla.

Fastest acceleration from 0–100 mph for a lawnmower

On 6 May 2019, W Series driver Jessica Hawkins (UK) swapped her racecar for *Mean Mower V2*, guiding it from 0–160 km/h (0–100 mph) in 6.29 sec in Klettwitz, Germany. The lawnmower, built by Honda and Team Dynamics (UK), was equipped with a four-cylinder 200-hp engine used by Honda's *Fireblade* sportbike.

First hybrid vehicle

The Lohner-Porsche *Semper Vivus* was constructed in 1900 at the Jacob Lohner and Company Coachworks in Vienna, Austria. It combined two "Systeme Porsche" electric hub motors with a pair of petrol engines, in what would today be called a "series hybrid" arrangement.

Fastest electric car (FIA-approved)

The *Venturi Buckeye Bullet 3* achieved a speed of 549.21 km/h (341.26 mph) over a two-way flying mile on 19 Sep 2016 at the Bonneville Salt Flats. Roger Schroer (USA) was behind the wheel. The electric car was designed and built by engineering students at Ohio State University's Center for Automotive Research, in partnership with French electric car designers Venturi.

Fastest tuk-tuk

On 13 Feb 2020, Ray Macdonald and Rojjaporn Lertworawanich (both THA) drove a modified three-wheeled autorickshaw to a speed of 130.45 km/h (81.05 mph) at Sangtawan airfield in Bangkok, Thailand. They flew past the mark of 119.58 km/h (74.30 mph) set on 13 May 2019 by the team of Matt Everard and Russell Shearman (both UK) at Elvington airfield in North Yorkshire, UK.

Most wins of the World Solar Challenge (Cruiser class)

The Cruiser class of the World Solar Challenge (see bottom) was introduced in 2013 to encourage development of practical solar vehicles. Entries are judged on criteria including energy efficiency, ease of access and passenger comfort. On 21 Oct 2019, Solar Team Eindhoven (NLD) claimed its fourth Cruiser title in four-seater *Stella Era*.

Fastest lap of the Nürburgring Nordschleife by an electric car

On 3 Jun 2019, Romain Dumas (FRA) drove the Volkswagen ID.R prototype around the iconic 20.81-km-long (12.93-mi) German circuit in 6 min 5.336 sec. The ID.R has two electric motors that generate a combined 500 kW (670 hp). It reportedly weighs less than 1,100 kg (2,500 lb) and has a 0–100 km/h (0–62 mph) time of 2.25 sec.

Largest parade of...

• **Mercedes-Benz cars**: 384, in Huizhou, Guangdong, China, on 28 Dec 2019. The Guangzhou office of IT company UNICLUB (CHN) took the parade on a scenic drive through the Nankun mountain range.

• **Harley-Davidson motorcycles**: 3,497, in Paris, Texas, USA, on 5 Oct 2019. The bikers came from all over the USA to ride alongside nomadic American motorcycle YouTuber Adam Sandoval.

• **Camping vehicles (RVs)**: 868, in Barcaldine, Queensland, Australia, on 26 May 2019. The event was organized by the Australian Motorhoming Lions Club.

• **Buses**: 503, in Prayagraj, Uttar Pradesh, India, on 28 Feb 2019. The local government was showing off the size of its fleet ahead of the arrival of Kumbh Mela festival pilgrims.

• **Ice-cream vans**: 84, at the annual gathering of British ice-cream van operators in Crewe, Cheshire, UK, on 16 Oct 2018. One of the trucks present was Edd China's **fastest electric ice-cream van** (see p.1).

Most wins of the World Solar Challenge

The World Solar Challenge is a biennial solar-powered car race across 3,020 km (1,876 mi) of the Australian Outback. Vattenfall Solar Team (NLD), based at the Delft University of Technology, won seven times between 2001 and 2017 (pictured). Their 2019 race ended in heartbreak when *Nuna X* caught fire while leading the race on the final day. No one was hurt, but it dashed the team's hopes for an eighth victory.

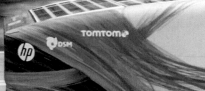

Transport

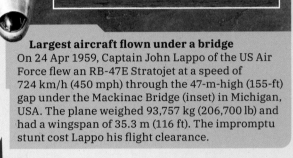

First supersonic airliner

The Soviet Tupolev Tu-144 made its first supersonic flight on 5 Jun 1969, four months before the Anglo-French Concorde did the same. The following year, the prototype Tu-144 reached 2,430 km/h (1,509 mph) during a test flight, making it the **fastest airliner**. Though it performed well in tests, the Tu-144's development was troubled and Concorde beat it to the title of **first supersonic passenger flight**, entering commercial service on 21 Jan 1976.

Highest helicopter landing

On 14 May 2005, fighter pilot Didier Delsalle (FRA) touched down at the summit of Everest (8,848 m; 29,029 ft) flying a Eurocopter AS350 B3. The exceptionally thin air at such high altitudes makes it difficult for helicopters to stay airborne, and nearly impossible for them to carry significant cargoes.

First oblique-wing aircraft

The NASA AD-1, which first flew on 21 Dec 1979, had a single wing joined to the fuselage by a pivot in the centre. Once in flight, it could be rotated up to 60°, meaning that the wing would be swept forward on one side of the plane and swept backward on the other. This design had been first proposed in the 1940s, but never implemented.

Longest duration non-stop scheduled flight

Singapore Airlines SQ21 has a scheduled flight duration of 18 hr 30 min and flies between Newark Liberty International Airport in New Jersey, USA, and Singapore Changi Airport. The first scheduled flight took place on 11 Oct 2018, with daily services following on 18 Oct. In Oct 2019, Qantas QF7879 made a 19-hr 16-min test flight from New York City, USA, to Sydney, Australia, although this is not yet a scheduled passenger service.

Longest streetcar/tram route (intra-city transport)

The 501 Queen in Toronto, Canada, is 24.5 km (15.2 mi) in length. This 24-hr, east–west line has an average of 52,000 passengers every day.

The oblique wing improved high-speed performance, but proved to be hard to control.

NASA 805

N805NA

Largest aircraft flown under a bridge

On 24 Apr 1959, Captain John Lappo of the US Air Force flew an RB-47E Stratojet at a speed of 724 km/h (450 mph) through the 47-m-high (155-ft) gap under the Mackinac Bridge (inset) in Michigan, USA. The plane weighed 93,757 kg (206,700 lb) and had a wingspan of 35.3 m (116 ft). The impromptu stunt cost Lappo his flight clearance.

Longest bus route

Peruvian company Ormeño operates a 6,200-km (3,852-mi) bus route – almost the same length as China's Yangtze River. It connects the Peruvian capital of Lima with Rio de Janeiro in Brazil. Known as the Trans Oceanica, its buses climb to 3,500 m (11,482 ft) on a 102-hr trip through the Amazon and Andes.

Longest bus ever

The articulated DAF Super CityTrain buses in the Democratic Republic of the Congo measured 32.2 m (105 ft) long and could accommodate 350 passengers. They weighed 28 tonnes (61,729 lb) unladen.

Largest private jet

Eleven models of the Boeing Business Jet 747-8 have been delivered to private customers since 2007. A snip for the super-wealthy at $364 m (£286 m), each jet leaves the factory in a "green" state – with no interior fittings aside from the cockpit, allowing luxury customization. A recent model, completed by Greenpoint Technologies (USA), boasts a stateroom, lounges, dining room and a palatial master bedroom (see insets). The 747-8 has a maximum take-off weight of 447,700 kg (987,000 lb).

BOEING BUSINESS JETS

In times of high demand, *The Ghan* can be extended to 44 carriages, increasing its length to 1,096 m (3,595 ft), or four times that of the *Titanic*.

Steam locomotive
On 3 Jul 1938, the "Class A4" No.4468 *Mallard* reached 201 km/h (125 mph) at Stoke Bank near Essendine in Rutland, UK. It was hauling seven coaches.

Maglev train
The Series L0 (A07) magnetically levitated (maglev) train attained a speed of 603 km/h (374.68 mph) on the Yamanashi Maglev Line in Japan on 21 Apr 2015.

The **fastest electric locomotive** is the multi-system electric 1216 050 (type ES 64 U4), which reached 357 km/h (221.83 mph) on 2 Sep 2006 on the high-speed line between Ingolstadt and Nuremberg in Germany.

Longest passenger train in scheduled service
The Ghan is a weekly sleeper service that covers the 54-hr journey between Adelaide and Darwin in Australia. Although the size of the train varies according to passenger numbers, a typical service comprises two locomotives and 30 carriages, giving an overall length of 774 m (2,539 ft).

Largest public-transit cable-car network
"Mi Teleférico" in La Paz, Bolivia, connects neighbourhoods in the famously mountainous Bolivian capital and its sister city of El Alto. As of 9 Mar 2019, when the Línea Plateada ("Silver Line") opened, the network had 33 stations along 10 cable-car lines, and a total track length of 33 km (20 mi).

FASTEST...

Transatlantic subsonic flight
At 4:17 a.m. on 9 Feb 2020, British Airways flight BA112 landed at London Heathrow Airport, having taken off from New York JFK only 4 hr 56 min earlier – around 1 hr 20 min ahead of schedule. This early arrival was made possible by Storm Ciara, which accelerated the west–east jet stream winds (see p.38) over the Atlantic to exceptionally high speeds, giving the airliner a boost.

Speed sailing
On 24 Nov 2012, Paul Larsen (AUS) reached 65.45 knots (121.21 km/h; 75.32 mph) in *Vestas Sailrocket 2* in Walvis Bay, Namibia. This is the highest speed reached under sail on water by any craft sailing more than 500 m (1,640 ft).

Speed by a hovercraft on water
Bob Windt (USA) drove a streamlined Universal UH19P hovercraft called *Jenny II* at 137.4 km/h (85.38 mph) at the 1995 World Hovercraft Championships in Peso de Régua, Portugal.

First solar-powered train
The Byron Bay Solar Train runs along a 3-km (1.86-mi) stretch of the previously disused Murwillumbah railway line between North Belongil Beach and Byron Beach in New South Wales, Australia. The train comprises a pair of vintage carriages with a 77-kW/h battery bank and 6.5 kW of thin-film solar panels on the roof.

Heaviest load lifted by a helicopter
The huge Russian Mil Mi-26 helicopter can lift anything from the remains of a woolly mammoth preserved in ice to a retired Tupolev Tu-134 airliner (pictured). The Mi-26's heaviest cargo was a mass of 56,768.8 kg (125,153 lb) that it hauled to 2,000 m (6,560 ft) in the air on 3 Feb 1982 near Moscow.

The SS *United States* was withdrawn from service in 1969. It is now moored in Philadelphia.

Fastest passenger liner
The SS *United States* reached speeds in excess of 44 knots (81.48 km/h; 50.63 mph) during sea trials, and in 1952 crossed the Atlantic at an average speed of 34.51 knots (63.91 km/h; 39.71 mph). The liner's speed was facilitated by its relatively light weight (a result of large amounts of aluminium used in its construction) and powerful 180,000-kW (241,000-hp) engines.

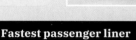

The fastest passenger liner to cross the Atlantic used to be awarded an unofficial yet prestigious accolade known as the "Blue Riband".

Tower

Formerly known as New Tokyo Tower, the Tokyo Skytree rises 634 m (2,080 ft) from the Sumida ward of the Japanese capital. The broadcasting and observation tower was completed in Feb 2012.

Twin buildings

The 88-storey Petronas Towers in Kuala Lumpur, Malaysia, are 451.9 m (1,482 ft) high. Opened in 1996, the towers are joined by a skybridge at levels 41 and 42.

Brick structure

The Anaconda Smelter Stack in Montana, USA, stands 169.2 m (555 ft) tall – 178.3 m (585 ft) including its foundation pedestal. The industrial chimney, part of the Washoe Smelter, was built using 2,446,392 bricks and completed on 1 Dec 1918. It is all that remains of the complex, and can be viewed only remotely on account of the poisonous heavy metals still present in the area.

Residential building

Situated in New York City, USA, 432 Park Avenue is the tallest single-function residential building at 425.5 m (1,396 ft). Its design was reportedly inspired by a 1905 trash can. This iconic address is set to be surpassed in 2020 by two taller residential buildings in New York City: Central Park Tower (472.4 m; 1,549 ft) and 111 West 57th Street (435.3 m; 1,428 ft).

Chimney

The GRES-2 Power Station in Ekibastuz, Kazakhstan, has a concrete stack standing 420 m (1,378 ft) tall. It is known locally as the "Cigarette Lighter" and weighs 60,000 tonnes (66,000 US tons). The power station is the beginning of the Ekibastuz–Kokshetau power transmission line, which has the **highest operating transmission voltage**: 1,150 kilovolts.

> The size-880 slipper owes its striking colour to 320 blue-tinted glass panels.

Building shaped like a shoe

The High-Heel Wedding Church in Chiayi, Chinese Taipei, measures 25.16 m long, 17.76 m high and 11.91 m wide (82 x 58 x 39 ft). The church, which does not hold religious services but acts as a wedding venue, is said to honour a local legend in which a girl's engagement was ended after she lost her legs to blackfoot disease.

Building

The Burj Khalifa (Khalifa Tower) measures 828 m (2,716 ft) tall. Developed by Emaar Properties, it officially opened on 4 Jan 2010 in Dubai, UAE. It is almost 200 m (656 ft) taller than its nearest rival, the Shanghai Tower, and twice as tall as the Empire State Building. Visitors with a head for heights can go to the 148th floor for At the Top, Burj Khalifa Sky – the **highest outdoor observation deck**, at 555.7 m (1,823 ft) – then descend to At.mosphere, which, at 441 m (1,147 ft), is the **highest restaurant**.

Cantilevered building

Opened in 2016, the King Power MahaNakhon is a 78-storey, 314.2-m (1,031-ft) mixed-use tower in Bangkok, Thailand. Thirty per cent of the building's total floor slab area is in cantilever span, with floors extending as much as 10 m (32 ft) outward from their vertical supports. A dramatic pixelated ribbon runs around the tower's exterior.

Cathedral spire

The Protestant Cathedral of Ulm in Germany has a 161.5-m-high (529-ft) spire. Although work on the building began in 1377, the tower in the west façade was not completed until 1890.

Pagoda

Completed in 2007, the 13-storey Tianning Pagoda in Changzhou, China, is 153.7 m (504 ft) tall. It is topped by a golden spire with a bronze bell that can be heard from a distance of 5 km (3 mi).

Hospital

The Li Shu Pui Block at the Hong Kong Sanatorium & Hospital stands 148.5 m (487 ft) tall. The 38-storey concrete and steel structure, built in 2008, is one of the largest private hospitals in China and has more than 400 beds.

Airport control tower

Tower West at Kuala Lumpur International Airport, Malaysia, measures 133.8 m (438 ft) tall and has 33 floors. Shaped like an Olympic torch, it was built as part of the airport's new KLIA2 terminal.

Grain silo

The Swissmill Tower in Zurich, Switzerland, is 118 m (387 ft) tall and can hold up to 35,000 tonnes (38,580 US tons) of grain. The huge silo took three years to build and was completed in Apr 2016.

Hindu temple

The 13-tiered gopura or gopuram (entrance tower) at the Sri Ranganathaswamy Temple on the Indian island of Srirangam reaches 72 m (236 ft) high. Dedicated to Ranganatha, a form of the Hindu deity Vishnu, the temple is more than 1,000 years old.

Castle

The apex of Neuschwanstein Castle, which overlooks the village of Hohenschwangau in Bavaria, Germany, rises 65 m (213 ft) above ground. It was built in the 19th century on the ruins of three other castles.

Cemetery

Located near São Paulo in Brazil, the Memorial Necrópole Ecumênica in Santos has 14 permanently illuminated storeys that rise 46 m (150 ft) above ground. The first burial took place here on 28 Jul 1984.

LED-illuminated façade

On 1 Jan 2019, New Year's revellers in Dubai, UAE, were treated to a dramatic light show on the Burj Khalifa, the world's **tallest building** (see above left). The LED-illuminated façade measured 790.8 m (2,594 ft). With a total area of 44,956.77 m² (483,910 sq ft), it was also the **largest LED-illuminated façade.**

Wooden pagoda

Located in Yingxian County, Shanxi, China, the Sakyamuni Pagoda of Fogong Temple has a height of 67.3 m (220 ft). It was constructed in 1056.

The **tallest wooden building** is Mjøstårnet, an 18-storey mixed-use structure in Brumunddal, Norway (inset). It is 85.4 m (280 ft) tall and is the work of Voll Arkitekter and builders HENT and Moelven Limtre (all NOR).

Unoccupied building

Construction on the Ryugyong Hotel in Pyongyang, North Korea, was halted in 1992. Despite reaching its full height of 330 m (1,082 ft), the building remains unfinished. It was built from reinforced concrete rather than lighter steel, which necessitated a pyramid-shaped design to support its upper levels.

Iron structure

The Eiffel Tower in Paris, France, is 300 m (984 ft) high, rising to 324 m (1,063 ft) to the tip of a TV antenna added in the 1950s. At the time of its inauguration on 31 Mar 1889, it was the tallest structure in the world; a title it would hold until the completion of New York's Chrysler Building on 27 May 1931.

Building in the shape of a picture frame

At 150.2 m (492 ft) tall and 95.5 m (313 ft) wide, the Dubai Frame towers over Zabeel Park in Dubai, UAE. Designed by Mexican architect Fernando Donis, the landmark's two towers are linked by a 48th-floor viewing gallery with a glass-floored walkway. It was completed on 1 Jan 2018.

Backyard Inventors

Largest water pistol
A super-sized soaker built by engineer Mark Rober and friends Ken Glazebrook, Bob Clagett and Dani Yuan (all USA) measured 1.22 m tall and 2.22 m long (4 ft x 7 ft 3 in) on 6 Nov 2017. Powered by a tank of pressurized nitrogen, it can fire a jet of water powerful enough to smash glass!

Smallest working drill
On 28 Nov 2017, Gaya Prasad Agarwal (IND) presented a working drill measuring 6.93 mm tall, 8.4 mm long and 6.4 mm wide (0.27 x 0.33 x 0.25 in).

Loudest bicycle horn
Tired of being cut up in traffic, Yannick Read (UK) created "The Hornster" – a modified freight-train horn powered by a scuba-diving tank built into the bike's frame. It produced a sound pressure level of 136.2 dB(A) on 13 Feb 2013 in Surrey, UK. A 150-dB noise is the same as a jet engine at 25 m (82 ft).

Highest-popping toaster
Fourteen-year-old Matthew Lucci (USA) turbocharged a toaster by adding a 12,000-rpm motor. It ejected a slice of toasted bread to a height of 4.57 m (15 ft) on 19 Nov 2012.

Smallest helicopter
Japanese inventor Gennai Yanagisawa (JPN) built the GEN H-4, a 70-kg (154-lb) helicopter with a rotor length of 4 m (13 ft). It consists of one seat and one power unit, and unlike traditional helicopters has two sets of contra-rotating rotors, eliminating the need for a balancing tail rotor.

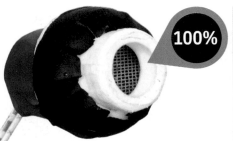

100%

Smallest vacuum cleaner
Engineering student Salvendar Ghansheed Baba (IND) takes waste materials and transforms them into miniature household appliances. His tiny vacuum cleaner (above) operates at 3.7 V, with its longest axis measuring 3.6 cm (1.4 in), as verified on 9 Apr 2019 in Vijayawada, India.

Smallest working circular saw
Another designer who thinks that small is beautiful is Lance Abernethy (NZ). On 23 Apr 2015, he 3D-printed a cordless circular saw of his own design measuring 14.3 x 18.9 x 10.6 mm (0.56 x 0.74 x 0.41 in). It was fitted with a 12-mm (0.47-in) working blade and powered by a hearing-aid battery.

Smallest road-legal car (non-production)
Austin Coulson (USA, pictured in 2013 with fiancée Lisa Stoll) built a car measuring 63.5 cm high, 65.4 cm wide and 126.4 cm long (2 ft 1 in x 2 ft 1.7 in x 4 ft 1.7 in). The vehicle was measured on 7 Sep 2012. It is licensed to be driven on public roads and has a speed limit of 40 km/h (25 mph).

Fastest sofa
On 26 Sep 2011, Glenn Suter (AUS) drove a motorized settee at 163.117 km/h (101.36 mph) at Camden Airport in New South Wales, Australia. The record attempt was organized by Australian drinks maker Ice Break. A coffee table was attached to the front of the mobile sofa as a method of breaking up the airflow to increase the vehicle's speed.

Fastest garden shed
Kevin Nicks (UK) converted a Volkswagen Passat into a motorized shed, refitting it with a 450-horsepower V6 twin-turbo Audi RS4 engine. On 22 Sep 2019, he took the shed to 170.268 km/h (105.800 mph), from a standing start, over a two-way measured mile (1.6 km) at Pendine Sands in Wales, UK.

BUILD-YOUR-OWN BOFFINS

Fastest pram
86.04 km/h (53.46 mph), built by Colin Furze (UK) and tested on 14 Oct 2012 at Shakespeare County Raceway in Stratford-upon-Avon, Warwickshire, UK

Fastest bathroom
68 km/h (42.25 mph), built by Edd China (UK) on 10 Mar 2011 in Milan, Italy. Bog Standard is a motorcycle and sidecar hidden under a bathroom set consisting of bathtub, sink and laundry bin

Largest Cozy Coupe
2.7 m (8 ft 10 in) long, built by John and Geof Bitmead (both UK), as measured on 14 Aug 2016 in Ambrosden, Oxfordshire, UK

Most powerful pencil sharpener
In 1999, Peter Svensson (SWE) re-engineered a pencil sharpener in style – with the addition of a 499.6-kw (670-hp) V12 engine borrowed from a tank. Although the engine worked at about 2,500 rpm, the machine was geared so that the sharpener operated at nearly normal speed.

Fastest robot to solve a Rubik's Cube
Albert Beer (DEU) spent an estimated 2,000 hours building a machine to crack the iconic puzzle cube in the blink of an eye. With the help of an algorithm, a microcontroller and six mechanical arms, "Sub1 Reloaded" solved a Rubik's Cube in 0.637 sec at an electronics trade fair in Munich, Germany, on 9 Nov 2016.

Largest functional microprocessor model
On 22 Jun 2016, software engineer James Newman (UK) finished work on a computer he calls the Megaprocessor. Instead of the nanometre-scale integrated circuits used in desktop computers, this machine is made from 42,370 pea-sized discrete transistors and measures 10 m (32 ft 10 in) wide and 2 m (6 ft 7 in) tall. The workings of the computer are shown using 10,500 LEDs.

Largest rideable hexapod robot
Mantis is a six-legged robot that stands 2.8 m (9 ft 2 in) tall and has a 5-m-wide (16-ft 4-in) leg span, as verified on 15 Nov 2017 in Wickham, Hampshire, UK. It was built by movie special-effects designer Matt Denton (UK), who can drive it from the cockpit or operate it remotely via an app. *Mantis* weighs 1.9 tonnes (4,188 lb) and is powered by a 2.2-litre (0.58-US-gal) turbo-diesel engine.

Tallest rideable motorcycle
A monster motorbike constructed by Fabio Reggiani (ITA) measures 5.10 m (16 ft 8 in) tall to the top of the handlebars – the same height as a giraffe. Weighing 5,000 kg (11,020 lb), *Big Bike* is powered by a 5.7-litre V8 motor. The chopper was ridden over a 100-m-long (328-ft) course at Montecchio Emilia in Italy on 24 Mar 2012.

Big Bike is six times the size of a standard chopper, with wheels taken from industrial excavators.

Fastest jet-powered go-kart
180.72 km/h (112.29 mph), test-driven by Tom Bagnall (UK) in York, North Yorkshire, UK, on 5 Sep 2017

www.diygt.org

Fastest monowheel motorcycle
117.34 km/h (72.91 mph), by the UK Monowheel Team and driver Mark Foster (all UK), who rode Trojan on 22 Sep 2019 at Elvington airfield in North Yorkshire, UK

Fastest motorized shopping trolley
113.29 km/h (70.4 mph), by Matt McKeown (UK) on 18 Aug 2013 in East Yorkshire, UK. The trolley had been fitted with a modified Chinook helicopter starter engine and a 250-cc Honda engine

Round-Up

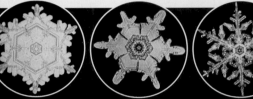

First photograph of a snowflake

Wilson Bentley (USA) spent 40 years taking pictures of thousands of snowflakes. His first successful photograph of an individual snow crystal was captured on 15 Jan 1885 on his family's farm in Vermont, USA. Bentley experimented with a glass-plate camera mounted on to a microscope to capture the delicate crystals in all their finery.

▶ Largest mirrored building

Situated at the UNESCO World Heritage Site Al-Hijra in Al-'Ula, Saudi Arabia, the 500-seat-capacity Maraya Concert Hall is covered by a wall of mirrors measuring a continuous 9,740 m² (104,840 sq ft). The building, constructed by the Royal Commission for Al-'Ula (SAU) and surveyed on 26 Dec 2019, dramatically reflects the area's volcanic landscape.

Deepest salvage

On 21 May 2019, the wreckage of a US Navy transport aircraft was recovered from the floor of the Philippine Sea some 5,638 m (18,500 ft) below the surface. The operation was carried out by a team from the US Navy Supervisor of Salvage and Diving (SUPSALV) using the deep-sea research ship RV *Petrel*.

Fastest elevator

The Guangzhou CTF Finance Centre in Guangdong, China, has an elevator capable of speeds of 75.6 km/h (47 mph). It can carry up to 21 people and can scale 95 floors in around 42 sec. The lift was designed by Hitachi Building Systems (JPN) and installed by Hitachi Elevator (CHN) on 10 Sep 2019.

First footage of molecular rotation

An international team of scientists assembled video footage of a rotating carbonyl sulphide molecule from 651 images captured over 125 trillionths of a second. The researchers from the Center for Free-Electron Laser Science, the University of Hamburg, the Max Born Institute (all DEU) and Aarhus University (DNK) published their results in *Nature* on 29 Jul 2019.

Largest aerial firework shell

On 8 Feb 2020, the Steamboat Springs Winter Carnival in Colorado, USA, closed in spectacular style by detonating a 1.26-tonne (2,797-lb) firework shell. The shell contained 380 individual comet fireworks and turned the sky red. It was the work of pyrotechnicians James Cowden Widmann, Eric Krug, Ed MacArthur and Tim Borden (all USA).

Rarest radioactive event observed

A research team looking for dark matter – the most elusive substance in the universe – happened to observe the decay of an isotope of xenon-124. It took place in the XENON1T instrument, which was submerged in water 1,500 m (4,921 ft) beneath the Gran Sasso mountain in Italy. Xenon-124 has a half-life of 1.8×10^{22} years – a trillion times the age of the universe. The XENON Collaboration's findings were published in *Nature* on 24 Apr 2019.

Heaviest weight lifted with glue

On 12 Jul 2019, adhesive manufacturer DELO (DEU) kept a 17.48-tonne (38,536-lb) truck suspended in the air for one hour with the aid of only 3 g (0.11 oz) of specially made glue in Windach, Germany. The vehicle was suspended from a crane via a bonded aluminium cylinder with a radius of just 3.5 cm (1.3 in).

Fastest 0–60 mph acceleration in an electric kart

On 9 Jun 2019, Luis Mengual (ESP) drove his all-wheel-drive (AWD) prototype kart from 0–60 mph (97 km/h) in 2.218 sec at the Kartodromo Internacional Lucas Guerrero in Valencia, Spain. Luis had spent two years building his electric-powered machine, which beat the previous record by 0.417 sec.

Want to see how Luis's kart compares to a seriously souped-up lawnmower? Turn to pp.166–67.

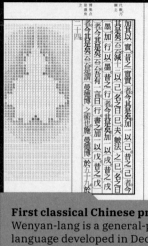

First classical Chinese programming language

Wenyan-lang is a general-purpose programming language developed in Dec 2019 by student Lingdong Huang (CHN) in Pittsburgh, Pennsylvania, USA. It reads as grammatically correct classical Chinese, rendering machine-readable code in the language of Confucius.

Largest 3D-printed boat

3Dirigo is a 7.72-m-long (25-ft 4-in) seaworthy vessel created by The University of Maine Advanced Structures and Composites Center (USA). The boat is named after the state of Maine's motto, "Dirigo" ("I guide"). It took 72 hr to print on 10 Oct 2019 in Orono, Maine, USA, and required the **largest polymer 3D printer** – with a maximum volume or "build envelope" of 343.61 m³ (12,134 cu ft).

First self-built functional LEGO® prosthetic arm

"Hand Solo", aka Andorra's David Aguilar, was born without a right forearm. He designed and built his own fully functioning arm using parts from a LEGO Technic helicopter set (#9396), completing the first version in 2017. David's most recent model, 2019's MK-IV, is a motorized limb with fingers that he controls by making subtle movements of his residual arm.

David's MK-IV prosthetic is built using pieces from the LEGO Technic Rough Terrain Crane set (#42082).

Washington, USA. The record attempt was made on Pi Day to demonstrate the power of Google Cloud's infrastructure.

Largest collection of washing machines

Retired engineer Lee Maxwell (USA) had amassed 1,350 unique washing machines as of 5 Aug 2019. He had restored all but six to working order, and has recently started building what he calls "Patent Demos" – small-scale working models of designs that were patented but either never built, or built but subsequently lost.

Most accurate value of pi

On 14 Mar 2019, Emma Haruka Iwao (JPN) calculated the mathematical constant π to 31,415,926,535,897 digits, with the support of Google (USA) in Seattle,

Best-selling smartphone brand

According to research carried out on 27 Feb 2020, Samsung (KOR) sold an estimated 260,247,100 smartphones in 2019. Samsung's nearest rival, Apple (USA), shifted 201,151,700 units during the same period.

Youngest co-discoverer of a circumbinary planet

Wolf Cukier (USA, b. 4 Jun 2002) was 17 years 27 days when he made the initial observations that led to the discovery of exoplanet TOI 1338 b. Wolf spotted the planet on 1 Jul 2019 while reading through a star database during an internship at NASA's Goddard Space Flight Center in Maryland, USA.

Highest-resolution radio telescope array

The Event Horizon Telescope (EHT) combines data from eight radio telescope arrays around the globe. It has a practical resolution of 43 microarcseconds – meaning it can focus on an object roughly equal in apparent size to an 8-cm-wide (3.1-in) disk on the surface of the Moon (as viewed from Earth). It was the EHT that provided the **first direct image of a black hole** (inset), as announced on 10 Apr 2019.

This supermassive black hole is located in the Messier 87 galaxy, 54 million light years from Earth.

○ HALL OF FAME

Andy Green

Whether it's cars, planes or even toboggans, if you want to go fast there's only one pilot you want behind the controls: British Wing Commander Andy Green.

Whether it's cars, planes or even toboggans, if you want to go fast there's only one pilot you want behind the controls: British Wing Commander Andy Green.

One Sunday in 1994, Andy read a newspaper article about a new land-speed record project looking for a driver. The team leader, Richard Noble, had hoped to go himself broken the land-speed record in *Thrust2* in 1983. Now he hoped to go even faster in *Thrust SSC* – a supersonic car powered by two Rolls-Royce Spey 202 jet engines capable of generating 222 kN (50,000 lbf) of thrust. And in Andy – a fighter pilot for the Royal Air Force (RAF) with a first-class degree in mathematics – he found the perfect driver.

After three years of development, the team took to the Black Rock Desert in Nevada, USA. On 15 Oct 1997, Andy drove *Thrust SSC*; *Thrust SSC* reached the Black Rock 202 jet speed of 1,227.985 km/h (763.035 mph), creating a sonic boom that could be felt 16 km (10 mi) away.

After three years of development, the team took to the Black Rock Desert in Nevada, USA. On 15 Oct 1997, Andy drove *Thrust SSC* at a speed of 1,227.985 km/h (763.035 mph), creating a sonic boom that could be felt 16 km (10 mi) away.

○ **fastest car (land-speed record)**
○ **first car to break the sound barrier**

Desert in Nevada, USA. On 15 Oct 1997, Andy drove *Thrust SSC* at a speed of 1,227.985 km/h (763.035 mph). *Thrust SSC* also became the **first car to break the sound barrier**, creating a sonic boom that could be felt 16 km (10 mi) away.

Fast-forward 23 years and Andy is once again behind the controls. This time, he's driving the land-speed record. This time, he's designed to again break land-speed record. Initial tests of the *Bloodhound LSR*, a rocket car designed to reach 1,000 mph, or 1,609 km/h. Initial tests (see below) are encouraging, and the hope is to make an official attempt in the coming year.

1

Bloodhound has been designed not only to break the land-speed record but also to inspire a new generation of children to take an interest in science and engineering.

The land speed record as measured over one mile is 1,227.985 km/h (763.035 mph). achieved by Andy Green (UK) driving Thrust SSC in the Black Rock Desert, Nevada, USA, on 15 October 1997

CERTIFICATE

GUINNESS WORLD RECORDS

A commemorative award to celebrate the 60th anniversary of Guinness World Records

OFFICIALLY

1955   2015

A.GREEN

ROYAL AIR FORCE

The only member of the Thrust SSC team who couldn't hear the car's sonic boom was Andy himself!

1: Testing *Bloodhound LSR* in 2019 in South Africa, where it reached a speed of 1,010 km/h (628 mph).

2: *Thrust SSC* breaks the **land-speed record** – and the sound barrier in 1997 – in the Nevada desert in 1997.

3: Andy takes on the Cresta Run bargain – in the RAF in the toboggan track in Switzerland in 2011, representing the **fastest** interservices Championships.

4: Celebrating breaking the **fastest diesel-engined car** record in 2006 (see below). *JCB Dieselmax* team in 2018.

5: Andy at the RAF Museum in 2018.

On 23 Aug 2006, at Bonneville Salt Flats in Utah, USA, Andy drove *JCB Dieselmax* at a speed of 563.418 km/h (350.092 mph) – the **fastest diesel-engined car**. Remarkably, he was not even in top gear.

Find out more about Andy in the Hall of Fame section at **www. guinnessworldrecords.com/2021**

Gaming

Largest prize pool for an esports tournament (single-player)
On 28 Jul 2019, the Arthur Ashe Stadium in New York City, USA, played host to the solo event finals of the *Fortnite* World Cup, with a prize pool of $15,287,500 (£12,338,400) at stake. The pot was shared among all 100 finalists, with even the last-placed finisher receiving $50,000 (£40,354). In front of a cheering crowd and up to 2 million viewers online, 16-year-old Kyle Giersdorf (USA, below), aka "Bugha", became the **first *Fortnite* Solo World Champion**, walking away with the $3-m (£2.4-m) top prize. The day before, the **first *Fortnite* Duo World Champions** had been crowned: "Nyhrox", aka Emil Bergquist Pedersen (NOR, bottom left), and "aqua", aka David Wang (AUT, bottom right).

"Bugha" underlined his new-found fame by appearing in a half-time commercial during Super Bowl LIV.

The gamer on the big screens is *Fortnite*-streaming superstar "Ninja" (aka Richard Tyler Blevins).

DESTINATIONS

The **largest esports prize pool for a tournament** was $34 m (£27.6 m), on offer for Valve's *Dota 2* championship The International 2019 on 20–25 Aug.

179

Speedruns

SPEEDRUN.COM

GWR on Speedrun.com
Listed here are the 60 most popular titles contested on Speedrun.com – the ultimate online leaderboard for speedrunning. We've teamed up with Speedrun.com to formally recognize speedrunning as a category in the GWR database and have created a series of unique challenges, which you can find at **speedrun.com/gwr**. All you need to do is get to the top of a leaderboard and take a screengrab to prove it, then follow the link to the GWR website and make your official application.

Top 60 most speedrun games on Speedrun.com

Game	Run type	Record holder	Time
A Hat in Time (PC)	Any%	"Enhu" (ARG)	36:07.7
Banjo-Kazooie (N64)	100%; N64	"Stivitybobo" (USA)	1:57:39
Bloodborne (PS4)	Any%; All Quitouts	"InSilico_" (IRL)	19:54
Celeste (PC)	Any%	"Marlin" (DEU)	27:0.7
CELESTE Classic (PC)	Any%	"Meep_Moop" (CAN)	1:43
Crash Bandicoot: N. Sane Trilogy (PC)	Crash Bandicoot; Any%	"DepCow" (USA)	42:10
Crossy Road (Android)	25 Hops; Mobile	"ENOOPS" (RUS)	3.8
Cuphead	All Bosses, Regular Difficulty, Legacy Version	"SBDWolf" (ITA)	23:16
Destiny 2 (PC)	Garden of Salvation	"Treezy" (UK), "purdy" (UK), "Intubate" (USA), "qassimks" (USA), "Crayonz" (USA), "Poots"	12:38
Diablo II: Lord of Destruction (PC)	Any% Normal; Softcore; Players 1; SOR	"Indrek" (EST)	1:04:44
Final Fantasy VII Remake (PS4)	Demo Any%; Normal	"desa3579" (DEU)	13:25
Getting Over It with Bennett Foddy (PC)	Glitchless	"Blastbolt"	1:13.2
Grand Theft Auto V (PC)	Classic%	"burhác" (HUN)	6:03:27
Grand Theft Auto: San Andreas (PC)	Any% (No AJS)	"Ielreset"	3:52:07
Guild Wars 2 (PC)	Spirit Vale; Vale Guardian; Restricted	"Deathlyhearts" (ROM), "qT Diablo", "Decados", "Codzka", "Tolgon", "Heldor", "qT Luigi", "BDaddl.7105", "qT Fennec", "eS Tim"	1:36
Hollow Knight (PC)	Any%; No Major Glitches	"fireb0rn" (CAN)	33:07
Human: Fall Flat (PC)	Any%; Solo	"Retr0virus11" (CAN)	8:49.6
Jump King (PC)	Any%	"Ny" (CHN)	4:24.7
Katana ZERO (PC)	All Stages; Normal; Katana	"Lastnumb3r" (POL)	15:57.7
League of Legends (PC)	Tutorial; Season 10; Part 1	"Xinipas" (BRA)	2:07
LEGO Star Wars: The Complete Saga (PC)	Any%; Solo	"WiiSuper" (USA)	2:42:27
Luigi's Mansion 3 (Switch)	Any%; Solo	"chris_runs" (AUT)	2:28:39
Mario Kart 8 Deluxe (Switch)	Nitro Tracks; Items; 150cc	"HitsujiOmochi" (JPN)	40:27
Minecraft: Java Edition (PC)	Any% Glitchless; Set Seed; Pre 1.9	"Illumina" (CAN)	4:56.7
New Super Mario Bros. Wii (Wii)	Any%	"FadeVanity" (UK)	24:28.3
Ori and the Blind Forest: Definitive Edition (PC)	All Skills, No Out of Bounds or Teleport Anywhere	"Lucidus"	27:26
Outlast (PC)	Any%; Main Game; PC	"HorrorDoesSpeedRuns" (USA)	8:12.2
Pencil Sharpening Simulator (PC)	Any%; 100 Pencils	"Jangoosed" (UK)	38:08

Celeste (Any%)
German gamer "Marlin" raced through the Matt Makes Games platformer on the PC in 27 min 0.7 sec. Released in Jan 2018, *Celeste* has proved instantly popular with speedrunners and had 7,049 runs submitted on Speedrun.com as of 22 Apr 2020 – the fifth most for any videogame.

Spyro the Dragon (Any%)
"ChrisLBC" (CAN) blitzed the PS2 platformer in 38 min 31 sec on 17 Jun 2018 and remains top of the leaderboard – if only by 1 sec.

"ChrisLBC" is also responsible for the **fastest Any% completion of *Spyro the Dragon* (*Spyro Reignited Trilogy*)** – just 6 min 9 sec, minus loads.

SpongeBob SquarePants: Battle for Bikini Bottom (100%)
On 3 Mar 2020, "SHiFT" (USA) saved Bikini Bottom from robot invasion in 1 hr 18 min 26 sec on Xbox. Released in 2003, the cartoon spin-off has gained cult status among speedrunners. With 4,243 runs, it is the 14th most popular game on Speedrun.com.

Ori and the Blind Forest: Definitive Edition (All Skills; No Out of Bounds or Teleport Anywhere)
On 12 Feb 2020, "Lucidus" navigated guardian spirit Ori – and companion Sein – through Moon Studios' 2016 expansion to the atmospheric platformer in 27 min 26 sec. The run knocked almost half a minute off the previous best.

Game	Category	Player	Time
Pokémon Red/Blue (Game Boy Player)	Any% Glitchless; ENG	"pokeguy" (USA)	1:45:21
Pokémon Sword/Shield (Switch)	Any%; ENG	"ringo777" (JPN)	4:04:13
Portal (PC)	Out of Bounds	"Shizzal" (USA)	6:53.9
Portal 2 (PC)	Single Player; Inbounds	"CantEven" (USA)	59:47.4
Refunct (PC)	Any%; Normal	"xzRockin" (USA)	2:42.4
Resident Evil 2 (PC)	PC; Leon A; Any%; Normal	"Se3cret" (COL)	48:44
Resident Evil 2 (2019) (PC)	New Game (PC); Leon; Standard; 120	"7rayD" (FIN)	52:10
Resident Evil 3: Nemesis (PC)	PC (TWN); Any%; Original	"Orchlon" (MNG)	40:55
Resident Evil 4 (Console)	New Game; PS4; Professional	"tanoshimu" (JPN)	1:36:03
ROBLOX: Speed Run 4 (PC)	No Skips; 5 Levels	"kriptopolis" (USA)	1:57.6
Sekiro: Shadows Die Twice (PC)	Shura Ending; PC; Unrestricted	"LilAggy" (USA)	21:19
SpongeBob SquarePants: Battle for Bikini Bottom (Xbox)	100%	"SHiFT" (USA)	1:18:26
Spyro the Dragon	Any%	"ChrisLBC" (CAN)	38:31
Super Mario 64 (N64)	120 Star; N64	"cheese" (ESP)	1:38:54
Super Mario Bros. (NES)	Any%	"Kosmic" (USA)	4:55.6
Super Mario Galaxy (Wii)	Any%; Mario	"Mr.CloudKirby" (USA)	2:31:21
Super Mario Maker 2 (Switch)	Story Mode (Any%); No Luigi Assist	"IamUncleSlam" (USA)	1:41:06
Super Mario Odyssey (Switch)	Any%; 1P	"Tyron18" (ITA)	58:36
Super Mario Sunshine (Wii)	Any%; Normal	"Weegee" (USA)	1:14:13
Super Mario World (SNES)	96 Exit	"Lui" (ITA)	21:57.4
Super Metroid (SNES)	Any%	"zoast" (USA)	40:56
The Legend of Zelda (NES)	Any% No Up+A; NES	"rcdrone" (USA)	28:15
The Legend of Zelda: A Link to the Past (SNES)	No Major Glitches; Any%	"RealAlphaGamer" (USA)	1:23:07
The Legend of Zelda: Breath of the Wild (Switch)	Any%	"sketodara01417" (JPN)	27:29.5
The Legend of Zelda: Ocarina of Time (N64)	Any%	"Zudu" (USA)	7:48.1
The Simpsons: Hit & Run (PC)	All Story Missions; PC	"LiquidWiFi" (AUS)	1:22:45
The SpongeBob SquarePants Movie (Xbox)	Any%	"Purple" (UK)	1:09:10
Titanfall 2 (PC)	Any%; Standard	"bryonato" (USA)	1:19:41
Tom Clancy's Rainbow Six Siege (PC)	Situations; Situation #01 - CQB Basics; Normal	"bezzles" (UK)	18.0
Undertale (Linux)	Neutral; 1.00-1.001	"Shayy" (USA)	55:37
Untitled Goose Game (Xbox One)	Any%	"Vitek" (USA)	2:11
Wii Sports Resort (Wii U)	All Sports	"Alaskaxp2" (USA)	16:35

Source: Speedrun.com; timings stated as hr:min:sec

Portal 2 (No Out of Bounds)

On 19 Jul 2019, "CantEven" (USA) completed Valve's puzzle-platformer in 59 min 47.4 sec while staying within the map boundaries. No one else has broken the 1-hr barrier.

With an approval rating of 97.48%, *Portal 2* remains the **highest-rated videogame on Steam**.

The Simpsons: Hit & Run (All Story Missions; PC)

"LiquidWiFi" (AUS) saved Springfield from disaster in 1 hr 22 min 45 sec. Developed by Radical Entertainment, the 22nd instalment in *The Simpsons* videogame franchise was released in 2003, and is an open-world action-adventure heavily influenced by *Grand Theft Auto III*.

Cuphead (All Bosses; Regular Difficulty; Legacy Version)

"SBDWolf" (ITA) ploughed through StudioMDHR's fiendish 2017 run-and-gun in 23 min 16 sec on the PC on 13 Jun 2019. He beat the previous record by just 2 sec. "Good run, happy for the moment being!" he wrote afterwards.

Super Mario Odyssey (Any%; No Assists)

"Tyron18" (ITA) completed Mario's 2017 world-hopping adventure on the Nintendo Switch (version 1.3.0) in 58 min 36 sec.

Super Mario Odyssey is the second most popular title on Speedrun.com, with 12,451 runs logged as of 22 Apr 2020. The game that beats it also features the popular plumber – see below.

The **most speedrun game** is *Super Mario 64* (Nintendo, 1996). As of 22 Apr 2020, 14,499 runs had been logged on Speedrun.com.

Action Adventure

Best-selling action-adventure videogame
Rockstar's felonious *Grand Theft Auto V* (2013) had racked up sales of more than 120 million units, according to figures released in Feb 2020 by its publisher, Take-Two Interactive. *GTA V*'s online mode alone generated more than $1 bn (£770 m) in just its first four years.

Largest cast for a videogame
A total of 1,200 actors appeared in the Wild West adventure *Red Dead Redemption II* (Rockstar Games, 2018). Around 500 of these provided motion-capture performances.

Most followers on Instagram for a videogame director
As of 30 Apr 2020, Hideo Kojima (JPN) had 1,193,983 followers on Instagram. The *Metal Gear* director released the dystopic action title *Death Stranding* through Kojima Productions in Nov 2019 (see right).

Most BAFTA award nominations for a videogame
The Last of Us (Naughty Dog, 2013) and its downloadable content, *Left Behind* (2014), received a total of 12 BAFTA nominations. The games won seven awards across two years, with a Best Performance double for Ashley Johnson, who played Ellie in both titles.

Most achieved Platinum trophy
As of 17 Mar 2020, a total of 182,420 players had obtained the "Enjoy Your Powers" Platinum trophy while playing *inFAMOUS: Second Son* (Sucker Punch Productions, 2014) on the PS4, according to PSNProfiles. To win the virtual prize, the game had to be played through at least twice, around 20 hr of work – relatively little for a dedicated gamer!

First console videogame with a "save" feature
The international release of the NES classic *The Legend of Zelda* (1987) used a cartridge with a battery-powered memory chip that could store the game state when the console was turned off. Thankfully, "save" soon became a standard feature of most games.

Most money pledged for a Kickstarter videogame
Fans of the epic action-RPG series *Shenmue* were left on a cliffhanger when the series was cancelled in 2001, after just two games. It was easy to understand why they rushed for their wallets when *Shenmue III* appeared on Kickstarter in 2015. The game raised $6.3 m (£4 m) on the crowdfunding site, and set a new record for the **fastest $1 m in pledges for a crowdfunded videogame** (1 hr 44 min). *Shenmue III* was finally released on 19 Nov 2019.

Most BAFTA award nominations for a videogame (single year)
In 2020, two titles were nominated for 11 BAFTA gaming awards: *Death Stranding* (Kojima Productions, 2019, top) and *Control* (Remedy Entertainment, 2019, above). At the live-streamed ceremony on 2 Apr, only the former picked up a trophy, for Technical Achievement. The games share a link through Hideo Kojima, who developed *Death Stranding* and has a voice cameo in *Control*.

Most critically acclaimed videogame
Released for the N64 in 1998, *The Legend of Zelda: Ocarina of Time* (Nintendo) is the only videogame to score 99% on Metacritic. The title brought the action-adventure gameplay and epic storytelling of the earlier *Zelda* games (see left) and combined them with stunning 3D graphics. IGN predicted that the game would "shape the action RPG genre for years to come".

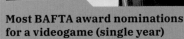

Ocarina of Time has been remastered for the GameCube (2002), Wii Virtual Console (2007) and 3DS (2011).

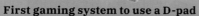

Platformers

Highest-rated platform videogame on Steam
Terraria (Re-Logic, 2011) is a 2D block-building game that features extensive amounts of combat and platforming. As of 23 Mar 2020, it had earned a rating of 96.77%, according to steamdb.info. With 425,831 positive reviews, it is also Steam's **most liked platform videogame**.

First use of cutscenes to tell a story in a videogame
Designed by Shigeru Miyamoto in Kyoto, Japan, the original *Donkey Kong* arcade game was released by Nintendo in Jul 1981. It contained a complete story told in cutscenes throughout the game: for example, the introductory animation showing Jumpman/Mario's girlfriend being abducted by the titular gorilla.

First Disney platform videogame
Mouse-branded side-scroller *Mickey Mousecapade* came out on the NES in 1988. It cleared a path for future Disney platform classics such as *DuckTales* (1989) and *Castle of Illusion Starring Mickey Mouse* (1990).

Most ubiquitous videogame character
Mario had appeared in 225 distinct videogame titles as of 23 Apr 2020, excluding remakes and re-releases. In addition to his 35 platforming adventures, Mario has also turned his hand to medicine (*Dr. Mario*), fine art (*Mario Artist: Paint Studio*) and all manner of sports, including tennis and kart racing. Mario has also made the **most appearances of a character on the top 50 best-selling videogames** – 14.

Most followed videogame character on Twitter
The official Twitter account for Sonic the Hedgehog (@sonic_hedgehog) had 5,853,082 followers as of 30 Apr 2020. This eclipsed Sega's own account, which had 1,805,238. Sonic's Twitter is well known for its posting style, which is done as though straight from the hedgehog's mouth.

Fastest completion of *Yoshi's Crafted World*
The big names in platforming all made the jump from 2D side-scrollers to 3D worlds in the mid-1990s, but in recent years some have chosen to hop back. Nintendo's 2019 side-scroller *Yoshi's Crafted World* has been a hit with both young gamers and

Most platform videogames starred in as a playable character
As of 26 Mar 2020, Sonic had been playable in 41 platform videogames – six ahead of Mario (see left). The hectic hedgehog debuted in the 1991 Sega Mega Drive classic *Sonic the Hedgehog*. In 2020, a film of the same name was released, with Ben Schwartz voicing the spiky speedster (above).

First gaming system to use a D-pad
The *Donkey Kong Game & Watch*, released in 1982, was a hugely influential piece of hardware. It replaced the heavy-duty control stick used in the 1981 *Donkey Kong* arcade machine with a compact "directional pad". This innovation allowed games such as *Donkey Kong* – the **first platform game** – to be played at home.

veteran platform fans, who have shunned the game's "mellow" mode in favour of the more challenging "classic" setting. Japanese speedrunner and Yoshi superfan "be_be_be_" was top of the leaderboard as of 11 Mar 2020, having completed the game in just 2 hr 20 min 57 sec.

Most crossover characters in a platform videogame
Fiendish indie platformer *Super Meat Boy* (Team Meat, 2010) features 18 playable cameo appearances from different gaming series, including *Half-Life* (Valve Corporation, 1998), *Braid* (Number None, 2008), *World of Goo* (2D Boy, 2008) and *Minecraft* (Mojang, 2011). The crossover was a heart-warming display of indie developer solidarity, and helped the game become a huge hit on both PC and consoles. In 2021, Meat Boy and Bandage Girl are set to return for the sequel, *Super Meat Boy Forever*.

Sports

Most Twitch channels for a sports videogame

At its peak on 6 Sep 2019, *NBA 2K20* (2K Sports) was being streamed simultaneously on 3,029 Twitch channels. There have been 21 main instalments in the *NBA 2K* series, which had shipped 90 million units as of 7 Apr 2020, according to VGChartz, making it the **best-selling basketball videogame series**.

Best-selling American football videogame series

As of 9 Mar 2020, an estimated 130 million units had been shipped of Electronic Arts' *Madden NFL* series. Named after the famous sportscaster, *John Madden Football* made its debut on 1 Jun 1988. *Madden NFL 20*, the most recent edition of the **longest-running sports videogame series**, was released on 2 Aug 2019 – 31 years 62 days later.

Most critically acclaimed sports videogame

Tony Hawk's Pro Skater 2 (Activision, 2000) on the PlayStation has earned a score of 98% on Metacritic. It is one of only four games (including *Soulcalibur*; see opposite) to have achieved this rating.

Best-selling sports videogame

Wii Sports, Nintendo's 2006 five-game compendium title featuring tennis, bowling, golf, boxing and baseball, had shipped 82.88 million units as of 7 Apr 2020.

Its popularity was boosted by the fact that it was bundled with the Wii for the console's release.

Best-selling sports videogame series

As of 7 Apr 2020, EA's *FIFA* titles had netted total sales of 282.4 million. *FIFA 20*, the 27th instalment in the series, was released on 27 Sep 2019.

The **highest-ranking *FIFA 20* esports player** is "Fnatic Tekkz", aka Donovan Hunt (UK), who had amassed 5,420 points playing the game on Xbox as of 9 Mar 2020.

Longest *FIFA* marathon

Chris Cook (UK) spent 48 hr 49 min 41 sec playing *FIFA 15* (EA Canada, 2014) on 5–7 Nov 2014 in London, UK. Towards the end of his attempt, Chris was resting his hands in buckets of ice between games!

Most critically acclaimed fitness videogame

Ring Fit Adventure (Nintendo, 2019) had worked up a score of 83% on Metacritic as of 9 Mar 2020. Players control their characters in this action RPG by wearing Ring-Con and Leg Strap accessories, which enable their movements to be monitored.

Most *FIFA 20 Ultimate Team* draft matches won in 24 hours

On 16–17 Mar 2020, Brandon Smith (UK) won 63 matches in 24 hr playing in Chichester, West Sussex, UK. Brandon, who live-streamed his record attempt to raise money for the Cancer Research and Young Minds charities, won every single match and a total of 15 drafts.

First official World Cup soccer game

Released in 1986, *World Cup Carnival* proved a critical own-goal for developers US Gold. It scored 0% in one review and was so easy that players could walk the ball into the net.

Longest-running horse-racing videogame series

On 12 Mar 2020, *Winning Post 9 2020* (Koei Tecmo) came out 26 years 289 days after the first title in the franchise. The original *Winning Post* was released for the Japan-only Sharp X68000 computer on 28 May 1993.

Talk of a "curse" for Madden cover stars was scotched by Patrick Mahomes' win at Super Bowl LIV (see p.216).

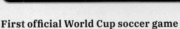

Longest single game of *Football Manager*

Sepp Hedel (DEU) completed 333 seasons on *Football Manager 2017* (Sports Interactive, 2016), as confirmed on 25 Sep 2019. He managed just three clubs, including a 200-year stint at Indian side Bengaluru FC. Sepp's virtual trophy cabinet groans with 729 cups and 258 league titles. He won 11,217 of 15,678 matches, scoring 42,672 goals.

Versus

Most critically acclaimed fighting videogame

The Dreamcast version of *Soulcalibur* (Namco, 1999) had a Metacritic score of 98% as of 3 Mar 2020. The weapons-based 3D fighter, the **most critically acclaimed Dreamcast game**, was in overall joint-second place on the review aggregator site. For the **most critically acclaimed videogame**, see p.182.

Most prolific fighting videogame series

There have been a total of 177 different *Street Fighter* games (including ports) since the original's release in 1987. This excludes crossover fighting games without "Street Fighter" in the title, such as *Marvel vs Capcom: Clash of Super Heroes* (1999), and also the *Puzzle Fighter* series.

Highest-ranked *Street Fighter V* player

As of 4 Mar 2020, "Tokido", aka Hajime Taniguchi (JPN), had accumulated a lifetime score of 335,813 playing Capcom's 2016 one-on-one battler, according to the fighting game site Shoryuken. Known for his mastery with Akuma, Hajime is referred to as one of the "Five Gods", a term coined for the players considered the most dominant and influential in fighting games.

First secret character in a fighting videogame

Mortal Kombat (Midway, 1992) had a hidden fighter named Reptile that players could unlock. They had to obtain two Flawless Victories in the "Pit" stage without blocking. This had to be done while a silhouette was visible in front of the Moon, which only occurred once every sixth game.

Largest character roster in a fighting game

Players of *Fire Pro Wrestling Returns* (Spike Chunsoft, 2005) could select from 327 characters. Owing to licensing issues, many of them were likenesses of real-life wrestlers from Japan, Mexico and the USA, who could be signed up for bouts such as the Exploding Barbed Wire Deathmatch.

Largest esports prize pool for a single tournament

The International *Dota 2* Championships 2019 had a total prize pot of $34,330,068 (£27,918,800). It grew from a base of $1.6 m (£1.3 m) thanks to in-game purchases available throughout the tournament to players around the world. The championships were held on 20–25 Aug 2019 at the Mercedes-Benz Arena in Shanghai, China.

Best-selling racing videogame series

High-octane street-racer franchise *Need for Speed* (EA) had shipped 150 million copies as of 2 Mar 2020. It had outsold Nintendo's *Mario Kart* series by almost 8 million units. There have been 24 titles between 1994's *The Need for Speed* and 2019's *Need for Speed: Heat*, making it the **most prolific racing videogame series**.

Fastest completion of the *Rocket League* GWR "Bouncing Shot Challenge"

Rocket League's (Psyonix, 2015) combination of cars and soccer is a favourite of record-breakers, so GWR has created a series of custom in-game records to test their reflexes. On 19 Nov 2019, Immanuel Sampath (IND) completed the "Bouncing Shot Challenge" in 59.39 sec at the WAFI mall in Dubai, UAE.

Best-selling fighting videogame

Super Smash Bros. Ultimate (Nintendo, 2018) had shipped 17.68 million copies as of 3 Mar 2020. It is the fifth instalment of the crossover franchise, in which characters from games such as *Super Mario* and *The Legend of Zelda* do battle.

The **highest-ranked *Super Smash Bros. Ultimate* player** is "MkLeo", aka Leonardo López Pérez (MEX, inset). He tops the leaderboards at Panda Global Rankings and Orionrank.

One famous face you won't see in *Super Smash Bros.* is the blocky 3D James Bond from 1997 N64 classic *GoldenEye 007*. Legal issues keep him off the roster.

Creative

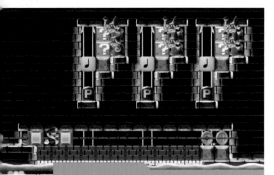

Least-cleared course in *Super Mario Maker*
Nintendo EAD's 2015 game creation system allows players to build and share their own *Super Mario* levels. As of 28 Feb 2020, the hardest to complete was "Lucky Draw" – cleared just 35 times from 19,569,423 attempts. Published on 29 Oct 2018 by gamer "Phenotype" (NZ), it is governed by a random luck. Players can only pray that the Magikoopas above Mario spawn coins to save him from the rising lava.

Longest time spent trying to beat a *Super Mario Maker* level
Before sharing a stage in *Super Mario Maker*, the creator has to prove that it can be completed. "ChainChompBraden", aka Braden Moor (CAN), began making "Trials of Death" in Jan 2016. More than 2,979 hours of gameplay later (that's equal to 124 days!), he was still trying to beat it. His creation requires pixel-perfect precision over eight minutes of gameplay.

Most starred course on *Super Mario Maker*
Created by "MK8" (USA), "Mission: Impossible" has been awarded 413,323 stars. Gamers have to guide Mario through the level in covert style, adopting disguises including a question block.

Most visited videogame created in *Roblox*
Roblox is an MMO gaming platform and sandbox videogame that allows users to create their own games for others to play and explore. As of 27 Feb 2020, "MeepCity" by "alexnewtron" had accrued 5,050,061,127 visits. "MeepCity" is an online hang-out where *Roblox* players can socialise or play simple games.

*all measurements taken on 2 Mar 2020, unless stated otherwise

Highest-rated videogame developed using *RPG Maker*
Rakuen (2017) had scored 84 out of 100 on Metacritic as of 25 Mar 2020. The game was created by singer-songwriter Laura Shigihara (JPN/USA) using the beginner-friendly game-development tool *RPG Maker*. It tells the story of a child who escapes to a fantasy world during a long stay in hospital.

Most thumbs-up received for a creation in *Dreams*
First published on 11 Feb 2020, "Art's Dream" is an interactive, movie-length story that had earned 52,281 signs of approval as of 28 Feb 2020. It was created by British game developers Media Molecule to demonstrate the possibilities offered by their game-creation and sharing platform *Dreams*.

In addition to full games, *Dreams* players can also make one-off character models or set pieces called sculptures. The **most**

Best-selling videogame
According to figures released by Microsoft in May 2019, sandbox game *Minecraft* (Mojang/Microsoft) has sold 176 million copies since its debut in 2011. In addition to these sales, *Minecraft* is distributed as a free-to-play game in China with an estimated 200 million downloads. As of Sep 2019, *Minecraft* had 112 million monthly active users.

Largest pixel art created in *Minecraft*
"Mysticlloyd", aka Lloyd Hancock (AUS), crafted a dramatic image of *Fairy Tail*'s mage Natsu Dragneel in *Minecraft* using 1,988,532 blocks. He began work on 25 Jul 2015 and completed the piece on 25 Oct 2018. Hancock had been inspired by seeing examples of pixel art on Twitch, including the work of previous record holder "Thorlar Thorlarian".

upvoted character model is "MechaWhale", created by "icecreamcheese". As the name would suggest, this is a whale with giant mechanical legs. It had been given 6,244 thumbs-up as of 25 Mar 2020.

Most liked indie videogame on Steam
Garry's Mod (Facepunch Studios, 2006) has received 491,538 positive reviews on Valve's digital distribution service. This physics-engine sandbox is the work of Garry Newman (UK).

Spring 2020 saw some students using *Minecraft* to recreate their closed schools, even putting on virtual graduations from self-isolation.

Puzzle

Most speed-run puzzle videogame
There had been 5,171 submitted runs of *Portal* (Valve Corporation, 2007) on Speedrun.com as of 28 Feb 2020.

Highest-rated puzzle videogame
World of Goo for the Nintendo Wii received a rating of 94 out of 100 on Metacritic, as verified on 28 Feb 2020. It was developed by 2D Boy (USA) and released on 13 Oct 2008.

Most concurrent players for a strategy game on Steam
On 26 May 2019, a total of 192,298 gamers did battle on *Total War: Three Kingdoms* (Sega, 2019). The turn-based game puts players in command of one of the warring factions during China's Three Kingdoms era.

First auto chess videogame
In auto chess players recruit armies to fight on a grid-shaped battlefield, with the ensuing carnage directed by the computer. The earliest example of this strategic sub-genre is *Dota Auto Chess*, developed by Drodo Studio as a mod for *Defense of the Ancients 2* (*Dota 2*) and released in Jan 2019.

First BAFTA award for a puzzle videogame
The Nintendo DS brain-booster *Dr Kawashima's Brain Training* won the Innovation category at the 2006 British Academy Video Games Awards. The game features a variety of challenges to test players' little grey cells, including Stroop tests and sudoku puzzles.

Most prolific puzzle-game series
Given the vast number of clones and legal grey areas, pinpointing an exact figure for the number of *Tetris* variants is a tricky process. However, on 1 Feb 2017, The Tetris Company revealed that there had been approximately 220 licensed and official variants of Alexey Pajitnov's classic puzzler.

First console VR puzzle game
On 13 Oct 2016, *Keep Talking and Nobody Explodes* was released for PlayStation VR. In this game, the player wearing the VR headset has to defuse a bomb using confusing instructions that only their friends can see.

First movie based on a puzzle videogame
On 19 Dec 2009, Level-5's *Professor Layton* series made its silver-screen debut in *Professor Layton and the Eternal Diva* (JPN/SGP). The anime recounted the adventures of the Professor and his self-proclaimed apprentice Luke as they searched for the secrets to eternal life.

Youngest *Tetris* world champion
Joseph Saelee (USA) won the Classic *Tetris* World Championship aged 16 on 21 Oct 2018. He defeated seven-time champion Jonas Neubauer in the final.
   Joseph is also responsible for the **highest score on NES *Tetris* (NTSC)** – 1,357,428 – which he set on 28 Dec 2019.

Most players in a single competitive puzzle videogame match
Released on 13 Feb 2019, *Tetris 99* for Nintendo Switch saw the iconic title adopt a battle-royale format, with a total of 99 gamers able to compete at arranging their tumbling tetrominoes. Clearing rows generates "garbage", which combatants can send to their opponents to clutter up their board.

Shooters

First FPS
Maze War was developed by Steve Colley, Greg Thompson and Howard Palmer (all USA) in 1973 on the Imlac PDS-1s at the NASA Ames Research Center in California, USA. This first-person shooter (FPS) allowed players on networked computers to hunt each other in a 3D maze. *Maze War* didn't get a commercial release until 1992.

Best-selling FPS
Counter-Strike: Global Offensive (Valve) had shipped 40 million units as of 9 Mar 2020. The franchise's fourth instalment was released in Aug 2012.

Most critically acclaimed FPS
Metroid Prime (Retro Studios/Nintendo, 2002), *Perfect Dark* (Rare, 2000) and *Halo: Combat Evolved* (Bungie, 2001) had all earned a Metacritic score of 97% as of 31 Mar 2020. The game with the most critic reviews – 70 – was *Metroid Prime* (above). It was the first game in the franchise to use a first-person perspective.

Most wins of *Fortnite Battle Royale*
"Mixer Ship" (USA) had racked up 14,540 wins on the free-to-play mass-melee phenomenon as of 1 Apr 2020. This was from a total of 32,774 matches, giving him a win ratio of 44.3%. The dead-eyed marksman had spent a total of 173 days 16 hr 58 min playing *Fortnite*, ending the hopes of 197,943 opponents.

Most hours viewed on Twitch for a videogame in one day
On 7 Apr 2020, a limited closed beta test for Riot Games' forthcoming shooter *Valorant* racked up a total of 34 million viewing hours on Twitch. Riot enabled streamers such as Jaryd "summit1g" Lazar and Félix "xQc" Lengyel to issue access keys to *Valorant* to their viewers while they also played the game.

Most wins of the *Overwatch* World Cup
South Korea won the first three editions of the *Overwatch* World Cup in 2016, 2017 and 2018. Their winning streak was ended by the USA in the 2019 semi-finals.

Most Twitch channels for a videogame
At its peak on 2 Feb 2019, there were 66,600 channels devoted to *Fortnite Battle Royale* (Epic Games, 2017) on the live-streaming platform Twitch.

Highest career earnings playing...*
• ***Counter-Strike: Global Offensive***: $1,764,521 (£1,418,050) by "Xyp9x", aka Andreas Højsleth (DNK).
• ***Call of Duty***: $810,909 (£651,684) by "Crimsix", aka Ian Porter (USA).
• ***Overwatch***: $219,730 (£176,585) by "Gesture", aka Hong Jae-hee, and "Profit", aka Park Joon-yeong (both KOR).
**All records correct according to esportsearnings.com as of 29 Apr 2020.*

First female in the *Overwatch* League
Kim "Geguri" Se-yeon (KOR) joined the Shanghai Dragons in Feb 2018. She rose to prominence playing *Overwatch* (Blizzard, 2016) as the Tank Hero Zarya, and is noted for the accuracy of her aim. In 2019, *TIME* selected Kim as one of its "Next Generation Leaders" for her esports achievements.

Best-selling FPS series
Activision Blizzard's *Call of Duty* series has shipped a total of 300 million units, as verified by VGChartz on 4 Feb 2020. Since its first release in 2003, the combat title has expanded its horizons from its initial World War II setting to the Vietnam War, modern conflicts and even outer space.

Call of Duty is also the **most prolific FPS series** with 29 titles, excluding DLC and expansions. In 2020, Activision Blizzard released *Call of Duty: Warzone* (pictured), a battle-royale-style addition to the series.

RPG

Most critically acclaimed RPG

As of 6 Mar 2020, *Mass Effect 2* (BioWare, 2010) for the Xbox 360 had blasted its way to a Metascore of 96 on Metacritic (based on 98 reviews). The action-packed role-playing game (RPG) enjoys artistic as well as critical acclaim; the Smithsonian American Art Museum featured the game in its 2012 exhibition *The Art of Videogames*.

Best-selling MMO videogame

Across its various expansions, the massively multiplayer online (MMO) *World of Warcraft* (Blizzard, 2004) had sold 36.9 million copies as of 5 Mar 2020.

World of Warcraft has also recorded the **most Twitch channels for an RPG videogame**, with a peak of 19,080 on 26 Aug 2019.

Best-selling tactical RPG

As of 5 Mar 2020, *Fire Emblem: Fates* (Intelligent Systems, 2015) had sold 2.94 million copies according to VGChartz. Developed as a swansong to the series, *Fates* sold many more units than its predecessor. It combines RPG play with tactical elements such as squad battles.

Longest-running RPG series

On 27 Sep 2019, *Dragon Quest XI S* (Square Enix) was released 33 years 123 days after the franchise's first game, *Dragon Quest*, appeared on 27 May 1986.

Best-selling RPG series

The *Pokémon* series had shifted 295.87 million units as of 5 Mar 2020, according to VGChartz. This total only includes RPGs – there have been other franchise spin-offs such as *Pokkén Tournament* (2016) and the hit mobile game *Pokémon GO* (2016), which has been downloaded more than a billion times.

The first game, *Pokémon Red, Green and Blue* (Game Freak, 1996), is the **best-selling RPG**. It alone has shifted 31.38 million units.

Most prolific RPG series

The *Final Fantasy* franchise (Square Enix, 1987–present) has a total of 61 titles. Though not all of its RPGs, such as *Chocobo's Dungeon*, bear the series' name, they feature the same recurring spells, items and magical creatures – not to mention the bumbling sword hunter, Gilgamesh.

Fastest 100% completion of *Baten Kaitos: Eternal Wings and the Lost Ocean*

On 24 Dec 2016, "Baffan" completed every quest and acquired every item in Namco's 2003 magical adventure in 341 hr 20 min 3 sec. This legendary 14-day speed run – one of the longest in gaming – owes its length to the need for some items to "upgrade" via real-time progressing. For example, it takes *c*. 336 hr for the "Shampoo" item to become "Splendid Hair"!

Most Golden Joystick awards won by a videogame

CD Projekt Red's action RPG *The Witcher III: Wild Hunt* (2015) has netted seven trophies at the long-running UK gaming awards. It won Most Wanted in 2013 and 2014, before adding Best Storytelling, Best Visual Design, Best Gaming Moment, Ultimate Game of the Year and Studio of the Year (for CD Projekt Red) in 2015.

The *Pokémon* franchise has earned an estimated $95 bn (£76 bn) over its lifetime – that's more than *Star Wars*!

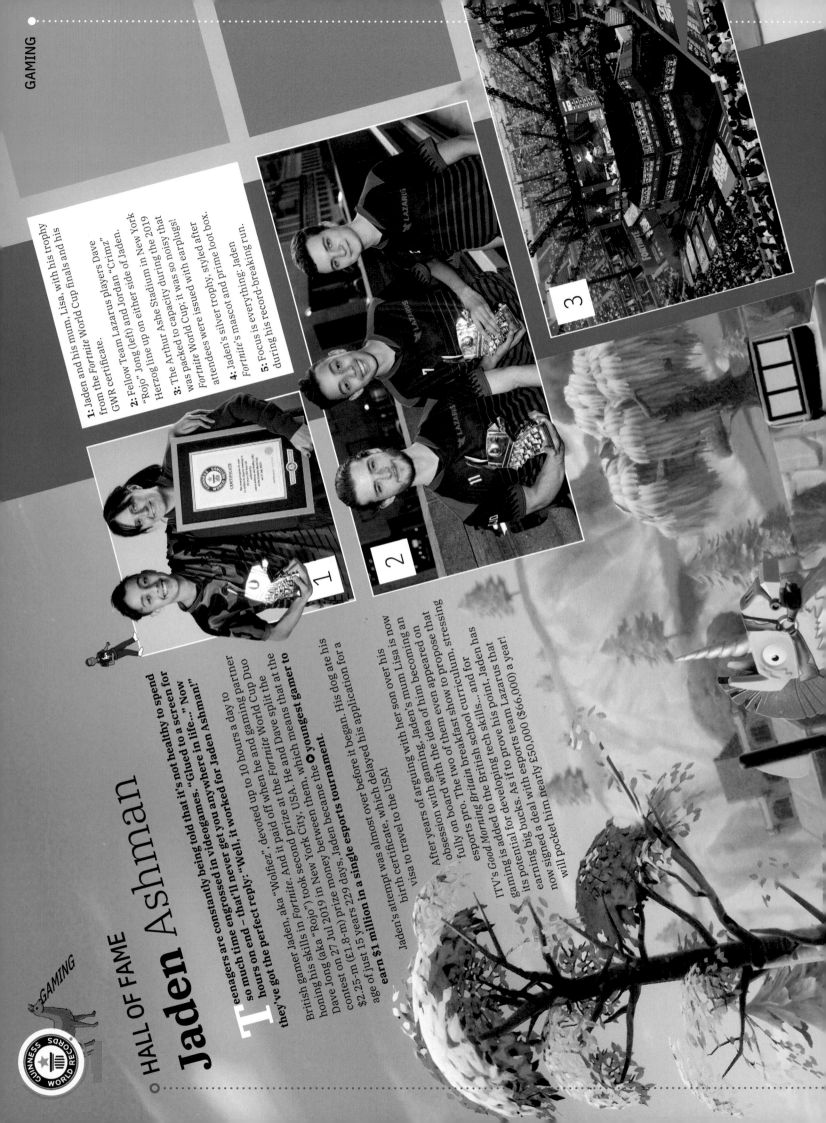

GUINNESS WORLD RECORDS

● HALL OF FAME

Jaden Ashman

Teenagers are constantly being told that it's not healthy to spend so much time engrossed in videogames. "Glued to a screen for hours on end – that'll never get you anywhere in life…." "Now they've got the perfect reply: "Well, it worked for Jaden Ashman!"

British gamer Jaden, aka "Wolfiez", devoted up to 10 hours a day to honing his skills in *Fortnite*. And it paid off when he and gaming partner Dave Jong (aka "Rojo") took second prize at the *Fortnite* World Cup Duo contest on 27 Jul 2019 in New York City, USA. He and Dave split the $2.25-m (£1.8-m) prize money between them, which means that at the age of just 15 years 229 days, Jaden became the ● **youngest gamer to earn $1 million in a single esports tournament.**

Jaden's attempt was almost over before it began. His dog ate his birth certificate, which delayed his application for a visa to travel to the USA!

After years of arguing with her son over his gaming, Jaden's mum Lisa is now becoming an obsession with gaming, the idea of him appeared on board with the two of them even to propose that fully on board. The two of them show to stressing esports pro. The breakfast school curriculum, and for ITV's *Good Morning Britain* breakfast show… and for gaming is added to the British tech skills…. and Jaden has its potential for developing tech point, Jaden has earning big bucks. As if to prove his esports team Lazarus that now signed a deal with prove big Lazarus that will pocket him nearly £50,000 ($66,000) a year!

1: Jaden and his mum, Lisa, with his trophy from the *Fortnite* World Cup finals and his GWR certificate.

2: Fellow Team Lazarus players Dave "Rojo" Jong (left) and Jordan "Crimz" Herzog line up on either side of Jaden.

3: The Arthur Ashe Stadium in New York was packed to capacity during the 2019 *Fortnite* World Cup; it was so noisy that attendees were issued with earplugs!

4: Jaden's silver trophy, styled after *Fortnite*'s mascot and prime loot box.

5: Focus is everything; Jaden during his record-breaking run.

CERTIFICATE

1

2

3

4

Fortnite's All Terrain Karts debuted in Season Five and accommodated a team of four.

Jaden's feat was made all the more remarkable by the fact that he used an Xbox One controller rather than a mouse. His choice to offer greater precision in his gameplay, thought to widely won him online plaudits (The latter is everywhere.) His controller players from controller players everywhere.

WOLFIEZ

RESPAWN

RESPAWN

5

Find out more about Jaden in the Hall of Fame section at www.**guinnessworldrecords.com/2021**

Above, Jaden holds a Rainbow Smash replica, one of Pickaxe styled after Fortnite's costliest harvesting tools.

The Lion King

Disney Theatrical Productions' stage-musical version of *The Lion King* – directed by Tony-winner Julie Taymor – is not only the world's **highest-grossing musical theatre show** but also the **most successful single entertainment title in box-office history**, having surpassed $9.1 bn (£6.9 bn). This includes grosses from its Broadway run along with those from overseas productions (pictured is the London cast), and domestic and international tours.

As of the week ending 1 Mar 2020, the Broadway production alone had grossed $1,680,389,582 (£1,310,480,000) since previewing in Oct 1997, making it the **most successful Broadway musical and Broadway production ever**. Pictured inset is Tshidi Manye, who plays Rafiki on Broadway.

The stage version of *The Lion King* has a book by Roger Allers and Irene Mecchi. It features songs by rock icon Elton John with lyrics by Tim Rice and other songwriters.

DESTINATIONS

The *Lion King's* original title was "The King of the Jungle", but it had to be changed. Why? Lions don't live in jungles!

At the **Movies**

Highest-grossing movie series (average)
In terms of mean gross per instalment, Marvel's *Avengers* series (USA, 2012–19) Hulk-smashes all the competition with $7,767,987,269 (£6.26 bn) earned across four releases. That works out at an average of $1.94 bn (£1.56 bn) per movie.

Most successful sports-movie franchise
The *Rocky* movies – *Rocky* (1976), *Rocky II* (1979), *III* (1982), *IV* (1985), *V* (1990), *Rocky Balboa* (2006), *Creed* (2015) and *Creed II* (2018; all USA) – had grossed $1,513,939,512 (£1.18 bn) worldwide as of 1 Mar 2020. The series charts the life of fictional boxer Robert "Rocky" Balboa, aka "The Italian Stallion" (portrayed by Sylvester Stallone), and, latterly, Adonis "Donnie" Creed (Michael B Jordan), the son of Balboa's best friend and former rival Apollo Creed.

AT THE OSCARS

Most nominations for a living person
As of 13 Jan 2020, composer John Williams (USA) had received 52 Academy Award nominations (winning five). His first came in 1968 for *Valley of the Dolls* (USA, 1967), and he has since gone on to be nominated, often multiple times, at 36 Oscar ceremonies, securing the record for the **most decades in which to receive a nomination** – seven. His 2020 nomination was for *Star Wars: The Rise of Skywalker* (USA, 2019).

Highest-grossing lead actor
The 29 movies starring Robert Downey Jr (USA) in the lead role have taken $14,380,708,898 (£11.60 bn) globally to date. These include his outings as Iron Man in the Marvel Cinematic Universe.

Downey Jr's fellow Avenger Scarlett Johansson (USA) is the **highest-grossing lead actress**. The 16 movies in which she has starred have taken $13,685,988,403 (£11.04 bn) worldwide.

Most bankable lead ensemble actor
The-Numbers.com uses its "Bankability Index" to rank the monetary value that an individual brings to a film. Chris Evans (USA, pictured in 2019's *Knives Out*) currently tops the chart as a lead ensemble actor, with $7,371,537 (£5.9 m) per movie. Boosting his status are nine credited (and two uncredited) appearances in Marvel movies. Below, you'll find a list of other Hollywood notables whose presence regularly tallies with box-office gold.

Most bankable...		
Actor	Tom Cruise (USA)	$22,186,586 (£17.9 m)
Actress	Emma Watson (UK)	$10,158,997 (£8.2 m)
Supporting actor	Jon Favreau (USA)	$14,092,784 (£11.3 m)
Supporting actress	Robin Wright (USA)	$7,436,541 (£6.0 m)
Lead ensemble actress	Scarlett Johansson (USA)	$8,484,169 (£6.8 m)
Director	Zack Snyder (USA)	$14,011,010 (£11.3 m)
Producer	Kathleen Kennedy (USA)	$15,643,296 (£12.6 m)
Composer	Alan Silvestri (USA)	$11,036,356 (£8.9 m)

All figures as of 1 Apr 2020

Highest-grossing R-rated movie
Joker (USA, 2019), starring Joaquin Phoenix, had earned $1,035,731,813 (£806.5 m) at the global box office by 25 Nov 2019. It is also the **first R-rated movie to gross $1 billion**, a figure it passed on the weekend of 16–17 Nov 2019. The "origin" movie offers one possible backstory for the title character – Batman's arch-nemesis – tracing his decline from well-meaning stand-up comedian to psychopathic villain. It was partly inspired by the 1988 graphic novel *Batman: The Killing Joke*, by Alan Moore and Brian Bolland.

Highest-grossing movie based on a videogame
As of 20 Apr 2020, *Pokémon: Detective Pikachu* (USA/JPN/UK/CAN, 2019) had grossed $433,005,346 (£346.2 m) at the worldwide box office. The film – the **first live-action *Pokémon* movie** – stars a deerstalker-hatted Pikachu (voiced by Ryan Reynolds), who teams up with Tim Goodman, a former Pokémon trainer, to help him find his missing father in Ryme City.

All box-office figures from The-Numbers.com as of 31 Mar 2020, unless otherwise indicated

Joaquin Phoenix won the Best Actor Oscar – his first from four nominations – at the 2020 Academy Awards; his powerful performance also earned him trophies at the BAFTAs, Golden Globes and Screen Actors Guild.

Highest-grossing actor at the global box office (supporting roles)
Films featuring Warwick Davis (UK) as a supporting actor have accumulated a box-office gross of $14,529,955,906 (£11.72 bn). Davis has appeared in some of cinema's biggest blockbusters of recent times, including several *Harry Potter* and *Star Wars* movies.

Most nominations for a director (living)
In 2020, Martin Scorsese (USA) received his ninth Academy Award nomination for *The Irishman* (USA, 2019). He had previously been nominated for cinematic *tours de force* such as *Raging Bull* (USA, 1980) and *The Departed* (USA, 2006). The latter won Scorsese his sole Oscar to date.

The **most nominated director** overall is William Wyler (DEU/CHE, 1902–81), who was acknowledged for Best Director 12 times (winning three) between 1936 and 1965. The **most Best Director wins** is four (from five nominations), by John Ford (USA, 1894–1973) between 1935 and 1952.

Most wins for an international movie
Three non-English-language films have each won four Oscars: *Fanny and Alexander* (SWE, 1982) in 1984; *Crouching Tiger, Hidden Dragon* (TPE, 2000) in 2001; and *Parasite* (KOR, 2019, see below) in 2020.

Highest-grossing film
Avengers: Endgame (USA, 2019) has grossed $2,797,800,564 (£2.25 bn). The superhero extravaganza is the fourth *Avengers* movie and the 22nd release in the Marvel Cinematic Universe. To date, only four other films have surpassed the $2-bn milestone at the global box office: *Avengers: Infinity War* (USA, 2018); *Star Wars Episode VII: The Force Awakens* (USA, 2015); *Avatar* (UK/USA, 2009); and *Titanic* (USA, 1997).

Highest-grossing spy movie series
The 26 movies in the *James Bond* franchise, from *Dr. No* (UK, 1962) to *Spectre* (UK/USA, 2015), have grossed $7,119,674,009 (£5.74 bn) at the worldwide box office to date. As a result of the COVID-19 crisis, the global launch of the 27th instalment, *No Time to Die* (UK/USA, with Daniel Craig, above), was postponed until Nov 2020.

The 007 highest-grossing *James Bond* movies	
Skyfall (2012)	$1,110,526,981 (£866 m)
Spectre (2015)	$879,620,923 (£771 m)
Casino Royale (2006)	$594,420,283 (£452 m)
Quantum of Solace (2008)	$591,692,078 (£445 m)
Die Another Day (2002)	$431,942,139 (£412 m)
The World is Not Enough (1999)	$361,730,660 (£366 m)
GoldenEye (1995)	$356,429,941 (£235 m)

Source: The-Numbers.com. All UK/USA. Figures not adjusted for inflation

First film to win Best International Feature Film and Best Picture Oscars
On 9 Feb 2020, *Parasite* (KOR, 2019) picked up both these coveted Academy Awards at the annual ceremony in Los Angeles, California, USA. Directed by Bong Joon-ho (inset), this black comedy/thriller sees the Kims, an impoverished family, pose as servants to infiltrate the household of a wealthy family, the Parks, highlighting social inequality in South Korea. The movie stars (left to right, below) Choi Woo-sik, Song Kang-ho, Jang Hye-jin and Park So-dam.

Highest-grossing movie series
In terms of a series of films with a single, linear narrative, the 12 movies in the *Star Wars* franchise have grossed $10,320,165,229 (£8.32 bn). Pictured is Daisy Ridley, who plays Rey in the most recent instalment, *The Rise of Skywalker* (USA, 2019). The 26 films in the Marvel Cinematic Universe (see above left) have grossed more than double that figure ($22,587,518,639; £18.22 bn), but don't fit into a consistent narrative arc in the same way.

Animated Movies

Most Oscars won in a lifetime
Animation legend Walt Disney (USA) won 26 Academy Awards between 1932 and 1969. He also received the **most Oscar nominations** – 64. His last one was tendered posthumously in 1969 for *Winnie the Pooh and the Blustery Day* (USA, 1968), which he won.

First animated movie nominated for the Best Picture Oscar
No feature-length animated films were nominated for the prestigious Best Picture Oscar until 1992, when Disney's *Beauty and the Beast* (USA, 1991) made the shortlist.

First animation nominated for a Best Foreign Language Film Oscar
Vals Im Bashir, aka *Waltz with Bashir* (ISR/DEU/FRA/USA, 2008), was nominated in 2009.

First anime movie to win an Oscar
Sen to Chihiro no kamikakushi, aka *Spirited Away* (JPN, 2001), was awarded the Oscar for Best Animated Feature on 23 Mar 2003.

As of 7 Jan 2020, the **highest-grossing Japanese animated movie** is romantic fantasy *Kimi no na wa*, aka *Your Name* (JPN, 2016), having taken $359,889,749 (£274.1 m). It was written and directed by Makoto Shinkai.

Highest-grossing remake
Jon Favreau's 2019 remake of Disney's *The Lion King* (USA, 1994; inset) has grossed $1,656,313,097 (£1.25 bn), overtaking the 2017 live-action remake of another Disney classic, *Beauty and the Beast* (USA, 1991). Although "filmed" by Disney's live-action division, all but one shot of *The Lion King* (USA, 2019) was created digitally by animators.

Most awards won by an animated short film
As of 31 Dec 2018, *Cuerdas* (ESP, 2014), written and directed by Pedro Solís García (ESP), had won 384 awards. It tells the story of a friendship between two children.

Widest movie release (opening weekend)
Released on 19 Jul 2019, Disney's remake of *The Lion King* opened at 4,725 cinemas in North America on its first weekend. (For more on *The Lion King*, see above.)

Most expensive colour animation cell
In 1999, a hand-painted cell from Disney's *The Band Concert* (USA, 1935), the first Mickey Mouse cartoon to be made in colour, was sold privately for a reported $420,000 (£259,657).

The **most expensive black-and-white animation cell** is a drawing from Disney's *The Orphan's Benefit* (USA, 1934), which raised $286,000 (£174,390) at Christie's in New York City, USA, on 16 May 1989.

Fastest animated movie to gross $1 billion (domestic)
Produced by Pixar, *Incredibles 2* (USA, 2018) took just 47 days to gross $1 bn in North America, the seventh animated film to

First animated movie to gross $1 billion
Released in Jun 2010, *Toy Story 3* (USA) had taken $1 bn at the worldwide box office by December of that year. It grossed $1,063,171,911 (£679.1 m) during the six months following its theatrical release.

Toy Story (USA, 1995) was the **first feature-length computer-animated movie**. At 1 hr 21 min, it remains the shortest movie in the franchise and the shortest film produced by Pixar so far.

Highest-grossing animated movie series
The four movies in the *Despicable Me* franchise released as of Jan 2020 have grossed $3,713,742,291 (£2.82 bn) at the worldwide box office. The most successful is *Minions* (USA, 2015), which has made $1,160,336,173 (£882.1 m). A fifth entry, *Minions: The Rise of Gru*, is scheduled for release on 3 Jul 2020.

All figures from The-Numbers.com, as of 7 Jan 2020, unless otherwise indicated

First animated movie

Vitagraph's *The Humpty Dumpty Circus* (USA, 1897) was conceived by the company's co-founder Albert E Smith (USA, b. UK). He borrowed his daughter's toy circus and used the stop-motion technique to film its acrobats and animals one frame at a time, changing their positions very slightly between shots.

Reynolds as the titular character – was the **first live-action *Pokémon* movie**. Find out more about this release on p.194.

The **highest-grossing animated film based on a videogame** is *The Angry Birds Movie* (USA/FIN, 2016), which has grossed $349,334,510 (£265.5 m) worldwide to date.

Most viewed animated movie trailer in 24 hours

Released on 13 Feb 2019, a teaser trailer for *Frozen II* (USA, 2019) was viewed 116.4 million times in its first 24 hours across multiple platforms. In doing so, it surpassed the 113.6 million views for the *Incredibles 2* trailer (USA, 2018), which was first shown on 18 Nov 2017.

Hans, Kristoff, Anna, Sven: the characters' names point to the writer whose story inspired *Frozen*...

have reached this landmark. The movie is a belated sequel to the acclaimed 2004 film featuring the superhero Parr family.

Incredibles 2 is also the **highest-grossing animation with an original screenplay**, having taken $1,242,805,359 (£944.8 m) to date. Only *Frozen* and *Frozen II* (see right) – inspired by the Hans Christian Andersen fairy tale "The Snow Queen" (1844) – have performed better at the box office.

Highest-grossing stop-motion movie

Aardman Animations' feature film *Chicken Run* (USA/UK/FRA, 2000) has taken $227,793,915 (£173.1 m) at the global box office to date.

Most movie spin-offs from a videogame series

Since its debut in 1996, Nintendo's *Pokémon* had inspired 22 feature-length animated films as of 7 Jan 2020. The premiere of *Pocket Monsters the Movie: Coco*, planned for Jul 2020, was postponed owing to COVID-19.

Released in 2019, *Pokémon: Detective Pikachu* (USA/JPN/UK/CAN) – starring Ryan

Longest Disney animated movie

With a running time of 124 min, Walt Disney's *Fantasia* (USA, 1940) is the longest of the studio's 58 animated features to date, and the only one with a running time of more than two hours. Hugely ambitious for its time, it's now seen as a landmark in animation. In one of its most famous sequences, Mickey Mouse appears in the tale of "The Sorcerer's Apprentice" (above).

Highest-grossing animated movie

Frozen II (USA, 2019; inset) has taken $1,324,788,837 (£1 bn) to date. It also achieved the **highest-grossing opening weekend for an animated movie**, with avid fans splashing out $358,200,000 (£278.9 m) on its debut (22–24 Nov).

Frozen (USA, 2013) – now bumped to second place in the list of all-time top-grossing animations – was co-directed and co-written by its creator, Jennifer Lee (USA), making it the **first film with a female director to gross $1 billion**.

197

Movie Memorabilia

Place your bids now for the most expensive props, costumes, posters and scripts ever sold at auction.*
*Buyer's premium included

Lot 1: Halter-neck dress with accordion pleats
Most expensive movie costume
The "Subway" outfit worn by Marilyn Monroe in a celebrated scene from *The Seven Year Itch* (USA, 1955). Originally bought by another Hollywood legend, Debbie Reynolds, in 1971 with the rest of Monroe's wardrobe from 20th Century Fox. Auctioned on 18 Jun 2011 at Profiles in History in California, USA. **$5,520,000 (£3,417,000)**

Lot 2: Acrylic panels, frame and 250 light bulbs
Most expensive piece of set
The disco platform on which John Travolta danced his way to film stardom in *Saturday Night Fever* (USA, 1977). Its 288 coloured squares, which flash in time to musical rhythms, cover 7.3 x 5 m (24 x 16 ft). Sold in Calabasas, California, USA, on 27 Jun 2017. **$1,200,000 (£942,130)**

Lot 3: Lion-skin costume with human-hair wig
Most expensive memorabilia from *The Wizard of Oz*
Designed by Hollywood couturier Adrian and worn by Bert Lahr in *The Wizard of Oz* (USA, 1939). One of only two made. Comes with a likeness of Lahr's face. "Discovered carefully bundled up in one of the oldest buildings on the MGM lot," reported auctioneer Bonhams. Sold on 24 Nov 2014 in New York City, USA. **$3,070,000 (£2,515,974)**

Lot 4: 140-page typescript annotated in turquoise ink. Some corners folded or snipped
Most expensive script from a movie
Audrey Hepburn's personal shooting script from *Breakfast at Tiffany's* (USA, 1961), including the actress's working notes. Bought by jewellers Tiffany & Co. on 27 Sep 2017 at Christie's in London, UK. **£632,750 ($851,515)**

Lot 5: Second-hand car. One careless owner
Most expensive *James Bond* memorabilia
One of four 1965 Aston Martin DB5s made for the early Bond films starring Sean Connery. Dubbed "The Most Famous Car in the World", its gadgets include a Browning machine gun in each bumper and retractable, bulletproof rear screen. Sold on 15 Aug 2019 at Sotheby's in Monterey, California, USA. **$6,385,000 (£5,292,980)**

Lot 6: Wooden fire axe. Blade still sharp
Most expensive horror-movie prop
The fire axe used by Jack Nicholson's character to break through a bathroom door in Stanley Kubrick's film *The Shining* (UK/USA, 1980). Sold on 1 Oct 2019 in London, UK. "Remains in excellent condition, with a few nicks and scratches present from use on Kubrick's notoriously long shooting days," according to the auction house.
£172,200 ($211,764)

Lot 7: Cinematic memento. Pin holes visible
Most expensive movie poster
A poster for *Dracula* (USA, 1931), one of only two known to exist with this design. Sold at auction in Dallas, Texas, USA, on 18 Nov 2017. Features the face of Hungarian actor Bela Lugosi, who portrayed the world's most famous vampire in the horror classic.
$525,800 (£397,706)

Lot 8: Latex bodysuit, ideal for Halloween
Most expensive movie monster suit
A "Xenomorph" suit worn on screen in director Ridley Scott's sci-fi horror movie *Alien* (UK/USA, 1979), sold at a Profiles in History auction in California, USA, on 5 Apr 2007. The iconic design is by Swiss artist H R Giger, whose macabre paintings were a key inspiration for the look of the film.
$126,500 (£64,059)

Lot 9: Fibreglass-and-foam headpiece
Most expensive movie mask
An original Darth Vader helmet and mask, worn by actor David Prowse in *The Empire Strikes Back* (USA, 1980). Sold in auction at Profiles in History in California, USA, on 26 Sep 2019, it was described by the auctioneers as a "holy grail of science-fiction movies". The mask was worn on screen during the iconic moment when Darth Vader reveals that – spoiler alert – he is Luke Skywalker's father.
$1,152,000 (£928,300)

Lot 10: Robot, assembled from salvaged parts
Most expensive *Star Wars* memorabilia
One of the original R2-D2 droids used in the first *Star Wars* movie in 1977. Sold on 28 Jun 2017 at an auction in California. The 109-cm-tall (3-ft 7-in) unit features parts added during the making of the original trilogy (1977–83), *The Phantom Menace* (USA, 1999) and *Attack of the Clones* (USA, 2002).
$2,760,000 (£2,164,150)

Lot 11: Custom-made, non-firing gun
Most expensive movie prop weapon
A BlasTech DL-44 "blaster" pistol used by Han Solo actor Harrison Ford in *Return of the Jedi* (USA, 1983). Previously owned for 35 years by *Star Wars* art director James Schoppe. Sold in New York City, USA, on 23 Jun 2018.
$550,000 (£414,389)

Music

Fastest Diamond certificate for a US digital single

On 22 Oct 2019, a remix of "Old Town Road" by Lil Nas X (b. Montero Hill; right), feat. Billy Ray Cyrus (both USA; left), was awarded a Diamond certificate by the Recording Industry Association of America to mark sales/streaming-equivalent sales of 10 million. The track had been released just 200 days earlier, on 5 Apr 2019. It also set a US record for **most weeks at No.1 for a single**: 19 weeks in a row between 13 Apr and 17 Aug 2019.

Highest annual earnings for a musician (current)

Taylor Swift (USA) earned $185 m (£145 m) in the year up to 1 Jun 2019, according to Forbes. Her 2018 *Reputation Stadium Tour* netted $266.1 m (£209.4 m) – the highest-grossing tour in US history. Also in 2019, Swift upped her total of **most American Music Awards won** to 29, picking up six gongs on 24 Nov.

Most consecutive No.1 debuts on the US albums chart

Rapper Eminem (b. Marshall Mathers III, USA) secured his 10th first-week chart-topper on the US *Billboard* 200 albums chart when *Music to be Murdered By* hit the No.1 spot for the week dated 1 Feb 2020. This is also the **most consecutive No.1s on the US albums chart**.

Most streamed track on Spotify (current)

"Señorita" by Shawn Mendes (CAN) and Camila Cabello (CUB/USA) was streamed more than 1 billion times on Spotify in 2019. As of 26 Feb 2020, the track had racked up 1,266,783,415 streams, putting it in the digital music service's 20 most popular songs of all time just eight months after it was released, on 21 Jun 2019.

The **most streamed track on Spotify** overall is held by Ed Sheeran's (UK) "Shape of You", which had 2,426,887,308 streams as of 20 Feb 2020. This put it some way ahead of second-place "rockstar" (2017) by Post Malone (see below), feat. 21 Savage, on 1,825,491,185 streams and "One Dance" (2016) by Drake, feat. Wizkid & Kyla, with 1,814,140,253 streams as of the same date.

The **most streamed track on Spotify in 24 hours (male)** is also claimed by Ed Sheeran, albeit shared with co-singer Justin Bieber (CAN). Their track "I Don't Care" was listened to 10,977,389 times on 10 May 2019; see the overall record opposite.

Most *Billboard* Latin Music Award wins for an artist in one year

Ozuna (b. Jan Carlos Ozuna Rosado, PRI) lived up to his reputation as the "New King of Reggaeton" by winning 11 *Billboard* Latin Music Awards on 25 Apr 2019. He had received 23 nominations in 15 categories and went on to claim an armful of gongs, including Artist of the Year. Ozuna's album *Odisea* crowned the Top Latin Albums chart for a record 46 weeks in 2017–18, a feat since equalled by a compatriot (see p.204).

Biggest-selling album (current)

Japanese vocal group Arashi's greatest hits album *5x20 All the BEST!! 1999–2019* sold 3.3 million copies in 2019, according to figures published by the International Federation of the Phonographic Industry. The 64-track, four-CD set was released on 26 Jun 2019 and outsold albums by Taylor Swift, BTS and Billie Eilish (see opposite).

Most US singles chart entries

"Oprah's Bank Account" became the 208th chart entry on the US *Billboard* Hot 100 for Drake (CAN) when it debuted at No.89 on the chart dated 21 Mar 2020. This was almost 11 years since his first, "Best I Ever Had". "Oprah's Bank Account" broke a tie with the cast of *Glee*, who amassed 207 Hot 100 hits between 2009 and 2013 – still the **most US singles chart entries by a group**.

Most streamed act on Spotify (current)

The music of rapper/singer Post Malone (b. Austin Post, USA) was streamed more than 6.5 billion times on Spotify in 2019. Four tracks – "rockstar", "Sunflower", "Better Now" and "Congratulations" – have been streamed more than 1 billion times each, with "rockstar" (1.8 billion) and "Sunflower" (1.3 billion) the second and eighth all-time most streamed songs on Spotify as of 20 Feb 2020; see the **most streamed tracks** above.

Among Post Malone's many tattoos are portraits on his fingers of musicians such as Elvis Presley, John Lennon and Kurt Cobain.

Most streamed track on Spotify in 24 hours

On 24 Dec 2019, Mariah Carey's (USA) festive hit "All I Want for Christmas Is You" was streamed 12,028,987 times. Three days earlier, the track provided Mariah, pictured alongside GWR's Michael Empric, with her 19th US *Billboard* Hot 100 chart-topper, giving her the **most US No.1 singles by a solo artist**.

Longest song to enter the *Billboard* Hot 100

"Fear Inoculum", the 10-min 21-sec title track from the fifth studio album by rock band Tool (USA), debuted at No.93 on the US singles chart on 17 Aug 2019. It was the first entry over 10 min to hit the Hot 100.

Most weeks at No.1 on the US Top Country Albums chart

By 2 Nov 2019, *This One's for You* by Luke Combs (USA) had spent 50 weeks at the No.1 spot on *Billboard*'s Top Country Albums chart. It shares this record with *Come on Over*, by Shania Twain (CAN).

Most weeks at No.1 on the US Hot Christian Songs chart

"You Say" by Lauren Daigle (USA) spent 66 non-consecutive weeks at the top of *Billboard*'s Hot Christian Songs chart between 28 Jul 2018 and 2 Nov 2019.

Oldest music video to reach 1 billion views on YouTube

The video for "Bohemian Rhapsody" by rock band Queen (UK) was viewed for the billionth time on 22 Jul 2019. The six-minute extravaganza – reportedly shot in just four hours on 10 Nov 1975, and originally posted to YouTube on 1 Aug 2008 – was 43 years 254 days old when it reached the milestone.

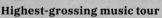

Highest-grossing music tour

The ÷ [*Divide*] *Tour* by UK singer-songwriter Ed Sheeran notched up a reported gross of $776.2 m (£631.3 m) between 16 Mar 2017 and 26 Aug 2019. Over the course of a marathon tour, taking in 255 shows on six continents, Sheeran played to 8,882,182 people – also the **highest attendance for a music tour**.

Youngest artist to win the "big four" Grammy Awards

Billie Eilish (USA, b. 18 Dec 2001) was 18 years 39 days old when she walked away with all four of the Grammys' general field categories on 26 Jan 2020. She won Album of the Year for *When We All Fall Asleep, Where Do We Go?* – the **most streamed album on Spotify (current)**, with 6 billion streams in 2019. Eilish also took home Song of the Year, Record of the Year and Best New Artist to become only the third performer to complete the sweep, after Christopher Cross in 1981 and Adele in 2012.

On 13 Feb 2020, aged 18 years 57 days, Eilish released the theme song for the upcoming 007 movie, *No Time to Die* (see p.195), making her the **youngest artist to record a *James Bond* movie theme**.

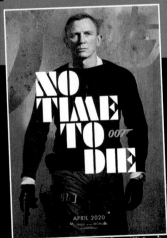

Most Grammy nominations for a female artist

Beyoncé (USA) has received a total of 70 Grammy nominations (including 13 with Destiny's Child) and has won 24 awards. She received four nominations for the 62nd Grammys – held on 26 Jan 2020 – and took home the gong for Best Music Film, for her concert movie *Homecoming* (USA, 2019).

Longest time for an album to return to No.1 in the UK

It took 49 years 252 days for *Abbey Road* by The Beatles (UK) to return to the summit of the UK's Official Albums Chart. Its initial 17-week run at the top came to an end on 31 Jan 1970, and in 2019, a 50th anniversary "stereo mix" – featuring previously unheard outtakes from the 1969 recording sessions – debuted at No.1 on the chart dated 10 Oct.

TV

Longest-serving TV soap star
British actor William Roache has played Ken Barlow in *Coronation Street* (ITV, UK) since the first episode on 9 Dec 1960 (inset). He appeared in episode 10,000 on 7 Feb 2020 – a run of 59 years 61 days.

Coronation Street is itself a record holder as the **longest-running TV soap opera**. A 60th-anniversary special of the much-loved show is scheduled for Dec 2020.

Highest-paid TV host
Dr Phil McGraw (USA) earned $95 m (£74.7 m) between 1 Jul 2018 and 1 Jul 2019, according to estimates by Forbes.

Talk-show star Ellen DeGeneres (USA) is the **highest-paid TV host (female)**. She earned $80.5 m (£63.3 m) in the same period.

Longest career as a game-show host for the same show
Pat Sajak (USA) has presented the syndicated evening edition of the US show *Wheel of Fortune* since 5 Sep 1983 – a total of 36 years 167 days as of 19 Feb 2020.

Longest-running animated TV series
First broadcast on 5 Oct 1969, anime series *Sazae-san* (JPN) celebrated its golden anniversary in 2019 and was still being aired as of Mar 2020. The **longest-running animated sitcom** is *The Simpsons* (FOX, USA), whose lead family enter the GWR Hall of Fame on pp.210–11.

Most Primetime Emmy Awards for...
• **Outstanding Drama Series**: Five US TV series have won this accolade four times: *Game of Thrones* (HBO, 2015–16, 2018–19), *Mad Men* (AMC, 2008–11), *The West Wing* (NBC, 2000–03), *LA Law* (NBC, 1987, 1989–91) and *Hill Street Blues* (NBC, 1981–84).

• **A Drama Series**: At the 71st Annual Primetime Emmy Awards on 22 Sep 2019, *Game of Thrones* won 12 awards, taking its total haul to a record 59. At the same ceremony, it garnered the **most Emmy nominations in one year (drama)** – 32.

Longest marathon TV talk show (team)
Between 12 and 15 Nov 2019, Sebastian Meinberg and Ariane Alter (both DEU) staged a 72-hr 5-min 11-sec chat show. The tireless TV presenters entertained a string of guests on the set of *Das schaffst du nie!* in Ismaning, Germany.

The success of *Game of Thrones* contributed to HBO earning the **most Emmy Award nominations for a network in a single year** at the 2019 ceremony – 137. Two other HBO shows, *Chernobyl* (see opposite page) and *Barry*, picked up 19 and 17 nominations respectively.

Most Nickelodeon Kids' Choice Awards won by a cartoon
SpongeBob SquarePants (Nickelodeon, USA) has taken the "Favorite Cartoon" gong 17 times at the Kids' Choice Awards; its last 12 wins have been consecutive. The series' most recent victory was secured at the 33rd ceremony held on 2 May 2020.

Most money pledged for a Kickstarter TV series project
A team from *Critical Role* (USA) – a weekly live-streamed tabletop role-playing series – attracted $11,385,449 (£8,709,300) in pledges from 88,887 backers between 4 Mar and 17 Apr 2019. The objective was to fund a 10-episode run of animated series *The Legend of Vox Machina*. When the crowd-funding project launched, its original goal was $750,000 (£567,500).

Edna became a "Dame" in the 1974 movie *Barry McKenzie Holds His Own*. The then-Australian prime minister, playing a cameo role, gave her the title.

Longest-running character portrayed by the same actor
As of 31 Dec 2019, Dame Edna Everage had been portrayed by comedian and Tony-Award-winning actor Barry Humphries (AUS) for 64 years 12 days. Humphries debuted the then-Mrs Everage on 19 Dec 1955 while on tour as an actor with The University of Melbourne's Union Theatre Repertory Company. Now a "Dame", Everage has enjoyed a steady career on television, on stage and in the movies, and continues to perform, despite a number of retirement concerts.

Highest Metacritic score for a TV series
These are the most acclaimed TV shows of the year from the past decade, according to Metacritic. The website calculates an average percentage ("Metascore") from professional critics' reviews. Here, it is followed by the user rating (out of 10).

2020	*BoJack Horseman* (Netflix, USA; above left): Season 6.5	93	9.2
2019	*Fleabag* (BBC, UK; above right): Season 2	96	8.7
2018	*Planet Earth: Blue Planet II* (BBC, UK)	97	8.2
2017	*The Leftovers* (HBO, USA): Season 3	98	9.1
2016	*Rectify* (Sundance TV, USA): Season 4	99	8.7
2015	*Fargo* (FX, USA): Season 2	96	9.2
2014	*Game of Thrones* (HBO, USA): Season 4	94	9.2
2013	*Enlightened* (HBO, USA): Season 2	95	7.6
2012	*Breaking Bad* (AMC, USA): Season 5	99	9.6
2011	*Breaking Bad* (AMC, USA): Season 4	96	9.5

Source: Metacritic.com

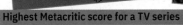

Most in-demand TV series debut
Chernobyl (HBO, USA), which premiered on 6 May 2019, enjoyed a 3.140 DEx/c. The drama follows the events of the disaster that occurred at the eponymous Soviet nuclear plant in Apr 1986 (see p.139) and the subsequent clean-up operation.

The **most in-demand superhero TV series** is *The Flash* (The CW, USA), with a 5.674 DEx/c. Hero Barry Allen (played by Grant Gustin, inset) is struck by a radioactive lightning bolt that endows him with superhuman speed.

Most in-demand TV series

Genre	Show	DEx/c
Based on a book and **overall**	*Game of Thrones* (HBO, USA)	12.686
Digital original	*Stranger Things* (Netflix, USA)	7.357
Sci-fi drama	*Stranger Things*	7.357
Based on a comic adaptation	*The Walking Dead* (AMC, USA)	5.727
Action & adventure	*The Flash* (The CW, USA)	5.674
Comedy	*The Big Bang Theory* (CBS, USA)	4.991
Sitcom	*The Big Bang Theory*	4.991
Teen drama	*Riverdale* (The CW, USA)	4.553
Medical drama	*Grey's Anatomy* (ABC, USA)	4.307
Remake of a previous series	*Shameless* (Showtime, USA)	3.978
Animated series	*Rick and Morty* (Adult Swim, USA)	3.859
Legal drama	*Suits* (USA Network, USA)	3.694
Horror	*American Horror Story* (FX, USA)	3.471
Children's show	*SpongeBob SquarePants* (Nickelodeon, USA)	3.319
Based on a film adaptation	*Westworld* (HBO, USA)	3.263
Anime	*One-Punch Man* (TV Tokyo, JPN)	2.990
Reality TV	*The Voice* (NBC, USA)	2.936
Variety show	*The Daily Show* (Comedy Central, USA)	2.546
Romantic drama	*Outlander* (Starz, USA)	2.515
Soap opera	*Dynasty* (The CW, USA)	2.262
Documentary	*Planet Earth* (BBC, UK)	1.395

Source: Parrot Analytics. Correct as of 18 Feb 2020

What is DEx/c?
To evaluate cross-platform demand for TV series, GWR has teamed up with data-analysis specialists Parrot Analytics. This company has devised a system of "television content demand measurement" to quantify the ways in which viewers engage with TV shows, analysing everything from streaming videos to hashtags and likes on social media. The more effort (i.e., time) a viewer devotes to a TV show, the higher the weighting. The "Demand Expressions per capita" (DEx/c) value represents the overall average daily global audience engagement with a show per 100 people in a set period.

Most Primetime Emmy Awards for...
• **Outstanding Host for a Reality or Competition Program**: four, by RuPaul Charles (USA, above) for *RuPaul's Drag Race* (Logo TV, VH1; USA). Shared with Jeff Probst of CBS's *Survivor* (both USA).
• **Online-Streaming Original Program**: 16, by *The Marvelous Mrs. Maisel* (Prime Video, USA) starring Rachel Brosnahan (right).

Most in-demand TV series
In 2019, *Game of Thrones* (HBO, USA) was once again the most popular TV show, according to data-science firm Parrot Analytics, with a rating of 12.686 DEx/c. The show, inspired by George R R Martin's *A Song of Ice and Fire* fantasy novels, premiered in 2011 and concluded in May 2019.

Social Media

Most videos to reach 1 billion views on YouTube by a musician

As of Feb 2019, Puerto Rican pop star Ozuna (b. Jan Carlos Ozuna Rosado) had seven music videos on YouTube with more than 1 billion views each. He also shares the record for the **most weeks at No.1 on** *Billboard***'s Top Latin Albums chart (male)**. His *Odisea* (2017) topped the list for 46 weeks, as did *X 100PRE* (2018) by fellow reggaeton artist Bad Bunny (b. Benito Antonio Martínez Ocasio, PRI).

Most viewed video online

The music video for "Despacito" by Luis Fonsi, feat. Daddy Yankee (both PRI), remains the most watched video, having amassed 6,731,095,978 views. It is also the **first YouTube video to reach 5 billion views**, a figure it passed on 4 Apr 2018.

Most viewed YouTube video in 24 hours

"Boy with Luv" by BTS (KOR), feat. Halsey (USA), is officially recognized by YouTube as the music video with the most views in a day – 74.6 million – on 12 Apr 2019. Three months later, however, it emerged that "Paagal" ("Mad") by Indian rapper Badshah (b. Aditya Singh) had accumulated a total of 75 million views in 24 hours after it was uploaded to YouTube on 10 Jul 2019. Controversially,

it was reported that "Badshah and his representatives had purchased adverts from Google and YouTube that embedded the video or directed fans to it in some other way," thereby inflating the viewing figures artificially. "Buying views" is common practice in the music industry, allowing acts to register views for their music videos by fans watching seconds of a linked advert. In the wake of this, YouTube is said to be re-evaluating the way its viewer-count technology works.

Most liked image on Instagram

The most popular photograph on the image-sharing website remains that of a brown, speckled egg, with more than 54.3 million likes as of 13 Apr 2020. It was first posted on 4 Jan 2019 by the Egg Gang, who are using it as a platform to support people suffering from stress and anxiety incurred by the pressures of social media.

Most followers on TikTok

Charli D'Amelio (USA) became the **first person with 50 million TikTok followers** on 22 Apr 2020. By 30 Apr, she had 52,037,851 fans. She reached the top spot in just 10 months, having begun uploading dance clips to the video platform in summer 2019.

TikTok's **most followed male** is Zach King (USA). His self-styled "digital sleight of hand" videos had won him 42,023,513 followers as of the same date.

Most followed duck on Instagram

The account "minnesotaduck", for Ben Afquack and owner Derek Johnson (USA), has accumulated 79,068 followers. The Pekin duck first went viral with a video showing him drumming with his feet.

Instagram's ▶ **most followed cat** is Nala, with 4,360,373 fans. The Siamese/Persian's story is one of rags to riches, having been adopted from a pet shelter in Los Angeles, California, USA. She now lives with Varisiri "Pookie" Methachittiphan and Shannon Ellis (both USA).

Highest-earning YouTube contributor (current)

According to estimates by Forbes, Ryan Kaji (b. Ryan Guan, USA) netted $26 m (£19.6 m) in the 12 months up to 1 Jun 2019. The eight-year-old first rose to fame with his unboxing channel "Ryan ToysReview". Now rebranded as "Ryan's World", it also includes family outings and fun science demos; it had accrued 24.8 million subscribers as of 1 May 2020.

Top 10 highest-earning YouTube stars of 2018–19		
Name	Earnings	Genre
1. Ryan Kaji (USA, left)	$26 m (£19.6 m)	Children
2. Dude Perfect (USA)	$20 m (£15.9 m)	Sports and stunts
3. Anastasia Radzinskaya (RUS, below)	$18 m (£14.3 m)	Children
4. Rhett & Link (aka Rhett McLaughlin and Charles Lincoln Neal, both USA)	$17.5 m (£13.9 m)	Comedy
5. Jeffree Star (aka Jeffrey Lynn Steininger Jr, USA)	$17 m (£13.5 m)	Make-up
6. "Preston" (aka Preston Arsement, USA)	$14 m (£11.1 m)	Gaming
=7. "PewDiePie" (aka Felix Kjellberg, SWE)	$13 m (£10.3 m)	Gaming
=7. "Markiplier" (aka Mark Fischbach, USA)	$13 m (£10.3 m)	Gaming
9. "DanTDM" (aka Daniel Middleton, UK)	$12 m (£9.5 m)	Gaming
10. "VanossGaming" (aka Evan Fong, CAN)	$11.5 m (£9.1 m)	Gaming

Source: Forbes; conversions as of 1 Jun 2019

Anastasia was born with cerebral palsy. Her parents began making videos of her to update friends and family on her health, which led to a series of hugely popular YouTube channels.

The enthusiasm for the *Friends* stars' debut on Instagram is likely related to a rumoured 25th-anniversary special of the hit sitcom.

Most followed Mixer channel
Professional gamer "Ninja" (aka Richard Tyler Blevins, USA) has 3,039,855 followers. Ninja moved from Twitch to Microsoft's Mixer on 1 Aug 2019 and instantly became the most popular channel there. However, despite his departure, he still boasts the **most followed Twitch channel** too, with 14.7-million-plus fans.

Ninja's is also the **most viewed Mixer channel**, with 59,432,637 views, putting him just ahead of Spanish gamer David Cánovas Martínez, who is better known as "TheGrefg".

Most liked person on Facebook (female)
The Facebook page of singer Shakira (b. Shakira Isabel Mebarak Ripoll, COL) has 99,930,971 likes. For Facebook's **most liked person**, see below.

Fastest time to reach 1 million followers on Instagram
Jennifer Aniston (USA) hit the 1-million mark in 5 hr 16 min on 15 Oct 2019. The actress attracted almost 5 million followers within 12 hr after her first post – a selfie with fellow *Friends* stars Lisa Kudrow, Courteney Cox, Matt LeBlanc, Matthew Perry and David Schwimmer. On 6 Feb 2020, Perry (inset) became the last of the gang to join Instagram, impressively racking up 4.4 million followers in a day.

Most subscribed YouTube channel
Record label and movie production company T-Series (IND) has amassed more than 138 million subscribers. Other YouTubers at the top of their respective categories, according to SocialBlade, include:
• **Comedy**: "PewDiePie" (SWE, see table opposite); 104 million subscribers.
• **Gaming**: "Fernanfloo" (aka Luis Fernando Flores Alvarado, SLV); 35.9 million subscribers.
• **Music**: Justin Bieber (CAN); 53.5 million subscribers.
• **Pets & animals**: "Brave Wilderness", hosted by Coyote Peterson (USA); 15.9 million subscribers.
• **Science & technology**: "Vsauce", hosted by Michael Stevens (USA); 15.6 million subscribers.

Most followers on Twitter
The former US president Barack Obama has 116,397,276 Twitter followers, more than anyone else on the microblogging platform. Canadian pop star Justin Bieber is currently in second place, with 111,255,013 followers.

The former overall holder, US singer-songwriter Katy Perry (b. Katheryn Hudson), is third on the listings, though her 108,506,809 fans do still make her the **most followed female on Twitter**.

Most followers on Weibo
Chinese singer, actress and TV presenter Xie Na has accumulated a total of 125,332,618 fans on the microblogging website, as confirmed by Weibo representatives on 25 Apr 2020.

Weibo's **most followed male** is TV star He Jiong (CHN), with 118,812,459 fans as of the same date. He has hosted the TV variety show *Happy Camp* for more than 20 years.

Most followers for a place on Twitter
The Twitter account for the Museum of Modern Art (@MuseumModernArt) in New York City, USA, has 5,381,330 followers, putting it just ahead of the UK's Tate galleries.

Most viewed new music video by a solo artist on YouTube in 24 hours
Taylor Swift (USA) attracted 65,200,000 views for "ME!", feat. Brendon Urie of Panic! at the Disco, on 27 Apr 2019.

Fastest time to reach 1 million followers on TikTok
On 25 Sep 2019, boy band BTS (KOR) took just 3 hr 31 min to amass 1 million fans on TikTok. The app allows users to upload their self-made videos – from dance and lip-synchs to magic tricks and parkour – and watch those of other performers. Videos have a time limit of 15 sec, though users can loop join them up to create a one-minute piece.

Most followers on Instagram (female)
Singer-songwriter Ariana Grande (USA) has attained 182,260,250 Instagram followers.

Juventus striker Cristiano Ronaldo (PRT) has the **most followers on Instagram**, with 214,941,702. His stellar success on the soccer pitch, including memorable spells with Manchester United and Real Madrid, has also seen Ronaldo become the **most liked person on Facebook**, with 122,525,916 thumbs-up.

Ariana Grande also enjoys the **most subscribers for a musician on YouTube (female)**, with 40.6-million-plus fans.

TOYS AND GAMES

Most expensive *Pokémon* trading card sold at auction

A "Pikachu Illustrator" Trainer Promo Hologram Trading Card sold for $195,000 (£150,704) on 23 Oct 2019 at Weiss Auctions in New York City, USA. Designed by Atsuko Nishida, the creator of Pikachu, it is one of 39 copies released in 1998 as prizes for an illustration contest.

Oldest board game

Boards used in the game senet (or "passing") have been found in pre-dynastic tombs at Abydos in modern-day Egypt, dating back as far as 3500 BCE. Two players moved a group of up to seven pieces along a board comprising three rows of 10 squares, and gameplay represented the journey to reunite with the Sun god. To win, players had to move their pieces past those of their opponent and off the board.

Largest collection of Monopoly boards

As of 5 Sep 2018, Neil Scallan (UK) owned 2,249 unique Monopoly sets, as confirmed in Crawley, West Sussex, UK. Neil began collecting localized editions of the board game as holiday souvenirs.

Fewest moves to complete a Rubik's Cube

Sebastiano Tronto (ITA) solved a 3x3x3 cube in 16 moves during the FMC ("Fewest Moves Count") event on 15–16 Jun 2019.

▶ Largest Rubik's Cube

On 18 Nov 2019, long-time Rubik's Cube fan Tony Fisher (UK) unveiled a super-sized version of the classic puzzle, with each side measuring 2.022 m (6 ft 7 in), in Ipswich, Suffolk, UK. The giant cube, which is completely functional, took around 330 hours for Tony to make from various plastic components, cardboard, springs and resin.

▶ Largest game of tag

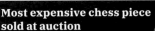

Fischer's and Fans of Fischer's (both JPN) assembled 10,908 people to play tag in Suita, Osaka, Japan, on 16 Sep 2019.

The **longest laser-tag marathon** lasted 26 hr 40 sec. It was staged on 22–23 Aug 2019 by Zap Zone in Canton, Michigan, USA.

Most expensive chess piece sold at auction

100%

A 12th-century "warder" figure carved from walrus ivory sold for £735,000 ($930,415) on 2 Jul 2019 at Sotheby's in London, UK. In 1964, it had been bought by an antiques dealer for just £5 ($14). The equivalent of a rook, or castle, the warder was one of five long-lost pieces from the so-called Lewis Chessmen, a hoard discovered on the Scottish isle of Lewis in Mar 1831. It is most likely of Nordic origin.

Largest board game

DKT is a game similar to Monopoly, but with the aim of repaying one's starting loan. On 22 Nov 2019, a 1,006.4-m² (10,833.8-sq-ft) game of DKT – around 13,400 times larger than a standard board – was unveiled by Junge Wirtschaft Steiermark, Wirtschaftskammer Steiermark, Bernd Liebminger and Christoph Kovacic (all AUT) in Graz, Austria.

Most contributors to a miniature LEGO®-brick city in eight hours

A total of 1,025 people helped to build a cityscape using some 380,000 LEGO bricks in Shanghai, China, on 22 Sep 2019. The construction project was overseen by Playable Design and Shanghai Tower, the world's second-tallest building (both CHN).

Largest LEGO-brick...

• **Diorama**: 21.04 m² (226.4 sq ft), built by Edgaras Račinskas (LTU) and Abhinav Sarangi (IND) at LEGO House in Billund, Denmark, on 23 Jun 2019. The display comprised around 540 miniature rooms that were assembled into a scene to celebrate the launch of LEGO's new *Tower* mobile game.

• **Model of Notre Dame**: 2.72 x 3.78 x 1.43 m (8 ft 11 in x 12 ft 4 in x 4 ft 8 in), built by Ivan Angeli at an event arranged by Wystawa Klocków (both POL). Unveiled in the Polish capital, Warsaw, on 9 Jan 2020, it used more than 400,000 LEGO bricks and commemorated the iconic cathedral that was devastated by fire in Apr 2019.

Most people solving Rubik's Cubes one-handed

On 23 Dec 2019, a total of 610 pupils at Chaoyang Primary School (CHN) each solved a 3x3x3 Rubik's Cube using just one hand at Capital Normal University in Beijing, China. All of the youngsters came from the first to sixth grade. It is a tradition at the school for students to be taught how to solve Ernő Rubik's renowned puzzles.

World Cube Association speedcubing records

Record	Single	Holder	Average	Holder
3x3x3	3.47	Yusheng Du (CHN)	5.53	Feliks Zemdegs (AUS)
2x2x2	0.49	Maciej Czapiewski (POL)	1.21	Martin Vædele Egdal (DNK)
4x4x4	17.42	Sebastian Weyer (DEU)	21.11	Max Park (USA)
5x5x5	34.92	Max Park	39.65	Max Park
6x6x6	1:09.51	Max Park	1:15.90	Max Park
7x7x7	1:40.89	Max Park	1:46:57	Max Park
3x3x3 blindfolded	15.50	Max Hilliard (USA)	18.18	Jeff Park (USA)
3x3x3 fewest moves	16	Sebastiano Tronto (ITA)	21	Cale Schoon (USA)
3x3x3 one-handed	6.82	Max Park	9.42	Max Park
3x3x3 with feet	15.56	Mohammed Aiman Koli (IND)	19.90	Lim Hung (MYS)
Clock	3.29	Suen Ming Chi (CHN)	4.38	Yunhao Lou (CHN)
Megaminx	27.22	Juan Pablo Huanqui (PER)	30.39	Juan Pablo Huanqui
Pyraminx	0.91	Dominik Górny (POL)	1.86	Tymon Kolasiński (POL)
Skewb	0.93	Andrew Huang (AUS)	2.03	Łukasz Burliga (POL)
Square-1	4.95	Jackey Zheng (USA)	6.54	Vicenzo Guerino Cecchini (BRA)
4x4x4 blindfolded	1:02.51	Stanley Chapel (USA)	1:08.76	Stanley Chapel
5x5x5 blindfolded	2:21.62	Stanley Chapel	2:27.63	Stanley Chapel
3x3x3 multi-blind*		Graham Siggins (USA) – solved 59 out of 60 cubes in 1 hr (59:46)		

*Correct as of 14 Feb 2020. Times in min:sec. *No average category for the multi-blind solves*

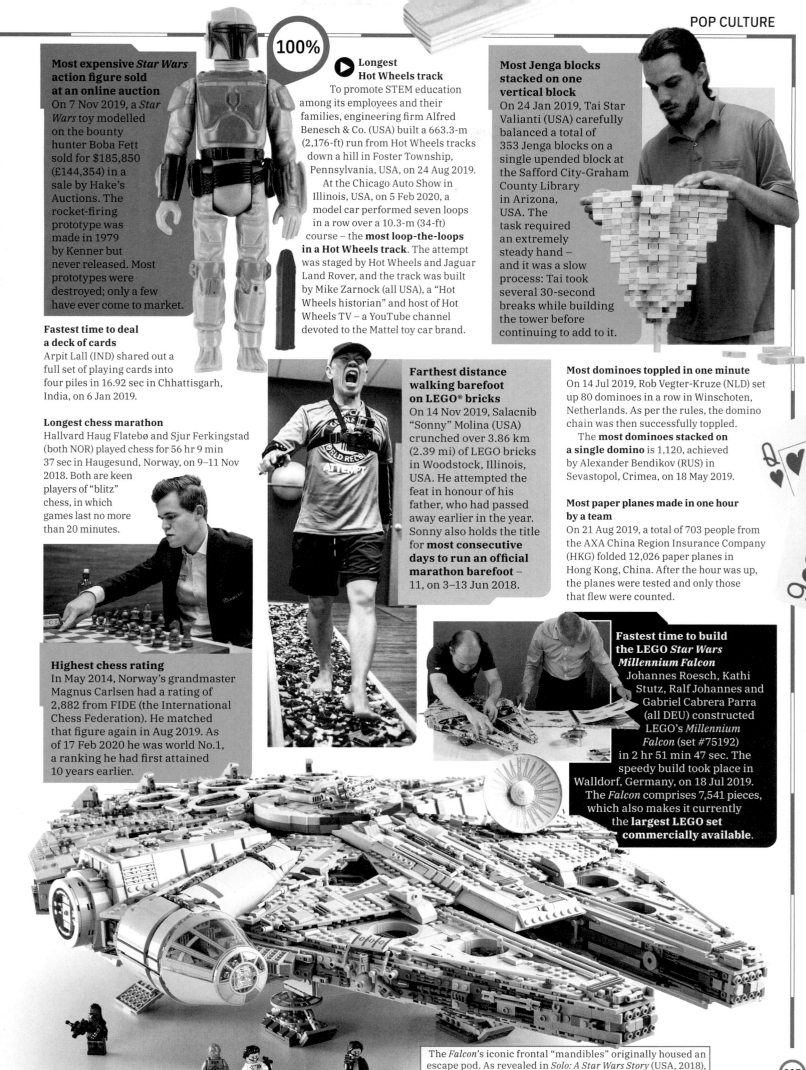

Most expensive *Star Wars* action figure sold at an online auction
On 7 Nov 2019, a *Star Wars* toy modelled on the bounty hunter Boba Fett sold for $185,850 (£144,354) in a sale by Hake's Auctions. The rocket-firing prototype was made in 1979 by Kenner but never released. Most prototypes were destroyed; only a few have ever come to market.

Fastest time to deal a deck of cards
Arpit Lall (IND) shared out a full set of playing cards into four piles in 16.92 sec in Chhattisgarh, India, on 6 Jan 2019.

Longest chess marathon
Hallvard Haug Flatebø and Sjur Ferkingstad (both NOR) played chess for 56 hr 9 min 37 sec in Haugesund, Norway, on 9–11 Nov 2018. Both are keen players of "blitz" chess, in which games last no more than 20 minutes.

Highest chess rating
In May 2014, Norway's grandmaster Magnus Carlsen had a rating of 2,882 from FIDE (the International Chess Federation). He matched that figure again in Aug 2019. As of 17 Feb 2020 he was world No.1, a ranking he had first attained 10 years earlier.

100%

▶ **Longest Hot Wheels track**
To promote STEM education among its employees and their families, engineering firm Alfred Benesch & Co. (USA) built a 663.3-m (2,176-ft) run from Hot Wheels tracks down a hill in Foster Township, Pennsylvania, USA, on 24 Aug 2019.
At the Chicago Auto Show in Illinois, USA, on 5 Feb 2020, a model car performed seven loops in a row over a 10.3-m (34-ft) course – the **most loop-the-loops in a Hot Wheels track**. The attempt was staged by Hot Wheels and Jaguar Land Rover, and the track was built by Mike Zarnock (all USA), a "Hot Wheels historian" and host of Hot Wheels TV – a YouTube channel devoted to the Mattel toy car brand.

Farthest distance walking barefoot on LEGO® bricks
On 14 Nov 2019, Salacnib "Sonny" Molina (USA) crunched over 3.86 km (2.39 mi) of LEGO bricks in Woodstock, Illinois, USA. He attempted the feat in honour of his father, who had passed away earlier in the year. Sonny also holds the title for **most consecutive days to run an official marathon barefoot** – 11, on 3–13 Jun 2018.

Most Jenga blocks stacked on one vertical block
On 24 Jan 2019, Tai Star Valianti (USA) carefully balanced a total of 353 Jenga blocks on a single upended block at the Safford City-Graham County Library in Arizona, USA. The task required an extremely steady hand – and it was a slow process: Tai took several 30-second breaks while building the tower before continuing to add to it.

Most dominoes toppled in one minute
On 14 Jul 2019, Rob Vegter-Kruze (NLD) set up 80 dominoes in a row in Winschoten, Netherlands. As per the rules, the domino chain was then successfully toppled.
The **most dominoes stacked on a single domino** is 1,120, achieved by Alexander Bendikov (RUS) in Sevastopol, Crimea, on 18 May 2019.

Most paper planes made in one hour by a team
On 21 Aug 2019, a total of 703 people from the AXA China Region Insurance Company (HKG) folded 12,026 paper planes in Hong Kong, China. After the hour was up, the planes were tested and only those that flew were counted.

Fastest time to build the LEGO *Star Wars* *Millennium Falcon*
Johannes Roesch, Kathi Stutz, Ralf Johannes and Gabriel Cabrera Parra (all DEU) constructed LEGO's *Millennium Falcon* (set #75192) in 2 hr 51 min 47 sec. The speedy build took place in Walldorf, Germany, on 18 Jul 2019. The *Falcon* comprises 7,541 pieces, which also makes it currently the **largest LEGO set commercially available**.

The *Falcon*'s iconic frontal "mandibles" originally housed an escape pod. As revealed in *Solo: A Star Wars Story* (USA, 2018), Han Solo jettisoned the unit and neglected to replace it.

Round-Up

Most Nickelodeon Kids' Choice Awards

At the 32nd Kids' Choice Awards held on 23 Mar 2019, US singer and actor Selena Gomez picked up her 11th "Blimp". Her latest win was Favorite Female Voice from an Animated Movie for playing Mavis in *Hotel Transylvania 3: Summer Vacation* (USA, 2018). This means she now ties with US actor Will Smith for most awards won by an individual. Some would argue that Gomez is ahead as two of Smith's were honorary titles.

Longest-running televised children's award show

The Nickelodeon Kids' Choice Awards (ViacomCBS, USA) debuted on 18 Apr 1988, and the latest show was broadcast on 2 May 2020 – a span of 32 years 15 days. The 2020 event was produced virtually owing to COVID-19.

Most searched-for...

At the end of each year, Google – the world's **largest search engine** – releases an annual *Trends* report, revealing its most popular search requests of the past 12 months. A few trending topics in 2019 were:
Male and **overall**: American football player Antonio Brown (USA).
Female: musician Billie Eilish (USA; see p.201).
Movie: *Avengers: Endgame* (USA, 2019; see p.195).
TV show: fantasy drama *Game of Thrones* (HBO, USA; see p.203).

Most public votes for a TV programme

An unprecedented 1,532,944,337 votes were cast online by viewers of *Big Brother Brasil 20* (Globo, BRA) on 29–31 Mar 2020. This smashed the mark of 132,311,283 votes that were received for the Season 11

finale of *American Idol* (FOX, USA), a record which had stood since 22–23 Mar 2012.

Longest West End run for a musical

Two shows vie for this title. *The Phantom of the Opera* has played at Her Majesty's Theatre in London's West End for 32 years since its premiere on 9 Oct 1986. *Les Misérables* had its West End debut at the Palace Theatre on 5 Dec 1985, but has moved location several times since. *Les Mis* closed on 13 Jul 2019 after 33 years and was replaced by a concert version at the Gielgud Theatre before

Most tracked group on Songkick

Rock band Coldplay (UK; lead singer Chris Martin, above) were being followed by 3,840,257 fans on live-music website Songkick as of 25 Feb 2020.

As of the same date, the **most tracked artist** overall was Rihanna (b. Robyn Rihanna Fenty, BRB), who was being tracked by 3,867,117 fans.

Most functional gadgets in a cosplay suit

Keith Dinsmore (USA) cosplays regularly as Gotham crime-fighter Batman, wearing a suit kitted out with 30 fully functioning gadgets, as documented in Portland, Maine, USA, on 24 May 2019. Among the tools at his disposal are a Batarang, a bluetooth headset, a tracking device, a fingerprint kit and, of course, a portable Bat signal.

Highest-grossing music festival (current)

The Outside Lands Music & Arts Festival (below), staged at Golden Gate Park in San Francisco, California, USA, on 9–11 Aug 2019, grossed $29,634,734 (£24,624,200), making it the year's top-earning festival. The event was headlined by Paul Simon, Childish Gambino and twenty one pilots.

Lollapalooza Brasil (inset) recorded the **most tickets sold for a music festival (current)**: 246,000. With a line-up including Arctic Monkeys, Kings of Leon and Sam Smith, it was held at Autódromo de Interlagos in São Paulo, Brazil, on 5–7 Apr 2019. Both records draw on data logged by the live-music trade publication *Pollstar*.

Youngest Hollywood executive producer

When the comedy film *Little* (USA) was released on 12 Apr 2019, its star and executive producer Marsai Martin (USA, b. 14 Aug 2004) was aged just 14 years 241 days. *Little* tells the story of a bullying boss who becomes a child again. The idea for the movie came while Martin was filming the TV series *Black-ish* (ABC, USA).

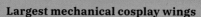

Nathan Sawaya, the creator of this remarkable set, is a multiple record holder who builds life-size LEGO models of everything from the Batmobile and superheroes to a *T. rex* skeleton.

Largest mechanical cosplay wings

Andy Holt (USA) created a pair of wings with a 5.84-m (19-ft 2-in) span for his take on the DC Comics superhero Hawkman. The wings are moved via linear actuators that are controlled using a handheld device. They were measured in Irvine, California, USA, on 24 Oct 2019.

re-opening in a new staging on 16 Jan 2020 at the Sondheim Theatre. As of 16 Mar, all London theatres were closed as part of the COVID-19 lockdown.

Highest annual earnings for an author

According to the most recent figures published by Forbes, *Harry Potter* creator J.K. Rowling (UK, see below) earned $92 m (£72.9 m) from 1 Jun 2018 to 1 Jun 2019.

The **highest-earning male author** is James

Patterson (USA), with a reported $70 m (£55.5 m) during the same period.

Highest annual earnings for a radio host

According to the same data set from Forbes, Howard Stern (USA) earned $93 m (£73.7 m) between 1 Jun 2018 and 1 Jun 2019.

Longest-held vocal note in a song (studio recording)

A professional rendition of the Benard Ighner classic "Everything Must Change"

– recorded in a private studio by singer and "vocal coach to the stars" Tee Green (UK) on 27 Mar 2011 – concludes with a same-pitch note that lasts for a lung-busting 39 sec.

Most issues by a letterer in a comic-book series

Since the debut of *Spawn* (Image Comics) in 1992, Tom Orzechowski (USA) has provided the lettering for 301 issues, as of #302 published on 6 Nov 2019. He also works on Marvel's *Uncanny X-Men*.

Fastest theatrical production

After only 11 hr 59 min of rehearsals, Rubber Chicken Theatre (UK) staged a production of *The Wedding Singer* on 16 Feb 2020. It was seen by a sold-out audience of 370 people at the Macrobert Arts Centre at the University of Stirling, UK.

Largest LEGO®-brick stage-set replica

On 19 Oct 2019, a 62.75-m² (675.4-sq-ft) recreation of the famous Central Perk coffee shop from TV sitcom *Friends* opened its doors in Las Vegas, Nevada, USA. Constructed by LEGO artist Nathan Sawaya, who was commissioned by Warner Bros. (both USA), it comprised almost 1 million bricks.

Highest-grossing Broadway play

No "straight" play – as opposed to a musical – has grossed more on Broadway than *Harry Potter and the Cursed Child*, which had taken $174,056,581 (£133,350,000) in its lifetime up to 8 Mar 2020. Written by Jack Thorne from a story conceived by Thorne, J.K. Rowling (right) and John Tiffany (all UK), the play picks up the story of the Boy Wizard in adulthood. James Snyder (left) currently plays the title role.

As of 8 Mar 2020, the play had sold 1,324,815 tickets across 783 performances on Broadway.

○ HALL OF FAME

The **Simpsons**

For 30 years, *The Simpsons* (FOX, USA) has held up a satirical mirror to modern American life. Homer, Marge, Bart, Lisa and Maggie have become household names… a small-town family who **conquered the world.**

The Simpsons made their TV debut in a series of short cartoons. They were conceived by cartoonist Matt Groening in 1987, in a series of short cartoons for *The Tracey Ullman Show*. They were conceived by cartoonist Matt Groening (USA, right), who named them after members of his own family. On 17 Dec 1989, his creations graduated to their own prime-time half-hour series with the episode "Simpsons Roasting on an Open Fire". *The Simpsons* earned instant acclaim, its characters becoming universally recognizable. In 1997, it surpassed *The Flintstones* (ABC, USA) as the **longest-running animated sitcom by episodes** — as of 22 Apr 2020, it had aired 680 episodes in 31 seasons.

In 2000, the Simpson family were afforded one of the highest honours in show business: their own star on the Hollywood Walk of Fame. Their critical plaudits – and catchphrases become the show continues to gain critical acclaim, the show continues to gain critical acclaim for the show by 22 Apr 2020. In Sep 2019, it extended its record for the **most Primetime Emmy Awards won by an animated TV series** to 34.

The Simpsons has also become famous for its celebrity guests, with everyone making special appearances from Katy Perry to Stephen Hawking. As of 22 Apr 2020, there had been 810 guest stars – the **most cameos in a TV series**. It seems even the biggest A-listers are happy to play a supporting role if it means getting a chance to share some screen time with Springfield's first family.

"I don't care about awards, but to be in the GWR book is really great"

1

Homer's catchphrase "d'oh" was included in the English Oxford English Dictionary in 2001.

Find out more about the Simpsons in the Hall of Fame section at **www.guinnessworldrecords.com/2021**

MATT GROENING

1: Springfield hits the big screen in *The Simpsons Movie* (USA, 2007).

2: Bart & co. as they first appeared in *The Simpsons* in 1987. In 2014, these proto-Simpsons returned for a ghostly cameo in the "Treehouse of Horror XXV".

3: Inside the Springsonian Museum of episode **largest collection of *The Simpsons* memorabilia** as of 2008. Cameron Gibbs (AUS), whose contained 2,580 different items – 203. **most tattoos of characters** Simpsons superfan Michael Baxter (AUS) displays the

4: *Simpsons* the **most animated series from an animated series** – 203.

5: On 13 Oct 2019, *Aquaman* star Jason Momoa made his debut cameo on the show.

The Simpson family are voiced by Dan Castellaneta (Homer), Julie Kavner (Marge), Nancy Cartwright (Bart) and Yeardley Smith (Lisa). Baby Maggie rarely speaks, but some of her pacifier sucking noises are provided by the show's creator, Matt Groening.

Sports

Most goals scored at the FIFA World Cup finals

No soccer player has scored more times at the FIFA World Cup than Brazil's iconic No.10, Marta (b. Marta Vieira da Silva). On 18 Jun 2019, she took her tally to 17 with a decisive penalty against Italy, surpassing German striker Miroslav Klose's total of 16. Marta scored on her World Cup debut on 21 Sep 2003 aged just 17, and she went on to win the Golden Boot in 2007 with seven goals. She has netted in a total of five tournaments – the **most FIFA World Cup finals scored in**, a record she shares with Canada's Christine Sinclair.

Marta has also amassed the **most wins of the Best FIFA Women's Player award** – six, between 2006 and 2018 (inset). Her closest rival is Birgit Prinz, a three-time winner in 2003–05 when the award was known as FIFA World Player of the Year.

Marta honed her skills playing in the street with improvised footballs made from plastic bags.

Soccer

Most international goals
Christine Sinclair scored 186 goals for Canada between 14 Mar 2000 and 4 Feb 2020. She surpassed Abby Wambach's **female** record of 184 with a brace against St Kitts & Nevis on 29 Jan 2020 (above). The **male** record is 109, by Iran's Ali Daei. Sinclair's tally includes the **most goals in a women's Olympic football tournament** – six, at London 2012.

Most international wins (male)
Sergio Ramos (ESP) had triumphed in 126 official international fixtures (excluding penalty shoot-outs) as of 18 Dec 2019. The no-nonsense defender made his debut for Spain in a 3–0 win over China in 2005, aged 18. He surpassed Iker Casillas' total of 121 wins during Spain's 3–0 victory over Sweden on 10 Jun 2019.

Most appearances in FIFA Women's World Cup finals
On 9 Jun 2019, Formiga (BRA, b. Miraildes Maciel Mota, 3 Mar 1978) took to the field for her seventh World Cup tournament. During Brazil's loss to hosts France on 23 Jun, she became the **oldest player at a FIFA Women's World Cup**, aged 41 years 112 days.

Most matches played at the FIFA Beach Soccer World Cup
Goalkeeper Mão (BRA, b. Jenílson Brito Rodrigues) played 50 games at the FIFA Beach Soccer World Cup between 2006 and 2019. He marked his 50th game with a goal during Brazil's loss to Russia on 28 Nov 2019.

Most Bundesliga title wins (individual)
In 2018/19, winger Franck Ribéry (FRA) secured his ninth German league title for Bayern Munich since 2007/08. After a 12-year stay at the club, Ribéry signed for Italian side Fiorentina in Aug 2019.

Bayern's 2018/19 win extended their record for the **most consecutive Bundesliga titles** to seven. The Bavarians have also registered the **most wins of the German top division** – 29, since 1931/32.

Most goals in a Chinese Super League season
Eran Zahavi (ISR) struck 29 times for Guangzhou R&F in the 2019 Chinese Super League season.

On 30 May 2019, Haaland hit nine goals in one game against Honduras at the FIFA U-20 World Cup.

Longest international career (male)
Andorran captain Ildefonso Lima Solà had played international soccer for 22 years 148 days, as of 17 Nov 2019. He made his debut on 22 Jun 1997, in what was only his country's second official fixture, a 4–1 defeat against Estonia in which he found the back of the net. Lima has accrued a total of 127 international caps, only the second Andorran, after Óscar Sonejee, to pass the 100-cap milestone.

Fastest hat-trick on debut in a Bundesliga match
Erling Braut Haaland (NOR) struck three times in 19 min 48 sec in his first game for Borussia Dortmund, against Augsburg on 18 Jan 2020. He came off the bench as a second-half substitute and took just 10 touches to record his hat-trick, as Dortmund won 5–3. Haaland (b. 21 Jul 2000) became the second-youngest player to score a German league hat-trick, after Eintracht Frankfurt's 18-year-old Walter Bechtold in 1965.

Youngest goalscorer in the UEFA Champions League
On 10 Dec 2019, FC Barcelona's Ansu Fati (ESP, b. GNB, 31 Oct 2002; left) struck against Inter Milan aged 17 years 40 days at the Stadio San Siro in Milan, Italy. The winger is the third-youngest scorer in La Liga history and also the **youngest player to score and assist in a La Liga game** – aged 16 years 318 days, against Valencia on 14 Sep 2019.

Most goals at the FIFA Beach Soccer World Cup
On 22 Nov 2019, Madjer (PRT, b. João Victor Saraiva) scored his 88th goal at the FIFA Beach Soccer World Cup during Portugal's 10–1 romp over Nigeria in Luque, Paraguay. The 42-year-old, who was appearing in his ninth World Cup tournament, went on to lift the trophy for the second time before announcing his international retirement.

Most wins of the Ballon d'Or
The Ballon d'Or is an annual award presented by *France Football* (jointly with FIFA in 2010–15) to honour the best player of the previous year. On 2 Dec 2019, Lionel Messi (ARG) was awarded his sixth trophy, moving one clear of rival Cristiano Ronaldo. Messi had scored 46 goals and made 17 assists for FC Barcelona and Argentina in 2019.

Most wins of the FIFA Women's World Cup
The USA secured their fourth Women's World Cup on 7 Jul 2019 with a 2–0 win over the Netherlands in Lyon, France. Player of the Match Megan Rapinoe (b. 5 Jul 1985, inset right) became the **oldest goalscorer in a Women's World Cup final**, aged 34 years 2 days.

The USA tore up the FIFA Women's World Cup record books throughout the 2019 edition, recording the **most consecutive wins** (12, across two tournaments), the **most goals in a tournament** (26) and the **highest margin of victory** (13–0, against Thailand on 11 Jun 2019).

Most goals in the UEFA Women's Champions League
Ada Hegerberg (NOR) struck 53 times for Stabæk, 1. FFC Turbine Potsdam and Olympique Lyonnais Féminin from 26 Sep 2012 to 30 Oct 2019. She overtook Anja Mittag's record of 51 in only her 50th appearance in the competition.

Hegerberg's teammate Wendie Renard (FRA) has recorded the **most UEFA Women's Champions League appearances** – 85, between 9 Aug 2007 and 16 Oct 2019.

Most Major League Soccer (MLS) goals
Chris Wondolowski (USA) hit 159 goals while playing for the Houston Dynamo and the San Jose Earthquakes between 30 Aug 2006 and 6 Oct 2019. He surpassed Landon Donovan's career tally of 145 goals with a four-goal blitz against the Chicago Fire on 18 May 2019.

Also in 2019, Carlos Vela (MEX) scored the **most goals in an MLS season** – 34, for Los Angeles FC – while Josef Martínez (VEN) recorded the **most consecutive MLS games with a goal** – 15, for Atlanta United from 24 May to 18 Sep. This excludes three games he missed while playing for Venezuela.

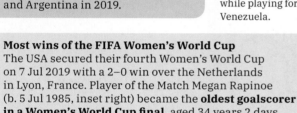

Most consecutive wins in the English top division
Liverpool racked up 18 league wins on the bounce between 27 Oct 2019 and 24 Feb 2020, equalling Manchester City's tally from 26 Aug to 27 Dec 2017. Despite their run ending with a 3–0 defeat to Watford on 29 Feb 2020, Liverpool looked set for their first league title since 1989/90 when the 2019/20 EPL season was halted owing to coronavirus.

Most English Premier League (EPL) goals by a foreign player
Manchester City's Sergio Agüero (ARG) had scored 180 league goals as of 8 Mar 2020. He moved past Thierry Henry's tally of 175 with three goals against Aston Villa on 12 Jan 2020, at the same time bagging the outright record for the **most EPL hat-tricks** – 12.

Highest margin of victory in an English top-division away win
Leicester City crushed Southampton 0–9 on 25 Oct 2019 at St Mary's Stadium in Hampshire, UK – the biggest top-flight away win since the Football League began in 1888.

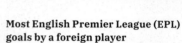

The USA conceded just three goals and were never behind at any point during the 2019 Women's World Cup.

American Football

All records are National Football League (NFL) and all current record holders are USA, unless otherwise indicated.

Fastest quarterback to reach 40,000 passing yards

On 20 Oct 2019, Matthew Stafford of the Detroit Lions reached 40,000 career passing yards in his 147th NFL game. That was four games quicker than the previous record holder, the Atlanta Falcons' Matt Ryan.

Fewest turnovers in a season (team)

The New Orleans Saints conceded only eight turnovers in 16 games in 2019. The previous lowest was 10.

Most career touchdown passes

Drew Brees threw 547 regular-season touchdown passes while playing for the San Diego Chargers and the New Orleans Saints between 2001 and 2019. He overtook Peyton Manning's total of 539 during the Saints' 34–7 win over Indianapolis on 16 Dec 2019.

On the same night, Brees also set the **highest completion percentage in a game** – 96.7%. He found his teammates with 29 out of 30 passes.

Most pass receptions in a season

Wide receiver Michael Thomas caught 149 passes while playing for the New Orleans Saints in the 2019 season. The previous record, 143, by Indianapolis's Marvin Harrison, had stood since 2002.

Longest first reception

On 8 Dec 2019, Olamide Zaccheaus grabbed a 93-yard touchdown catch on his debut NFL reception for the Atlanta Falcons during a 40–20 win over the Carolina Panthers.

Most consecutive playoff appearances (team)

On 4 Jan 2020, the New England Patriots made their 11th appearance in a row in postseason. Despite going down 20–13 to the Tennessee Titans, quarterback Tom Brady extended his **postseason** records for **most games** (41), **touchdown passes** (73), **completed passes** (1,025) and **passing yards** (11,388).

Youngest player to reach 50 sacks
On 8 Dec 2019, Danielle Hunter (JAM, b. 29 Oct 1994) recorded his 50th career sack aged 25 years 40 days. Hunter, a defensive end for the Minnesota Vikings, beat the mark of Robert Quinn (25 years 167 days, set in 2015) during Minnesota's 20–7 win over the Detroit Lions.

Most career points

Kicker Adam Vinatieri scored 2,673 points while playing for the New England Patriots and the Indianapolis Colts between 1996 and 2019. Vinatieri has also recorded the **most field goal attempts** – 715; he surpassed Morten Andersen's total of 709 on 17 Nov 2019, during the Colts' 33–13 defeat of Jacksonville.

Most rushing yards gained in a season by a quarterback
Lamar Jackson rushed for 1,206 yards for the Baltimore Ravens during the 2019 season. He surpassed Michael Vick's mark of 1,039 from 2006. Jackson, who also led the league in touchdown passes (36), went on to become only the second-ever unanimous selection for the NFL Most Valuable Player (MVP) award.

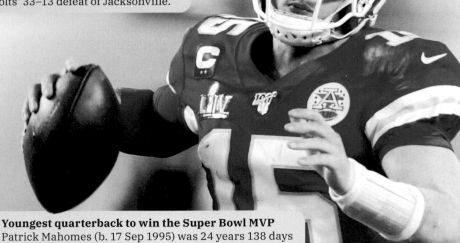

Youngest quarterback to win the Super Bowl MVP

Patrick Mahomes (b. 17 Sep 1995) was 24 years 138 days when he was named MVP at Super Bowl LIV on 2 Feb 2020. The quarterback had guided his Kansas City Chiefs to a 31–20 victory over the San Francisco 49ers.

On 12 Jan 2020, Mahomes equalled Doug Williams' record for the **most touchdown passes thrown in a single quarter of a postseason game**. He threw four during the second quarter to spark the Chiefs' 51–31 comeback victory over the Houston Texans.

Heaviest player to catch a touchdown pass in a regular-season game
Tipping the scales at 347 lb (157 kg; 24 st 11 lb), defensive tackle Vita Vea caught a touchdown pass for the Tampa Bay Buccaneers against the Atlanta Falcons on 24 Nov 2019.

The **postseason** record was set on 19 Jan 2020, by 321-lb (145-kg; 22-st 13-lb) Dennis Kelly for the Tennessee Titans against the Kansas City Chiefs.

The only operational franchises to have played in the first NFL season in 1920 are the Arizona Cardinals (as the Chicago Cardinals) and the Chicago Bears (as the Decatur Staleys).

Ice Hockey

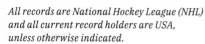

All records are National Hockey League (NHL) and all current record holders are USA, unless otherwise indicated.

Oldest goaltender to win on regular-season debut
On 22 Feb 2020, David Ayres (CAN, b. 12 Aug 1977) made a fairytale NHL debut aged 42 years 194 days during the Carolina Hurricanes' 6–3 win over the Toronto Maple Leafs in Ontario, Canada. Ayres – a former minor-league player, and the Maple Leafs' emergency back-up goaltender – took to the ice for Carolina when both of their goaltenders were injured.

Most career blocked shots
Brent Seabrook (CAN, above centre) had blocked 1,998 shots for the Chicago Blackhawks as of 17 Feb 2020. Blocked shots began being officially tracked by the NHL during the 2005/06 season. Seabrook has played more than 1,000 games alongside Duncan Keith – the first defencemen duo to pass that milestone in NHL history.

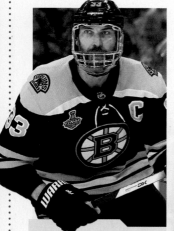

Most Game 7 appearances
On 12 Jun 2019, Boston Bruins defenceman Zdeno Chára (SVK) played in his 14th deciding Game 7 of the Stanley Cup playoffs. The Bruins were defeated by the St Louis Blues in Game 7 of the Stanley Cup Finals.
In Game 6, on 9 Jun, Chára (b. 18 Mar 1977) became the **oldest defenceman to score in the Cup Finals**, aged 42 years 83 days.

Longest road winning streak by a rookie goaltender
Ilya Samsonov (RUS) won 10 consecutive games away from home during his first season for the Washington Capitals between 4 Oct 2019 and 31 Jan 2020. He made his NHL debut against the New York Islanders at Uniondale's Nassau Coliseum, making 25 saves as the Capitals won 2–1.

Most seasons to finish as top scorer
Alex Ovechkin (RUS) ended the 2018/19 season as goal leader for the eighth time in the NHL, striking 51 times. The Washington Capitals winger moved ahead of seven-time top scorer Bobby Hull.
On 29 Oct 2019, Ovechkin extended his record for **most regular-season overtime goals** to 23, during a 4–3 win over the Toronto Maple Leafs.

Most career face-offs won
As of 17 Feb 2020, Patrice Bergeron (CAN) had won 11,976 face-offs while playing for the Boston Bruins since the 2005/06 season, when the NHL began officially tracking face-off statistics.

Most goaltenders used in a season
The Philadelphia Flyers called on eight goaltenders during the 2018/19 season: Brian Elliott, Carter Hart, Calvin Pickard, Cam Talbot (all CAN), Michal Neuvirth (CZE), Anthony Stolarz, Alex Lyon and Mike McKenna all started.

Most points won by a team without reaching the playoffs
Three sides have earned 96 points without making the playoffs: the Boston Bruins (2014/15), the Florida Panthers (2017/18) and the Montreal Canadiens (CAN, 2018/19).

Most wins in a season (team)
The Tampa Bay Lightning won 62 games during the 2018/19 season, equalling the mark set by the Detroit Red Wings in 1995/96. The Lightning claimed the President's Trophy for the first time, only to be swept 4–0 by the Columbus Blue Jackets in the first round of the Stanley Cup playoffs.

NHL regular-season team records

Most...	Number	Team	Season
Standings points	132	Montreal Canadiens (CAN)	1976/77
Goals	446	Edmonton Oilers (CAN)	1983/84
Assists	738	Edmonton Oilers	1985/86
Ties	24	Philadelphia Flyers	1969/70
Losses	71	San Jose Sharks	1992/93
Shootouts	21	Washington Capitals	2013/14
Shootout wins	15	Edmonton Oilers	2007/08

Basketball

First WNBA player to record a "50-40-90" season
In 2019, Elena Delle Donne of the Washington Mystics hit 51.5% of her field goals (220 of 427), 43% of her three-pointers (52 of 121) and 97.4% of her free throws (114 of 117). She became only the ninth player to record a "50-40-90" season, joining eight NBA players. Her free-throw percentage is the highest recorded by any of the nine.

All records are National Basketball Association (NBA) and all current record holders are USA, unless otherwise indicated.

Most finals MVP awards won with different teams
Kawhi Leonard earned his second NBA Finals MVP award with the Toronto Raptors in 2019, having previously won with the San Antonio Spurs in 2014. He matched Kareem Abdul-Jabbar (Milwaukee Bucks and the Los Angeles Lakers) and LeBron James (Miami Heat and the Cleveland Cavaliers).

Longest postseason game
On 3 May 2019, the Portland Trail Blazers topped the Denver Nuggets 140–137 in four overtime periods in Game 3 of their Western Conference semi-final series. They equalled the four OTs played by the Boston Celtics and the Syracuse Nationals on 21 Mar 1953.

Most games won by a coach
As of 10 Mar 2020, Gregg Popovich had racked up 1,442 victories (including 170 in the playoffs) as coach of the San Antonio Spurs. On 13 Apr 2019, he passed Lenny Wilkens' mark of 1,412. Popovich is the **longest-tenured coach with one team** – the 2019/20 NBA season was his 24th at the Spurs.

Most points scored in a postseason quarter (team)
The Philadelphia 76ers scored 51 points in the third quarter of Game 2 of their Eastern Conference playoff series against the Brooklyn Nets on 15 Apr 2019. They equalled the 51 points scored by the Los Angeles Lakers in the fourth quarter against the Detroit Pistons on 31 Mar 1962.

The **most points scored in a Finals quarter (team)** is 49, by the Cleveland Cavaliers on 9 Jun 2017. The **most points scored in a quarter (team)** is 58, by the Buffalo Braves at the Boston Celtics on 20 Oct 1972.

Largest comeback in playoff history
The LA Clippers overcame a 31-point deficit to beat the Golden State Warriors 135–131 in Game 2 of their first-round Western Conference matchup on 15 Apr 2019. This topped a 29-point rally by the LA Lakers over the Seattle Supersonics in Game 4 of the 1989 Western Conference semi-finals.

Most All-Star Game starts
LeBron James made 16 consecutive All-Star Game starts between 20 Feb 2005 and 16 Feb 2020. He claimed the record outright from Kobe Bryant (inset), to whom numerous tributes were made following his death in a helicopter crash on 26 Jan 2020. Bryant shares with Bob Pettit the **most All-Star Game MVP wins** – four, in 2002, 2007, 2009 and 2011. The award now bears Bryant's name in honour of his achievements.

Most points scored in a game by a non-starting player
Jamal Crawford (b. 20 Mar 1980) scored 51 points off the bench for the Phoenix Suns in a 120–109 loss to the Dallas Mavericks on 9 Apr 2019. It was the highest since starts were first recorded in the 1970/71 season. At 39 years 20 days, Crawford became the **oldest player to score 50+ points in a game**.

Most siblings to play in the same game
On 28 Dec 2019, a game between the New Orleans Pelicans and the Indiana Pacers became a family affair as brothers Justin, Jrue and Aaron Holiday all took to the court. Jrue claimed the bragging rights, his Pelicans winning 120–98.

Most WNBA career double-doubles
Sylvia Fowles recorded her 158th career double-double during the Minnesota Lynx's 75–62 win against the Phoenix Mercury on 14 Jul 2019. She finished with 14 points and 13 rebounds.

Most three-point field goals in a WNBA game (individual)
Kelsey Mitchell sank nine three-pointers for the Indiana Fever in a 104–76 win over the Connecticut Sun on 8 Sep 2019. She matched the feat of Kristi Toliver for the Washington Mystics on 10 Sep 2017.

The **most three-point field goals in a WNBA game (team)** is 18, by the Washington Mystics during their 107–68 victory over the Indiana Fever on 18 Aug 2019 in Washington, DC, USA.

Baseball

Fewest innings to reach 1,500 strikeouts for a pitcher
Stephen Strasburg of the Washington Nationals struck out 1,500 batters in 1,272 1/3 innings between 8 Jun 2010 and 2 May 2019. He recorded 14 strikeouts on an unforgettable debut against the Pittsburgh Pirates, and has battled back from injuries to reach the landmark figure faster than any other player.

Most consecutive games with at least one home run (team)
The New York Yankees went deep 31 games in a row between 26 May and 30 Jun 2019 – the latter, a 12–8 win over the Boston Red Sox at the London Stadium, UK.

The **longest team home-run streak to start a season** is 20 games, by the Seattle Mariners in 2019. They smashed the previous record of 14 by the Cleveland Indians in 2002.

Most at-bats without recording a hit
Chris Davis of the Baltimore Orioles set a modern-day (i.e., post-1900) record for a non-pitcher by going hitless in 54 consecutive at-bats over the 2018 and 2019 seasons. The streak started on 15 Sep 2018 and ended with a single against the Boston Red Sox on 13 Apr 2019. Davis broke the unwanted record of 46 straight at-bats by Eugenio Vélez in 2010–11.

Highest-paid player
On 18 Dec 2019, pitcher Gerrit Cole joined the New York Yankees from the Houston Astros on a contract worth $324 m (£245 m) over nine years – $36 m (£27 m) a year. Cole's average annual salary beat the previous MLB record of $35.5 m (£26.7 m), by Los Angeles Angels outfielder Mike Trout in a 12-year deal signed on 20 Mar 2019.

All records are Major League Baseball (MLB) and all current record holders are USA, unless otherwise indicated.

Fewest innings to reach 2,000 strikeouts for a pitcher
Chris Sale struck out 2,000 batters in 1,626 career innings. He passed the previous best of 1,711 1/3 innings by Pedro Martínez when he fanned Cleveland's Oscar Mercado while pitching for the Boston Red Sox on 13 Aug 2019.

Pitcher with most consecutive scoreless games
Ryan Pressly had a scoreless streak of 40 games while relief pitching for the Houston Astros over a 38-innings span from 15 Aug 2018 to 24 May 2019. He passed the mark of 38 games established by the Atlanta Braves' Craig Kimbrel between 14 Jun and 8 Sep 2011.

Most consecutive World Series games hitting a home run
On 22 Oct 2019, George Springer went deep in his fifth consecutive World Series game while playing for the Houston Astros against the Washington Nationals at Minute Maid Park in Houston, Texas, USA. His Game 1 drive off Tanner Rainey took Springer one clear of Hall of Fame members Reggie Jackson and Lou Gehrig.

Springer's previous homers came during the 2017 World Series, when he also equalled the **most home runs in a single World Series** record of five, shared by Jackson (in 1977) and Chase Utley (2009).

Most home runs in a game (aggregate)
On 10 Jun 2019, the Arizona Diamondbacks and the Philadelphia Phillies combined for 13 home runs at Citizens Bank Park in Philadelphia, Pennsylvania, USA. The D-backs hit eight homers to the Phillies' five, and won the game 13–8.

Fewest games to hit 10 home runs
After just one at-bat in 2018, Aristides Aquino (DOM) of the Cincinnati Reds launched a blitz of 10 dingers between 1 and 16 Aug 2019 – his first 16 MLB games. He hit three in one game, against the Chicago Cubs. Aquino, nicknamed "The Punisher", beat the mark of 17 games set by the Philadelphia Phillies' Rhys Hoskins in 2017.

Most teams played for in a season
On 4 Aug 2018, Oliver Drake took to the mound for the Minnesota Twins, his fifth different team of the season. The right-handed pitcher was on the Opening Day roster for the Milwaukee Brewers, before being sold to the Cleveland Indians on 5 May. He then pitched for the Los Angeles Angels and the Toronto Blue Jays before joining Minnesota.

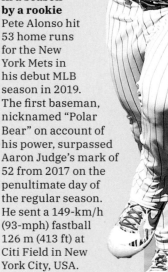

Most home runs in a season by a rookie
Pete Alonso hit 53 home runs for the New York Mets in his debut MLB season in 2019. The first baseman, nicknamed "Polar Bear" on account of his power, surpassed Aaron Judge's mark of 52 from 2017 on the penultimate day of the regular season. He sent a 149-km/h (93-mph) fastball 126 m (413 ft) at Citi Field in New York City, USA.

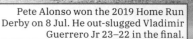

Pete Alonso won the 2019 Home Run Derby on 8 Jul. He out-slugged Vladimir Guerrero Jr 23–22 in the final.

Rugby

Most wins of the Hong Kong Sevens
Established in 1976, the Hong Kong Sevens is widely considered to be the most prestigious tournament on the World Rugby Sevens Series circuit. Fiji secured their fifth consecutive and 19th overall title on 7 Apr 2019, defeating France 21–7. Their nearest rivals, New Zealand, have won 11. Fiji are reigning Olympic sevens champions, having won the event at Rio 2016.

Most tries scored in the Champions Cup
On 24 Nov 2019, Chris Ashton (UK) recorded his 40th try in European Rugby's top-tier competition (previously known as the Heineken Cup). He had scored eight for Northampton Saints, 29 for Saracens, two for RC Toulon and, most recently, one for Sale Sharks.

Most World Rugby Sevens Series tournament appearances
James Rodwell (UK) played for England in 93 sevens tournaments from 2009 to 2019. He surpassed D J Forbes's record of 89 on 26–27 Jan 2019 in Hamilton, New Zealand.
The **most games in the World Rugby Women's Sevens Series** is 219, by Kayla Moleschi (CAN) as of 11 Feb 2020.

Whitelock is the **fastest player to 100 international rugby union caps** – 8 years 67 days from debut.

Most appearances in Rugby World Cup tournaments
On 22 Sep 2019, Sergio Parisse lined up for Italy for their 47–22 win over Namibia – his fifth consecutive World Cup since 2003. He matched the feat of Samoa's Brian Lima between 1991 and 2007, and Mauro Bergamasco (ITA) between 1999 and 2015.
Parisse also holds the record for the **most appearances in the Five/Six Nations** – 69. He surpassed Irish centre Brian O'Driscoll's mark of 65 during Italy's match against Scotland on 2 Feb 2019.

Most brothers to score a try in a Rugby World Cup game
On 2 Oct 2019, Beauden, Jordie and Scott Barrett all touched down during New Zealand's 63–0 win over Canada in Ōita, Japan. The Barretts became the first trio of brothers to start in the same Rugby World Cup match since Elisi, Manu and Fe'ao Vunipola played for Tonga against Scotland on 30 May 1995. Ken, Tusi and George Pisi featured for Samoa against South Africa on 26 Sep 2015, but only Ken started the game.

Fastest Rugby World Cup drop goal
Dan Biggar (UK) kicked a drop goal for Wales after just 36 sec of their game against Australia on 29 Sep 2019 in Tokyo Stadium, Japan. Wales went on to win a thrilling game 29–25.

Most appearances in the National Rugby League
Cameron Smith (AUS) had played 413 games for the Melbourne Storm in the NRL as of 21 Mar 2020. He became the first player to reach 400 appearances on 13 Jul 2019, when the Storm defeated the Cronulla-Sutherland Sharks 40–16. Smith also has the **most career NRL points** – 2,616. He has scored 45 tries and kicked 1,216 goals.

Most Rugby Union World Cup wins
On 2 Nov 2019, South Africa lifted the Webb Ellis Cup for the third time after a rampant 32–12 victory over England in Yokohama, Japan. Previously winners in 1995 and 2007, they matched the feat of New Zealand (1987, 2011 and 2015). Remarkably, the Springboks are yet to concede a try in a World Cup final.

Most consecutive matches won at the Rugby World Cup
All Black second row Sam Whitelock (NZ) was victorious in 18 Rugby World Cup matches in a row between 9 Sep 2011 and 19 Oct 2019. He lifted the trophy in 2011 and 2015. His run finally came to an end in the 2019 World Cup semi-final, when New Zealand were defeated 19–7 by England on 26 Oct.

Youngest player to appear in a Challenge Cup final
Hollie Dodd (UK, b. 26 Jul 2003) played in the Women's Challenge Cup final aged 16 years 1 day on 27 Jul 2019 in Greater Manchester, UK. Dodd was a national ballroom dance champion before taking up rugby league. Her Castleford Tigers Women team lost out to Leeds Rhinos Women 16–10 on the day.

Tennis

Most prize money won at a single tournament
On 3 Nov 2019, Ashleigh Barty (AUS) defeated Elina Svitolina 6–4, 6–3 to win the Women's Tennis Association Finals – and pocketed $4.42 m (£3.41 m). The World No.1 became only the fifth debutante to win the event, staged in 2019 at the Shenzhen Bay Sports Center in China.

Youngest female player to make the Wimbledon main singles draw through qualifying (open era)
On 27 Jun 2019, Cori "Coco" Gauff (USA, b. 13 Mar 2004) came through the final round of qualifying for the Wimbledon Championships in London, UK, aged 15 years 106 days. She went on to beat five-time Wimbledon singles champion Venus Williams before falling in Round 4.

Most Grand Slam singles matches won
As of 28 Jan 2020, Roger Federer (CHE) had won 362 singles matches at Wimbledon and the Australian, French and US Opens. In beating Kei Nishikori at Wimbledon on 10 Jul 2019, Federer became the **first male player to win 100 singles matches at a Grand Slam tournament**.
  According to estimates by Forbes, Federer earned $93.4 m (£74 m) in the 12 months up to 1 Jun 2019 – the **highest annual earnings for a tennis player ever**.

The **most men's tennis tournament titles** is 109, by Jimmy Connors (USA) between 1972 and 1996.

Most Australian Open men's singles titles
On 2 Feb 2020, Novak Djokovic (SRB) claimed his eighth title at Melbourne Park, beating Dominic Thiem in five sets. Djokovic also became the **first male tennis player to win an open-era Grand Slam singles title in three different decades**. He won his first Australian Open in 2008 and landed 15 Grand Slams in the 2010s.
  Djokovic's 17th major title left him just three shy of the **most Grand Slam men's singles titles** – 20, by his Swiss rival Roger Federer (see below).

Longest Wimbledon singles final
Novak Djokovic and Roger Federer served up a 4-hr 57-min final at the Wimbledon Championships on 14 Jul 2019. Djokovic saved two match points on his opponent's serve before prevailing 7–6, 1–6, 7–6, 4–6, 13–12, in the **first Grand Slam men's singles final to feature a final-set tie-break**.

Most Grand Slam singles tennis tournaments played consecutively
The 2020 Australian Open witnessed the 72nd consecutive Grand Slam appearance of Feliciano López (ESP). His run began at the 2002 French Open.
  The **most Grand Slam singles tournaments played** is 85, by Venus Williams (USA) between 1997 and 2020.

Most ATP Masters 1000 singles titles won
Rafael Nadal (ESP) has won 35 Association of Tennis Professionals (ATP) Tour Masters 1000 tournaments. His most recent success came at the 2019 Rogers Open on 11 Aug, when he defeated Russia's Daniil Medvedev 6–3, 6–0 in the final. Nadal has also recorded the **most consecutive years winning an ATP title** – 17 (2004–20).

First deaf player to win a main-draw match on the ATP Tour
On 20 Aug 2019, Lee Duck-hee (KOR) defeated Henri Laaksonen 7–6, 6–1 in the first round of the Winston-Salem Open at Wake Forest University in North Carolina, USA. The sound a tennis ball makes when striking the racket can give an opponent clues as to the type of shot being played; Lee overcomes this by visually studying his opponent's swing and the way he makes contact with the ball.

Most Grand Slam wheelchair titles
At the 2020 Australian Open, Shingo Kunieda (JPN) won the men's singles to secure his 44th wheelchair Grand Slam (comprising 23 singles and 21 doubles titles). Kunieda matched the tally of Esther Vergeer (NLD), who claimed 21 singles and 23 doubles titles between 2002 and 2012.

Longest span of Grand Slam singles finals
At the US Open on 7 Sep 2019, Serena Williams (USA) reached her 33rd Grand Slam singles final 19 years 361 days after her first, on 11 Sep 1999. Williams (b. 26 Sep 1981) lost 6–3, 7–5 to 19-year-old Bianca Andreescu (CAN, b. 16 Jun 2000) in a match with the **greatest age difference for a Grand Slam singles final (open era)** – 18 years 264 days.

Combat Sports

belts since 13 Sep 2014, making her the **longest-reigning four-belt undisputed world boxing champion** – 5 years 78 days, as of 30 Nov 2019.

Pacquiao is the only boxer to have held a world title in four different decades.

Most individual gold medals won at the IBJJF World Championship
In 2019, Marcus Almeida (BRA) claimed his 12th and 13th titles at the International Brazilian Jiu-Jitsu Federation World Championship (aka the Mundials). He has won seven ultra-heavyweight and six open-class titles.

The **most individual gold medals (female)** is nine, achieved by Beatriz Mesquita (BRA) from 2012 to 2019. She has collected seven lightweight and two open-class titles.

Most gold medals won on the IJF World Tour
On 24 Oct 2019, Kosovo's Majlinda Kelmendi won her 18th gold medal on the International Judo Federation World Tour, at the Abu Dhabi Grand Slam. All Kelmendi's titles have come in the women's -52 kg category.

The **most medals won on the IJF World Tour** is 36, by Urantsetseg Munkhbat (MNG) from 17 Dec 2010 to 8 Feb 2020. She has won 11 golds, 11 silvers and 14 bronze in the women's -48 kg and -52 kg categories.

Oldest welterweight boxing world champion
Manny Pacquiao (PHL, b. 17 Dec 1978) claimed the WBA welterweight title aged 40 years 215 days on 20 Jul 2019. He won the belt with a split-decision win over Keith Thurman. One of boxing's most decorated fighters, Pacquiao has won the **most world titles in different weight divisions** – eight.

Fastest *ippon* on the IJF World Tour
In judo, *ippon* is a winning score awarded for a decisive move. On 21 Sep 2019, Sharofiddin Boltaboev (UZB) won his -81 kg second-round match against Nai Rigaqi with a perfect *tai otoshi* throw in 2.88 sec at the IJF Grand Prix in Tashkent, Uzbekistan. He went on to claim his first IJF World Tour gold medal.

Oldest medallist at an IJF World Tour event
Sabrina Filzmoser (AUT, b. 12 Jun 1980) won a bronze in the women's -57 kg category aged 39 years 30 days at the IJF Budapest Grand Prix in Hungary on 12 Jul 2019.

The **oldest gold medallist** is Miklós Ungvári (HUN, b. 15 Oct 1980), aged 37 years 300 days, on 11 Aug 2018.

Most bouts undefeated by a boxing world champion
On 25 Oct 2019, Wanheng Menayothin (aka Chayaphon Moonsri, THA) improved his professional record to 54 wins from 54 bouts. He beat Simphiwe Khonco in his 12th defence of the WBC minimumweight title.

The **most bouts undefeated by a female boxing champion** is 36, by Cecilia Brækhus (NOR, b. COL). She has held the WBO, WBA, IBF and WBC welterweight

Fewest fights to become a four-belt undisputed world boxing champion
On 13 Apr 2019, Claressa Shields (USA) defeated WBO champion Christina Hammer to become undisputed middleweight champion in her ninth professional fight. Shields had won two belts at super middleweight in her fourth fight before dropping down to middleweight. On 10 Jan 2020, she added the vacant WBC and WBO super welterweight titles by beating Ivana Habazin – the **fewest fights to become a three-weight boxing world champion**.

Not content with dominating women's boxing, as of 2020 Shields was considering a move into MMA.

Most sabre titles at the World Fencing Championships (female)

On 20 Jul 2019, Olga Kharlan (UKR) won her fourth world championship title, defeating her rival Sofya Velikaya 15–14 in Budapest, Hungary. Kharlan had previously won in 2013–14 and 2017. Alongside foil and épée, sabre is one of the three disciplines of modern fencing.

Most ONE Championship successful title defences

Bibiano Fernandes (BRA) recorded his eighth defence of the ONE Championship bantamweight title on 13 Oct 2019.

At the same event, atomweight Angela Lee (SNG, b. CAN) extended the **female** record to four with with a fifth-round submission of Xiong Jingnan.

Most World Taekwondo Championships titles (female)

At the 2019 World Taekwondo Championships, Bianca Walkden (UK) won her third heavyweight world championship title with a controversial victory over Shuyin Zheng, forcing her into a series of penalties that led to her disqualification. Walkden joined triple world champions Jung Myoung-sook, Cho Hyang-mi (both KOR) and Brigitte Yagüe (ESP).

Most gold medals won in the Karate1 Premier League

On 24 Jan 2020, Ryo Kiyuna (JPN) claimed his 19th men's kata gold medal in the league run by the World Karate Federation (WKF). He had suffered just two defeats in 21 competitions since 2012. Kiyuna has also recorded the **most wins of the men's kata at the WKF Karate World Championships** – three consecutively, in 2014–18 – equalling his mentor Tsuguo Sakumoto (JPN, 1984–88), Michaël Milon (FRA, 1994–96, 2000) and Luca Valdesi (ITA, 2004–08).

The **most medals won in the Karate1 Premier League** is 35, by Sandra Sánchez (ESP) in the women's kata from 10 Jan 2014 to 28 Feb 2020. Her tally includes 17 golds, only two behind Kiyuna.

Longest-reigning *yokozuna*

Hakuhō Shō (JPN, b. Munkhbat Davaajargal, MNG) occupied the highest rank in sumo for 76 consecutive *basho* (tournaments) from Jul 2007 to Mar 2020. The previous longest streak was 63, by Kitanoumi Toshimitsu between 1974 and 1985.

At the 2020 Spring *basho* in Osaka, Japan, Hakuhō increased his total of **most sumo top-division championship wins** to 44. It was his second title since attaining Japanese citizenship.

Most wins (female)

On 14 Dec 2019, Amanda Nunes (BRA, above right) won her 12th bout in the Ultimate Fighting Championship (UFC), defeating Germaine de Randamie via unanimous decision at UFC 245. It was Nunes's 10th win on the bounce – the **most consecutive fight wins (female)**.

The reigning bantamweight and featherweight champion, Nunes is also the **first female fighter to hold two titles simultaneously**.

Most wins

Donald "Cowboy" Cerrone (USA) emerged victorious from the octagon 23 times between 5 Feb 2011 and 4 May 2019. He claimed his 23rd UFC victory with a unanimous decision over Al Iaquinta on 4 May 2019 in Ottawa, Ontario, Canada.

On 15 Feb 2020, Jim Miller (USA) tied Cerrone's record for **most fights** – 34.

Most wins by submission

Charles Oliveira (BRA) made 14 opponents tap out between 1 Aug 2010 and 14 Mar 2020. His most recent submission came at UFC Fight Night 170 in Brasilia, Brazil, where he defeated Kevin Lee with a guillotine choke. It was Oliveira's 16th win before the bell – the **most finishes**, tied with Donald Cerrone.

Most wins (title bouts)

On 8 Feb 2020, Jon "Bones" Jones (USA) won his 14th title bout with a unanimous decision over Dominick Reyes at UFC 247. He moved one clear of the record by Georges St-Pierre (CAN). To date, Jones has won every title bout in which he has fought, with an additional victory at UFC 214 subsequently ruled a no-contest when Jones violated the UFC's anti-doping policy.

Most consecutive knockouts (female)

On 18 Oct 2019, Maycee Barber (USA) KO'd her third consecutive opponent – in only her third UFC fight. Barber, known as "The Future", matched the feat of Cris Cyborg (BRA/USA, b. Cristiane Justino Venâncio) – who also knocked out her first three UFC opponents – and Amanda Nunes.

Longest total fight time

Frankie Edgar (USA) had spent a total of 7 hr 15 min 51 sec fighting in the octagon as of 21 Dec 2019. He had contested 26 bouts, racking up 17 wins.

Most world titles held simultaneously in different weight divisions

On 8 Jun 2019, flyweight champion Henry Cejudo (USA) beat Marlon Moraes for the bantamweight title. Cejudo – the **first athlete to win an Olympic and UFC world title** – matched Conor McGregor (IRL), Daniel Cormier (USA) and Amanda Nunes in holding two UFC belts at the same time.

Highest attendance

On 6 Oct 2019, UFC 243 drew 57,127 fans to Marvel Stadium in Melbourne, Victoria, Australia. The previous highest attendance had also been set at the same venue in Australia.

Most significant strikes landed

Max Holloway (USA) has landed 2,071 significant strikes in his 22 UFC bouts. At UFC 231 on 8 Dec 2018, featherweight Holloway unleashed the **most significant strikes landed in a match** – 290 – against Brian Ortega. Significant strikes are defined by FightMetric as "all strikes at distance, and power strikes in the clinch and on the ground".

Fastest wins in UFC

Fastest...	Time	Record holder	Opponent	Date
Knockout	5 sec	Jorge Masvidal (USA)	Ben Askren	6 Jul 2019
Knockout (female)	16 sec	Ronda Rousey (USA)	Alexis Davis	5 Jul 2014
		Germaine de Randamie (NLD)	Aspen Ladd	13 Jul 2019
Title fight	13 sec	Conor McGregor (IRL)	José Aldo	12 Dec 2015
Title fight (submission)	14 sec	Ronda Rousey	Cat Zingano	28 Feb 2015

Cricket

Most runs in a Twenty20 (T20) International (female)

On 2 Oct 2019, Alyssa Healy (AUS) scored 148 not out in a T20 match against Sri Lanka in New South Wales, Australia. Her knock included 19 fours and 7 sixes, and was her maiden century in the format. She reached triple figures in 46 balls – behind only the West Indies' Deandra Dottin (38 balls, against South Africa on 5 May 2010) for the **fastest international century (female)**.

Most wickets taken in a Cricket World Cup

Pace bowler Mitchell Starc (AUS) dismissed 27 batsmen in 10 matches – at an average of 18.59 runs per wicket – at the 2019 Cricket World Cup. His total included five-wicket hauls against the West Indies on 6 Jun and New Zealand on 29 Jun.

On 20 Jun, Australia and Bangladesh combined for the **most runs in a Cricket World Cup match (aggregate)** – 714 – at Trent Bridge in Nottingham, UK. Australia hit 381 and won by 48 runs.

Highest 10th-wicket partnership to win a first-class match

On 16 Feb 2019, Kusal Perera and Vishwa Fernando (both LKA) snatched victory from the jaws of defeat with an unbroken stand of 78 runs against South Africa at Kingsmead in Durban, South Africa. Perera added 67 while Fernando chipped in with six as Sri Lanka won the Test by one wicket.

Most wickets taken in a single over

Three cricketers have taken five wickets in a six-ball over in a professional match: Neil Wagner (NZ), for Otago in the Plunket Shield on 6 Apr 2011; Al-Amin Hossain (BGD), for the UCB-BCB XI in the Victory Day T20 Cup on 26 Dec 2013; and Abhimanyu Mithun (IND), for Karnataka in the Syed Mushtaq Ali Trophy on 29 Nov 2019.

Youngest bowler to take a Test match hat-trick

Pakistani paceman Naseem Shah (b. 15 Feb 2003) took three wickets with successive deliveries aged 16 years 359 days on 9 Feb 2020. Shah claimed the scalps of Bangladesh's Najmul Hossain Shanto (lbw), Taijul Islam (lbw) and Mohammad Mahmudullah (caught at slip) at Rawalpindi Cricket Stadium in Pakistan.

Most hundreds in a Cricket World Cup

India opener Rohit Sharma scored five centuries in nine matches at the 2019 Cricket World Cup. His top score was 140, recorded against Pakistan on 16 Jun. He finished with a tournament average of 81 runs, while his total of 648 was the third highest ever. The **most runs in a Cricket World Cup** is 673, by Sachin Tendulkar (IND) in 2003.

Most sixes by a player in a T20 International

Hazratullah Zazai (AFG) clubbed 16 sixes during his 62-ball innings of 162 not out against Ireland on 23 Feb 2019 in Dehradun, India. Together with fellow opener Usman Ghani, Zazai produced an opening stand of 236 runs – the **highest partnership in a T20 International (male)**.

Best bowling figures in a T20 International

Nepal's Anjali Chand took six wickets for no runs in 13 balls in a South Asian Games match against the Maldives in Pokhara, Nepal, on 2 Dec 2019. She took three wickets in her first over and recorded a hat-trick – all on her international debut.

Highest team score in a T20 International

On 20 Jun 2019, Uganda Women posted a score of 314 for 2 against Mali Women in a Kwibuka Women's T20 Tournament match at Gahanga International Cricket Stadium in Kigali, Rwanda.

First Cricket World Cup final won after a super over

On 14 Jul 2019, England claimed their first Cricket World Cup in extraordinary fashion at Lord's in London, UK. Tied with New Zealand on 241 runs after 50 overs, the two sides each played a "super over" to determine the winner. Having once again matched each other's score – both hitting 15 runs from six balls – England were declared the winners, after scoring more boundaries in the match (26 to 17). Earlier in the tournament, England captain Eoin Morgan (inset) had hit the **most sixes by a player in a One-Day International** – 17, against Afghanistan on 18 Jun.

Ball Sports

Most Fistball Men's World Championships
A game of European origin that dates back to Roman times, fistball is similar to volleyball, although the ball can only be struck with the fist or arms (rather than an open hand) and is allowed to bounce after each contact. Germany secured its 12th world championship title on 17 Aug 2019 in Winterthur, Switzerland, defeating Austria in the final by 4 sets to 0.

Most consecutive wins of the Ladies Real Tennis World Championship
On 26 Jan 2019, Claire Fahey (UK) claimed her fifth real tennis singles world title in a row since 2011. She defeated Isabel Candy 6–0, 6–0 at Ballarat Tennis Club in Victoria, Australia. Fahey is also a five-time ladies' doubles champion.

Most ITTF World Tour singles titles (male)
Ma Long (CHN) has won 28 singles titles on the International Table Tennis Federation World Tour. Ma, nicknamed "The Dragon", claimed his most recent title at the China Open on 2 Jun 2019. He has also recorded the **most wins of the men's singles Grand Finals** – five, in 2008–09, 2011 and 2015–16.

Most consecutive Gaelic football All-Ireland Final wins
On 14 Sep 2019, Dublin collected their fifth Sam Maguire Cup in a row. They defeated Kerry 1–18 to 0–15 in a replay at Croke Park in Dublin, Ireland.
Kerry can still lay claim to the **most All-Ireland Final wins**, having racked up 37 victories between 1903 and 2014.

Most consecutive wins of the ITTF World Tour Grand Finals (singles)
At the 2019 table tennis Grand Finals, Chen Meng (CHN) won her third title in a row with a 4–1 victory over Wang Manyu. She equalled the feat of Liu Shiwen (CHN) in 2011–13.

Most wins of the World Indoor Lacrosse Championship
Canada secured its fifth Cockerton Cup on 28 Sep 2019 with a 19–12 defeat of the Iroquois Nationals at the Langley Events Centre in British Columbia, Canada. The Canadians have won every World Indoor Lacrosse Championship to date, and are yet to lose a single match at the tournament.

Most tournament appearances at the Netball World Cup
Rhonda John-Davis (TTO) appeared at her sixth Netball World Cup during Trinidad and Tobago's 76–45 defeat to South Africa on 12 Jul 2019. The wing attack has also played basketball at international level.

Most FIBA Basketball World Cup assists
Ricky Rubio (ESP) increased his career tournament assists to 130 at the 2019 Fédération Internationale de Basketball World Cup in Beijing, China. He guided Spain to the trophy and was named MVP.

Most Women's EHF Handball Champions League FINAL4 goals
The FINAL4 stage of the Women's EHF Champions League comprises the semi-finals and final of the competition. On 12 May 2019, Nycke Groot (NLD) scored her 57th FINAL4 goal as her side Győri Audi ETO KC defeated Rostov-Don to secure its third consecutive title.

Most World Handball Player of the Year awards
Cristina Neagu (ROM) has been named International Handball Federation Women's World Player of the Year four times: for 2010, 2015, 2016 and 2018. Left-back Neagu finished as top scorer in the 2017/18 EHF Champions League with 110 goals for CSM București.
The **most World Handball Player of the Year awards (male)** is three, by Mikkel Hansen (DNK) and Nikola Karabatić (FRA, b. Yugoslavia).

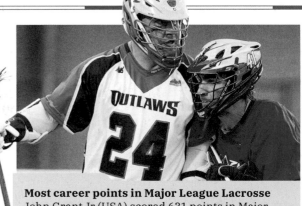

Most career points in Major League Lacrosse
John Grant Jr (USA) scored 631 points in Major League Lacrosse (MLL) between 2001 and 2019. Aged 44, the attackman returned with the Denver Outlaws after a three-year hiatus. He broke Paul Rabil's record of 596 points during Denver's 18–16 defeat of the Atlanta Blaze on 8 Jun 2019. Grant Jr's tally includes the **most MLL goals**: 387.

Most wins of the Volleyball Women's World Cup
China romped to their fifth World Cup title with a perfect 11–0 record in the 2019 round-robin tournament, staged in Japan on 14–29 Sep. They had previously won the competition – run by the Fédération Internationale de Volleyball – in 1981, 1985, 2003 and 2015. Captain Zhu Ting (No.2, above) became the first two-time World Cup MVP.

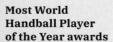

Neagu is the top scorer at the European Women's Handball Championship, with 237 goals.

Auto Sports

Fastest Formula One pit stop

Red Bull Racing (AUT) completed a pit stop on Max Verstappen's car in 1.82 sec at the Brazilian Grand Prix on 17 Nov 2019. It was the third time that the Red Bull team had broken the record that season, having previously set fastest times in successive grands prix in the UK and Germany.

Longest time between Formula One points

On 28 Jul 2019, Robert Kubica (POL) finished in 10th place at the 2019 German Grand Prix to record his first championship point since 14 Nov 2010 – a gap of 8 years 256 days. Kubica's career was interrupted by a devastating crash at the Ronde di Andora rally in 2011, which left him with severe injuries including a partially severed right forearm.

Youngest winner of an IndyCar race

On 24 Mar 2019, Colton Herta (USA, b. 30 Mar 2000) triumphed aged 18 years 359 days at the IndyCar Classic in Austin, Texas, USA. On 22 Jun 2019, he also became the **youngest person to achieve an IndyCar pole position** – 19 years 84 days – at the REV Group Grand Prix at Road America in Elkhart Lake, Wisconsin, USA.

Hamilton hits new heights

In 2019, Lewis Hamilton (UK) sealed his sixth Formula One world title for Mercedes. He is chasing down the record for **most championships** – seven – held by Michael Schumacher (DEU, inset). Other Schumacher records in Hamilton's sights are the **most race wins** – 91 – and the **most wins at the same grand prix** – eight, at the French Grand Prix from 1994 to 2006. Hamilton already has the **most pole positions** – 88 – and the **most consecutive starts** – 250. He has not missed a race since his Formula One debut on 18 Mar 2007.

Most pole positions in a Grand Prix motorcycle career

Marc Márquez (ESP) qualified fastest in 90 Grand Prix motorcycle races between 16 May 2009 and 19 Oct 2019. The eight-time world champion claimed pole 62 times in MotoGP (overtaking Mick Doohan's record of 58), 14 times in Moto2 and 14 times in the 125 cc class.

Most Formula One grand prix starts by a constructor

As of the end of the 2019 season, Scuderia Ferrari (ITA) had started 991 races in Formula One. The team, nicknamed "The Prancing Horse" after its logo, competed in its first race at the 1950 Monaco Grand Prix. Ferrari has gone on to record the **most Formula One grand prix wins** – 238. Its first victory came at the 1951 British Grand Prix, with Argentinian driver José Froilán González behind the wheel; the most recent win came at the 2019 Singapore Grand Prix, courtesy of Sebastian Vettel.

Youngest person to achieve a MotoGP pole position

On 4 May 2019, Fabio Quartararo (FRA, b. 20 Apr 1999) qualified fastest at the Spanish MotoGP in Jerez de la Frontera, Spain. Aged 20 years 14 days, he claimed the record from Marc Márquez (see left), who took revenge by winning the race.

Most wins in NHRA (Pro Stock Motorcycle class)

Six-time Pro Stock Motorcycle champion Andrew Hines (USA) won 56 races between 2002 and 14 Oct 2019.

Most National Hot Rod Association wins

As of 3 Feb 2020, John Force (USA) had won 151 races in the Funny Car class of NHRA drag racing. He went winless in his first nine seasons before claiming his maiden victory in Jun 1987, and went on to win the Funny Car championship a record 16 times. Force reached his landmark 150th win at the Northwest Nationals on 4 Aug 2019 (pictured).

The first official NHRA race was held in Apr 1953 on a fairground parking lot in Pomona, California, USA.

Fastest Isle of Man TT sidecar race
Brothers Ben and Tom Birchall (both UK) completed a three-lap race around the Isle of Man TT course in 57 min 24.005 sec on 3 Jun 2019. They were riding a 600 LCR Honda.

Most races at the World Rally Championship (individual)
Jari-Matti Latvala (FIN) drove in 209 World Rally Championship (WRC) races from 14 Nov 2002 to 13 Feb 2020. He overtook Carlos Sainz's record of 196 at Rally Sweden on 14 Feb 2019.

Latvala (b. 3 Apr 1995) also remains the **youngest WRC race winner**, aged 22 years 313 days at Rally Sweden on 10 Feb 2008.

Fastest lap in the 24 Hours of Le Mans
On 15 Jun 2019, Mike Conway (UK) completed a lap of the Circuit de la Sarthe in Le Mans, France, in 3 min 17.297 sec. His team's Toyota TS050 Hybrid led for much of the race, only to lose the lead in the final hour owing to issues replacing a slow puncture.

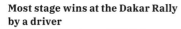

First W Series championship winner
Jamie Chadwick (UK) won the inaugural W Series in 2019, with two victories in six races at the women-only Formula Three-level championship. Chadwick went on to gain a seat as a development driver for Formula One team Williams. To date, only two women have qualified for a Formula One race, with the **most starts (female)** being accrued by Lella Lombardi (ITA). She drove in 12 grands prix between 1 Mar 1975 and 15 Aug 1976.

Most NASCAR race victories
Kyle Busch (USA) won 209 stock car races across NASCAR's three divisions between 14 May 2004 and 21 Feb 2020. He overtook the legendary racer Richard Petty (USA, inset), whose 200 victories from 28 Feb 1960 to 4 Jul 1984 were all achieved in NASCAR's top-tier Cup Series – giving him the **most Cup Series wins**. Busch has 56 Cup Series victories to his name, but has also recorded the **most Xfinity Series wins** – 96 – and the **most Truck Series wins** – 57.

Fastest speed in an NHRA Top Fuel race (1,000-ft track)
The daughter of NHRA legend John (see below left), Brittany Force (USA) is a champion Top Fuel driver and record-breaker in her own right. On 1 Nov 2019, she reached a speed of 544.23 km/h (338.17 mph) at the Dodge NHRA Nationals in Las Vegas, Nevada, USA.

Force has also set the **lowest elapsed time in an NHRA Top Fuel race** – 3.623 sec, on 14 Sep 2019 in Mohnton, Pennsylvania, USA.

Fastest speed in an NHRA Pro Mod car race
On 22 Jun 2019, Erica Enders (USA) achieved a speed of 420.39 km/h (261.22 mph) during qualifying at the NHRA Nationals in Norwalk, Ohio, USA. Enders had to escape her Chevy Camaro when it burst into flames immediately after her run.

The **lowest elapsed time in an NHRA Pro Mod race** is 5.643 sec, by Steve Jackson (USA) on 17 Mar 2019 in Gainesville, Florida, USA.

Most Superbike World Championship titles
In 2019, Kawasaki Racing Team's Jonathan Rea (UK) claimed his fifth consecutive world championship title – putting him one clear of Carl Fogarty. Rea has also notched up the **most Superbike World Championship race wins** – 89, from 21 Jun 2009 to 1 Mar 2020.

Most stage wins at the Dakar Rally by a driver
Stéphane Peterhansel (FRA) has won 80 stages of the annual off-road rally since 1988. He claimed four at the 2020 event, which was held in Saudi Arabia. Peterhansel has recorded the **most Dakar Rally wins (motorcycle)** – six – and the **most Dakar Rally wins (car)** – seven, alongside navigator Jean-Paul Cottret (FRA).

The **most Dakar Rally motorcycle wins by a manufacturer** is 18, by KTM (AUT) consecutively between 2001 and 2019. The rally was cancelled in 2008.

Most Formula E race wins
On 13 Jul 2019, Sébastien Buemi (CHE) won his 13th career race in the electric-powered motorsport championship at the New York City ePrix. His first victory came in Formula E's third-ever race. Buemi, world champion in 2015/16, also holds the record for the **most Formula E pole positions** – 14 – between 10 Jan 2015 and 13 Jul 2019.

Target Sports

Highest score in ISSF 10 m air rifle (male)

On 30 Aug 2019, Yu Haonan (CHN) won his first International Shooting Sport Federation (ISSF) World Cup gold in style, racking up a record score of 252.8 in the men's 10 m air rifle final. As he was aged just 20, this was also a world junior record. The competition was held at the Centro Militar de Tiro Esportivo in Rio de Janeiro, Brazil.

Oldest bowler in a PBA tour event

Carmen Salvino (USA, b. 23 Nov 1933) played in the Professional Bowlers Association (PBA) Tournament of Champions aged 86 years 75 days on 6 Feb 2020 at AMF Riviera Lanes in Fairlawn, Ohio, USA. A founder member of the PBA and 17-time titlist, Salvino (pictured in 2019) was competing in his 734th PBA event. He finished 59th out of 62 entrants.

Most wins of the World Women's Snooker Championship

Reanne Evans (UK) claimed her 12th world championship on 23 Jun 2019, defeating Nutcharut Wongharuthai 6–3 in the final at the Hi-End Snooker Club in Bangkok, Thailand. Evans's previous titles came in 2005–14 and 2016.

Most points scored in 50 m 36-arrow outdoor recurve archery (male)

Kim Woo-jin (KOR) shot a score of 352 out of 360 on 6 Oct 2019 at the 100th National Sports Festival in Seoul, South Korea. The previous record of 351 points, set by Kim Kyung-ho, had stood for 22 years, making it the longest-standing outdoor archery record.

Most points scored in 70 m 72-arrow outdoor recurve archery (female)

On 10 Jun 2019, Kang Chae-young (KOR) shot 692 out of 720 during the ranking round at the World Archery Championships in 's-Hertogenbosch, Netherlands. In outdoor target archery, the 72-arrow round is a preliminary used to ascertain seedings for the head-to-head matchplay rounds.

Most century breaks in a professional snooker match (individual)

Judd Trump (UK) compiled seven centuries during his 18–9 win over John Higgins in the final of the 2019 World Snooker Championship on 5–6 May. This equalled the feat of Stephen Hendry (UK) in the final of the 1994 UK Championship, and Ding Junhui (CHN) during the semi-final of the 2016 World Snooker Championship.

Together, Trump and Higgins combined for 11 centuries in their heavy-scoring encounter: the **most century breaks in a match (combined)**.

Most Archery World Cup wins

Two archers have won five titles at the Archery World Cup: Brady Ellison (USA, above) in the men's recurve in 2010–11, 2014, 2016 and 2019; and Sara López (COL, below) in the women's compound in 2014–15 and 2017–19.

For Ellison, victory capped a stellar year in which he had also set the **most points in 70 m 72-arrow outdoor recurve archery (male)** – 702, in the preliminary ranking round of the Pan American Games on 7 Aug 2019 in Lima, Peru.

Highest score in para shooting men's 10 m air pistol (SH1)

Indian marksman Rahul Jakhar took gold at the World Shooting Para Sport World Cup with a score of 240.1 in Osijek, Croatia, on 28 Jul 2019. Shooters competing in the SH1 classification can support the weight of their firearm themselves and shoot using a rifle or pistol.

Most titles at the World Indoor Bowls Championships

Alex Marshall (UK) won 14 indoor bowls world championship titles between 1995 and 2019. This includes the **most open singles titles** – six – together with six men's doubles and two mixed doubles titles. Marshall secured his 14th title with victory in the men's doubles alongside Paul Foster on 21 Jan 2019 at Potters Resort in Great Yarmouth, Norfolk, UK.

Early Olympic archery events had competitors aiming at targets placed atop poles and even at live birds!

Most wins of the Mosconi Cup

The Mosconi Cup is an annual men's nine-ball pool match between the USA and Europe. The USA are ahead by 13 wins to 12, following their 11–8 victory on 25–28 Nov 2019 in Las Vegas, Nevada, USA.

First woman to win a match at the PDC World Darts Championship

On 17 Dec 2019, Fallon Sherrock (UK) created darts history at Alexandra Palace in London, UK. She defeated Ted Evetts 3–2 in their first-round Professional Darts Corporation world championship match, hitting six 180s on her way to victory.

Sara López holds three archery scoring world records, including the **most points scored in a 1,440 round (compound, female)** – 1,424.

Golf

Most LPGA Tour wins in a year

Mickey Wright (USA) won 13 titles, including two majors, on the 1963 Ladies Professional Golf Association Tour. She retired in 1969 aged just 34, having claimed 82 Tour titles and 13 majors. These included the **most wins of the Women's PGA Championship** – four – and **most wins of the US Women's Open Championship** – four, tied with Betsy Rawls (USA). A golfing pioneer noted for her iconic swing, Wright died on 17 Feb 2020.

Fastest hole of golf (individual)

On 25 Jun 2019, four golfers vied to break Ruben Holgado Guerrero's record of 1 min 33.4 sec to complete a single hole. To qualify for the GWR title, the hole – the par-five 10th at the Real Club de Golf Guadalmina in Marbella, Spain – had to play at least 500 yards, and each player had to finish carrying the same number of clubs with which they started. Belgium's Thomas Detry won the day, holing out in 1 min 29.62 sec.

Most PGA Tour tournament victories

On 28 Oct 2019, Tiger Woods (USA) won his 82nd title on the PGA Tour at the Zozo Championship in Chiba, Japan. Twenty-three years had passed since Woods' first victory, at the 1996 Las Vegas Invitational. He equalled the mark of Sam Snead (USA), whose official tally of 82 PGA Tour wins was achieved between 1936 and 1965.

Lowest total score at the PGA Championship (first 36 holes)

Brooks Koepka (USA) reached the halfway stage of the 2019 PGA Championship on 128 strokes, following rounds of 63 and 65 on 16–17 May 2019 at Bethpage Black Course on Long Island, New York, USA. His opening round equalled the **lowest score in a round at the PGA Championship** – shared by 16 golfers – and was his second round of 63 in consecutive years. Koepka went on to claim his fourth major title – incredibly, out of just six wins on the PGA Tour.

Lowest total score at the US Open by an amateur

On 16 Jun 2019, Viktor Hovland (NOR) finished the US Open on 280 (69, 73, 71, 67; 4 under par) at Pebble Beach Golf Links in California, USA. He broke the record of 282, set by Jack Nicklaus in 1960. Hovland turned professional shortly afterwards.

Largest margin of victory at the Solheim Cup (four-ball match)

Two pairings have won a Solheim Cup four-ball match by 7 & 5 (i.e., seven strokes up with five holes to play). In 2019, Ally McDonald and Angel Yin (both USA) beat Anna Nordqvist and Caroline Hedwall to match the margin of victory achieved by Pat Hurst and Rosie Jones (both USA) against Lisa Hackney and Sophie Gustafson in 1998.

Most consecutive holes without a bogey

Ko Jin-young (KOR) played 114 holes of professional golf without dropping a shot on 3–29 Aug 2019. She topped Tiger Woods' record of 110 consecutive bogey-free holes from 2000. Ko's historic streak – through which she went a total of 41 under par – finally ended at the ninth hole of her first round at the Cambia Portland Classic.

Most wins of the Senior Open Championship

On 28 Jul 2019, Bernhard Langer (DEU) secured his fourth Senior Open Championship at the Royal Lytham & St Annes Golf Club in Lancashire, UK. He finished two strokes clear of the field. Langer's win increased his tally of **most PGA Tour Champions major victories** to 11. As of 26 Feb 2020, he had also accrued the **highest career earnings on the PGA Tour Champions**: $28,913,842 (£22,289,500).

Most wins of the Walker Cup

Officially established in 1922, the biennial Walker Cup is a 10-man amateur team competition contested by the USA and Great Britain & Ireland. The USA recorded its 37th victory on 7–8 Sep 2019, at Royal Liverpool Golf Club in Merseyside, UK.

Smallest winning margin at the Solheim Cup

On 15 Sep 2019, Europe secured a thrilling last-gasp triumph in the Solheim Cup when wildcard pick Suzann Pettersen holed a 7-ft putt on the last to win the trophy. They defeated the USA 14½ points to 13½, their winning margin of one point matching that of the victorious US team at the 2015 Solheim Cup (who also won by 14½ to 13½).

Lowest total score at The Open Championship (first 54 holes)

On 18–20 Jul 2019, Shane Lowry (IRL) played the first three rounds of The Open in 197 strokes (67, 67, 63; 16 under par) at Royal Portrush in County Antrim, Northern Ireland, UK. Lowry went on to claim the Claret Jug with a final round of 72. For the lowest 72-hole scores at the majors, see below.

Lowest major tournament total scores

Major	Winner	Year	To Par	Score
The Masters	Jordan Spieth (USA)	2015	-18	270 (64,66,70,70)
	Tiger Woods (USA)	1997		270 (70,66,65,69)
PGA Championship	Brooks Koepka (USA)	2018	-16	264 (69,63,66,66)
US Open	Rory McIlroy (UK)	2011	-16	268 (65,66,68,69)
The Open Championship	Henrik Stenson (SWE)	2016	-20	264 (68,65,68,63)

In 2019, Royal Portrush staged The Open for just the second time. The **most times to host The Open** is 29, by St Andrews in Scotland, UK.

Track & Field

WORLD ATHLETICS CHAMPIONSHIPS
The 17th edition of the biennial global athletics competition was held in Doha, Qatar, on 27 Sep–6 Oct 2019.

Oldest medallist
On 28–29 Sep 2019, João Vieira (PRT, b. 20 Feb 1976) won silver in the men's 50 km race walk aged 43 years 221 days. Vieira described the race, which began at 11.30 p.m. owing to the heat, as "hell".

Most appearances
Jesús Ángel García (ESP) has competed in 13 world championship 50 km race walks since 1993. On 28–29 Sep 2019, at the age of 49, he finished eighth. García won a career total of one gold and three silver medals at the championships.

The **most appearances (female)** is 11, by Susana Feitor (PRT) in the 10 km and 20 km race walks between 1991 and 2011.

Youngest medallist (field event)
Yaroslava Mahuchikh (UKR, b. 19 Sep 2001) won a silver medal in the women's high jump aged 18 years 11 days on 30 Sep 2019. The Ukranian crowned a breakthrough year in which she had already become the **youngest winner at a Diamond League meeting (female)**, aged 17 years 226 days, on 3 May 2019.

At the world championships, Mahuchikh had to settle for silver behind Mariya Lasitskene (RUS), whose clearance of 2.04 m (6 ft 8 in) completed a perfect scorecard with no foul jumps. It was Lasitskene's third consecutive world title – the **most high jump gold medals (female)**.

The **most high jump gold medals (male)** is two, by two athletes: Javier Sotomayor (CUB) in 1993 and 1997, and Mutaz Essa Barshim (QAT) in 2017 and 2019.

Most men's hammer gold medals at the World Athletics Championships
On 2 Oct 2019, Paweł Fajdek (POL) secured his fourth consecutive world championship title. His four legal throws were the largest of the competition. Despite his domination of the men's hammer at the world championships, as of 2019 Fajdek had yet to reach an Olympic final.

Most gold medals won at the World Athletics Championships
Allyson Felix (USA) won 13 world championship golds between 2005 and 2019. She moved clear of Usain Bolt's record of 11 with her win in the 4 x 400 m mixed relay on 29 Sep 2019, and also ran in the heats of the USA's victorious women's 4 x 400 m relay team. Felix's career tally of 18 medals (with three silver and two bronze) is also the **most world championship medals**.

Most gold medals in an individual event (female)
On 29 Sep 2019, Jamaican sprinter Shelly-Ann Fraser-Pryce claimed her fourth women's 100 m world championship title. She equalled the feat of Valerie Adams (NZ) in the shot put consecutively in 2007–13; Brittney Reese (USA) in the long jump in 2009–13 and 2017; and Anita Włodarczyk (POL) in the hammer throw in 2009 and 2013–17.

The **most gold medals won in an individual event (male)** is six, by Sergey Bubka (UKR) in the pole vault consecutively between 1983 and 1997.

Most siblings in the same event
On 30 Sep 2019, brothers Jakob, Filip and Henrik Ingebrigtsen (all NOR) lined up for the final of the men's 5,000 m. Jakob won the family honours but finished out of the medals, in fifth place. The Ingebrigtsens matched the feat of Jonathan, Kevin and Dylan Borlée (all BEL), who ran in the 4 x 400 m relay at the 14th World Athletics Championships on 15 Aug 2013 in Moscow, Russia.

Fastest 100 m (T12, male)
On 13 Jun 2019, Salum Ageze Kashafali (NOR, b. COD) ran 100 m in 10.45 sec at the Bislett Games in Oslo, Norway. This is the fastest 100 m ever run by any para athlete. Kashafali came to Norway as a refugee from the Democratic Republic of Congo aged 11 and was diagnosed with a degenerative eye disease the following year. A keen footballer, he switched to running at the age of 17.

Kashafali had previously broken the T12 100 m record on 24 May 2017 in his first race as a para athlete.

Fastest one mile (female)
Sifan Hassan (NLD, b. ETH) won the women's mile in 4 min 12.33 sec at a Diamond League meeting on 12 Jul 2019 in Monaco. She broke Svetlana Masterkova's record of 4:12.56, which had stood for almost 23 years. On 17 Feb 2019, Hassan had set the **fastest 5 km (women-only race)** – 14 min 44 sec – also in Monaco.

Fastest wheelchair 100 m (T34, female)
On 10 Nov 2019, Hannah Cockroft (UK) secured her 11th world championship gold medal with victory in the women's T34 100 m in 16.77 sec.

Fastest 200 m (T36, female)
Shi Yiting (CHN) broke the world record twice in the same day on 9 Nov 2019. She clocked 28.54 sec in the heats of the women's T36 200 m and 28.21 sec in the final.

Fastest 400 m (T12, male)
Morocco's Abdeslam Hili pipped his compatriot and former world champion Mahdi Afri at the line to take gold in 47.79 sec on 9 Nov 2019.

Highest pole vault
Armand Duplantis (SWE, b. USA) cleared a height of 6.18 m (20 ft 3.3 in) on 15 Feb 2020 at the Müller Indoor Grand Prix in Glasgow, UK. The 20-year-old, nicknamed "Mondo", had broken Renaud Lavillenie's **indoor** and **outdoor** pole vault record of 6.16 m (20 ft 2.5 in) the previous weekend, only to go a further centimetre higher in Glasgow.

Fastest 400 m (T62, male)
On 15 Nov 2019, Johannes Floors (DEU) completed a lap of the track in 45.78 sec. Five days earlier, he had clocked the **fastest 100 m (T62, male)** – 10.54 sec – in the heats, before going on to secure another gold in the final. Floors is a double amputee who runs on prosthetic legs.

Farthest long jump (T44, male)
In the men's T64 long jump final on 13 Nov 2019, T44 athlete Mpumelelo Mhlongo (ZAF) leapt 7.07 m (23 ft 2 in) – a record in his class. He had to settle for a bronze medal this time, as T64 record holder Markus Rehm (DEU) took gold with 8.17 m (26 ft 9 in). Mhlongo has a club foot and a shorter right leg owing to amniotic band syndrome.
On 11 Nov 2019, Mhlongo completed the **fastest 100 m (T44, male)** in 11 sec flat.

Farthest long jump (T62, female)
Fleur Jong (NLD) leapt 5.21 m (17 ft 1 in) on 30 Aug 2019 at the World Para Athletics Grand Prix in Paris, France. She also ran the **fastest 100 m (T62, female)** – pictured – in 13.16 sec, only for Sara Andrés Barrio (ESP) to better it with 12.90 sec on 12 Nov 2019. Double amputee Jong completed a remarkable comeback from surgery: as late as Mar 2019, she could not walk, having had bone shaved from her left leg stump in 2018.

Sally Gunnell (UK) is the only other women's 400 m hurdler to have won Olympic and world titles and broken the world record.

Fastest 400 m hurdles (female)
On 4 Oct 2019, Dalilah Muhammad (USA) won gold at the World Athletics Championships in 52.16 sec in Doha. The Olympic champion improved on her own mark of 52.20 sec, which she had set at the US Nationals on 28 Jul 2019. Later that year, Muhammad was crowned Women's Athlete of the Year by World Athletics (formerly the IAAF).

Farthest shot put (F37, female)
On 9 Nov 2019, Lisa Adams (NZ) won the shot put with a throw of 14.80 m (48 ft 6 in). It was her first world title, just two years after taking up the sport. Adams, who has cerebral palsy, is the sister of double-Olympic shot put champion Valerie Adams (see opposite page).

Farthest shot put (F32, male)
Li Liu (CHN) won gold in Dubai with a throw of 12.05 m (39 ft 6 in) on 13 Nov 2019. He beat the previous record by almost a metre.

WORLD PARA ATHLETICS CHAMPIONSHIPS
The ninth edition of the global para sport competition was held on 7–15 Nov 2019 in Dubai, UAE. For more information on Paralympic classification go to **guinnessworldrecords.com**.

Fastest 100 m (T47, male)
Petrúcio Ferreira dos Santos (BRA) ran 10.42 sec in the heats for the 100 m on 12 Nov 2019. He went on to top an all-Brazilian podium in the final, taking gold in 10.44 sec.

Most Diamond League titles won (male)
Two men have won seven Diamond League titles: pole vaulter Renaud Lavillenie (FRA) in 2010–16 and triple jumper Christian Taylor (USA) in 2012–17 and 2019 (pictured). Taylor earned his latest title with a winning jump of 17.85 m (58 ft 6 in) at the season finale in Brussels, Belgium, on 6 Sep 2019.

Marathons

Fastest-run 50 km (female)*
On 1 Sep 2019, Alyson Dixon (UK) broke a 30-year-old record in her first ultramarathon, clocking 3 hr 7 min 20 sec at the International Association of Ultrarunners (IAU) 50 km World Championships in Brașov, Romania. Frith van der Merwe's record of 3 hr 8 min 39 sec had stood since 1989.

Just seven days later, Dixon followed up by running the **fastest half marathon in superhero costume (female)** – 1 hr 18 min 26 sec – at the Great North Run in Newcastle, Tyne and Wear, UK. She sported an original Wonder Woman costume.

Fastest-run marathon (T46, male)
Michael Roeger (AUS) recorded a time of 2 hr 19 min 33 sec on 19 Jan 2020 at the Houston Marathon in Texas, USA. Roeger, who was born without the lower part of his right arm, became the first ambulant para-athlete to break the 2:20 barrier – in only his second marathon race.

pending ratification by the IAU

Farthest distance run in 24 hours (female)*
On 26–27 Oct 2019, Camille Herron (USA) ran 270.116 km (167.842 mi) at the IAU 24 Hour World Championship in Albi, France. She bested her own mark by around 8 km (5 mi). Herron also holds records for the **farthest distance run in 12 hours (female)** – 149.130 km (92.665 mi) – and the **fastest-run 100 miles (female)** – 12 hr 42 min 40 sec.

Fastest-run marathon (female)
On 13 Oct 2019, Brigid Kosgei (KEN) ran the Chicago Marathon in 2 hr 14 min 4 sec in Illinois, USA, breaking Paula Radcliffe's record of 2 hr 15 min 25 sec from 2003. Kosgei finished almost 7 min ahead of the rest of the field. Her time would have been the outright marathon record up to 1964.

Fastest-run 100 miles (male)*
On 24 Aug 2019, Zach Bitter (USA) ran 100 mi in just 11 hr 19 min 13 sec at the "Six Days in the Dome – The Redux" event in Milwaukee, Wisconsin, USA. Having broken one record, Bitter kept running for another 40 min to improve on his own mark for the **farthest distance run in 12 hours (male)*** – 168.792 km (104.882 mi).

Fastest-run Tokyo Marathon (female)
On 1 Mar 2020, Lonah Chemtai Salpeter (ISR, b. KEN) ran the Tokyo Marathon in Japan in 2 hr 17 min 45 sec. She took 2 min off the previous fastest time, running the sixth-fastest women's marathon in history. The field was limited to fewer than 200 elite athletes owing to the COVID-19 outbreak.

Virgin LONDON MARATHON money 2020

With the 2020 London Marathon postponed following the COVID-19 outbreak, GWR looks back over some of the records set by fleet-footed fancy-dress runners during our 12 years of partnership with the event (all UK, unless stated):

Book character (male)
David Stone as Dracula in 2012 – 2:42:17

Fairy (male)
Martin Hulbert in 2012 – 2:49:44

School uniform (male)
Steven Nimmo in 2014 – 2:50:17

Sailor (male)
Stephen Richardson in 2013 – 2:52:32

Lifeguard (male)
Terry Midgley in 2015 – 2:55:54

Roman soldier (male)
David Tomlin in 2012 – 2:57:00

Viking (male)
Paul Richards in 2017 – 3:03:11

Star Wars character (male)
Mathieu Lavedrine as an X-wing pilot in 2018 – 3:05:27

Bottle (male)
Charlie Long in 2016 – 3:09:37

Police uniform (male)
Paul Swan in 2011 – 3:09:52

Doctor (female)
Victoria Carter in 2015 – 3:13:23

Postbox (male)
Matthew Collins in 2019 – 3:14:32

School uniform (female)
Sophie Wood in 2013 – 3:14:34

In a wedding dress (female)
Sarah Dudgeon in 2014 – 3:16:44

Circus strongman (male)
Steven Reading in 2016 – 3:19:30

In cricket kit
Subhashis Basu in 2015 – 3:20:46

In a two-person costume
Michael Odell (CHE) and Guy Dunscombe as a horse and jockey in 2018 – 3:25:17

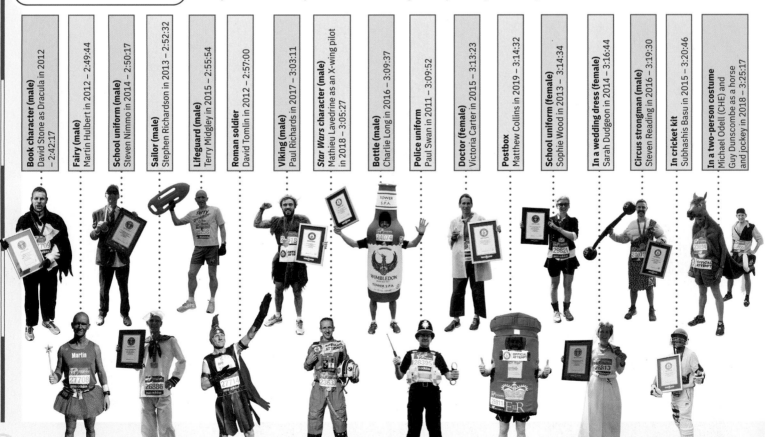

Fastest time to complete the IRONMAN® World Championship

On 12 Oct 2019, Germany's Jan Frodeno secured his third IRONMAN World Championship in 7 hr 51 min 13 sec in Hawaii, USA. He completed the 3.8-km (2.4-mi) swim in 47:31, the 180-km (112-mi) bike ride in 4:16:03 and the 42.1-km (26.2-mi) marathon in 2:42:43.

Fastest-run marathon (T12, male)

El Amin Chentouf (MAR) ran the London Marathon in 2 hr 21 min 23 sec on 28 Apr 2019. He knocked 10 sec off his own record for the T12 class, which is for visually impaired athletes.

Most wins of the Great North Run

Mo Farah (UK, b. SOM) claimed his sixth consecutive title at the UK half marathon on 8 Sep 2019, in a personal-best 59 min 7 sec.

In the women's race, Brigid Kosgei won in 1 hr 4 min 28 sec. However, as the Great North Run course did not meet official World Athletics criteria, the **fastest-run half marathon (female)** remains 1 hr 4 min 51 sec, set by Joyciline Jepkosgei (KEN) on 22 Oct 2017 in Valencia, Spain.

Youngest winner of the Boston Marathon wheelchair division (male)

On 15 Apr 2019, Daniel Romanchuk (USA, b. 3 Aug 1998) won the men's wheelchair race at the Boston Marathon aged 20 years 255 days. He took the title in 1 hr 21 min 36 sec. First staged on 19 Apr 1897, the Boston Marathon is the **oldest continuously-run annual marathon**.

Romanchuk also holds track records in the men's T54 category for the **fastest wheelchair 800 m** – 1 min 29.66 sec, recorded on 16 Jun 2018 – and the **fastest wheelchair 5,000 m** – 9 min 42.83 sec, set on 2 Jun 2019.

Fastest-run half marathon

On 15 Sep 2019, Geoffrey Kamworor (KEN) won the Copenhagen Half Marathon in Denmark in 58 min 1 sec. He prioritized his record attempt over participation in the 2019 IAAF World Championships, and was rewarded with a time 17 sec inside the previous best.

Fastest-run marathon distance

On 12 Oct 2019, Eliud Kipchoge (KEN) made history by running 26.2 mi (42.1 km) in 1 hr 59 min 40 sec at the INEOS 1:59 Challenge in Vienna, Austria. He broke the 2-hr barrier with the help of 41 in-out pacemakers arranged in an inverted "V" formation around him. As standard competition rules were not followed, Kipchoge's **fastest-run marathon** record remains 2 hr 1 min 39 sec, set on 16 Sep 2018 in Berlin, Germany.

Witch (female)
Nicola Nuttall in 2017 – 3:26:13

In a graduation gown (female)
Kelly Murphy in 2015 – 3:32:08

Zombie (female)
Charlotte Österman (SWE) in 2018 – 3:39:25

Fruit (female)
Lorna Pursglove as a chilli pepper in 2017 – 3:41:25

Gingerbread person (female)
Cat Dascendis in 2017 – 3:46:55

In military dress (male)
Olivier Hamar (FRA) in 2013 – 3:47:14

Elvis (female)
Elizabeth Sampson in 2019 – 3:49:53

Astronomical body (male)
Philip Rose as the Sun in 2019 – 3:52:40

In a tent (male)
Oscar White in 2019 – 3:57:05

Mascot (female)
Rachel Bown as Brain Tumour Support's Mr Hippo in 2016 – 3:58:57

Shoe (female)
Lucie Barney in 2013 – 4:40:56

Three-dimensional toy (male)
Bob Johnson as Mr Potato Head in 2018 – 4:59:30

Hula-hooping
Sasha Kenney (SVN) in 2012 – 5:05:57

On crutches
John Sandford Hart in 2011 – 6:24:48

In a bomb-disposal suit
Iain Church in 2015 – 6:28:06

Marching band
Huddersfield Marathon Band in 2014 – 6:56:48

Swimming

Fastest S8 100 m backstroke (female)
At the 2019 World Para Swimming Championships in London, UK, Alice Tai (UK) won the S8 100 m backstroke in 1 min 8.04 sec – one of a total of seven gold medals. It capped a stellar year: on 6–9 Jun 2019, she had set seven world records at a single meet in Berlin, Germany, including the **fastest S8 50 m freestyle (female)** – 28.97 sec. Tai was born with severe bilateral talipes (club foot) and has undergone more than a dozen operations.

Fastest long course 4 x 200 m freestyle relay (female)
On 25 Jul 2019, the Australian team of Ariarne Titmus, Madison Wilson, Brianna Throssell and Emma McKeon claimed gold at the FINA World Championships in 7 min 41.50 sec. They beat a record set by China in 2009 during the "supersuit era", when athletes could wear low-friction non-textile swimsuits.

FASTEST...

Long course 200 m butterfly (male)
On 24 Jul 2019, Kristóf Milák (HUN) won his first world championship gold medal in 1 min 50.73 sec in Gwangju, South Korea. He broke Michael Phelps's record of 1 min 51.51 sec, which had stood for a decade.

Other world records to fall in Gwangju included the **fastest long course 200 m breaststroke (male)** – 2 min 6.12 sec, by Anton Chupkov (RUS) on 26 Jul – and the **fastest long course 4 x 100 m women's medley relay** – 3 min 50.40 sec, by the US team of Regan Smith (backstroke), Lilly King (breaststroke), Kelsi Dahlia (butterfly) and Simone Manuel (freestyle) on 28 Jul.

Short course 100 m backstroke (female)
On 27 Oct 2019, Minna Atherton (AUS) set the first world record at an International Swimming League (ISL) meet when she swam a short course 100 m backstroke in 54.89 sec in Budapest, Hungary. Short course races are held in a 25-m-long pool; long course races in a 50-m pool.

At the ISL Grand Final on 20 Dec 2019, Daiya Seto (JPN) of the Energy Standard team clocked the **fastest short course 400 m individual medley** – 3 min 54.81 sec.

Short course 4 x 50 m medley relay (mixed)
On 5 Dec 2019, the Russian team of Kliment Kolesnikov (backstroke), Vladimir Morozov (breaststroke), Arina Surkova (butterfly) and Maria Kameneva (freestyle) won gold in 1 min 36.22 sec at the European Short Course Swimming Championships in Glasgow, UK.

Fastest long course 200 m backstroke (female)
Regan Smith (USA) touched home in 2 min 3.35 sec at the FINA World Championships in Gwangju on 26 Jul 2019. The 17-year-old set three world records in three days. On 28 Jul, she swam the **fastest 100 m backstroke (female)** – 57.57 sec – and was also part of the USA's **fastest 4 x 100 m women's medley relay** team (see bottom left).

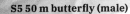

Most FINA world records (current)
As of 19 Feb 2020, Caeleb Dressel (USA) had set the fastest time in seven swimming events. He has overtaken Michael Phelps, whose number of current world records has dropped from seven to four. Dressel swam the **fastest long course 100 m butterfly (male)** in 49.50 sec on 26 Jul 2019, and a day later helped set the **fastest long course 4 x 100 m freestyle relay (mixed)** – 3 min 19.40 sec. On 20 Dec 2019, he added the **fastest short course 50 m freestyle (male)** – 20.24 sec – at the ISL Grand Final in Las Vegas, Nevada, USA.

S5 50 m butterfly (male)
Lichao Wang (CHN) swam a single length in 31.52 sec on 12 Sep 2019 at the World Para Swimming Championships. He followed up with the **fastest S5 50 m backstroke (male)** – 32.59 sec – two days later. Wang lost both of his arms following an electrical accident at the age of eight.

S9 100 m freestyle (male)
On 9 Sep 2019, Simone Barlaam (ITA) won one of his four world championship gold medals in 54.10 sec in London, UK. He also set S9 records for the **fastest 50 m freestyle** (24 sec flat) and **fastest 100 m backstroke** (1 min 1.22 sec). Barlaam was born with a deficiency of the right femur.

Peaty swam the fastest long course 50 m breaststroke (male) – 25.95 sec – on 25 Jul 2017.

Fastest long course 100 m breaststroke (male)
On 21 Jul 2019, Adam Peaty (UK) won his semi-final of the men's 100 m breaststroke in 56.88 sec at the FINA World Championships. He achieved his "Project 56" goal of becoming the first swimmer to break the 57-sec barrier. Peaty has dominated the 100 m breaststroke, winning the 2016 Olympic title, recording the 18 fastest times ever swam and setting the world record on five occasions.

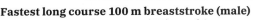

Water Sports

Fastest speed women's sailing (nautical mile)

On 10 Jun 2019, windsurfer Heidi Ulrich (CHE) reached a speed of 37.62 knots (69.67 km/h; 43.29 mph) over a nautical mile at the Prince of Speed event in La Palme, France. The record was ratified by the WSSRC.

Farthest freediving dynamic apnea with fins (female)

On 13 Oct 2019, Magdalena Solich-Talanda (POL) swam 257 m (843 ft) underwater on one breath at the Hydro Dynamic event in Vienna, Austria. She reclaimed the record from her compatriot, Agnieszka Kalska.

Fastest men's kite surfing speed (nautical mile)

Roberto Douglas (USA) reached 39.04 knots (72.30 km/h; 44.92 mph) over 1 nautical mi (1.8 km; 1.1 mi) on 10 Jun 2019 in La Palme, France.

Marine Tlattla (FRA) set the **women's** record of 35.86 knots (66.41 km/h; 41.26 mph) at the same event on 22 Jun. Both records were verified by the World Sailing Speed Record Council (WSSRC).

Most Canoe Slalom World Championships gold medals (female)

Jessica Fox (AUS, b. FRA) won 10 titles at the ICF Canoe Slalom World Championships between 2013 and 2019. Seven of her wins came in the solo canoe (C1) and kayak (K1) classes – the **most individual gold medals**. Her other three victories came in the C1 team category.

Most gold medals won at the FINA World Championships (female)

Artistic swimmer Svetlana Romashina (RUS) has won 25 world championship gold medals since 2005, including four as a reserve. She claimed three in 2019: solo free routine, duet free routine and duet technical routine. Romashina has won every world and Olympic final she has entered.

Most Women's Water Polo World Championships

On 26 Jul 2019, the USA sealed their sixth women's title with an 11–6 victory over Spain in Gwangju, South Korea. They became the first team, male or female, to claim three consecutive gold medals at the World Aquatics Championships.

The USA have also claimed the **most wins of the Women's Water Polo World League** – 13, between 2004 and 2019. Serbia hold the **men's** record with 10, between 2007 and 2019.

Fastest 2,000 m single sculls para-row (male)

On 1 Sep 2019, Roman Polianskyi (UKR) won the PR1 M1X final in 9 min 12.990 sec at the World Rowing Championships in Linz-Ottensheim, Austria.

The **fastest 2,000 m coxed four para-row (mixed)** is 6 min 49.240 sec, by Ellen Buttrick, Giedre Rakauskaite (b. LTU), James Fox, Oliver Stanhope and cox Erin Wysocki-Jones (all UK) on 29 Aug 2019, also in Linz-Ottensheim.

Oldest participant in the University Boat Race

Since 1829, Oxford and Cambridge have contested an annual Universtity Boat Race along the River Thames in London, UK. On 7 Apr 2019, James Cracknell (UK, b. 5 May 1972) rowed for Cambridge aged 46 years 337 days. He was 10 years older than the previous oldest rower to compete. Cambridge beat Oxford in a time of 16 min 57 sec to record its 84th victory – the **most wins of the University Boat Race**.

Fastest C1 500 m canoe sprint (female)

On 23 Aug 2019, Alena Nazdrova (BLR) clocked a time of 2 min 0.73 sec at the International Canoe Federation (ICF) Canoe Sprint and Paracanoe World Championships in Szeged, Hungary.

Highest score slalom waterskiing (female)

Regina Jaquess (USA) waterskiied 4.5 buoys on a 10.25-m line at 55 km/h (34 mph) on 6 Jul 2019 in Duncanville, Alabama, USA.

Deepest freediving constant weight with bi-fins (male)

New bi-fins categories in the constant weight division were established by freediving federation AIDA on 1 Jan 2019. On 5 Aug 2019, Alexey Molchanov (RUS) dived to 110 m (360 ft 10 in) at the Caribbean Cup in Roatán, Honduras.

The **female** record is 92 m (301 ft 10 in), by Alenka Artnik (SVN) on 11 Jun 2019 in Panglao, Philippines. Bi-fins are an unconnected pair of fins worn on each foot, as opposed to a single monofin.

Fox overtook her mother, Myriam, to become the most successful female canoe slalom world champion.

Winter Sports

Most race wins at the FIS World Cup

Amélie Wenger-Reymond (CHE) was victorious in 147 races at the Fédération Internationale de Ski (FIS) World Cup between 18 Mar 2007 and 8 Feb 2020. To date, she is one of only three skiers to rack up 100 victories in the competition, together with Marit Bjørgen (114, in cross-country) and Conny Kissling (106, in freestyle).

Most wins of the men's relay at the World Ski Orienteering Championships

On 24 Mar 2019, Russia secured their 10th men's relay title in Piteå, Sweden. They had won the gold medal in the biennial competition every year since 1998, bar 2009 and 2011.

Most wins of the FIS Freestyle World Cup (male)

Mikaël Kingsbury (CAN) claimed his ninth consecutive Freestyle World Cup in 2019/20, winning seven out of 10 competitions. He extended his record for **most career event wins (male)** to 62 (44 in the mogul category and 18 in the dual mogul).

On 9 Feb 2019, Kingsbury equalled the **most gold medals at the FIS Freestyle World Ski Championships** – four. He matched the feat of Kari Traa (NOR) between 2001 and 2003 and Jennifer Heil (CAN) from 2007 to 2011.

Most World Alpine Ski Championships gold medals (male)

On 17 Feb 2019, Marcel Hirscher (AUT) claimed his seventh world championship title with victory in the men's slalom in Åre, Sweden. He matched the tally of Anton "Toni" Sailer (AUT) in 1956–58. Hirscher has won three slalom, one giant slalom, one combined and two team events.

In Sep 2019, Hirscher announced that he was retiring, ending a glittering career that included the **most FIS Alpine Ski World Cup overall titles** – eight consecutively, from 2011/12 to 2018/19.

Most FIS Alpine Ski World Cup slalom race wins

Mikaela Shiffrin (USA) recorded 43 slalom race victories at the FIS Alpine Ski World Cup between 20 Dec 2012 and 29 Dec 2019. She surpassed the **male** record of 40 wins – by Ingemar Stenmark (SWE) – on 23 Nov 2019 in Levi, Finland.

Most individual starts in FIS Ski Jumping World Cup competitions

Ski jumper Noriaki Kasai (JPN, pictured in 2019) competed in 569 FIS World Cup events from 17 Dec 1988 to 2 Feb 2020. Kasai had won 17 career events and made the podium 63 times. He had also made the **most Winter Olympic appearances** – eight, from Albertville 1992 to Pyeongchang 2018.

Most wins of the World Para Ice Hockey Championships

On 4 May 2019, the USA equalled Canada's total of four world championship titles with a 3–2 overtime victory over their great rivals in Ostrava, Czech Republic. The tournament, known as the IPC Ice Sledge Hockey World Championships up to 2016, was first held in Nynäshamn, Sweden, in 1996.

Fastest speed skating 5,000 m (female)

On 15 Feb 2020, Natalya Voronina (RUS) won gold in 6 min 39.02 sec at the ISU World Single Distances Speed Skating Championships in Salt Lake City, Utah, USA. She improved on Martina Sáblíková's time of 6 min 41.18 sec, set earlier in the event.

At the same championships on 14 Feb, Graeme Fish (CAN) set the **fastest 10,000 m** – 12 min 33.86 sec. He broke the previous world record by almost 3 sec.

Also on 14 Feb, the Japanese team of Miho Takagi, Nana Takagi and Ayano Sato completed the **fastest women's six-lap team pursuit** in 2 min 50.76 sec.

Most gold medals at the ISU World Single Distances Speed Skating Championships

Sven Kramer (NLD) won his 21st Single Distances championship title on 15 Feb 2020. Together with Douwe de Vries and Marcel Bosker, he skated the **fastest men's eight-lap team pursuit** – 3 min 34.68 sec.

The **most gold medals (female)** is 16, by Martina Sáblíková (CZE) between 2007 and 2020. Sáblíková has won six titles over 3,000 m and 10 titles at 5,000 m.

Most wins of the ISU World Team Trophy

The ISU World Team Trophy is a team figure skating competition, with each side comprising eight skaters. The USA lifted its fourth trophy since 2009 on 13 Apr 2019 in Fukuoka, Kyushu, Japan.

Fastest short track speed skating 500 m (female)

On 3 Nov 2019, Kim Boutin (CAN) won her 500 m quarter-final in 41.936 sec at the ISU Short Track Speed Skating World Cup event in Salt Lake City, Utah, USA. This is one of a host of skating records set at the high-altitude Utah Olympic Oval, where skaters face less air resistance; the track is also harder and faster on account of there being less oxygen in the ice.

Short track speed skating began in the USA and Canada at the beginning of the 20th century. It became an official Olympic event in 1992.

Most wins of the Women's Bandy World Championship

Similar to ice hockey, bandy is contested by teams of 11 players on a soccer-pitch-sized rink, using a ball instead of a puck. Sweden's women secured their ninth world championship title on 22 Feb 2020, defeating Russia 3–1 in the final. They have won every tournament bar 2014, when they lost to Russia in the final, also 3–1.

The **most wins of the Men's Bandy World Championship** is 14, by the Soviet Union from 1957 to 1991.

Most skeleton race wins at the IBSF World Cup (male)

Between 8 Feb 2008 and 15 Feb 2020, Latvia's Martins Dukurs was victorious in 54 World Cup races. He claimed his ninth skeleton World Cup title in 2019/20, with eight in a row from 2009/10 to 2016/17.

Highest total score in ice dance figure skating

On 22–23 Nov 2019, ice dancers Gabriella Papadakis and Guillaume Cizeron (both FRA) amassed a total score of 226.61 points at the NHK Trophy in Sapporo, Hokkaidō, Japan. This comprised the the **highest rhythm dance score** – 90.03 – and the **highest free dance score** – 136.58, for an aerobics-themed routine set to "Fame" (inset).

Highest figure skating total score (female)

On 6–7 Dec 2019, Alena Kostornaia (RUS) won the ISU Grand Prix of Figure Skating Final with a total score of 247.59 points in Turin, Italy. This included the **highest short programme score (female)** – 85.45.

Also in Turin, Nathan Chen (USA) won his third consecutive Grand Prix Final with the **highest total score (male)** of 335.30. This included the **highest free skating score (male)** – 224.92, for a routine in which he landed five quadruple jumps.

The runner-up behind Chen, Yuzuru Hanyu (JPN), achieved the **highest short programme score (male)** – 111.82 – on 7 Feb 2020 in Seoul, South Korea.

Most individual skeleton titles at the IBSF World Championships (female)

Tina Hermann (DEU) has won three individual titles at the International Bobsleigh & Skeleton Federation World Championships. She claimed her third on 29 Feb 2020 in Altenberg, Germany. Hermann has also won two gold medals in the mixed team event (in 2015 and 2016).

Fastest speed skating 1,000 m

On 15 Feb 2020, Pavel Kulizhnikov (RUS) won gold in the men's 1,000 m in 1 min 5.69 sec at the International Skating Union (ISU) World Single Distances Speed Skating Championships in Salt Lake City, Utah, USA. He became the first man to break 1:06 and was described by silver medallist Kjeld Nuis as being "in a league of his own".

First quadruple flip jump in a figure skating competition (female)

On 7 Dec 2019, 15-year-old Alexandra Trusova (RUS) landed a four-revolution flip jump at the ISU Grand Prix of Figure Skating Final in Turin, Italy. Trusova has been at the vanguard of a group of young female figure skaters transforming the sport by adding more acrobatically demanding jumps to their routines. See below for each first by jump.

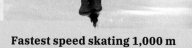

Trusova made her senior debut in style on 21 Sep 2019, becoming the first female skater to land three quad jumps in a routine.

First figure skating quadruple jumps

Quadruple jump	Date	Skater	Location
Toe loop (male)	25 Mar 1988	Kurt Browning (CAN)	Budapest, Hungary
Salchow (male)	7 Mar 1998	Timothy Goebel (USA)	Lausanne, Switzerland
Salchow (female)	14 Dec 2002	Miki Ando (JPN)	The Hague, Netherlands
Lutz (male)	16 Sep 2011	Brandon Mroz (USA)	Colorado Springs, USA
Flip (male)	22 Apr 2016	Shoma Uno (JPN)	Spokane, USA
Loop (male)	30 Sep 2016	Yuzuru Hanyu (JPN)	Montreal, Canada
Toe loop (female)	10 Mar 2018	Alexandra Trusova	Sofia, Bulgaria
Lutz (female)	12 Oct 2018	Alexandra Trusova	Yerevan, Armenia

Cycling

Fastest 200 m time trial (female)
Kelsey Mitchell (CAN) won the flying sprint in 10.154 sec on 5 Sep 2019 at the Pan-American Track Cycling Championships in Cochabamba, Bolivia.

The next day, Nicholas Paul (TTO) set the **fastest 200 m time trial (male)** in 9.100 sec. Cochabamba's altitude of 2,558 m (8,392 ft) means lower air resistance, enabling riders to go even faster.

Fastest men's 750 m team sprint*
On 26 Feb 2020, the Netherlands (Jeffrey Hoogland, Harrie Lavreysen and Roy van den Berg) rode three laps in 41.225 sec at the UCI Track Cycling World Championships in Berlin, Germany.

Fastest C1 200 m time trial (male)*
On 31 Jan 2020, Ricardo Ten Argilés (ESP) won gold in 12.325 sec at the Para-cycling Track World Championships in Milton, Ontario, Canada. A former Paralympic swimming gold medallist, Argilés only took up track cycling in 2017. He had both his arms and one leg below the knee amputated after a childhood accident.

Farthest one hour unpaced standing start
On 16 Apr 2019, Victor Campenaerts (BEL) shattered one of track cycling's most prestigious records when he rode 55.089 km (34.230 mi) in 60 min in Aguascalientes, Mexico. He added 563 m (1,847 ft) to Bradley Wiggins' distance from 7 Jun 2015, which had withstood nine other attempts to beat it.

Most wins of the Tour de France's points classification
Since 1953, points have been awarded to Tour de France riders according to their final position on each stage, with extra points for intermediate sprints during certain stages. Peter Sagan (SVK) has won the points classification seven times, in 2012–16 and 2018–19.

Sagan also extended his record for the **most Tour de Suisse stage wins** to 17. He won stage 3 of the 2019 race on 17 Jun, maintaining his record of winning at least one stage in every year he had competed.

Fastest men's 4 km team pursuit*
On 27 Feb 2020, the Danish team of Lasse Norman Hansen, Julius Johansen, Frederik Madsen and Rasmus Pedersen won gold at the UCI Track Cycling World Championships in 3 min 44.672 sec. They broke the world record three times in two days in Berlin, Germany, setting fastest times in qualification and the first round before going even quicker in the final.

Youngest winner on the UCI World Tour
Remco Evenepoel (BEL, b. 25 Jan 2000) triumphed in the Clásica San Sebastián in Spain on 3 Aug 2019 aged 19 years 190 days. Riding for Deceuninck – Quick-Step, Evenepoel became the third-youngest winner of a classic cycling race, after Victor Fastre (18 years 362 days) and Georges Ronsse (19 years 102 days), in the 1909 and 1925 Liège–Bastogne–Liège respectively.

Fastest C3 200 m time trial (female)*
Wang Xiaomei (CHN) set a time of 12.853 sec on 31 Jan 2020 at the Para-cycling Track World Championships. She smashed Paige Greco's record of 13.250 sec from the previous year's event (see below).

Highest score in artistic cycling (male, single)
Lukas Kohl (DEU) scored 214.10 points for his routine on 5 Oct 2019 at the German Masters in Weil im Schönbuch, Germany.

The **women's single** record is 195.35 points, by Milena Slupina (DEU) on 7 Sep 2019 in the preliminary round of the German Masters in Murg, Germany.

Most men's cross-country titles at the UCI Mountain Bike & Trials World Championships
Nino Schurter (CHE) has been crowned men's cross-country world champion eight times, in 2009, 2012–13 and 2015–19. He secured his fifth consecutive title on 31 Aug 2019 at Mont-Sainte-Anne Bike Park in Quebec, Canada.

In 2019, Schurter also equalled Julien Absalon's (FRA) mark of **most UCI Mountain Bike World Cup cross-country titles** – seven.

pending ratification by the Union Cycliste Internationale (UCI)

Fastest C3 3 km individual pursuit (female)
On 14 Mar 2019, Paige Greco (AUS) set a time of 4 min 0.026 sec during qualifying for the women's C3 individual pursuit at the 2019 Para-cycling Track World Championships in Apeldoorn, Netherlands. Greco, who has cerebral palsy, set three world records in two days, including the **fastest C3 500 m time trial (female)** – 39.442 sec – on 15 Mar.

X Games

Most gold medals in BMX Street
Garrett Reynolds (USA) claimed 11 BMX Street golds between 2008 and 2019. He won his first on his event debut, aged 18, and has made the podium in every X Games BMX Street competition since. His total haul of 15 medals includes two silvers and a bronze, along with a gold from the 2016 Real BMX event.

Most medals in summer disciplines (female)
Skateboarder Letícia Bufoni (BRA) won 11 medals between 2010 and 2019. These comprise five golds, three silvers and three bronze – all bar one in Skateboard Street. Bufoni claimed her fifth gold, and 11th overall medal, on 1 Jun 2019 at X Games Shanghai 2019 in China.

Bufoni shares the record for **most Skateboard Street gold medals (female)** – four – with Elissa Steamer (USA), who triumphed in 2004–06 and 2008.

Most Skateboard Street gold medals
On 2 Jun 2019, Nyjah Huston (USA) won his 10th Skateboard Street title since 2011 with a final-round score of 94.00 at X Games Shanghai. Huston has also won skateboarding gold in Real Street (Los Angeles 2012) and Best Trick (Minneapolis 2019), together with four silvers and two bronze.

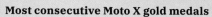

Most consecutive Moto X gold medals
On 1 Aug 2019, rider Jarryd McNeil (AUS) cleared a height of 12.1 m (40 ft) at X Games Minneapolis to seal his fourth consecutive gold in the Step Up competition.

The **most Moto X medals** is 19, accrued by Nate Adams (USA) between X Games Los Angeles 2003 and X Games Austin 2015.

First 1260 on a skateboard
On 3 Aug 2019, Mitchie Brusco (USA) landed a 1260 (three-and-a-half-rotation aerial spin) during the Skateboard Big Air event at X Games Minneapolis 2019. Despite his ground-breaking trick, Brusco had to settle for silver behind Elliot Sloan at US Bank Stadium in Minnesota, USA.

The **first 900** remains one of the most iconic moments in X Games history. The two-and-a-half aerial spin was landed by skateboard legend Tony Hawk (USA) at X Games Five on 27 Jun 1999 in San Francisco, California, USA.

The **first 1080** was performed by Tom Schaar (USA) on 26 Mar 2012 at Woodward West in Tehachapi, California, USA. He was aged just 12 at the time.

Most Snowboard Slopestyle gold medals
At X Games Aspen 2020, Jamie Anderson (USA) claimed her sixth gold in Snowboard Slopestyle. She had previously triumphed in 2007–08, 2012–13 and 2018.

Anderson has amassed the **most X Games medals (female)** with 17. She is just three behind the outright winter-discipline holder, Mark McMorris (see right).

Most medals in winter disciplines
At X Games Norway on 7–8 Mar 2020, snowboarder Mark McMorris (CAN) claimed a gold medal in Big Air and a silver in Slopestyle – his 19th and 20th career medals at the X Games. He surpassed the total of 18 set by Shaun White (USA), although White still holds the **most winter-discipline gold medals** – 13. McMorris's achievements are all the more remarkable for the fact that he had to battle back from a near-fatal crash in Mar 2017, which left him with numerous internal injuries.

Most skiing medals
Henrik Harlaut (SWE) won 12 skiing medals (seven gold and five silver) from 2013 to 2020. He surpassed Tanner Hall's tally of 11 with a victory in Ski Big Air at X Games Aspen on 24 Jan 2020.

Most medals by a teenager
On 26 Jan 2020, Kelly Sildaru (EST, b. 17 Feb 2002) claimed her ninth X Games medal aged 17 years 343 days. She matched Shaun White (USA, b. 3 Sep 1986) – who won his ninth medal aged 19 years 147 days at Winter X Games 10 on 28 Jan 2006 – and Nyjah Huston (USA, b. 30 Nov 1994) – who did likewise aged 19 years 190 days at X Games Austin on 8 Jun 2014.

Sildaru's total includes the **most medals at a Winter X Games (female)** – three, which she won at X Games Aspen 2019. She matched the feat of Jennie Waara (SWE) in 1997.

Youngest athlete
Gui Khury (BRA, b. 18 Dec 2008) was only 10 years 225 days old when he competed in the Skateboard Vert elimination round at X Games Minneapolis on 31 Jul 2019. Khury landed his first 900 (a two-and-a-half-revolution aerial spin) at the age of eight, and landed another on his X Games debut in Minneapolis.

Youngest medallist
On 2 Aug 2019, Cocona Hiraki (JPN, b. 26 Aug 2008) claimed a silver medal aged 10 years 341 days in the Women's Skateboard Park competition at X Games Minneapolis. Hiraki finished runner-up behind 13-year-old Misugu Okamoto, in what was the youngest field in X Games history.

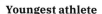

Round-Up

Most Women's World Floorball Championships

On 15 Dec 2019, Sweden claimed its ninth world title with a 3–2 overtime victory against hosts Switzerland in Neuchatel. During the tournament, Swedish forward Anna Wijk set a new record for the **most career points at the Women's World Floorball Championships** – 88, since 2009.

Fastest 15 m speed climb (female)

On 19 Oct 2019, Aries Susanti Rahayu (IDN) scaled a 15-m (49-ft) climbing wall in 6.995 sec in Xiamen, China. She beat the previous record holder, Song Yi Ling, in the speed final of the International Federation of Sport Climbing World Cup.

Most gold medals won by a nation at an IWF World Championships

China won 29 golds at the 2019 International Weightlifting Federation World Championships in Pattaya, Thailand, matching their record tally from 1997. Six lifters won all three golds in their categories (snatch, clean & jerk and total). Among them were 19-year-old sensation Li Wenwen (left) – who lifted the **heaviest +87 kg total (female)** of 332 kg (731 lb 14 oz) – and Li Fabin (below), who set the **heaviest 61 kg total (male)** – 318 kg (701 lb 1 oz).

The **individual** record for golds is 22, by Soviet Vasily Alekseyev and Naim Süleymanoğlu (BUL/TUR).

Fastest finswimming 100 m surface (female)

On 27 Jun 2019, Ekaterina Mikhailushkina (RUS) swam 100 m in 38.06 sec at the CMAS Finswimming Senior European Championships in Ioannina, Greece. Surface finswimmers swim through the water using a mask, snorkel and monofin.

At the same event, Zuzana Hraskova (SVK) completed the **fastest finswimming 400 m bi fins (female)** in 3 min 44.65 sec on 29 Jun.

Fastest ILSF 200 m Super Lifesaver (female)

Prue Davies (AUS) touched home in 2 min 20.05 sec at the German Cup 2019 in Warendorf, Germany, on 23 Nov. The event requires competitors to dive to retrieve a submerged manikin and tow it to the finish edge. It is monitored by the International Life Saving Federation (ILSF).

Heaviest Paralympic powerlift (-107 kg, male)

Sodnompiljee Enkhbayar (MNG) lifted 247 kg (544 lb 8 oz) on 18 Jul 2019 at the World Para Powerlifting Championships in Nur-Sultan, Kazakhstan.

Other powerlifting records to fall in Nur-Sultan included the **women's -41 kg** – 104.5 kg (230 lb 6 oz), by Zhe Cui (CHN) on 13 Jul – and the **women's -79 kg** – 142 kg (313 lb), by Bose Omolayo (NGA) on 17 Jul. On 18 Jul, Folashade Oluwafemiayo (NGA) set the **women's -86 kg** record with a lift of 150 kg (330 lb 11 oz).

Most consecutive horse racing jump race wins

Altior, a thoroughbred trained by five-time Champion Trainer Nicky Henderson, won 19 jump races in a row between 10 Oct 2015 and 27 Apr 2019. With his win of the Celebration Chase at Sandown in Surrey, UK, he overtook Big Buck's record of 18. The streak ended on 23 Nov 2019, when Altior was beaten by Cyrname.

First married squash world champions

On 15 Nov 2019, Tarek Momen (EGY) was crowned the 2019/20 Professional Squash Association (PSA) men's world champion in Doha, Qatar. He matched the feat of his wife, Raneem El Welily (EGY), who became PSA women's world champion on 17 Dec 2017.

Most wins of the Optimist World Championship

The Optimist is a class of single-handed sailing dinghy used by children up to the age of 15. On 15 Jul 2019, Marco Gradoni (ITA) won his third world championship in a row. In honour of his achievement, the 15-year-old was voted male Sailor of the Year on 29 Oct 2019, becoming the youngest-ever recipient of the award.

Most individual all-around titles at the Rhythmic Gymnastics World Championships

Dina Averina (RUS) claimed her third consecutive rhythmic gymnastics all-around world title in 2019. Averina joined an exalted list of three-time champions: Maria Gigova, Maria Petrova (both BUL), Yevgeniya Kanayeva and Yana Kudryavtseva (both RUS).

Most badminton men's singles titles in a season

Kento Momota (JPN) claimed 11 singles titles between 3 Mar and 15 Dec 2019. His wins included the All England Open Badminton Championships, the Badminton World Federation (BWF) World Championships and the BWF World Tour finals – where Momota surpassed Lee Chong Wei's 2010 single-season record of 10 titles.

Most women's singles medals won at the Badminton World Championships

P V Sindhu (IND) and Zhang Ning (CHN) have both won five world championship medals in the women's singles event. Sindhu matched Ning's total with her first gold medal, earned in a 38-min final victory against Nozomi Okuhara on 25 Aug 2019.

MOST WINS OF THE...

Trampoline Gymnastics World Championships (consecutive men's individual titles)

On 1 Dec 2019, Gao Lei (CHN) secured his fourth men's individual world title in a row in Tokyo, Japan. He moved clear of Russia's Alexander Moskalenko, who won three in 1990–94.

World Korfball Championship

The Netherlands secured its 10th World Korfball Championship by defeating Belgium 31–18 on 10 Aug 2019 in Durban, South Africa. The two sides have contested every final since the event began in 1978. The Netherlands has won every one, bar 1991.

World Orienteering Championships long-distance event (male)

Olav Lundanes (NOR) won his sixth long-distance title on 14 Aug 2019. He finished the 16.6-km-long (10.3-mi) course, complete with 26 controls, in a time of 1 hr 30 min 9 sec in Østfold, Norway. It was Lundanes's fourth consecutive victory in the event, previously known as the "individual" or "classic distance".

Red Bull Cliff Diving World Series (male)

Gary Hunt (UK) won five out of seven competitions in 2019 to wrap up his eighth title. Runner-up in 2009, 2013 and 2017, Hunt has never finished lower than second in the series.

Most wins of AFL's Norm Smith Medal

The player judged the "best on ground" in the Australian Football League Grand Final is awarded the Norm Smith Medal. Richmond's Dustin Martin won his second medal in three years on 28 Sep 2019, joining Gary Ayres, Andrew McLeod and Luke Hodge (all AUS) as the only two-time recipients.

Most wins of the Red Bull Cliff Diving World Series (female)

In 2019, Rhiannan Iffland (AUS) secured her fourth consecutive Red Bull Cliff Diving World Series title with the first-ever unbeaten season. She won all seven competitions (with one stop, in Dublin, not counting towards overall points). Iffland, who comes from a trampolining background, triumphed in her debut series in 2016 as a wildcard entry.

Before cliff diving, Iffland spent three years performing as an acrobatic diver on cruise ships.

Iffland launches herself from a rock pinnacle at the Small Lagoon on Miniloc Island in the Philippines during the 2019 Cliff Diving World Series.

While performing her Biles II backflip, Simone leaps approximately twice her own height in the air.

SPORTS

o HALL OF FAME

Simone Biles

A t the age of just 23, Simone Biles. Her gymnastic power. And not content with dominating the boundaries of the possible, in her sport. Her explosive power. And not content with dominating the boundaries of the possible, in her sport. **combine dominating the boundaries of the possible, in her sport.** the all-time sporting greats. Her gymnastic power. And not **is redefining the boundaries of the possible, in her sport.**

Simone was born on 14 Mar 1997, and first tried gymnastics aged six. At 16, she won two golds at the 2013 World Artistic Gymnastics Championships. And in 2019, she became the third woman to win five golds at a single world championships (pictured), taking her career tally to 19: the **most World Artistic Gymnastics Championships gold medals.** This includes three silvers and three bronze – 25. With the addition in world championship history evolving. Most the **most medals, Simone also has four skills named after **World individual **Gymnastics all-around titles** (five). Simone now has the **most medals in world championships** Championships **Championships** taking her career

Beyond the medals, Simone keep gymnastics evolving. Most her – proof of her desire to keep the Biles (H), a double twisting double somersault dismount from three twists. the Biles II, a double backflip with three twists.

One record is the most Olympic gold Simone's reach is the **most Olympic gold** medals **(female)** – nine, by Soviet gymnast Larisa Latynina. Simone won four golds at Rio 2016, but with the 2020 Olympics delayed, will she get the chance to add to her total?

Find out more about Simone in the Hall of Fame section at **www.guinnessworldrecords.com/2021**

1: Simone blew away the competition at the 2016 Olympics, achieving the **highest margin of victory in an Olympic all-around final (female)** – 2.100.

2: At the US National Gymnastics Championships on 11 Aug 2019, Simone performed the **first triple-double in gymnastics competition**...

3: ... and also the **first double-double dismount on beam**, two days earlier.

4: Simone with her first Laureus World Sportswoman of the Year award in 2017.

5: Celebrating all-around gold at her first World Championships in 2013, aged 16.

Simone is a three-time winner of the Laureus World Sports Award for Sportswoman of the Year (2019 and 2020). She is one of three female athletes to claim the prestigious trophy more than once – in 2017 (pictured). Only tennis player Serena Williams (USA) has won more, with four (2003, 2010, 2016 and 2018) – the **most Laureus World Sportswoman of the Year awards.**

Bold entries in the index indicate a main entry on a subject; **BOLD CAPITALS** indicate an entire chapter

GWR 2021 has been compiled from applications from the public but also submissions from a global network of institutions and experts, whom we'd like to thank. Find a full list at www.guinnessworldrecords. com/about-us/partners.

8000ers.com
Eberhard Jurgalski has developed the system of "Elevation Equality", a method of classifying mountain ranges and peaks. His website has become the main source of altitude statistics for the Himalayas and Karakoram ranges.

American Society of Ichthyologists and Herpetologists
The ASIH was founded in 1913 and is dedicated to the scientific study of fishes, amphibians and reptiles. It aims to increase knowledge about these organisms and to support young scientists in these fields.

Archaeology in the Community
Established by Dr Alexandra Jones, this not-for-profit – based in Washington, DC, USA – promotes the study and public understanding of archaeological heritage through informal educational programmes and community events.

Berkeley Seismology Lab
Professor Michael Manga is chair of Earth and Planetary Science at UC Berkeley – also home of the Berkeley Seismology Lab – in California, USA. He specializes in volcanic eruptions and geysers on Earth and other planets.

British Microlight Aircraft Association
Approved by the Civil Aviation Authority, the BMAA looks after the interests of microlight pilots and enthusiasts in the UK. It is chaired by Rob Hughes, who is also 1st Vice-President to the FAI Microlight & Paramotor Commission.

CANNA UK National Giant Vegetables Championship
Every September, Martyn Davis welcomes expert growers to the Malvern Autumn Show held in Worcestershire, UK. Martyn ensures all the vegetables comply with the strict criteria and are measured appropriately.

Channel Swimming Association
The CSA supports swimmers with the logistics of crossing the Strait of Dover and has been the governing body of Channel swimming since 1927. The CSA only ratifies swims that are conducted under its rules and that are accompanied by its observers.

Council on Tall Buildings and Urban Habitat
Based in Chicago, Illinois, USA, the Council on Tall Buildings and Urban Habitat is the world's leading resource for professionals focused on the design, construction and operation of tall buildings and future cities.

Desert Research Institute
Dr Nick Lancaster is Research Professor Emeritus of the DRI in Nevada, USA, where his specialisms are desert geomorphology and the impacts of climate change on desert regions.

DogFest
DogFest is the UK's ultimate summer festival for dogs, held each year at three locations. Visitors can get involved in activities including dock diving and flyball. In 2019, GWR attended the event with its live "Record Barkers" show to scout for new canine talent.

ESPN X Games
Since its inception in 1995, ESPN's X Games have become the leading action-sports competition, spotlighting the world's best action-sports athletes in BMX, skateboard and Moto X in the summer as well as the crème de la crème of skiing, snowboarding and snowmobiling at its winter events.

Foundation for Environmental Education
With members in 77 countries, the Denmark-headquartered FEE is the world's largest organization of its kind. Its globally recognized Green Key and Blue Flag initiatives promote the protection of natural resources.

Gareth Jones' Lab
GJL conducts research on ecology, conservation biology and animal behaviour, with a particular focus on bats. Professor Jones has published around 300 scientific papers; his work ranges from acoustics to tracking animal movements.

Gerontology Research Group
Established in 1990, the GRG's mission is to slow and ultimately reverse ageing via the application and sharing of scientific knowledge. It also keeps the largest database of supercentenarians (people aged 110+), a division that is managed by Robert Young.

Great Pumpkin Commonwealth
The GPC cultivates the growing of giant pumpkins – as well as other prodigious produce – by establishing universal standards and regulations that ensure quality of fruit and fairness of competition across the world.

International Ice Swimming Association
Founded by Ram Barkai, the IISA was formed in 2009 with a vision to formalize swimming in icy water. It has put in place a set of rules to allow for maximum safety measures and to regulate swim integrity in terms of distance, time and conditions.

International Mineralogical Association
The IMA consists of 39 member societies across six continents. Its mandate ranges from streamlining the nomenclature and classification of minerals to the preservation of mineralogical heritage.

International Ornithologists' Union
The IOU is a member-supported global organization dedicated to research in avian biology from ecosystems to molecules, linking basic and applied research, and nurturing education and outreach. Its current president, tenured between 2018 and 2022, is Dr Dominique Homberger.

International Slackline Association
The ISA aims to support and develop slackline communities of all sizes, as well as providing governance for slacklining as a competitive sport.

International Society of Limnology
Founded in 1922, SIL is devoted to the study of inland waters (e.g., lakes, rivers and inland seas), with some 1,250 members from 70 countries. Dr Tamar Zohary has been General Secretary-Treasurer since 2013.

IUCN SSC Small Mammal Specialist Group
The Small Mammal Specialist Group (part of the International Union for Conservation of Nature) is a global network of scientists and conservationists who share a passion for rodents, shrews, moles, hedgehogs and tree shrews.

IUCN World Commission on Protected Areas
The IUCN's WCPA is the world's premier network of protected-area expertise. Administered by IUCN's Global Programme on Protected Areas, it boasts more than 2,500 members, spanning 140 countries.

Marine Megafauna Foundation
The MMF was created in 2009 to research, protect and conserve the populations of threatened marine megafauna around the world. Ocean giants that fall under its remit include whales, sharks, rays and sea turtles.

Metacritic
Since 2001, Metacritic has distilled opinions from the world's most respected and reliable entertainment critics into an easy-to-understand rating for films, music, games and TV.

MonumentalTrees.com
Tim Bekaert is the administrator of MonumentalTrees.com, a community website listing thousands of girth and height measurements for noteworthy trees, as well as photos and location details of otherwise undocumented remarkable specimens.

National Museum of Computing
The National Museum of Computing at Bletchley Park in Oxfordshire, UK, is an independent charity housing a vast collection of functional historic computers such as *Colossus*, the **first code-breaking computer**, and the **oldest working digital computer**, the *WITCH*.

National Oceanic and Atmospheric Administration
NOAA's reach extends from the surface of the Sun to the depths of the ocean floor as it works to keep the public informed of the changing environment around them. Its scope ranges from daily weather forecasts and severe storm warnings to coastal restoration and marine-commerce support.

National Pet Show
The UK's National Pet Show is an annual event held each November at the National Exhibition Centre in Birmingham. It's attended by all manner of domestic animal professionals, including those with expertise in dogs, cats, birds, reptiles, rodents, livestock and even insects.

National Speleological Society
The NSS is a non-profit membership organization dedicated to the scientific study, exploration, protection and conservation of caves and karst.

Natural History Museum Vienna
Dr Ludovic Ferrière is a geologist and expert on meteorites and impact craters. He is chief curator of the prestigious meteorite and impactite collections at the Natural History Museum Vienna in Austria.

Ocean Rowing Society
The ORS was established in 1983 by Kenneth F Crutchlow and Peter Bird, later joined by Tom Lynch and Tatiana Rezvaya-Crutchlow. The organization documents all attempts to row the oceans and major bodies of water, and classifies, verifies and adjudicates ocean-rowing achievements.

Parrot Analytics
Parrot Analytics is the leading global content demand analytics company for the modern multi-platform TV business. The company currently tracks more than 1.5 billion daily expressions of demand in over 100 languages.

Paul Zimnisky Diamond Analytics
Paul Zimnisky is a leading global diamond industry analyst. His research is used by financial institutions, governments and universities.

Roller Coaster DataBase
The RCDB is a repository of theme-park statistics started by Duane Marden in 1996. It now features more than 5,000 rollercoasters. GWR is kept "in the loop" by RCDB researcher Justin Garvanovic.

Royal Botanic Gardens, Kew
Kew Gardens in London, UK, is a world-famous scientific organization, globally respected for its outstanding collections as well as its scientific expertise in plant diversity, conservation and sustainable development. It was accredited as a UNESCO World Heritage Site in 2003.

School of Ants Australia
Dr Kirsti Abbott is an ant ecologist who runs School of Ants in Australia, a citizen-science project that aims to document the diversity and distribution of ants in urban landscapes.

Scott Polar Research Institute
The SPRI of Cambridge University, UK, was formed in 1920 as a memorial to those who died during Captain Scott's 1910–13 South Pole expedition. Its resources, including a vast library, cover the entire Arctic and Antarctic.

Speedrun.com
Speedrun.com provides leaderboards, resources, forums and more for speedrunning – the act of playing a videogame with the intent of completing it as quickly as possible. The site has amassed a database of more than 930,000 runs across 16,648 games.

The Cornell Lab
Directed by Dr Holger Klinck, the Center for Conservation Bioacoustics at The Cornell Lab of Ornithology in Ithaca, New York, USA, is a team of scientists, engineers and students working on a wide variety of terrestrial, aquatic and marine bioacoustic research projects.

The H J Lutcher Stark Center for Physical Culture & Sports
Based at the University of Texas in Austin, USA, the Stark Center is directed by Professor Jan Todd and houses the world's foremost collection dedicated to physical culture.

The International Cat Association
TICA® is the world's largest genetic registry of pedigreed and household pet cats. It supports the health and welfare of all domestic cats through education, and promotes proper care to the owners of millions of cats worldwide.

The Numbers
The-Numbers.com is the web's biggest database of cinema box-office information, with figures on more than 38,000 movies and 160,000 people in the film industry. It was founded in 1997 by Bruce Nash and is visited by more than 8 million people every year.

UK Timing Association
The UKTA was established in 2013 when personnel from Straightliners Ltd and SPEE3D Ltd joined forces to enhance and promote land-speed record-breaking in Britain and Europe. It ensures that land-speed contenders can compete under all governances.

University College London: The Bartlett School of Architecture
Iain Borden is Professor of Architecture & Urban Culture at The Bartlett School at UCL London, UK. He has authored more than 100 books and articles, including numerous titles on architects, buildings and cities.

University of Liverpool: Integrative Genomics of Ageing Group
Dr João Pedro de Magalhães leads the Integrative Genomics of Ageing Group at the UK's University of Liverpool, focusing on the genetic, cellular and molecular mechanisms of ageing. He also manages the AnAge database, logging the oldest animals in captivity.

University of Southern California
Primatologist Dr Craig Stanford is the Professor of Anthropology and Biological Sciences at the University of Southern California, USA. He has conducted field research on primates in East Africa, Asia and South America.

VGChartz
Established in 2005 by Brett Walton, VGChartz is a business intelligence and research firm. It publishes over 7,000 unique weekly estimates relating to videogaming hardware and software sales, and hosts an ever-expanding game database with over 40,000 titles.

Whale and Dolphin Conservation
WDC is the leading global charity dedicated to the conservation and protection of whales and dolphins. It defends cetaceans against the threats they face through campaigns, lobbying, advising governments, conservation projects, field research and rescue.

World Cube Association
The WCA governs competitions for mechanical puzzles that are operated by twisting groups of pieces, such as the Rubik's Cube. Its mission is to have more competitions in more countries with more people, all participating under fair and equal conditions.

World Memory Sports Council
The mind sport of memory was founded in 1991 by Tony Buzan and Raymond Keene OBE. The 10 disciplines which formed the basis of the first competition have since been adopted worldwide as the basis for all competitive memory contests.

World Meteorological Organization
Dr Randall Cerveny is a President's Professor in Geographical Sciences who specializes in weather and climate. He has held the position of Rapporteur of Weather and Climate Extremes for the WMO since 2007.

World Open Water Swimming Association
Founded by Steven Munatones in 2005, WOWSA is the international governing body for the sport of open-water swimming. It provides membership and certification programmes as well as publications and online resources.

World Sailing Speed Record Council
The WSSRC was recognized by the International Yacht Racing Union (now World Sailing) in 1972. The council of experts draws members from Australia, France, Great Britain and the USA.

World Sport Stacking Association
As the official global governing body for the fast-paced pastime of sport stacking, the WSSA promotes the standardization and advancement of the discipline's rules, records and events.

World Surf League
The WSL is dedicated to celebrating the world's best surfing on the best waves. It has been championing competitive surfing since 1976, running more than 180 global events annually.

World UltraCycling Association
WUCA (formerly known as UMCA) is a non-profit organization dedicated to supporting ultra-cycling across the world. It holds the largest repository of cycling records for all bike types and certifies records for its members.

ZSL Institute of Zoology
The Institute of Zoology is the academic research division of the Zoological Society of London in the UK. It is a world-renowned research centre at the cutting edge of conservation science.

Solar System
Claire Andreoli, Mark Aston, Ravi Kumar Kopparapu, Timur Kryachko, Catherine l'Hostis & Marc Fulconis, Jonathan McDowell, Carolyn Porco, Peter Schultz, Scott S Sheppard

Natural World
Nikolai Aladin, Andrew Baldwin, Nellie Barnett, Michael Caldwell, Anton Chakhmouradian, Karen Chin, Peter Clarkson, Gerardo Aguirre Diaz, Wenyuan Fan, Rory Flood, Mike Fromm, Robert Headland, Vincent Johan van Hinsberg, Robert Holzworth, Dan Laffoley, Mathieu Morlighem, David Peterson, Simon Poppinga, Stephen Pyne, Alan Robock, Ryan Said, Marc Schallenberg, Roger Seymour, John Sinton, Jon Slate, John Smellie, David J Smith, Thomas Speck, Chris Stokes, Brian Toon, Maximillian Van Wyk De Vries, Paul Williams

Animals
Tycho Anker-Nilssen, Joseph Bump, Chris Carbone, Dan Challender, William Crampton, Phil Currie, Dyan deNapoli, Tanya Detto, Coen Elemans, Christo Fabricius, Peter Flood, Eva Fuglei, Semyon Grigoriev, Adam Hartstone-Rose, Matthew Hayward, Jutta Heuer, Craig Hilton-Taylor, Dominique Homberger, Blanca Huertas, Simon Ingram, Paul Johnsgard, Stephen Kajiura, Alec Lackmann, Robin Moule, Christopher Murray, Mark O'Shea, Aniruddh D Patel, W Scott Persons, Robert Pitman, Grigory Potapov, Liz Sandeman, Kate Sanders, Karl P N Shuker, Heather Sohl, Katharina Sperling, Arnaud Tarroux, Samuel Turvey, Oliver Wearn, Richard Weigl, Becky Williams, Alan Wilson, Harald Wolf, Trevor Worthy, Jhala Yadvendradev

Humans
Edward Bell, Donald Rau, Nancy Segal, Kira Westaway, Robert Young

Recordmania / Against the Clock
Andrew Aldridge, Martyn Davis, Todd Kline, Ian Woodcock

Adventurers
Ned Denison, Thaneswar Guragai, Rob Hughes, Steve Jones, Pádraig Mallon, Richard Meredith-Hardy, David Monks, Larry Oslund

Culture & Society
Amanda Abrell, Stuart Ackland, Alexis Albion, Alaia Berriozabal, Aliza Bran, Lauren Clement, Mike Dunn, Marshall Gerometta, Sophie Bachet Granados, Hannah Hess, Ioanna Iordanou, Alexandra Jones, Darren Julien, "Matt L", Peter Marsters, Valerie Miller, Chris Moran, Alistair Pike, Harro Ranter, Barry Roche, Monique Turner

Pop Culture / Gaming
Dick Fiddy, Jane Klain, Dan Peel, James Proud, Matthew White

Technology
Evan Ackerman, Michael Blakemore, Inge Buytaert, Martin Campbell-Kelly, Jessie Clark, Nigel Crowe, Stephen Fleming, Justin Garvanovic, Andrew Good, Veselin Kostov, Judi Lalor, Beck Lockwood, Beatriz Alcalá López, Sam Mason, Fran Read, Gary Settles, Jules Tipler, Richard Wynne, Hua Zhao

Sports
Tom Beckerlegge, Grace Coryell, David Fischer, Matthew White

ACKNOWLEDGEMENTS

Editor-in-Chief
Craig Glenday

Layout Editors
Tom Beckerlegge,
Rob Dimery

Managing Editor
Adam Millward

Editor
Ben Hollingum

**Proofreading
& fact-checking**
Matthew White

**Head of Publishing
& Book Production**
Jane Boatfield

**Head of Pictures
& Design**
Fran Morales

Picture Researcher
Alice Jessop

Design
Paul Wylie-Deacon
and Rob Wilson
at 55design.co.uk

Production Director
Patricia Magill

Production Coordinator
Thomas McCurdy

Production Consultants
Roger Hawkins,
Florian Seyfert

Cover Design
Rod Hunt

Indexer
Marie Lorimer

Head of Visual Content
Michael Whitty

Original Photography
Mustapha Azab,
Adam Bettcher,
Michael Bowles,
Peter Gaunt,
Paul Michael Hughes,
Craig Mitchelldyer,
Johanna Morales
Rodríguez,
Kevin Scott Ramos,
Alex Rumford

Reprographics
Res Kahraman at
Born Group

Printing & Binding
MOHN Media Mohndruck
GmbH, Gütersloh,
Germany

British Library Cataloguing-in-publication data: a
catalogue record for this book is available from the British
Library
UK: 978-1-913484-01-9
US: 978-1-913484-00-2
US PB: 978-1-913484-02-6
Middle East: 978-1-913484-05-7
Australia: 978-1-913484-07-1

Records are made to be broken – indeed, it is one of the
key criteria for a record category – so if you find a record
that you think you can beat, tell us about it by making
a record claim. Always contact us before making a
record attempt.

Check www.guinnessworldrecords.com regularly
for record-breaking news, plus video footage of record
attempts. You can also join and interact with the Guinness
World Records online community.

Sustainability
The trees that are harvested to print *Guinness World
Records 2021* are carefully selected from managed
forests to avoid the devastation of the landscape.

The paper contained within this edition is
manufactured by Stora Enso Veitsiluoto,
Finland. The production site is PEFC Chain-
of-Custody certified and operates within
environmental systems certificated to ISO
14001 to ensure sustainable production.

PEFC/04-31-1033

minus
52%
CO$_2$

Thanks to innovative use of combined heat and power
technology, up to 52% less CO$_2$ was emitted in printing this
product when compared with conventional energy use.

  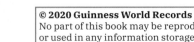 

OFFICIALLY
AMAZING

THE JIM PATTISON GROUP

Global President: Alistair Richards
Governance
Alison Ozanne
Finance: Jusna Begum, Elizabeth
Bishop, Jess Blake, Lisa Gibbs, Lucy
Hyland, Kimberley Jones, Maryana
Lovell, Sutha Ramachandran,
Jamie Sheppard, Scott Shore,
Andrew Wood
Legal: Raymond Marshall, Kaori
Minami, Mehreen Moghul
**People, Culture & Office
Management:** Jackie Angus,
Alexandra Ledin, Stephanie Lunn,
Swarna Pillai, Monika Tilani
IT & Operations
Rob Howe
Data Analytics: Kevin Allen
Digital Technology: Veronica Irons,
Alex Waldu
IT: Céline Bacon, Manu Bassi, John
Cvitanovic, Diogo Gomes, Karen
Lean, Benjamin Mclean, Cenk
Selim, Alpha Serrant-Defoe
Central Record Services: Lewis
Blakeman, Adam Brown, Megan
Bruce, Betsy Cunnett, Tara
El Kashef, Mark McKinley, Sheila
Mella Suárez, Will Munford, Emma
Salt, Will Sinden, Luke Wakeham,
Dave Wilson

Content & Product
Katie Forde
Brand & Product Management:
Lucy Acfield, Juliet Dawson,
Rebecca Lam, Emily Osborn,
Louise Toms
Demand Generation:
James Alexander-Dann
Design: Fran Morales, Alisa Zaytseva
Visual Content: Sam Birch-Machin,
Karen Gilchrist, Jesse Hargrave,
Matthew Musson, Joseph O'Neil,
Catherine Pearce, Alan Pixsley,
Jonathan Whitton, Michael Whitty
Website & Social Content:
Aitana Marín, Dominic Punt,
Connie Suggitt, Dan Thorne

Corporate Communications
Sam Fay, Doug Male

Creative
Paul O'Neill

Publishing
Nadine Causey
Editorial: Craig Glenday,
Ben Hollingum, Adam Millward

Marketing: Nicholas Brookes,
Lauren Johns
PR: Jessica Dawes, Amber-
Georgina Gill, Jessica Spillane
Production: Jane Boatfield,
Patricia Magill, Thomas McCurdy
Sales: Helene Navarre, Joel Smith

Beijing Consultancy
Marco Frigatti
Brand & Content Marketing:
Echo Zhan
Client Account Services:
Catherine Gao, Chloe Liu, Tina
Ran, Amelia Wang, Elaine Wang,
Ivy Wang, Jin Yu
Commercial Marketing: Theresa
Gao, Lorraine Lin, Karen Pan
Event Production: Fay Jiang,
Reggy Lu
Legal: Paul Nightingale, Jiayi Teng
**People, Culture & Office
Management:** Crystal Xu, Joan
Zhong, Nina Zhou
PR: Yvonne Zhang
Records Management: Ted Li,
Vanessa Tao, Charles Wharton,
Angela Wu, Alicia Zhao

Dubai Consultancy
Talal Omar
Brand & Content Marketing:
Mohamad Kaddoura
Client Account Services: Naser
Batat, Mohammad Kiswani,
Kamel Yassin
Commercial Marketing:
Shaddy Gaad
Event Production: Daniel Hickson
**People, Culture & Office
Management:** Monisha Bimal
PR: Hassan Alibrahim
Records Management: Reem
Al Ghussain, Karen Hamzeh

London Consultancy
Neil Foster
Client Account Services:
Nicholas Adams, Tom Albrecht,
Sonia Chadha-Nihal, Fay Edwards,
Soma Huy, Irina Nohailic,
Sam Prosser, Nikhil Shukla
Event Production:
Fiona Gruchy-Craven
Commercial Marketing:
Stine McNeillis, Iliyan Stoychev,
Amanda Tang
PR: Lisa Lambert
Records Management:
Andrew Fanning, Matilda Hagne,

Paul Hillman, Daniel Kidane,
Christopher Lynch, Francesca Raggi

Miami Consultancy
Carlos Martinez
Client Account Services:
John David, Carolina
Guanabara-Hall, Ralph Hannah,
Jaime Rodriguez
Commercial Marketing: Laura
Angel, Luisa Fernanda Sanchez
PR: Alice Pagán
Records Management: Raquel
Assis, Maria Fernanda De la Vega
Diaz, Joana Weiss

New York Consultancy
Alistair Richards
Brand & Content Marketing:
Nick Adams, Michael Furnari,
Claire Elise Stephens, Kristen
Stephenson
Client Account Services:
Mackenzie Berry, Brittany
Carpenter, Justin Frable, Danielle
Levy, Nicole Pando, Kim Partrick,
Michelle Santucci
Commercial Marketing: Billy
George, Morganna Nickoff,
Jete' Roach, Rachel Silver
Event Production: Dan Reyes
**People, Culture & Office
Management:** Jennifer Olson
PR: Rachel Gluck, Amanda Marcus,
Liz Montoya
Records Management:
Spencer Cammarano, Chrissy
Fernandez, Maddison Kulish,
Ryan Masserano, Hannah Ortman,
Callie Smith, Kaitlin Vesper

Tokyo Consultancy
Kaoru Ishikawa
Brand & Content Marketing:
Masakazu Senda
Client Account Services:
Minami Ito, Wei Liang, Takuro
Maruyama, Yumiko Nakagawa,
Masamichi Yazaki
Commercial Marketing:
Momoko Cunneen, Aya McMillan,
Hiroyuki Tanaka, Eri Yuhira
Event Production: Yuki Uebo
**People, Culture & Office
Management:** Emiko Yamamoto
PR: Kazami Kamioka
Records Management:
Aki Ichikawa, Mai McMillan,
Momoko Omori, Naomi-Emily Sakai,
Koma Satoh, Lala Teranishi

Picture credits

1 Paul Michael Hughes/GWR; **2** Rod Hunt, Shutterstock, Paul Michael Hughes/GWR; **3** Paul Michael Hughes/GWR, Shutterstock, Alamy, Getty, Hake's Auctions; **4 (UK)** Neal Street Productions/BBC One, Dymond/Thames/Syco/Shutterstock; **4 (US)** Lorenzo Bevilaqua/ABC Entertainment; **5 (AUS/NZ)** John Gadsby/Capture the Light Photography; **5 (MENA)** Emirates Airlines; **5 (UK)** Orchard; **5 (US)** Hulu, Getty; **6 (AUS/NZ)** Alamy, Shutterstock; **6 (UK & US)** Sonja Horsman/GWR, Paul Michael Hughes/GWR; **7 (AUS & NZ)** Ben Beaden/Australia Zoo; **7 (MENA)** The Cool Box Studio, Hywell Waters/Warner Bros., Warner Bros.; **7 (UK & US)** Getty, TikTok, Shutterstock, Emma Sohl/Capture the Light Photography; **8** Rod Hunt, Brett D. Meister; **9** Michael Bowles/GWR; **10** Shutterstock, Alamy; **11** The Lions Share, Olin Feuerbacher/USFWS, Alamy, Shutterstock; **12** Shutterstock; **14** NASA/JPL, NASA, NASA/USGS/Arizona State University/Carnegie Institution of Washington/JHUAPL; **15** JAXA/ISAS/DARTS/Damia Bouic, RISDE, Shutterstock, JPL/NASA; **16** Glenn Schneider, Gregory H. Revera, NASA, Paul van Hoeydonck, Shutterstock; **18** NASA/JPL-Caltech/University of Arizona, NASA/JPL/USGS, Shutterstock, NASA; **19** ESA/DLR/FU Berlin, NASA/Goddard Space Flight Center Scientific Visualization Studio, NASA/JPL/Cornell University, Maas Digital LLC; **20** NASA/JPL, NASA/JPL/DLR, NASA/ESA & John T. Clark; **21** NASA/JPL, NASA, NASA/JPL-Caltech/SwRI/MSSS/Gerald Eichstädt, Seán Doran; **22** NASA/JPL-Caltech/Space Science Institute, Scott S. Sheppard; **23** NASA/JPL-Caltech Space Science, NASA/JPL, NASA/JPL-Caltech/Space Science Institute, NASA/JPL/Space Science Institute; **24** NASA/JPL-Caltech, NASA/JPL/USGS, NASA/JPL/Kevin M. Gill/Jason Major, Alamy, NASA/JPL; **25** NASA/JPL, NASA; **26** JAXA, NASA, ESA; **27** NASA/Johns Hopkins Applied Physics Laboratory, Yulia Zhulikova, NASA/ESA/D. Jewitt/J. DePasquale, Shutterstock; **28** Ranald Mackechnie/GWR, NASA; **29** Christina Korp; **30–31** Shutterstock; **32** Getty, Alamy, Shutterstock, Expedition with Steve Backshall, UKTV Dave; **33** Alamy, Shutterstock; **34** Shutterstock, Alamy; **35** Alamy, Shutterstock; **36** Shutterstock, Yuzhen Yan/Department of Geosciences, Princeton University, Alamy; **37** NASA, Christian Pondella/Red Bull Content Pool, NWS Aberdeen, SD, Alamy; **38** Getty, Alamy, NOAA; **39** Anton Yankovyi, NASA, Getty, Shutterstock; **40** Alamy, Shutterstock, Getty; **41** Getty, Alamy, Shutterstock; **42** Lou Jost, Alamy; **43** Shutterstock, MFdeS, Alamy; **44** Alamy; **45** Shutterstock; **46** Rod Hunt, Alamy, Shutterstock, Getty; **47** Pavel Novak; **48–49** Ben Beaden/Australia Zoo; **50** Alamy, Shutterstock; **51** A. Fifis/Ifremer, B. Trapp/agefotostock, Alamy, Shutterstock, Rod Hunt; **52** Shutterstock, Alamy; **53** Getty, Alamy, Rod Hunt, Shutterstock; **54** Alamy, Shutterstock, Getty; **55** Charles J. Sharp, Shutterstock, Alamy; **56** Alamy, Shutterstock; **57** Alamy, Mark V. Erdmann/BluePlanetArchive.com, Shutterstock; **58** Alamy, Shutterstock; **59** Erin Buxton, Alamy, Shutterstock; **60** Anthony Thillien, Paul Michael Hughes/GWR, Shutterstock, Alamy; **61** Alamy, Shutterstock; **62** Rod Hunt; **63** Kevin Scott Ramos/GWR; **64** Shutterstock, Matthias Wittlinger/Ulm University, Alamy; **65** Amanda Kelley, Anselmo d'Affonseca/Instituto Nacional de Pesquisas da Amazônia; **66** Jane Goodall Institute, Robert Ratzer, Shutterstock, Michael Neugebauer, Alamy; **68–69** Kevin Scott Ramos/GWR, Rod Hunt; **70** Getty, Shutterstock; **71** College of Physicians of Philadelphia, SWNS, Shutterstock; **72** Kevin Scott Ramos/GWR, James Ellerker/GWR, Getty, Paul Michael Hughes/GWR; **73** Getty, Shutterstock; **74** Kevin Scott Ramos/GWR, James Ellerker/GWR, Rod Hunt, Getty; **75** Ranald Mackechnie/GWR, Lorne Campbell/Guzelian, Paul Michael Hughes/GWR; **76** Tom Stromme/Tribune, Paul Michael Hughes/GWR, Getty, Rod Hunt; **77** Richard Bradbury/GWR, Maria Elisa Duque/GWR, Johanna Morales Rodríguez/GWR, Getty; **78** Paul Michael Hughes/GWR; **79** Paul Michael Hughes/GWR; **80** Getty, Ryan Schude/GWR; **81** Alamy, Shutterstock; **83** Getty, Adam Bettcher/GWR, Rod Hunt; **84** John Wright/GWR, Paul Michael Hughes/GWR; **85** Dinore Aniruddhasingh, Daw Photography; **86–87** Paul Michael Hughes/GWR; **88** Ranald Mackechnie/GWR, Shutterstock; **89** Paul Michael Hughes/GWR; **90** Paul Michael Hughes/GWR; **91** Paul Michael Hughes/GWR, Eigil Korsager, Shutterstock; **92** Richard Bradbury/GWR; **93** Paul Michael Hughes/GWR; **94** Mustapha Azab/GWR, Rod Hunt; **95** Paul Michael Hughes/GWR, Shutterstock; **96** Alamy, Paul Michael Hughes/GWR, Getty, Rod Hunt; **97** Kevin Scott Ramos/GWR, Paul Michael Hughes/GWR, John Wright/GWR; **98–99** Kevin Scott Ramos/GWR; **100** Alamy, Stuart Purfield; **101** Shutterstock, Rod Hunt; **102** Harald Stampfer, Paul Michael Hughes/GWR; **103** Paul Michael Hughes/GWR; **104** Shutterstock; **105** Shutterstock; **108** Kevin Scott Ramos/GWR; **109** Shutterstock; **110** Ryan Schude/GWR, John Wright/GWR; **111** Unrah Jones/Courtesy Sotheby's, SCP Auctions, Alamy, Kevin Scott Ramos/GWR; **112** Marialivia Sciacca; **113** Shutterstock; **114** Katie Klercker; **115** Josef Holic, Alex Rumford/GWR; **116** Paul Fishwick; **117** Drew Gardner/GWR, Miguel Quintanilla; **120** Tom Lovelock/Silverhub for Prudential RideLondon, Alp Baranok, Paul Michael Hughes/GWR, Rod Hunt; **122** Getty, Shattner Kanjiranthigal Joy, Richard Bradbury/GWR, Rod Hunt; **123** Getty; **124** Shutterstock, Getty; **126–27** Getty; **128** Alamy, Fabio Buitrago, Reuters, Getty, Shutterstock; **129** Ratno Sardi/Griffith University, Maxime Aubert, SWNS, Shutterstock; **130** Rod Hunt; **131** Alamy, Shutterstock; **132** MIT Architecture Machine Group, Germanisches Nationalmuseum, Shutterstock; **133** Rod Hunt, Bridgeman Images, Shutterstock; **135** Getty, Mark Bowen/Scripps National Spelling Bee, Kevin Scott Ramos/GWR, Shutterstock, Rod Hunt; **136** USAF, Getty; **137** The History Center, Central Intelligence Agency, Shutterstock; **138** NOAA, Alamy, Getty, Shutterstock; **139** Reuters, Getty, Shutterstock, Alamy; **140** Rod Hunt, Shutterstock, Manistee Fire Dept., Getty; **141** Alamy, Shutterstock; **142** The Trustees of the Natural History Museum, *TIME*, Rod Hunt; **143** Getty, Shutterstock, Alamy; **144** Rod Hunt, Shutterstock, Chris Garrison, Lotus Eyes Photography; **146** Alamy, Shutterstock; **147** Shutterstock; **148** SWNS, Kelvin Trautman, U.S. Air Force, Shutterstock; **149** Gabe Souza, Getty, NOAA, Shutterstock; **150** Alamy, Shutterstock; **151** Shutterstock, Alamy, Getty; **152** Ben Duffy, Shutterstock; **153** Shutterstock, Getty, Alamy; **154** Alamy, Getty; **155** Alamy, Shutterstock, Getty; **156** Rod Hunt, Shutterstock; **157** Dean Coopman, Shutterstock; **158** Adrian Lam, Getty, Shutterstock; **159** Talisker Whisky Atlantic Challenge/Atlantic Campaigns, Hamish Frost, Alamy, Tamara Stubbs; **160** The Five Deeps Expedition; **161** The Five Deeps Expedition, Rod Hunt; **162** JCB; **163** JCB; **164** Alamy, Shutterstock; **165** Shutterstock; **166** Richard Bradbury/GWR; **167** Volkswagen, Porsche, STE/Bart van Overbeeke, Shutterstock, Rod Hunt; **168** Shutterstock, NASA, Greenpoint Technologies; **169** Shutterstock, SS United States Conservancy; **170** Shutterstock; **171** Alamy, Shutterstock; **172** James Ellerker/GWR, Rod Hunt, Ranald Mackechnie/GWR, Paul Michael Hughes/GWR, Richard Bradbury/GWR; **173** Richard Bradbury/GWR, Paul Michael Hughes/GWR; **174** The Metropolitan Museum of Art; **175** Lingdong Huang, Pau Fabregat, ESO/C. Malin, EHT Collaboration; **176** Bloodhound LSR, Shutterstock, fotoswiss/cattaneo, JCB; **177** Paul Michael Hughes/GWR, Alamy, Rod Hunt; **178** Getty; **179** *Fortnite*; **180** Speedrun.com; **181** Shutterstock; **183** Alamy; **185** Getty, Matt Schmucker; **188** Riot Games, Rod Hunt, Shanghai Dragons; **190** Paul Michael Hughes/GWR, Alamy; **191** Paul Michael Hughes/GWR, Phil Penman/News Licensing, Shutterstock, Rod Hunt; **194** Brinkhoff-Mögenburg, Deen van Meer, Rod Hunt, Shutterstock, Alamy; **195** Alamy, Shutterstock; **196** Shutterstock, Alamy, Disney; **197** Shutterstock, Disney, Alamy; **198** Courtesy of Bonhams, Shutterstock, Alamy, Courtesy of RM Sotheby's; **199** Shutterstock, Courtesy of Profiles in History, Alamy, Courtesy of Bonhams; **200** Alamy, Getty, Shutterstock; **201** Denise Truscello, Shutterstock, Getty, Alamy; **202** Shutterstock, Alamy, Rod Hunt; **203** Shutterstock, Alamy; **204** Getty, Kevin Scott Ramos/GWR; **205** Getty, Shutterstock; **206** Rod Hunt, Getty, Shutterstock; **207** Shutterstock, Paul Michael Hughes/GWR; **208** Shutterstock, Will Wohler, Josh Withers, Getty; **209** Matthew Murphy, Getty; **210** Alamy; **211** Alamy; **212–13** Getty, Rod Hunt; **214** Getty, Shutterstock; **215** Shutterstock, Getty; **216** Alamy, Shutterstock, Getty; **217** Shutterstock, Getty; **218** Shutterstock, Getty; **219** Alamy, Shutterstock, Getty; **220** Getty, Shutterstock; **221** Getty, Alamy, Shutterstock; **222** Shutterstock; **223** Shutterstock, Getty; **224** Getty, Shutterstock; **225** Getty, Alamy; **226** Shutterstock, Getty, Alamy; **227** NHRA, Getty, Gold and Goose/LAT Images, Alamy; **228** ISSF Sports, Alamy, Alan Petersime, Getty; **229** Getty, Shutterstock; **230** Getty, Alamy; **231** D. Echelard, Getty, Shutterstock; **232** IAU, Athletics Australia, Shutterstock; **233** Shutterstock, Alamy; **234** Alamy, Shutterstock; **235** Marius van de Leur, Getty, Alamy, Alex St. Jean; **236** Getty, World Para Ice Hockey, Shutterstock; **237** Alamy, Shutterstock; **238** Getty, Shutterstock, Simon Wilkinson/SWpix.com; **239** ESPN Images; **240** Getty, Matias Capizzano, IWF, Alamy; **241** Getty, Dean Treml/Red Bull Content Pool; **242** Alamy, Shutterstock; **243** Alamy, Shutterstock; **244** Rod Hunt; **246** Rod Hunt; **248** Rod Hunt; **252** Rod Hunt

Official adjudicators

Camila Borenstain, Joanne Brent, Jack Brockbank, Sarah Casson, Dong Cheng, Swapnil Dangarikar, Casey DeSantis, Brittany Dunn, Kanzy El Defrawy, Michael Empric, Pete Fairbairn, Victor Fenes, Christina Flounders Conlon, Fumika Fujibuchi, Ahmed Gabr, John Garland, Andrew Glass, Sofia Greenacre, Iris Hou, Louis Jelinek, Andrea Karidis, Kazuyoshi Kirimura, Lena Kuhlmann, Maggie Luo, Solvej Malouf, Mike Marcotte, Ma Mengjia, Shaifali Mishra, Rishi Nath, Anna Orford, Kellie Parise, Pravin Patel, Justin Patterson, Glenn Pollard, Natalia Ramirez, Stephanie Randall, Cassie Ren, Susana Reyes, Philip Robertson, Paulina Sapinska, Tomomi Sekioka, Hiroaki Shino, Lucia Sinigagliesi, Tyler Smith, Brian Sobel, Richard Stenning, Şeyda Subaşı Gemici, Carlos Tapia Rosas, Lorenzo Veltri, Xiong Wen, Peter Yang

Acknowledgements

55 Design Ltd (Hayley Wylie-Deacon, Tobias Wylie-Deacon, Rueben Wylie-Deacon, Linda Wylie, Vidette Burniston, Lewis Burniston), After Party Studios (Richard Mansell, Callum McGinley, Joshua Barrett, Matt Hart, Ben Doyle), Agent Fox Media (Rick Mayston), Ahrani Logan, Alexandra Boanta, Andrew Davies, ATN Event Staffing US, Banijay Germany (Steffen Donsbach, Sven Meurer, Sina Oschmann), Banijay Group (Carlotta Rossi Spencer, Joris Gijsbertse, Elodie Hannedouche), Banijay Italy (Gabriela Ventura, Esther Rem, Francesca De Gaetano, Maria Spreafico, David Torrisi, Giulia Arcano, Riccardo Favato, Alessandra Guerra, Giorgia Sonnino, Elena Traversa, Silvia Gambarana, Simona Frau, Silvia Gambarana, Popi Albera), Blue Kangaroo (Paul Richards), Brett Haase, Bruce Reynolds, Campaign UK (Sarah Virani), Canada Running Series, Codex Solutions Ltd, D&AD (Sammi Vaughan), Dan Biddle, Daniel Chalk, Dude Perfect, Entertainment Tonight, FJT Logistics Ltd (Ray Harper, Gavin Hennessy), Games Press, Georgia Young, Gianluca Schappei, Giraffe Insights (Maxine Fox and Sadie Buckingham), Gracie Lewis, Highlights, the Hilditch family (Lorraine, Mirren, Amber & Tony), ICM (Michael Kagan), Inspired Media (Liam Campbell), Integrated Colour Editions Europe Ltd (Roger Hawkins, Susie Hawkins), Jack Lewis, Jonathan Glazier, Jordan Hughes, LA Marathon (Rafael Sands), *Let's Make a Deal*, *Live with Kelly and Ryan* (Photos: David M. Russell, ABC Entertainment; Lorenzo Bevilaqua, ABC Entertainment; Andrea Lizcano, ABC Entertainment), Mariah Carey, Caesar's Palace (Photos: Denise Truscello), Mina Choe, Mohn Media (Theo Loechter, Fynn-Luca Lüttig, Christin Moeck, Jonas Schneider, Jeanette Sio, Reinhild Regragui), Normanno Pisani, Orchard TV (Robert Light, Adrian Jones, Rhidian Evans, Bleddyn Rhys), Orla Langton, Prestige Design, Production Suite (Beverley Williams), Rachael Greaves, Rebecca Buchanan-Smith, Ripley Entertainment (Steve Campbell, John Corcoran, Ryan DeSear, Suzanne DeSear, Megan Goldrick, Rick Richmond, Andy Taylor, Christie Coyle, William Anthony, Sophia Smith), Ripley's Believe It or Not! Times Square, Rob Partis, S4C (Rhodri ap Dyfrig, Tomos Hughes), Sally Wilkins, Science North (Guy Labine, Julie Moskalyk, Ashley Larose, Troy Rainville, Kirsti Kivinen, Michael Tremblay, Roger Brouillette, Emily Macdonald, Darla Stoddart, Bryen McGuire), Stora Enso Veitsiluoto, Tee Green, The Drum (Gordon Young), The Lion's Share, Todd McFarlane and Image Comics, United Nations Development Programme (Boaz Paldi), Victoria Grimsell, *Wheel of Fortune*, YouGov

Country codes

ABW	Aruba
AFG	Afghanistan
AGO	Angola
AIA	Anguilla
ALB	Albania
AND	Andorra
ANT	Netherlands Antilles
ARG	Argentina
ARM	Armenia
ASM	American Samoa
ATA	Antarctica
ATF	French Southern Territories
ATG	Antigua and Barbuda
AUS	Australia
AUT	Austria
AZE	Azerbaijan
BDI	Burundi
BEL	Belgium
BEN	Benin
BFA	Burkina Faso
BGD	Bangladesh
BGR	Bulgaria
BHR	Bahrain
BHS	The Bahamas
BIH	Bosnia and Herzegovina
BLR	Belarus
BLZ	Belize
BMU	Bermuda
BOL	Bolivia
BRA	Brazil
BRB	Barbados
BRN	Brunei Darussalam
BTN	Bhutan
BVT	Bouvet Island
BWA	Botswana
CAF	Central African Republic
CAN	Canada
CCK	Cocos (Keeling) Islands
CHE	Switzerland
CHL	Chile
CHN	China
CIV	Côte d'Ivoire
CMR	Cameroon
COD	Congo, DR of the
COG	Congo
COK	Cook Islands
COL	Colombia
COM	Comoros
CPV	Cape Verde
CRI	Costa Rica
CUB	Cuba
CXR	Christmas Island
CYM	Cayman Islands
CYP	Cyprus
CZE	Czech Republic
DEU	Germany
DJI	Djibouti
DMA	Dominica
DNK	Denmark
DOM	Dominican Republic
DZA	Algeria
ECU	Ecuador
EGY	Egypt
ERI	Eritrea
ESH	Western Sahara
ESP	Spain
EST	Estonia
ETH	Ethiopia
FIN	Finland
FJI	Fiji
FLK	Falkland Islands (Malvinas)
FRA	France
FRG	West Germany
FRO	Faroe Islands
FSM	Micronesia, Federated States
GAB	Gabon
GEO	Georgia
GHA	Ghana
GIB	Gibraltar
GIN	Guinea
GLP	Guadeloupe
GMB	Gambia
GNB	Guinea-Bissau
GNQ	Equatorial Guinea
GRC	Greece
GRD	Grenada
GRL	Greenland
GTM	Guatemala
GUF	French Guiana
GUM	Guam
GUY	Guyana
HKG	Hong Kong
HMD	Heard and McDonald Islands
HND	Honduras
HRV	Croatia (Hrvatska)
HTI	Haiti
HUN	Hungary
IDN	Indonesia
IND	India
IOT	British Indian Ocean Territory
IRL	Ireland
IRN	Iran
IRQ	Iraq
ISL	Iceland
ISR	Israel
ITA	Italy
JAM	Jamaica
JOR	Jordan
JPN	Japan
KAZ	Kazakhstan
KEN	Kenya
KGZ	Kyrgyzstan
KHM	Cambodia
KIR	Kiribati
KNA	Saint Kitts and Nevis
KOR	Korea, Republic of
KWT	Kuwait
LAO	Laos
LBN	Lebanon
LBR	Liberia
LBY	Libya
LCA	Saint Lucia
LIE	Liechtenstein
LKA	Sri Lanka
LSO	Lesotho
LTU	Lithuania
LUX	Luxembourg
LVA	Latvia
MAC	Macau
MAR	Morocco
MCO	Monaco
MDA	Moldova
MDG	Madagascar
MDV	Maldives
MEX	Mexico
MHL	Marshall Islands
MKD	North Macedonia
MLI	Mali
MLT	Malta
MMR	Myanmar (Burma)
MNE	Montenegro
MNG	Mongolia
MNP	Northern Mariana Islands
MOZ	Mozambique
MRT	Mauritania
MSR	Montserrat
MTQ	Martinique
MUS	Mauritius
MWI	Malawi
MYS	Malaysia
MYT	Mayotte
NAM	Namibia
NCL	New Caledonia
NER	Niger
NFK	Norfolk Island
NGA	Nigeria
NIC	Nicaragua
NIU	Niue
NLD	Netherlands
NOR	Norway
NPL	Nepal
NRU	Nauru
NZ	New Zealand
OMN	Oman
PAK	Pakistan
PAN	Panama
PCN	Pitcairn Islands
PER	Peru
PHL	Philippines
PLW	Palau
PNG	Papua New Guinea
POL	Poland
PRI	Puerto Rico
PRK	Korea, DPRO
PRT	Portugal
PRY	Paraguay
PYF	French Polynesia
QAT	Qatar
REU	Réunion
ROM	Romania
RUS	Russian Federation
RWA	Rwanda
SAU	Saudi Arabia
SDN	Sudan
SEN	Senegal
SGP	Singapore
SGS	South Georgia and South SS
SHN	Saint Helena
SJM	Svalbard and Jan Mayen Islands
SLB	Solomon Islands
SLE	Sierra Leone
SLV	El Salvador
SMR	San Marino
SOM	Somalia
SPM	Saint Pierre and Miquelon
SRB	Serbia
SSD	South Sudan
STP	São Tomé and Príncipe
SUR	Suriname
SVK	Slovakia
SVN	Slovenia
SWE	Sweden
SWZ	Swaziland
SYC	Seychelles
SYR	Syrian Arab Republic
TCA	Turks and Caicos Islands
TCD	Chad
TGO	Togo
THA	Thailand
TJK	Tajikistan
TKL	Tokelau
TKM	Turkmenistan
TMP	East Timor
TON	Tonga
TPE	Chinese Taipei
TTO	Trinidad and Tobago
TUN	Tunisia
TUR	Turkey
TUV	Tuvalu
TZA	Tanzania
UAE	United Arab Emirates
UGA	Uganda
UK	United Kingdom
UKR	Ukraine
UMI	US Minor Islands
URY	Uruguay
USA	United States of America
UZB	Uzbekistan
VAT	Vatican City
VCT	Saint Vincent and the Grenadines
VEN	Venezuela
VGB	Virgin Islands (British)
VIR	Virgin Islands (US)
VNM	Vietnam
VUT	Vanuatu
WLF	Wallis and Futuna Islands
WSM	Samoa
YEM	Yemen
ZAF	South Africa
ZMB	Zambia
ZWE	Zimbabwe

Stop Press

The following entries were approved and added to our database after the official closing date for this year's submissions.

Most football touches while wearing 5-kg ankle weights in one minute
On 1 Mar 2019, football freestyler Ben Nuttall (UK) performed 217 touches of a football in 60 sec while his feet were strapped with 5-kg (11-lb) ankle weights. The feat took place during a GWR Facebook Live event in London, UK.

Largest mobile-phone sentence
Realme (IND) spelled out the sentence "Proud to be young" using 1,024 cell phones in New Delhi, India, on 16 Mar 2019.

Largest dice word
Realty ONE Group (USA) recreated their "ONE" logo out of 11,111 dice at the MGM Grand Hotel in Las Vegas, Nevada, USA, on 25 Mar 2019. More than 200 employees contributed to the project, which took in excess of 100 hours to plan and approximately six hours to make.

Most nationalities in a soccer-training session
On 31 May 2019, Gazprom Football for Friendship (RUS) brought together soccer players from 57 nations to practise their skills in Madrid, Spain. The session took place on the day before the city hosted the Champions League final.

Tallest sandcastle
Skulptura Projects GmbH (DEU) sculpted a 17.65-m-tall (57-ft 11-in) sandcastle in Binz, Germany, on 5 Jun 2019.

Most consecutive fifties scored by a captain in an ICC World Cup tournament (male)
India's captain Virat Kohli posted five consecutive half-centuries during the 2019 Cricket World Cup in England and Wales between 9 and 30 Jun. His scores of 82 (vs. Australia), 77 (vs. Pakistan), 67 (vs. Afghanistan), 72 (vs. West Indies) and 66 (vs. England) helped him towards a total of 443 runs in nine matches.

Longest bathtub
Koop-Brinkmann GmbH (DEU) presented a bath 19.47 m (63 ft 10 in) long in Drebber, Germany, on 7 Jul 2019. A team of 20 people worked for more than two months in order to complete the titanic tub.

Largest guitar-effect pedal board
Sweetwater Sound and Rob Scallon (both USA) unveiled a board with 319 effects pedals in Fort Wayne, Indiana, USA, on 9 Jul 2019.

Highest vocal note (male)
Amirhossein Molaei (IRN) sang an F# in the eighth octave (F#8; 5,989 Hz) in Tehran, Iran, on 31 Jul 2019.

Most threshing machines operating simultaneously
François Latour (CAN) ran 243 threshing machines at once in St-Albert, Ontario, Canada, on 11 Aug 2019.

Largest orthopaedic cast
NorthShore Orthopaedic & Spine Institute (USA) displayed a 1.99-m³ (70.27-cu-ft) leg cast in Skokie, Illinois, USA, on 24 Aug 2019.

Most expensive cheese sold at auction
On 25 Aug 2019, the Regulatory Council DOP Cabrales (ESP) sold a block of Cabrales – a semi-hard, strong-tasting blue cheese – for €20,500 ($22,830; £18,572) in Asturias, Spain.

Most LED lights lit simultaneously
Iulius Town (ROM) arranged for a concert audience to illuminate 7,235 LED wristbands in Timişoara, Romania, on 31 Aug 2019.

Longest distance danced in a conga line
On 4 Sep 2019, a 10-person conga line danced 22.4 km (13.9 mi) in Bournemouth, Dorset, UK. The performers were Jonathan Dunne, Zoe Meaton, Jemma Finlay, Jo Bridle-Brown, Seb Ridout, Rachael Eastment, Mark Kearns, Heidi Dempsey, Janet Brassington and Sally Duckmanton (all UK).

Longest inner-tube/mat water slide
Outdoor adventure park Sim Leisure ESCAPE (MYS) unveiled a 1,111-m-long (3,645-ft) water slide in Penang, Malaysia, on 6 Sep 2019. The slide has been fitted with double rings so that two people can ride together.

Largest dog photoshoot
Nestlé Purina PetCare (RUS) brought together 710 dogs for a photoshoot in Moscow, Russia, on 14 Sep 2019.

Largest tarte Tatin
The Ville de Lamotte-Beuvron (FRA) unveiled a 308-kg (679-lb) tarte Tatin in Sologne, France, on 15 Sep 2019. The attempt was organized in celebration of the 120th anniversary of the sweet pastry, which originated at the Hôtel Tatin in the town.

Largest inflatable aqua park
PT Ecomarine Indo Pelago (IDN) and Wibit Sports GmbH (DEU) created a 28,900-m² (311,077-sq-ft) inflatable water park in Bali, Indonesia, as verified on 19 Sep 2019.

Most fonts identified in one minute
Mahgul Faheem (PAK) correctly picked out 37 different fonts in 60 sec in Karachi, Pakistan, on 20 Sep 2019.

Longest charcuterie board
Datassential (USA) prepared a 45.73-m-long (150-ft 0.4-in) charcuterie board laden with food in Chicago, Illinois, USA, on 24 Sep 2019. It took two people 24 hours to fill the board with more than 180 kg (400 lb) of meat, cheese and deli delights.

Largest arancino
METRO Italia Cash and Carry S.p.A. (ITA) cooked up a 32.72-kg (72-lb 1-oz) rice ball in Catania, Italy, on 5 Oct 2019. It was later donated to a food bank.

Most people wearing high-visibility vests
On 10 Oct 2019 – World Mental Health Day – a total of 2,499 people donned hi-vis vests for an event organized by Mental Health Australia (AUS). The gathering took place in Townsville, Queensland, Australia. The vests were donated by hardware chain Bunnings Warehouse.

Most people buzzing simultaneously
Delaware State University (USA) brought together 1,661 students and alumni to make a communal buzzing sound on 19 Oct 2019. The feat was staged in Dover, Delaware, USA.

On the same day, they achieved the **most people waving a foam finger simultaneously**: 1,709.

Largest special stamp
On 30 Oct 2019, to mark the 85th anniversary of Donald Duck's first appearance in a cartoon, The Walt Disney Company Italia created a postage stamp measuring 4.11 m² (44.23 sq ft). Presented in Lucca, Italy, it showed Donald and his car against a background of the Italian peninsula.

Largest Filipino folk dance
On 31 Oct 2019, the province of Sorsogon in the Philippines united 7,127 dancers to perform a Pantomina sa Tinampo.

Largest gape
Phillip Angus (USA) has a distance of 9.52 cm (3.75 in) between his upper and lower incisors, as verified in Boyertown, Pennsylvania, USA, on 5 Nov 2019.

Oldest Santa's grotto
The World's Famous Grotto Ltd has operated in Liverpool, UK, for 123 years, as verified on 16 Nov 2019.

Most push-ups on fingertips with a 60-lb pack in one minute
On 17 Nov 2019, Irfan Mehsood (PAK) carried out 39 push-ups on fingertips in Dera Ismail Khan, Pakistan. He wore a 60-lb (27.2-kg) pack on his back.

Longest marathon hula-hooping
Jenny Doan (AUS) hula-hooped for 100 hr in Chicago, Illinois, USA, from 19 to 23 Nov 2019. The feat raised money for Mental Health America, which promotes mental wellbeing and provides support to those with mental illness.

Longest line of banknotes
On 11 Dec 2019, Beauséjour Family Crisis Resource Centre (CAN) created a 7,435.57-m-long (24,394-ft 10-in) line of dollar bills in Moncton, New Brunswick, Canada. It comprised 50,206 notes. The record raised CAN$251,030 ($189,673; £144,078) to provide a new shelter for victims of domestic violence.

Longest toast relay
A line of 1,300 participants took part in a drinks toast arranged by Coca-Cola Thailand at Siam Square in Bangkok, Thailand, on 12 Dec 2019. Each person was served an array of local cuisine and a bottle of Coke to raise a toast to the event.

Most people hugging soft toys simultaneously
Maxicare Healthcare Corporation (PHL) recruited 654 individuals to give soft toys a cuddle at SM by the Bay in Pasay City, the Philippines, on 15 Dec 2019.

Fastest 10-km swim in open water (one arm)
On 19 Dec 2019, Elham Sadat Asghari (IRN) swam 10 km (6.2 mi) using just one arm in 4 hr 58 min 32 sec in Chabahar, Iran.

Highest-altitude drive by an electric car
A Kona Electric made by Hyundai Motor India

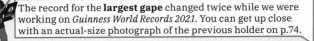

The record for the **largest gape** changed twice while we were working on *Guinness World Records 2021*. You can get up close with an actual-size photograph of the previous holder on p.74.

reached 5,771 m (18,933 ft) above sea level at Sawula Pass in Tibet Autonomous Region, China, on 8 Jan 2020. The 925-km (574-mi) drive over rough, snow-covered terrain took eight days, in the face of high winds and sub-zero temperatures.

Oldest person to ski to both Poles
Zdeněk Chvoj (CZE, b. 16 Mar 1948) reached the South Pole aged 71 years 302 days on 12 Jan 2020. He had previously skied to the North Pole, arriving on 20 Apr 2018, a journey made more arduous by his having to bypass open water and dodge polar bears.

Largest serving of beans and rice
A 1,995-kg (4,398-lb) helping of beans and rice was dished up by the Department of Tourism and Civil Aviation, Himachal Pradesh (IND) at Tattapani village in Mandi, India, on 14 Jan 2020.

Longest cake
On 15 Jan 2020, Bakers Association Kerala (IND) presented a 5.3-km-long (3.2-mi) chocolate-covered sponge cake at Thrissur in Kerala, India. Once the record was ratified, the cake was consumed by onlookers.

Tallest stack of eggs
Mohammed Abelhameed Mohammed Muqbel (YEM) stacked three eggs – one on top of the other – in Kuala Lumpur, Malaysia, on 16 Jan 2020. After hours of practice, he was able to arrange all three so that their combined centre of mass was directly above the stack's very small base.

Largest layered dip
BUSH'S® Beans (USA) created a 493-kg (1,087-lb) dip, as ratified in Chicago, Illinois, USA, on 17 Jan 2020. Ten different BUSH's seven-layer dips were piled on each other: Veggie, Cuban, Caprese, Loaded Baked Potato, Buffalo Chicken, Mediterranean, Fiesta, Spicy, Barbecue and Classic.

Youngest driver to win a Formula E race
Maximilian Günther (DEU, b. 2 Jul 1997) won the Santiago ePrix aged 22 years 200 days in Santiago, Chile, on 18 Jan 2020. This championship is for single-seater electric cars.

Fastest time to model five balloon sculptures blindfolded
Wearing a blindfold, Ryan Tracey (IRL) took just 43.64 sec to make a balloon dog, sword, snail, flower and caterpillar on the set of *Britain's Got Talent* in London, UK, on 20 Jan 2020.

Largest Burns supper
On 24 Jan 2020, a group of 926 participants assembled for a Burns supper arranged by Scotmid Co-op (UK) in Edinburgh, UK. A traditional celebration of the life and work of Scotland's national poet Robert "Rabbie" Burns, the meal formed part of a celebration of Scotmid's 160th anniversary.

Earliest known pollinating bee
On 29 Jan 2020, the discovery of a tiny female specimen belonging to the new species *Discoscapa apicula* was reported in *Palaeodiversity*. It was found in Myanmar, embedded in a lump of *c.* 100-million-year-old amber from the mid-Cretaceous period. Scientists have theorized that the bee flew into resin that then hardened into amber, trapping it.

Largest chocolate-nut bar
Hershey (USA) produced an outsized bar of REESE'S TAKE 5 weighing 2,695 kg (5,943 lb) on 31 Jan 2020. It was ratified in the brand's eponymous home town in Pennsylvania, USA, and beat a giant SNICKERS® bar made by Mars Wrigley that had only recently set a new world record. It was created to promote REESE'S first Super Bowl advert.

Most expensive leg of ham
As of 3 Feb 2020, Japan's Taishi Co., Ltd were selling an Iberian bellota ham for 1,429,000 yen ($13,183; £9,982).

Largest onion bhaji
Oli Khan and a team from Surma Takeaway Stevenage (both UK) cooked up a 175.48-kg (386-lb 13.8-oz) onion bhaji in London, UK, on 4 Feb 2020.

Most northerly pop-up commercial internet broadcast
Europa Plus CJSC and SINTEC Lubricants (both RUS) conducted an internet broadcast at 78.06208°N in Barentsburg, Svalbard and Jan Mayen, Norway, on 7 Feb 2020.

Most people making sensory bottles at once
Sensory bottles are tools that assist people who have developmental disabilities, by helping to calm their breathing and regulate emotion. Damar Services Inc. (USA) assembled 662 individuals to make these sensory aids in Indianapolis, Indiana, USA, on 8 Feb 2020.

Farthest indoor triple jump (female)
Yulimar Rojas (VEN) performed a 15.43-m (50-ft 7.4-in) triple jump at the Meeting Villa de Madrid in Spain on 21 Feb 2020.

Most people doing the baby shark dance routine
Trudel Alliance SEC (CAN) assembled 782 people for a baby shark dance on 23 Feb 2020. The event was part of the FDL Fest at Fleur de Lys Centre Commercial in Quebec City, Canada.

First anaerobic multicellular animal
The fish parasite *Henneguya salminicola* is a tiny multicellular species of myxozoan (an aquatic parasite). Unlike all other animals, its cells do not contain any mitochondria, the organelles that convert oxygen into energy. It apparently obtains its energy via anaerobic (non-oxygen-driven) means, presumably deriving it from its host species – salmon in Alaska, USA. The discovery was described in the journal *PNAS* on 24 Feb 2020.

Longest line of pancakes
Kenwood Ltd (UK) served up a 130.84-m-long (429-ft 3-in) line of pancakes at Tottenham Hotspur Stadium in London, UK, on 25 Feb 2020. They were later shared out by The Felix Project, a charity tackling food waste and hunger.

Longest career as a surgeon
Mambet Mamakeev (KGZ) performed surgery for 67 years 181 days, as verified on 29 Feb 2020 in Bishkek, Kyrgyzstan. Dr Mamakeev's long service has seen him awarded the prestigious title of Honorary Citizen of the Republic of Kyrgyzstan.

Largest protein bar
Grenade® (UK) Ltd served up a 239-kg (526-lb 14-oz) protein bar in Solihull, West Midlands, UK, on 4 Mar 2020.

Farthest distance to pull a vehicle in 12 hours (team)
Between 4 and 5 Mar 2020, a team from 3 Regiment, Royal Logistic Corps (UK) pulled a van 76.38 km (47.46 mi) at Blenheim Palace in Oxfordshire, UK. The van weighed nearly 1.8 tonnes (3,968 lb) and the team worked in rotation.

Farthest shot put (F37, female)
Para athlete Lisa Adams (NZ) produced a 15.28-m (50-ft 1-in) shot put on 7 Mar 2020. She was competing in an F37-category contest at the New Zealand Track & Field Championships in Christchurch, New Zealand.

Oldest red panda in captivity
When he died on 10 Mar 2020, Taylor (b. 7 Jun 1998) – a red or lesser panda (*Ailurus fulgens*) – was aged 21 years 277 days. In the wild, the species' lifespan is nearer 10 years. Taylor lived at ZooMontana in Billings, USA.

Smallest dinosaur
Based on only a skull that was found in northern Myanmar, the newly discovered species *Oculudentavis khaungraae* ("eye-tooth bird") is the smallest known Mesozoic dinosaur. According to the findings, published in *Nature* on 11 Mar 2020, this bird-like dinosaur would have been roughly the same size as today's **smallest bird**,

the bee hummingbird (*Mellisuga helenae*), males of which can measure 57 mm (2.2 in), including bill and tail, and may weigh less than 2 g (0.07 oz).

Longest marathon TV talk show
Alexandru Raducanu hosted a 72-hr 18-min chat show on Canal 33 Network SRL (both ROM) in Bucharest, Romania, between 14 and 17 Mar 2020.

Most tunnel-boring machines operating simultaneously in a single project
The Russian company JSC Mosinzhproekt ran 23 tunnel excavators at the same time while working on the Moscow Metro on 18 Mar 2020.

Longest breakwater
Daewoo Engineering & Construction Co. Ltd (KOR), GCPI (IRQ) and TECHNITAL (ITA) built a 14.523-km-long (9.02-mi) breakwater in Al Faw Grand Port, Basra, Iraq, as confirmed on 2 Apr 2020.

Oldest rhesus macaque in captivity
A rhesus macaque (*Macaca mulatta*) named Isoko – a resident of Kyoto City Zoo in Japan – celebrated her 42nd birthday on 15 Apr 2020. The typical lifespan for the species is 25 to 30 years. The oldest known specimen previous to Isoko lived to 40 years old.

Highest attendance for a concert in a videogame
The "Astronomical" event hosted by *Fortnite* (Epic Games, 2017) and Travis Scott (both USA) attracted 12.3 million concurrent viewers on 24 Apr 2020.

Most visitors to a virtual pub
Crowdfunder (UK) drew 6,321 users to "The Covid Arms" on 1 May 2020. To be counted towards the record, patrons had to buy a virtual pint. The gathering raised over £32,000 ($40,060) for the National Emergencies Trust Coronavirus Appeal and was an effort to bring people together virtually in the UK lockdown to support local pubs. Good health!

At a typical Burns supper you could expect to dine on haggis (cooked sheep offal) with mashed neeps (swedes, yellow turnips or rutabagas) and tatties (potatoes). And to complete the setting, a dram of whisky on the side.

Where's **Wadlow?**

GUINNESS WORLD RECORDS 2021

For the cover of this year's book, we wanted to do something a bit different… To celebrate the "Discover Your World" theme, we asked the award-winning illustrator Rod Hunt to create a superlative metropolis and cram it with as many record-breakers as possible.

Rod is well-known for his busy, retro-style cartoons, which are rich in colour and detail. And as you've seen, he's risen to the challenge and squeezed in some 200 record holders, including Robert Wadlow (USA), the **tallest man ever**. Wadlow may have stood 272 cm (8 ft 11.1 in), but his mini avatar (right) is rather more tricky to find!

Listed below are 20 more record holders that feature on the front and back of the book (see the inside covers for a version without any text). How quickly can you find them all?

For an interactive, clickable version of the cover that lists everyone featured, visit **guinnessworldrecords.com/2021**

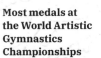

Tallest full Mohican/Mohawk
Joseph Grisamore (USA): 108.2 cm (3 ft 6.5 in). *See p.83*

Most medals at the World Artistic Gymnastics Championships
Simone Biles (USA): 25. *See p.242*

Highest-grossing spy movie series
James Bond (UK/USA): $7.11 bn (£5.69 bn). *See p.195*

Loudest burp
Paul Hunn (UK): 109.9 decibels. *See p.82*

Fastest circumnavigation of Australia by sail boat
Lisa Blair (AUS): 58 days 2 hr 25 min. *See p.157*

First person to visit Earth's highest and lowest points
Victor Vescovo (USA): *See p.160*

Youngest female with a full beard
Harnaam Kaur (UK, b. 29 Nov 1990): 24 years 282 days. *See p.72*

Shortest man (mobile)
Edward "Niño" Hernández (COL): 72.1 cm (2 ft 4.3 in). *See p.77*

Farthest wheelchair ramp jump
Aaron Fotheringham (USA): 21.35 m (70 ft). *See p.124*

Longest gum-wrapper chain
Made by Gary Duschl (USA): 32.55 km (20.22 mi). *See p.98*

Youngest drone cartographer
Nathan Lau (USA, b. 25 Sep 2004): 14 years 202 days. *See p.132*

Fastest bathroom
Built by Edd China (UK): 68 km/h (42.25 mph). *See p.172*

Most money raised by a charity walk
Captain Tom Moore (UK): £32.79 m ($40.82 m). *See p.80*

Shortest woman
Jyoti Amge (IND): 62.8 cm (2 ft 0.7 in). *See p.84*

Greatest distance skied solo, unassisted and unsupported in Antarctica
Richard Parks (UK): 3,700 km (2,299 mi). *See p.159*

Longest-running wild-primate study
Started by Jane Goodall (UK): 60 years. *See p.66*

Youngest X Games athlete
Gui Khury (BRA, b. 18 Dec 2008): 10 years 225 days. *See p.239*

Longest hair
Xie Qiuping (CHN): 5.627 m (18 ft 5.5 in). *See p.83*

Youngest gamer to earn $1 million in an esports tournament
Jaden Ashman (UK): 15 years 229 days. *See p.190*

Longest domestic cat
Barivel (ITA): 120 cm (3 ft 11.2 in) *See p.62*

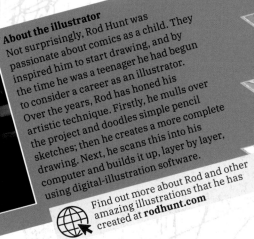

About the illustrator
Not surprisingly, Rod Hunt was passionate about comics as a child. They inspired him to start drawing, and by the time he was a teenager he had begun to consider a career as an illustrator. Over the years, Rod has honed his artistic technique. Firstly, he mulls over the project and doodles simple pencil sketches; then he creates a more complete drawing. Next, he scans this into his computer and builds it up, layer by layer, using digital-illustration software.

Find out more about Rod and other amazing illustrations that he has created at **rodhunt.com**